Modernity and Its Discontents

Modernity and Its Discontents

Making and Unmaking the Bourgeois from Machiavelli to Bellow

Steven B. Smith

Yale UNIVERSITY PRESS

NEW HAVEN & LONDON

Yale University Press books may be purchased in quantity for educational, business, or promotional use. For information, please e-mail sales.press@yale.edu (U.S. office) or sales@yaleup.co.uk (U.K. office).

Set in Adobe Garamond and Stone Sans types
by Westchester Publishing Services.
Printed in the United States of America.

Library of Congress Control Number: 2015957288
ISBN: 978-0-300-19839-3 (cloth : alk. paper)

A catalogue record for this book is available from the British Library.

This paper meets the requirements of
ANSI/NISO Z39.48-1992 (Permanence of Paper).

10 9 8 7 6 5 4 3 2 1

*To Susan
Life, Dance, Love*

Fashion a teacher for yourself. Meaning to say, even if he were not suited to be a teacher to you, nevertheless, make him into a teacher for yourself so that you conceive of him that he is teaching, because of this you shall succeed in the study of wisdom.
—Moses Maimonides, *The Commentary to Mishnah Aboth*

The educator himself must be educated.
—Karl Marx, *Theses on Feuerbach*

Contents

Preface

Modernity is a problem. It is a word that means many things to many people. It is the name of both a process (modernization) and a state of affairs. The term first gained currency in the sixteenth and seventeenth centuries with the "quarrel between the ancients and moderns" over the proper models of artistic production, but it quickly morphed into a debate over a range of phenomena from philosophy to politics to economics. Modernity came to be associated with the sovereign individual as the unique locus of moral responsibility, the separation of state and civil society as distinct realms of authority, the secularization of society or at least the lessening of the public role of religion, the elevation of science and scientific forms of rationality as the standard for knowledge, and a political regime based on the recognition of rights as the sole basis of its legitimacy.

My own point of departure begins with modernity as the site of a unique type of human being, one entirely unknown to the ancient and medieval worlds that I want to call the *bourgeois*. I realize that the term "bourgeois" is contested and currently out of favor, but it is something I would like to resurrect. I use this term not in the Marxist sense to mean owners of "the means of production" but to indicate members of an urban middle class that began to think of itself as constituting a distinctive culture with a distinctive way of life and set of moral characteristics. Among the traits that characterize this bourgeois way of life are the desire for autonomy and self-direction, the aspiration to live independently of the dictates of habit, custom, and tradition, to accept moral institutions and practices only if they pass the bar of one's critical intellect, and to accept ultimate responsibility for one's life and actions. The characteristics attributed to this new kind of individual by writers as diverse as Machiavelli, Montaigne, Descartes, Hobbes, Spinoza, and many others included the qualities of generosity, courage, nobility, love of fame, and self-assertion that together constituted a new morality of the individual. These are traits of character that arose initially in the early modern period and are uniquely attached to the constitutional democracies of the West.

The character traits described above have come to be most fully identified with the American way of life. Our founding documents—the Declaration of Independence and the Constitution—take modern philosophy, the philosophy of individual rights, government by consent, and the sovereignty of the people as their point of departure. Our way of life virtually forces us to ask whether a regime founded upon such a philosophy can long endure. The form of government devoted to the protection of life, liberty, and the pursuit of happiness is without doubt one of the most profound and precious accomplishments of modernity, and yet it leaves, perhaps deliberately so, many questions unanswered. What is happiness? Is it to be discovered more in the chase or in the catch? Is happiness equivalent to pleasures of the moment or in the experience of some higher order goal like virtue or contemplation? Is the idea of the pursuit of happiness a universal aspiration of all human beings or does it address the needs of a specific and perhaps very limited sector of humanity?

No pain, no gain, as the saying goes. Our political regime—the regime dedicated to the pursuit of happiness—is beset with dissatisfaction. It may seem strange that the most powerful and prosperous society that has ever existed should be given over to fits of self-doubt, but as a famous economist once said, there is no such thing as a free lunch. The quest for autonomy has been depicted by its critics as a form of "subjectivity" or ruthless aggressiveness used to control nature and dominate others; the claims made on behalf of trade and commerce have been depicted as a defense of rapacious capitalism and mindless consumerism; even the achievements of democracy have been presented as a sterile wasteland of philistinism and conformity. The thesis that I develop in this book is that modernity has created within itself a rhetoric of antimodernity that has taken philosophical, literary, and political forms. How did the idea of the bourgeois, once considered virtually synonymous with the free and responsible individual, become associated with a kind of low-minded materialism, moral cowardice, and philistinism? It is this dialectic that I hope to explore.

Any account of modernity potentially pulls in endless directions with many detours and pit stops along the way, but for reasons discussed below, I begin with Machiavelli. Machiavelli's claim to have mastered *fortuna* and discovered "new modes and orders" put us on the road to the idea of progress as the master trope by which modernity understands itself. The idea of progress is what principally defines "us" as moderns different from "them" as premoderns. The ancient political philosophers and historians—Herodotus, Thucydides, Plato, Polybius—all conceived of history as an endless cycle of regime change that followed a more or less eternal order. History was for them a matter of reshuffling a fixed deck. Modernity began with the audacious idea that we could break this endless pattern of birth, growth, and decay and, what is more, do so not through divine or supernatural intervention but through our own unaided efforts. Machiavelli and those who chose to follow him saw politics as a work of art, a testimony to human initiative and creativity.

The idea of progress was given classic expression by the thinkers of the Enlightenment—Descartes, Hobbes, Spinoza, Kant, and others—who saw in the idea of progress the promise of an unprecedented form of liberation. The idea of progress applied to the life of the mind in its quest to achieve certainty and overcome paralyzing bouts of doubt and despair, to the life of society as it seeks to banish or abolish popular forms of ignorance and superstition in order to achieve a stable, balanced, and prosperous civil order, and finally to history as a whole in humankind's ascent to a utopian vision of material well-being and peace among the nations as overseen by a system of international law. Modernity considered here is hardly all of a piece. It might be more accurate to speak of modernities. It includes everything from liberal modernity that values tolerance, commerce, and self-discovery to the more ambitious plans for large-scale social engineering, achieving of rationalist perfectionism, and the transformation of the nation-state into a world federation or even a world state.

It would not be long until modernity was confronted with its doppelgän-ger. Modernity would morph into its opposite, sometimes referred to as the Counter-Enlightenment. The Enlightenment's boast to have created an "age of taste" appeared to its critics beginning around the mid-eighteenth century as a world of hypocrisy, shallowness, and duplicity. Beginning with Rousseau, critics of civil society increasingly found this new civilization—bourgeois civilization—to be intolerably dull, flat, and conformist. What began as a trickle soon became a wave. The middle-class democracies that arose in the wake of the American and French Revolutions came to be regarded as the home of everything from Marx's world of unfettered "commodity fetishism," to Nietzsche's "last man," to Weber's "rationalized world," to Heidegger's anon-ymous *das Man*. What had been viewed as the home of progress and enlighten-ment by modernity's founders was seen by its critics as a barren landscape of cultural impoverishment and moral and spiritual decline. Modernity had given rise to a comprehensive discourse of antimodernity.

But just as modernity was not of a piece, neither was antimodernity. The best critics of modernity—those from whom we have most to learn—are not those who have engaged in a kind of "negative dialectic" but those like Alexis de Tocqueville, who accepted modern democracy as a given but hoped to deepen it with practices and values from earlier moral, political, and religious traditions, like Isaiah Berlin, who has nourished the monism of Enlighten-ment rationalism with the sense of pluralism and diversity that comes from Counter-Enlightenment romanticism, and like Leo Strauss, who has en-riched our understanding of modernity through a spirited engagement and selective appropriation of themes drawn from classical antiquity. These think-ers all understood that modernity, by which they meant the principles of the Enlightenment—the demand for equality, the aspiration to autonomy, the restless quest for happiness—needed to be enriched by sources outside itself if it was to remain viable. Only an educated middle class—what Hegel had called the *Bildungsbürgertum*—could preserve modernity from its self-destructive inner tendencies.

This book is divided into two main sections. The first main section, "Mo-dernity," deals with some of the classic themes and texts of early modernity, beginning with Machiavelli on the new "protean" manner of individualism, Hobbes and Spinoza on the secularization of society, Descartes and Franklin on the creation of the modern idea of the self, Kant on the globalization of human rights, and Hegel on civil society and the culture of free "subjectiv-ity." The second main section, "Our Discontents," deals with some of the great critics of the modern project, beginning with Rousseau's critique of the culture of refinement and the arts, Tocqueville's account of a new kind of democratic despotism, Flaubert's passionate diatribe against the world of the modern bourgeois, and Nietzsche's subtle undermining of the idea of progress, with its influence on the apocalyptic visions of Georges Sorel, Georg Lukács, Martin Heidegger, and Carl Schmitt. These are followed by chapters dealing with Isaiah Berlin and Leo Strauss, both of whom provide profound reconsiderations of the trajectory of the modern. I then consider two extraordinary images of modernity in the literary imagination. Giuseppe di Lampedusa's *The Leopard* is a stoical reflection on the world of modern democracy as told through the prism of his aristocratic ancestor contemplating the unification of Italy and the end of the old order; Saul Bellow's *Mr. Sammler's Planet* is an assessment of contemporary America as revealed by a Holocaust survivor living in New York. Bellow's book is often taken for an angry, dyspeptic assault on the New Left and the sexual revolution of the 1960s, which it is in part, but it is also, as I argue, a call to embrace the common world that we inhabit.

The title of this book is obviously drawn from Freud's *Civilization and Its Discontents*. The similarity ends there. Freud believed that civilization was based on our capacity to repress or sublimate our instinctual desires. This rendered us the sick or neurotic animal. I have no intention of offering such a sweeping explanation. The sources of our discontents are far wider and more various than any single, much less psychiatric, explanation can do justice. To be sure, every successful society requires individuals to defer gratification and take a longer view of what contributes to their own and their collective well-being, but anyone who believes that Plato, Kant, Jane Austen, and Saul Bellow are case studies of instinctual repression is capable of believing anything. I do not believe that modern men and women are necessarily less well adjusted or more disabled than their counterparts in the past. We are just more vocal in expressing our grievances. This dissatisfaction with ourselves is part and parcel of what it means to be modern. We are, or at least have become, the sum of our discontents.

ACKNOWLEDGMENTS

Like Molière's M. Jourdain, who at the age of forty suddenly discovered that he had been speaking in prose his whole life, it was not until considerably later that I realized I had been thinking about modernity without really knowing it. What is the modern, how does it differ from what preceded it, and what does it hold for the future—these questions have been with me since long before I became fully aware of them.

The theme of *Modernity and Its Discontents* has been informed by the conviction that the critique of modernity is at least as essential as our belief in the humane and civilizing project of the modern West. By modernity I mean broadly the regime that assigns priority to science and scientific modes of rationality, to the marketplace as the definitive allocator of goods and services, to representative forms of democracy as the most advanced form of political rule, and preeminently to the individual as the supreme locus of moral and political authority. That these ideas and institutions have become in different ways problematic scarcely needs saying. Why and how modernity has become a problem to itself—and what to do about it—is the theme of this book.

Every book is a labor of love, and this one has been no exception. The true benefactors of any work are ultimately one's friends. It is to my colleagues and students who have heard the arguments expressed here, and have either silently or vocally expressed their support or dissent, that I owe the greatest debts. These include my *chers collègues* Bryan Garsten, Karuna Mantena, and Hélène Landemore in the Yale Department of Political Science. My friends Howard Bloch, Giuseppe Mazzotta, David Bromwich, and Anthony Kronman have all served as wonderful conversation partners and occasionally coteachers. I would also like to acknowledge those from whom I have learned a great deal over the years, including (in no particular order) Nathan Tarcov, Michael Mosher, Aurelian Craiutu, Ran Halévi, and Joshua Cherniss. I would especially like to thank Amy Gais for reading the entire manuscript and making valuable suggestions. The person to whom the book is dedicated is the one from whom I have learned the most.

Some chapters included here appeared earlier in slightly different form. These are "An Exemplary Life: The Case of René Descartes," *Review of Metaphysics* 57, no. 3 (2004); "The Political Teaching of Lampedusa's *The Leopard*," *Yale Review* 98, no. 3 (2010); and "Mr. Sammler's Redemption," *Yale Review* 99, no. 2 (2011).

Part One **Introduction**

Chapter 1 Modernity in Question

Mon Dieu! Qu'est-ce que ce monde.
—Last words of M. de Cinq-Mars

The concept of modernity is a distinctively modern idea. What else could it be? The term "modernity" seems to ask the question, Modern in relation to what? Obviously, something that came before. No one living in the fifth century BCE thought of himself or herself as "ancient" or in the tenth century as "medieval," whereas we all consider ourselves to be modern—and in some cases postmodern—men and women. If terms like "modern" and "modernity" mean anything at all, they must be terms of distinction. Furthermore, the distinction between the ancients and the moderns is inevitably tied to the problem of the legitimacy of the modern world. On what does modernity's legitimacy rest? This might seem a paradox. To even raise the issue of the legitimacy of modernity seems a fool's errand. We inhabit modernity the way fish swim in water. It is simply the environment in which we live and act. Yet this is not quite the case.

The difference between the ancients and the moderns is not merely a question of temporal horizons. Modernity is a mentality. Of course, there have been many efforts to establish the origins of modernity or to somehow date its beginnings. Some have traced it back to the age of exploration and the discovery of the New World, beginning in the fifteenth century, others to the scientific revolution of Harvey, Galileo, and Newton, and still others to the philosophical innovations of Descartes, Hobbes, and Spinoza with their quest for new rational foundations for knowledge.[1] Modernity has been associated with the end of the devastating wars of religion that wracked Europe throughout the sixteenth century and brought about the beginnings of our modern theories of secularism and toleration.[2] It has been identified with the social and political revolutions of 1689, 1776, and 1789 that for the first time introduced the language of equality and the rights of man.[3] Some have identified it with the new artistic and aesthetic developments associated with the high modernism of writers like Proust, Joyce, and James. Virginia Woolf memorably declared that human nature itself changed "on or about December 1910."[4]

The problem of modernity concerns not only its origin but also its meaning. Is the idea of modernity a coherent one? On one influential account, we have simply lost confidence in modernity. Modernity or "the modern project" rested on a certain claim to universality, that its achievements in the domain of science, politics, and law could serve as a model for humanity. The confidence in the humane and civilizing project of modernity was expressed in such documents as the French Declaration of the Rights of Man and the Citizen and the United Nations' Universal Declaration of Universal Human Rights. The very terms in which these documents expressed themselves suggested a universal society based upon equal human rights and consisting of a league of nations devoted to maintaining the health, safety, and prosperity of its citizens. Today, however, leading opinion has increasingly lost confidence in these goals. This is in part due to the legacy of Marxism and postcolonialism that regards this mission as a thinly veiled (or perhaps not so veiled) form of Western imperialism seeking to impose its way of life on the developing world. It is also due to the influence of historicism or relativism that views all such claims to universalism as a disguised species of particularism. Modernity is merely one historical configuration now showing signs of exhaustion. Modernity, on this account, is on the cusp of giving rise to a new dispensation of history sometimes described as postmodernity, but exactly what this will look like is by no means certain.

Modernity has become less a cause for celebration than a reason for doubt. It is a register of the questions we feel about ourselves. Our belief in the fundamental benevolence of the West has been challenged by the rise of a series of oppositional ideologies—communism, fascism, and more recently political Islam, or "Islamism"—all of which claim to respond to a moral and spiritual void at the core of modernity. On this account, modern liberal democracy is the regime devoted to the satisfaction of our worldly desires. Its very materialism has become a cause of anxiety. This has meant especially sidelining or "privatizing" values of ultimate concern. In the language of John Rawls and his school, liberalism must remain neutral to comprehensive moral doctrines—doctrines about the good life, what makes life worth living, and so on—as being inherently controversial and therefore outside what reasonable citizens might agree to. As a result, modern democracy has been accused of failing to answer or even to raise the most fundamental problems of life. It is the materialism and technologism of modern democracy that has once again become a problem.

The Rawlsian conception of a world where rational citizens set aside their most deeply cherished moral conceptions for the sake of achieving a political modus vivendi—an "overlapping consensus" in Rawls-speak—coincided nicely with the claims about an "end of history" where the danger of war between the developed states had all but disappeared. The end of history thesis was never really about history but about the justification of political order. It was based on a revival of the Hegelian belief that the liberal democratic order represented the final form of political justification capable of providing a completely satisfying and fully civilized way of life. Democracies were supposed to represent the highest form of political development toward which all other regimes were either rapidly or slowly evolving. This doctrine appeared at just the moment when the ascendant market democracies of the West seemed to be achieving total dominance over their ideological competitors.

The utopian belief that with the end of the Cold War we were entering a period of democratic peace in which ethnic tensions would wither away and "soft power" could be used to resolve conflicts between states came to a stunning denouement on the morning of September 11, 2001. We find ourselves once again mired in the bloody and conflict-ridden domain of history. The hopeful vision of a global civil society designed to ensure perpetual peace seems to have foundered on the shoals of a political reality that has proved far more recalcitrant than previously believed. A resurgent nationalism and ethnic tribalism in Russia and the Middle East has made a mockery of the claim that we have all become—or are on our way to becoming—liberal democrats. Once again we find ourselves in the bloody and conflict-ridden domain of history. Modernity has come to appear less "modern" than it is often believed to be.

These problems force us to return to the beginnings of modernity in order to see better what is at stake. The birth of modernity began inauspiciously with a literary debate called in England "the battle of the books" and in France the *querelle des anciens et des modernes.* This was initially a dispute about whether modern authors should continue to be bound by the rules of aesthetics and literary composition that had held since the time of Aristotle. Were we simply pygmies standing on the shoulders of giants or could modern writers create works of their own that could rival or even surpass the greatest works of the classical world? The argument seems absurd today. What would be the point of arguing whether Shakespeare is superior or inferior to Homer or Milton to Aeschylus? But what began as a literary quarrel soon spread to areas as wide as religion, science, morality, economics, and politics. Francis Bacon, one of the most aggressive modernists, mischievously argued that those we call the ancients are not ancient at all. They belong to the childhood of humanity. We of the present are the true ancients because we have a longer wealth of history and experience upon which to draw.[5] Knowledge advances with time, and it is we latecomers who have made greater contributions to the sum total of human knowledge. At the core of this debate was a belief that modernity is characterized by constant change, constant revolutions in knowledge, and that human life after these revolutions will be better than it was before and will be subject to continual betterment in the future.

MODERNITY AS PERMANENT REVOLUTION

The first author to confront this quarrel in a systematic and comprehensive manner was a Florentine, Niccolò Machiavelli. In the fifteenth chapter of *The Prince* Machiavelli threw down the gauntlet and declared himself forthrightly on the side of the moderns. "I depart from the orders of others," Machiavelli confidently averred. "But since my intent is to write something useful to whoever understands it, it has appeared to me more fitting to go directly to the effectual truth of the thing than to the imagination of it. And many have imagined republics and principalities that have never been seen or known to exist in truth; for it is so far from how one lives to how one should live that he who lets go of what is done for what should be done learns his ruin rather than his preservation."[6]

Machiavelli's claim here was to put politics on a new—a modern— foundation, to give it a realism that it had not previously possessed, to free it from the illusions of the imagination, and to provide a different and to some degree "lower" conception of human nature that would be more in accord with actual human behavior. On Machiavelli's telling of the story, the ancients were utopians, dreamers, who believed in an orderly cosmos and tried to figure out what was the appropriate human place within it, whereas the proper task of knowledge is to make nature serve our ends. He presents himself as the bearer of a new truth—*alla verità effetuale della cosa* (the effectual truth of things)— that is concerned not with how things ought to be but with how things are. It is knowledge of the "is" rather than the "ought" that is important. Machiavelli's realism is often associated with a related claim that he is the founder of a new "science" of politics. By science is meant the causal analysis of facts and their relations, where causes are understood to be not the Aristotelian study of ends but efficient causes or the study of means. It would be based on a new appreciation for empiricism, an inductive spirit, that limits itself to what can be seen, observed, measured, and quantified. The new Machiavellian political science would be a science of power.

Machiavelli was not so much a modern as a prophet of modernity. His language remains replete with biblical allusions to prophecy, enslavement, liberation, and future redemption. Like Moses, he pointed the way to, even if he never fully arrived at, the Promised Land. He audaciously compared himself to Christopher Columbus, who had discovered a new continent, even if it was not entirely clear what he had found. Machiavelli helped to introduce a new trope by which modern people understand themselves in relation to the ancients, namely, progress. The ancients, on this account, were largely dependent on nature or *fortuna*. The founding of Rome, Machiavelli tells us, was a stroke—a very good stroke—of luck. But armed with the right science or the right understanding of nature and history, we can free ourselves from dependence on fortune. To be modern means to take affairs into our own hands, to achieve through our own unaided efforts what in the past had been consigned to the province of wish, prayer, or even the endless cycle of history. It is not as if people in ancient times were incapable of imagining a world better than the one they inhabited, they simply did not know how to achieve it. For the first time, we will be able do freely and self-consciously what the ancients could hope to achieve only through chance. By following a deliberate plan of action,

we can do through "reflection and choice"—to use Alexander Hamilton's felicitous phrase—what in the past had been the result of "accident and force."[7]

For those who allied themselves with this program, modernity came to
be regarded as synonymous with progress. Progress—or what today goes by
the name progressivism—implies a certain attitude toward change. Certainly,
the ancient writers understood the importance of change, but typically they
regarded it as synonymous with corruption or decay. History is cyclical, oscil-
lating between periods of freedom and despotism, civilization and barbarism.
Periods of peace and freedom were certainly possible, but there was no reason
to believe they would last forever. Progressives, on the other hand, believe that
change is, on the whole, change for the better. Progress means a preference
for the present to the past and for the future to the present. Older theories
and doctrines were ranked as mere "predecessors" or "precursors" of the present and therefore evaluated as either contributions to or impediments of future
progress. The scientific revolutions of the sixteenth and seventeenth centuries
provided the most tangible evidence for this belief in progress. Science, for
the first time, came to be seen as a cumulative enterprise, a slow, steady accre-
tion of knowledge that is in principle illimitable. There is no knowing where
scientific progress may lead. We can only say that because all knowledge is
provisional and subject to future revision, science is susceptible to infinite
progress. And just as science has progressed beyond anything imaginable in
previous times, so it was believed that the human condition might be susceptible to infinite improvement. Science is simply the standard that could be
applied to every human endeavor. We are entering a new age—the age of
Enlightenment—that promised to submit not only nature but all social, political, and religious authorities to the sovereign control of reason and experiment.

To be sure, no one imagined that the cause of progress would be unimpeded.
Standing over and against the belief in progress stood the whole complex of
theological politics embodied in the role of the church as the organizer-in-
chief of our terrestrial lives. For centuries, the word of God and God's earthly
interpreters in the church remained the unquestioned source of authority. In
the case of conflict between the church and the worldly authorities, whom
should one follow? To be progressive meant to oppose the "the kingdom of
darkness," as it was called by Thomas Hobbes in the final part of *Leviathan,*
as a shorthand for the power of the clergy, above all the Roman and Presbyterian clergy. Priestcraft designated the whole system of theological politics
in which religious leaders used their powers to pursue their own interests to

the detriment of both good government and true religion. It was the independence of the clergy—its claim to serve as the ultimate arbiter of opinion—that early Enlightenment critics like Hobbes and Spinoza saw as the chief cause of civil war and the deliberate cruelty of inquisitorial politics.

The critique of priestly politics was the presupposition of the emergence of national states in the sixteenth and seventeenth centuries. The concept of sovereignty that Hobbes was the first to develop as the cornerstone of modern politics grew out of the radical critique of biblical politics. The critique of religion was not merely a historical aside but (as we will see later in this book) the elementary precondition for the modern state conceived as a sovereign, autonomous political form. It was from the putative fact of revelation that priests and their surrogates claimed their title to rule. The belief in biblical revelation could not but pose a profound challenge to the national state as the absolute sovereign over its own internal affairs. For Hobbes, Bodin, Spinoza, and Locke, a whole new politics was necessary that would make a relapse into theological politics impossible. Theirs was to be a form of secular politics that would submit theology to political control, or in the famous phrase of the Treaty of Westphalia, *cuius regio, eius religio;* henceforth the head of each state would have the right to determine the religion of the state. These states were sovereign in the sense that they would be masters of their own affairs; they would put an end to the designs of a universal church, and deserve the respect of other states in a new international system.

Correlative to the emergence of the sovereign state was the emergence of the sovereign individual. No longer were men and women considered to be tied to a family, a polis, a guild, an estate, or a religious order; they were regarded as "by nature" free and equal individuals, at liberty to consent to whatever social and political arrangements seemed rational. Henceforward, the individual, free from all sources of tradition, was to be the locus of both moral and political authority. There arose consequently a new protean conception of the "self" as consisting of the capacities of willing and choosing, of free agency, and an awareness that we are dependent, not on God, but on ourselves alone to realize our own unique character. This new idea of the individual cut off from divine purpose or any assigned place in an ordered cosmos seemed to many a frightening prospect, but to others like Pico della Mirandello, Cervantes, Montaigne, Pascal, Charron, and Hobbes, it seemed something of inestimable worth.

Descartes is generally and correctly read as the founder of modern philosophy, the person who set the questions with which all later philosophers would have to contend. This is true, but it neglects the fact that Descartes also developed the modern conception of the self involved in a lengthy voyage of discovery. Descartes's *cogito ergo sum*—I think therefore I am—gave philosophical voice to this new individualism. Underlying Descartes's famous discussions of hyperbolic doubt and the rules of method is a story of self-education, of his rejection of the books and studies of his elders, of his removal from society to the famous stove-heated room where beginning on November 10, 1619, he engaged in contemplation for three lonely days, of his decision to adopt a policy of resoluteness in action, and then of his wanderings and adventures before he finally settled in Amsterdam, where he could pursue his philosophy unbothered by the intrusions of those around him. Descartes's story is *the* modern story told many times over in such classic works of modern self-discovery as Daniel Defoe's *Robinson Crusoe,* John Bunyan's *Pilgrim's Progress,* and Benjamin Franklin's rollicking account of himself as the original self-made man in his *Autobiography.*

The central claim of the Enlightenment and its progeny, however, was the belief that the increase in knowledge—especially scientific knowledge—will necessarily lead to a better condition of society. The Enlightenment was a project of education. The massive French *Encyclopédie* published under the direction of Diderot and d'Alembert was a barometer of the view that where advances in science go, advances in morality and politics are sure to follow. The modern age was to be an age of unprecedented freedom. To halt or reverse the increase in knowledge would be to halt the advance of human freedom. The advance of knowledge means emancipation not only from theological prejudice and superstition but also from the regimes of throne and altar that had ruled European politics for centuries. Since the optimum condition for the progress of knowledge requires communication between peoples, or at least between scientists and researchers from different nations, there emerged a preference for "open societies," that is, societies that have enshrined freedom of commerce and exchange, but above all freedom of belief and opinion. Societies that not merely tolerate but actually encourage the widest latitude for freedom of thought are the ones most likely to share in the new age of progress.

The great revolutions of the early modern age were all undertaken in the name of the progressive ideals of equality and human rights. These ideals found expression in the regimes dedicated to such classic modern principles as life, liberty, property, and the pursuit of happiness. America was the first truly modern nation, that is, the first nation self-consciously established on the principles of modern philosophy. The Declaration of Independence, the Constitution, and Lincoln's Gettysburg Address express those universal principles that are said to hold for all people everywhere. It was in America that the doctrines of early modernity first came to roost. The founders of modern philosophy explained modern politics in terms of a history of mankind, a long struggle of ascent from the state of nature to civil society. This was a story about how an original condition of fear and anxiety, poverty and ignorance, came to be replaced by way of a social contract with guaranteed legal protections of person and property. By civil society was meant a certain type of civilization whose pillars were property, science, and commerce. It was the transition from natural society to civil society that formed the basis for the great Enlightenment theories of history given expression by Locke, Kant, and Condorcet.

The very idea of progress came to be inseparable from the great revolutionary movements of the modern world. Revolution had initially signified circulation, in the naturalistic sense of a return to a fixed point of origin. Polybius used the word *anacyclosis* to indicate the cyclical overturning of a state and its return to first principles. The ancient idea of revolution was conservative, in the sense of a return to first principles as suggested by the prefix "re" in the word *revolutio*. What distinguishes modernity is its claim of revolution as the absolute new beginning point. Revolutions were to be the veritable engines of human progress from which there could be no return. Revolution itself, rather than being seen as a rebellion against an ancient and venerable tradition, or even as a restoration of a noble beginning, was viewed as the harbinger of a better future. The progress of history may be thought of as a linear development, as conceived by Kant and Condorcet, or through dialectical stages, as imagined by Hegel and Marx, but this does not change the inexorable forward motion of the historical process. Revolutions came to be seen not simply as singular events in time but as a process of acceleration that drives history relentlessly forward, even despite the intentions of political actors. It was but a single step to see the whole of world history as a site of permanent revolution.

THE DIALECTIC OF ENLIGHTENMENT

The difference between the ancients and the moderns is often framed in terms of a quarrel. Yet the very terms seem to risk anachronism. A quarrel implies a debate, a conversation. How can there be a quarrel when one of the sides is not even present to carry it on? To speak more precisely, the very concept of modernity implies a break with historical tradition, with preceding patterns of thought and practice. This naturally raises a host of questions. What justified this break, and what makes it legitimate? What was so wrong with the past to make such a breach necessary? And is such a break even conceptually possible? The idea that modernity represents some absolute new beginning where the old is replaced by the new seems epistemologically naïve. Did the founders of modernity not continue to speak and write in the same language as their predecessors and therefore, even unwittingly, carry on certain common meanings and usages? In a similar vein, historians have shown that modern concepts and categories are themselves dependent upon earlier Christian ideals. For example, modern idioms of revolution and human progress are said to be merely "secularizations" of theological conceptions of new beginnings and eschatological visions of an end of time. In many respects we may not be as modern as we think. If these objections carry weight, this seems to cast doubt upon the very legitimacy of the modern project.[8]

The attempt to open the debate about the legitimacy of modernity has gone under a variety of different names, but for want of a better one, I prefer to call it the Counter-Enlightenment. The term "Counter-Enlightenment" was not coined by but is most widely associated with the name of Isaiah Berlin.[9] Berlin used the term in a manner that was more or less synonymous with the romantic reaction to the Enlightenment. The Enlightenment, he argued, was wedded to an unduly reductionist and monistic theory of human nature according to which human behavior is conceived as fundamentally uniform across time and space and therefore subject to common laws of explanation that hold true everywhere. Even today this remains the official view of the social sciences, which consider human nature as constant over time, responding to one or a very few number of variables. The Counter-Enlightenment, by contrast, insisted on the variety of distinct national cultures, conceived as organic bodies that develop according to their own internal principles, or what Montesquieu referred to as "the general spirit of a nation" that shapes its distinctive laws, customs, and institutions. The Counter-Enlightenment did not so much discover as rediscover the importance of national character, the idea that Spartans and Athenians, Greeks and Persians, Germans and Italians act on different understandings of the world and that these understandings cannot be reduced to the same uniform laws of behavior. There is, in fact, a pluralism or diversity of cultures according to which not only our secondary characteristics but even our fundamental human attributes—our heart, soul, and mind—are shaped by the inescapably complex texture of history and social life that we inhabit. The Counter-Enlightenment was inseparable from the rise of this new "historical consciousness."

I do not want so much to dispute Berlin's use of the term "Counter-Enlightenment"—I shall discuss it at some length later on—but rather to use the term in a somewhat more capacious manner to describe the movement of return that led to a reconsideration and deepening of the idea of modernity itself. My thought is something like the following. For each movement of modernity, there has developed a comprehensive counternarrative. The idea that modernity is associated with the secularization of our institutions has given rise to fears about the rationalization and "disenchantment" of the world; the rise of a market economy and the commercial republic gave way in turn to an antibourgeois mentality that would find expression in politics, literature, art, and philosophy; the idea of modernity as the locus of individuality and free subjectivity gave rise to concerns about homelessness, anomie, and alienation; the achievements of democracy went together with fears about conformism, the loss of independence, and the rise of the "lonely crowd"; even the idea of progress itself gave rise to a counterthesis about the role of decadence, degeneration, and decline. These are not so much antimodern conceptions as they are part of the structure of modernity itself. Modernity has become inseparable from the doubts we feel about it. This continual back and forth between modernity and its critics seems to validate what two German critics, Max Horkheimer and Theodor Adorno, may have been getting at when they spoke of a "dialectic of enlightenment."[10]

There is much to this thesis. Modernity could never entirely immunize itself from the very processes of critical inquiry that brought it into being. It was only a matter of time until the critical spirit that had once been turned against the past would be turned against modernity itself, creating its own forms of disaffection with the present. Modernity carries with it the same seeds of skepticism and doubt about its own project that it once brought to its examination of its classical and medieval forebears. In fact, I want to suggest that to be modern is to exhibit a whole range of uncertainties and pathologies, from Locke's sense of "uneasiness," Rousseau's "amour-propre," Hegel's "unhappy consciousness," and Kierkegaard's "anxiety" to Tocqueville's "*inquiétude*," Marx's "alienation," and Weber's "disenchantment." This skepticism has even led some to question the very foundations of modernity and to ask whether its victories have not been prematurely declared. The idea of modernity gave way to a set of related fears about the end of history, the emergence of the "last man," and the rise of the postmodern. It has been argued, with some overstatement to be sure, that the principal beneficiaries of the Enlightenment have been the "totalitarian democracies" of the twentieth century whose vast schemes of social engineering were said to have drawn their inspiration from Enlightenment conceptions of the plasticity of human nature and the recasting of society.[11]

Hegel and Marx were certainly right on one point. Every thesis contains its own antithesis. Every Enlightenment produces its Counter-Enlightenment. This is not to say that the Counter-Enlightenment was simply a movement of reaction. To be sure, there were and have always been reactionaries who think it possible to turn back the historical clock, to restore a lost world that existed at a privileged moment. But this was not the aim of the most profound agents of the Counter-Enlightenment. Their goal was not to restore a world that was lost but to create a more accelerated form of the new. Beginning in Germany in the last quarter of the eighteenth century, the Counter-Enlightenment started as a reaffirmation of the nation or national idea as something higher, nobler, and more worthy of esteem than cosmopolitanism. The particular was conceived as something greater than the universal because rooted in the insight that moral perfection is only possible in a small society, one held together by bonds of trust, friendship, and civic pride. This countermovement, as I have called it, has taken many forms, from the humane and liberal pluralism of Herder and Burke, to the romantic and aesthetic reaction of novelists and poets who regarded bourgeois society as entirely immersed in material affairs and therefore blind to the areas of beauty and human nobility, to the often violent and chiliastic repudiations of anarchists and revolutionaries who saw in modernity a "totalizing" or homogenizing culture that could not tolerate true individualism, difference, and particularity. These nihilistic repudiations have ranged from Joseph de Maistre's call for a counterrevolution to nationalist and collectivist appeals coming from Germany, Russia, and parts of the contemporary Middle East that claim to assert their authentic and indigenous cultures in opposition to what they regard as the artificial and soul-destroying materialism of the West.

The Counter-Enlightenment often took the form of apocalyptic narratives of decline and fall. From Max Nordau's *Degeneration,* Georges Sorel's *Illusions of Progress,* and Oswald Spengler's (mistranslated) *Decline of the West* to Alasdair MacIntyre's *After Virtue* and Francis Fukuyama's *The End of History and the Last Man*—these works all declared the end of the Enlightenment often by turning the idea of progress against itself. They regarded progress not as the master narrative of human history in its rise from barbarism to civilization but as one type of historical consciousness—one weltanschauung—among many that was now coming to its natural and inevitable end. Today these narratives of decline have only proliferated, even if they are likely to be more social scientific and less apocalyptic. Works that predict the imminent or future decline of Western civilization include Ian Morris's *Why the West Rules—For Now,* Niall Ferguson's *Civilization: The West and the Rest,* Thomas Friedman and Michael Mandelbaum's *That Used to Be Us,* and George Packer's *The Unwinding.* Each of these works predicts—sometimes woefully, sometimes not—not only an end of Western civilization but the possible return of a new kind of barbarism. These predictions have fortunately not come to pass—at least not yet—although their warnings are worth taking seriously.

THE PROBLEM OF THE BOURGEOIS

Like the origins of modernity, the origins of the Counter-Enlightenment are the subject of endless debate. Who or what set off this protest movement? A convenient, but by no means uncontroversial, place to begin is the year 1750, which witnessed the publication of Jean-Jacques Rousseau's *Discourse on the Sciences and the Arts.* Rousseau's *First Discourse,* as it became known, was a response to an essay question posed by the learned Academy of Dijon on whether the progress of the arts and sciences had contributed to moral progress. Rousseau answered with a decisive no. The century of progress, he argued, was not all in one direction. Progress in some areas has meant backsliding or even decay in others. "Our souls have become corrupted," Rousseau complained, "in proportion as our sciences and our arts have advanced toward perfection."[12] Scientific and technological progress could go hand in hand with a certain kind of moral corruption. Rousseau did not write as a know-nothing or as a kind of Luddite rejecting modernity in toto. His goal was not to condemn the culture of the sciences and the arts but to protect them from the inevitable vulgarization that comes with using them as an instrument for public education. It was just as important to protect the true Enlightenment from the corruptions of society as it was to protect society from exposure to the fruits of the Enlightenment.

The Counter-Enlightenment, as the term suggests, began as a movement of opposition or reaction against the twin engines of modernity—science and commerce. The new natural science with its mathematically inspired method was presented as the model for all forms of knowledge. Science was progressive in the sense that both its methods and its conclusions could be passed down from generation to generation and therefore provide a solid foundation for future research. What did not measure up to the scientific means of exactitude could simply no longer be considered knowledge. Just as science hoped to limit the power of the imagination from engaging in metaphysical flights of fancy, so commerce was regarded as taming and pacifying the unruly passions and appetites, especially the desires for war, conquest, and domination. According to its advocates, the new commercial regimes found in Great Britain and the United States represented a safe and sane alternative to the ancien régime with its visions of moral grandeur, disdain for mundane employments, and preoccupation with intangible goals like glory and honor.[13]

At the core of the Counter-Enlightenment was a critique of a new kind of civilization that Rousseau characterized by terms like "uniformity," "duplicity," and "hypocrisy." Civilization was, above all, distinguished from culture. While civilization was associated with the development of the arts and sciences, cultures were distinguished by their distinctive folk minds or original genius as revealed in their language, poetry, music, and dance. Civilization was shallow; culture was deep. Civilizations could be ranked as "higher" or "lower" depending on their degree of social and economic development, but only cultures can be deemed "authentic" or "inauthentic." The idea of culture has never completely lost its original meaning as the culture of the soil—agriculture—while civilization presupposes the transformation of human beings into bourgeois and city dwellers. There can be primitive or rustic cultures, but there is no such thing as a rustic civilization. Even Kant, the great apostle of the Enlightenment, could acknowledge some truth in Rousseau's charge. "We are cultivated to a high degree by art and science," Kant wrote. "We are *civilized* to the point of excess in all kinds of social courtesies and proprieties. But we are still a long way from the point where we could consider ourselves *morally* mature."[14]

It was not civilization as such that Rousseau protested against but a certain form of civilization that can be summed up in a phrase: bourgeois civilization. This form of civilization had produced a new kind of human being, the bourgeois, who was polite, civil, and refined but also craven, false, and insincere. The concept of the bourgeois was something coined by Rousseau. I do not mean that he invented the term—long before him, Molière wrote a play entitled *Le bourgeois gentilhomme*—only that Rousseau gave the word its popular currency. In the opening book of *Emile* Rousseau defines the bourgeois as follows: "He who in the civil order wants to preserve the primacy of nature does not know what he wants. Always in contradiction with himself, always floating between his inclinations and his duties, he will never be either man or citizen. He will be good neither for himself nor for others. He will be one of these men of our days: a Frenchman, an Englishman, a bourgeois. He will be nothing."[15]

The bourgeois, as described in this passage, is someone in between. It is not just to be a member of the middle class caught between the aristocracy above and the peasantry below. To be bourgeois is to live neither purely for oneself nor purely for others. It is to be caught between duties and desires, or in Rousseau's phrase to be "in contradiction" with oneself. The bourgeois is a victim of what the sociologists call "status anxiety." It is to be caught in between the natural man—the savage of the state of nature—and the citizen who is capable of acts of extraordinary courage and self-sacrifice, both of whom exhibit a certain wholeness or integrity. It was the allegedly contradictory nature of bourgeois society and the search for an authentically coherent form of life that would contribute so much to the power of the Marxist rhetoric in the following century. For Rousseau and later Marx, the modern state dominated by the science of political economy and an ethic of utility and self-interest lacked both heroic greatness and the rudiments of social justice.

The term "bourgeois" did not enter the political vocabulary until Marx, who borrowed much of his vocabulary from Rousseau. The word is most famously associated with the *Communist Manifesto,* where Marx described modern history as a titanic struggle between the two great social classes, the bourgeoisie and the proletariat. But even for Marx the term was not entirely negative. He praised the bourgeois class for introducing the element of constant novelty and revolutionizing the conditions of existence, for its destruction of "venerable prejudices" and the creation of new forms of life ("All that is solid melts into air").[16] He distinguished between the early heroic period of the bourgeoisie in its struggle against the feudal aristocracy and the contemporary decadent phase of development where the bourgeoisie simply acts in defense of its own interests. The bourgeois is in Marx's analysis the same as the capitalist, and the rule of the bourgeoisie came to mean for Marx a form of civilization based on the oppression or exploitation of the working class. To be bourgeois means to be a heartless exploiter of one's neighbor and the products of the earth. It comes to be associated with absolute oppression, absolute injustice, and therefore absolute evil.

It was not Marx but Nietzsche who made the war on the bourgeois a virtual rallying cry. Like all the great haters of the bourgeoisie, Nietzsche, like Marx, was a product of the bourgeois class, one the scion of generations of Protestant pastors, the other a lawyer's son. Both were recipients of the ultimate passport to bourgeois respectability—the Ph.D. The phenomenon of the self-hating bourgeois is surely one of the most arresting psychological phenomena of the modern age, giving rise to an extraordinarily rich literature with some unforgettable characters. (Why are there no examples of the self-hating aristocrat or the self-hating peasant?) Nietzsche brought this kind of bourgeois hatred to a pitch of perfection, tracing the ideals of modern civilization back to their English origins.

Three passages from among many can serve to illustrate the association of modern civilization with its English philosophical roots. The first is from Heinrich Heine, the most cosmopolitan German of his generation, who treated Locke as the source of materialism and a mechanistic theory of the mind. "French philosophers chose John Locke as their master," he wrote. "He was the savior they needed. His *Essay Concerning Human Understanding* became their gospel, and they swore by it. . . . He turned the human mind into a kind of calculating machine; the whole human being became an English machine."[17] Similarly, Heine's contemporary Marx associated the modern market economy with English ideas about free trade and the ethic of utility. "There alone," he sardonically remarked, "rule Freedom, Equality, Property, and Bentham."[18] Or consider one further example from Nietzsche: "They are no philosophical race, these Englishmen; Bacon signifies an attack on the philosophical spirit; Hobbes, Hume and Locke a debasement of the value of the concept of philosophy for more than a century . . . it was Locke of whom Schelling said understandably, '*je meprise Locke.*'"[19]

The German contempt for Locke, the quintessential Englishman, says it all. No less than Heine and Marx, Nietzsche associated the English philosophy of Hobbes, Locke, and Bentham with the rise of a new type of bourgeois society based on the ideas of the rights of man and the greatest happiness for the greatest number. These concepts that played such a significant role in the creation of liberal democracy were seen by all three of the sources just cited to represent the degradation of society by reducing a longing for the noble and the great to something unpoetic, unaesthetic, and of course utterly materialistic. One finds in Nietzsche's unforgettable portrait of "the last man" in *Thus Spoke Zarathustra* a depiction of the type of human being who will be the inhabitant of the mass democracies of the future, a world in which races and cultures will disappear, where there will be neither ruling nor being ruled ("both require too much exertion"), neither rich nor poor, neither love nor hate, and where the only real passion will be for comfortable self-preservation. This is a universal society of free, equal, and prosperous individuals that Nietzsche could regard only with contempt.[20]

Nietzsche's fears about the last man fed the imagination of some of Europe's leading philosophers, who saw it not as a projection of certain trends or tendencies of modern society but as an actual description of present-day reality. Nietzsche's greatest disciple, Martin Heidegger, spoke of the "inauthenticity" of everyday life dominated by "the they" (*das Man*). The very impersonality of this new form of being testified to its "averageness" and "leveling down" of all possibilities. He uses the Enlightenment's term for the public or publicity (*Öffentlichkeit*)—a word suggesting openness, transparency, and civil society—to depict a world that has become permeated by idle chatter, superficial opinion, or what today would be called "buzz."[21] Although Heidegger did not explicitly relate his critique of publicity to the institutions of representative democracy, his contemporary Carl Schmitt found no problem in depicting parliamentary government as the regime dominated by a kind of endless talk without the ability to act. Schmitt enjoyed quoting the Spanish jurist Donoso Cortés's sarcastic reference to the bourgeoisie as *una clasa discutidora*—a discussing class, or a "chattering class"—to show the attempt to shift all political activity to the plane of conversation.[22] It would be only a step from here to Schmitt's embrace of an ethics of pure decisionisim, in which choice is no longer the consequence of deliberation but has become an irrational and groundless act of will.

It did not take long for Nietzsche's culture critique to finds its way to America.[23] The concept of the bourgeois may belong to the high European tradition of literature and philosophy, but it has its distinctively American offshoots that focused on fears of conformity, the disappearance of the rugged individualist, and a pervasive averageness associated with what is often contemptuously called Middle America. Sinclair Lewis's novel *Babbit,* not read so much any longer, gave rise to the term "Babbitry" to describe the small-town American of the 1920s who joins civic booster clubs and praises the virtues of membership. The journalist H. L. Menken coined the term "booboisie"—a combination of boob and bourgeois—to describe the typical democratic everyman. And more recently *New York Times* columnist David Brooks in his book *Bobos in Paradise*—a combination of bohemian and bourgeois—parodied the term to describe today's high-end consumer Yuppies who engage in conspicuous consumption while paying lip service to liberal values: the kind of people who put an environmental bumper sticker on the back of their suburban

SUV. Books and films from Sherwood Anderson's *Winesburg Ohio* to Alexander Payne's *Nebraska* depict an American modernity that is increasingly heartless, intolerant, repressive, and suffocatingly provincial.

But the Counter-Enlightenment also told another story, not just of decadence, but of a possible liberation. The story has been told many times and in countless ways about modernity's discovery of history and the historical method. The Counter-Enlightenment showed that the very idea of modernity was itself a product of history, no longer the absolute moment of a vast metanarrative but a distinct "moment" whose force might even now be spent. Modernity itself may be surpassed by a leap into an absolutely new and yet unknown (because unknowable) dispensation of history. The point of this act of excavation was not simply inspired by a messianic longing to "force the end" or issue in a new postmetaphysical era, although it took this form in the writings of Heidegger and other postmodernists. The Counter-Enlightenment was initially a movement of return, to excavate the foundations of modernity, to see where modernity began and what resources could be discovered to prevent its self-dissolution. Such a return was inspired not simply by a nostalgia for the old or a love of the past for its own sake but by the deepest and most enduring human desire: the desire to see for ourselves, with our own eyes, as it were, and not simply on the authority of others what modernity had concealed from view.

MODERNITY AND ITS DOUBLES

The question that I want to pose is this. How is it possible to retain a critical stance toward modernity and yet resist the temptation of radical negation? If the Counter-Enlightenment has been modernity's doppelgänger from the beginning, how should the challenge be met? The first step is to realize that the standard picture of modernity, embraced by both its advocates and its critics, is not in every respect accurate. The Enlightenment and its Counter-Enlightenment critics are not so much antagonists as copartners in the modern project. They represent modernity's doubles. Modernity is not monolithic, and it contains many competing strands. Dissatisfaction with—indeed, alienation from—modernity is itself a characteristically modern pose. How better to express one's modernity than by voicing one's discontent with it? But the critique of modernity need not result in wholesale rejection.

The best defenders of modernity have often been precisely those who have taken a page from the Counter-Enlightenment and yet have not been led to embrace fascism or other kinds of "reactionary modernism."[24] There are ways of challenging the dominance of the Enlightenment without sliding down the slippery path to nihilism and bourgeois self-hatred. The author who comes closest to capturing this sensibility is Alexis de Tocqueville. Perhaps because he was an aristocrat, he displayed none of the bourgeois sense of anxiety and alienation exhibited by the likes of Rousseau, Flaubert, Marx, and Nietzsche. Tocqueville gave vivid expression to the fears about the age of equality. He was profoundly skeptical of the great middle-class democracies with their materialism, love of comfort, and belief in unlimited progress. Yet Tocqueville's work contains nothing of the spirit of *ressentiment*—the incurable desire for revenge—that Nietzsche saw as the besetting sin of the modern age. He saw democracy as a historical inevitability, but one that could still be moderated by practices and institutions favorable to liberty.

One example among many can serve as an illustration. Tocqueville recognized that the modern democratic age would be based on an ethic of self-interest, or what he called "self-interest well understood."[25] By self-interest well understood Tocqueville did not mean avarice or greed—it is not Gordon Gekko's famous "greed is good" in Oliver Stone's *Wall Street*—but rather a concept comprising the totality of human aspirations. Self-interest well understood suggested enlightenment, reflection, and a spirit of cool calculation with respect to the manner in which these aspirations were pursued. Self-interest, when well understood, could also serve as the basis for certain civic virtues, not, to be sure, the high aristocratic virtues of beauty, nobility, and self-sacrifice, but a set of lower-order, more mundane, "bourgeois" virtues, such as cooperation, moderation, tolerance, and self-mastery. Such virtues were not to be sneezed at. Tocqueville did not rail against self-interest as something petty, narrow, or vulgar or view it, as did the followers of Kant, as a kind of perversion of ethics. Rather he saw it as responsible for certain excellences of heart and mind most fitting for an age of democracy.

Another thinker who imbibed much of Tocqueville's understanding of modernity was the German émigré philosopher Leo Strauss. Strauss may have done more than any thinker of the twentieth century to revive a serious engagement with Plato and classical political philosophy. In particular he resisted the facile association of Plato with totalitarianism that became especially widespread after World War II. His views of the ancients were complex. Strauss did not see them as a simple alternative to the problems of modern liberal democracy, nor did he see them as providing the first, hesitant baby steps toward the evolution of modern democracy. He insisted that although the ancients could not provide ready-made answers for the problems of today, the premodern thought of the Western tradition—in both its classical and medieval variants—could provide crucial theoretical support for modern liberal democracy by recalling it to its often-forgotten premodern roots.

Strauss developed these ideas most vividly in his thoughts on the future of liberal education. Liberal education, as he conceived it, is etymologically related to the virtue of liberality that originally meant generosity or openness. A liberal democracy, therefore, was a political regime open to education of a very rare, if not to say rarified, kind, a regime that was both democratic and had acquired some of the characteristics previously associated with aristocracy.[26] A liberal democracy is therefore a species of what the ancients called a "mixed regime" precisely for its blending of democratic and aristocratic principles, that is, a regime where the fruits of liberal education are in principle available to everyone. This remained especially true, Strauss believed, of the United States and Great Britain, where the tradition of liberal education and the virtues of public service continued to be cultivated in the great universities, like Oxford and Yale.

But as Strauss knew, liberal education was for all practical purposes the preserve of a minority—he preferred the deliberately old-fashioned term "gentlemen"—who in the conditions of modern democracy could serve as a counterfoil to the pressures of mass culture. Modern education was increasingly losing touch with its foundations in the ancients and becoming ever more technical and specialist in nature. Rather than serving as a counterfoil to mass democracy, modern education was becoming its handmaiden. Only an education in the classics or the "great books" could provide modern men and women with the taste for excellence that they were being unjustly denied. "Liberal education," Strauss wrote, "is the ladder by which we try to ascend from mass democracy to democracy as originally meant. Liberal education is the necessary endeavor to found an aristocracy within democratic mass society."[27] For comments such as these, Strauss has often been characterized as an elitist and an enemy of democracy. Yet he preferred to describe himself as a friend of liberal democracy, who, precisely because he was a friend, did not permit himself to become a flatterer.

At its best, the Counter-Enlightenment has helped to initiate a conversation between the two sides to the debate between modernity and its critics that was prematurely cut short. The purpose in revitalizing such a debate is not to declare one side the victor over the other—what would such victory even look like?—but to discover what we moderns have still to learn or at least to discover what is important not to forget. In fact, as writers like Tocqueville and Strauss appreciated, the breach between modernity and its doubles was never quite as complete as some of the early moderns tended to claim. Important areas of continuity as well as discontinuity continue to exist and to play themselves out in often-fruitful results. It is to help keep this conversation alive that I have written this book.

Part Two **Modernity**

Chapter 2 Machiavelli's *Mandragola* and the Protean Self

Each man behaves according to his own intellect and imagination.
—Niccolò Machiavelli

It will surprise no one—I shall simply repeat a well-received opinion—if I say that Machiavelli is the founder of modern political science.

To be sure, long before Machiavelli, the ancient writers had attempted to establish a science of politics. Plato, Aristotle, Polybius, and Cicero had engaged in serious and systematic efforts to organize and clarify the data of political life, to establish rules and laws by which different regimes come into being and pass away. The failure of the ancients, so it was alleged, came not from their efforts to establish a science of politics but from their want of method in attempting to do so. It is the charge of methodological naïveté that was brought against the ancients by Machiavelli, Bacon, Descartes, Hobbes, and others seeking to put knowledge on a new, more secure foundation.

The idea that Machiavelli is the founder of modern political science is by no means self-evident. He seems to make none of the bold experimental moves more frequently associated with Descartes and Hobbes. His most famous book, *The Prince,* follows a traditional genre of "mirror of princes" that goes back to Xenophon; his longest and greatest book, *Discourses on Livy,* takes the form of a commentary on the first ten books of the Roman historian Livy. What could be more traditional? Yet Machiavelli's modernity consists less in his methodological innovations than in his call to break from the traditional authority of his predecessors.

Machiavelli's modernity is expressed in his preference for novelty, for the new over the old, for the bold and experimental over the tried and true. His embrace of novelty is also tied to his realism, to the "effectual truth of the thing" rather than the imagination. By the effectual truth, he means knowledge of the "is" rather than the "ought," of the way things actually work as opposed to how they ought to be. This is the prior move that made all later methodological innovations possible, namely, Machiavelli's attempt to determine the rules of political life solely from political life rather than subordinating it to the demands of morality, theology, or metaphysics. But Machiavelli's realism should not be mistaken for Aristotle's conception of a statesman who knows how to establish, or reestablish, order in conflict-ridden situations. Machiavelli's praise of the effectual truth is followed by his famous (or infamous) judgment that the prince who hopes to succeed must learn how "not to be good," in other words, learn to break the established rules and conventions. The prince who follows Machiavelli's advice will be not simply a reformer but a revolutionary who establishes his authority de novo.

Machiavelli's modernity is most often expressed in his conception of the new prince who is the bringer of "new modes and orders," someone on the order of the great founder legislators of the past like Moses, Lycurgus, Cyrus, and Romulus.[1] Machiavelli's appeal to these classical models concealed the fact that his prince expressed a new, highly idealized, conception of the statesman, at once individual, autonomous, and self-legislating. Machiavelli thought of politics as a work of art, as a product of will and artifice, of certain newfound powers of creativity and human agency. He was a product of Renaissance Florence and a contemporary of Michelangelo and Leonardo.[2] The term "Renaissance" may mean rebirth, but the period was a time of extraordinary innovation. The Renaissance was not just a recovery of the old; it was a harbinger of the new. In fact Nietzsche's contemporary, the historian Jacob Burckhardt, remains the most perceptive analyst of this new disposition that assumed the proportions of a new protean image of human nature, a combination of individuality, an unprecedented flowering of the "free personality," and a new attention to the value of private life.[3]

This protean quality of individuality and self-expression came alive in fifteenth-century Italy initially with Boccaccio and Pico della Mirandola. It can be discovered in writers like Rabelais, who explored it with unparalleled enthusiasm, Cervantes, who created the first modern novel of self-discovery, and Descartes, who discovered the lonely interiority of his *cogito ergo sum*. The spirit of the enterprising individual seeking his intellectual and material fortune and responsible to himself alone can similarly be found in the novels of Bunyan and Defoe, the politics of Locke and Bernard Mandeville, and the autobiographies of Franklin and Rousseau. Consider only Hobbes's attempt to capture the protean character of experience in his "Verse Life":

> Then I four years spent to contrive which way
> To pen my book *De Corpore* night and day;
> Compare together each corporeal thing,
> Think when the known changes of forms do spring.
> Inquire how I compel this *Proteus* may,
> His cheats and artifices to display.[4]

Machiavelli's term for this protean quality of self-creation is *fantasia*. This is one of the most suggestive, but also most underrated, terms in Machiavelli's psychological lexicon. Machiavelli might seem to be a critic of fantasia as associated with utopianism and imaginative flights of fancy, but in fact the concept also suggested for him the power of individual human agency responsible for the great diversity of individual personalities. It is a term often identified with human creativity by which persons are enabled to act out their own ambitions and fulfill their own individuality. Machiavelli's judgments are often dictated less by prudence than by aesthetics and expanding the limits of the possible. Fantasia has a deliberately "theatrical" quality about it, enabling Machiavelli to view politics as the sphere of spectacle.[5]

Machiavelli's assertion of this new individuality did not remain at the plane of high politics only. Among the institutions that is the most enduring and the most essential to the maintenance of political life is the family. Yet *The Prince* and the *Discourses* pay scant attention to the role of the family. This would seem to be a glaring omission, but the family is not altogether absent in Machiavelli's work. Machiavelli takes the theme of the family with the utmost seriousness, although not necessarily in the place that most readers would expect to find it, namely, in his comic masterpiece *Mandragola*.[6] Here we find Machiavelli applying the same methods of innovation, novelty, and audacity to private life as he does to the founding of states. At the core of the work is even a confounding of public and private life. The work is nothing less than the founding of Machiavelli's new family values.

ISTORICO, COMICO, ET TRAGICO

Most readers are probably unaware that Machiavelli was not only the author of important political treatises but also a poet and playwright who wrote one of the most popular and still widely performed comedies of the Renaissance. *Mandragola*—originally entitled *Messer Nicia* or *Commedia di Callimico e di Lucrezia*—was written in 1518, although it was probably read to friends gathered in the Orti Oricellari even before it was performed. The play has never lacked admirers. According to Voltaire, it was "perhaps worth more than all the comedies of Aristophanes," while Macaulay proclaimed it "superior to the best of Goldoni and inferior only to the best of Molière."[7] It was adapted as an opera and was revived for the New York stage in the 1970s with a young, then unknown, actor named Tom Hanks playing the part of Callimico. Ever since the play's first performance, efforts have been made to relate Machiavelli's comic masterpiece to his political teachings. In what respect does Machiavelli here present his political teachings in a comic form? How do the characters of *Mandragola* express actual historical persons or events? How does this domestic comedy of fraud and deception corroborate Machiavelli's claim to be the discoverer of "new modes and orders"?

In a letter to his friend Francesco Guicciardini, Machiavelli described himself as "historian, comic, and tragedian" (*istorico, comico, et tragico*).[8] Terms like "historian" and "tragedian" readily seem to apply, but we do not usually think of Machiavelli as a comic writer. While his political writings often reveal brilliant flashes of wit and irony, we tend to be more impressed by the seriousness with which he takes politics, and in fact a case could be made that his writings have a closer resemblance to tragedy than comedy. There is nothing funny about Machiavelli's depiction of the decline, even the decadence, of modern Italy. Machiavelli's heroes, like Cesare Borgia and Castruccio Castracani, are all failures who are often overwhelmed by the power of *fortuna*. Even his exhortations to imitate the great deeds of the Roman, Greek, and Hebrew heroes seem bound to fail given what Machiavelli regards as the corruption of the age in which he lives.[9]

Yet at the same time, these tragic elements are easily overstated. Machiavelli confidently predicts that it is possible to master and control *fortuna*. Rather than giving way to despair, he believes it is possible not only to imitate the Romans but to exceed them, to do through planning and forethought what they achieved only through chance. Machiavelli's work arouses in its readers a sense of optimism and confidence that the future belongs to them. Comedies, as we all know, appeal more to the young, who especially enjoy seeing the veil of respectability removed from their elders, and it is to the young—in fact the very young (*giovanissimi*)—to whom Machiavelli addresses his work.[10]

According to Machiavelli's biographer Roberto Ridolfi, the time when Machiavelli wrote the *Mandragola* remains "one of the most obscure periods of his life," even though "studded with his masterpieces."[11] The context of *Mandragola* is presented in the Prologue to the play. "This is your Florence," Machiavelli tells the audience, the Florence of his day (Prologue). He makes clear that his present-day Florence is a place where virtue goes unrewarded and where people are more eager to blame others for their plight than to work and struggle to improve themselves. The author, he writes, is "not of great fame." Machiavelli alludes to the fact of his political exile, noting that "he is trying with these vain thoughts to make his wretched time more pleasant, because he has nowhere else to turn his face; for he has been cut off from showing with other undertakings other virtue, there being no reward for his labors" (Prologue). Machiavelli presents the play as a diversion—a pleasant diversion, to be sure—from the serious business of politics. But how like Machiavelli would it be to disguise his most serious teachings in the form of a lighthearted comedy about domestic life?

Machiavelli's jesting tone also contains a real sense of sorrow and bitterness, coming from his political disappointments, perhaps from the failure of *The Prince* to gain an audience. This appears in the Prologue to *Mandragola* where he expresses a kind of proud contempt for those who are his superior in rank and nobility:

> Yet, if anyone thinks that by speaking ill,
> He can hold the author by his hair
> And discourage him or make him draw back a bit,
> I warn him, and say to such a one
> That the author knows how to speak ill as well as he,
> And that this was his first art;
> And that, in every part

Of the world where *sì* [Italian] is sounded,
He doesn't stand in awe of anyone,
Even though he might play the servant to one
Who can wear a better coat than he can. (Prologue)

LUCRETIA AND LUCREZIA

Machiavelli's play is itself a comic retelling of a pivotal event from Roman history: the rape of Lucretia.[12] This story occupies a central moment in Livy's account of the transition from the Roman monarchy to the republic. On Livy's telling of the story, a group of young Roman princes are sitting around their battle encampment bragging about the virtue of their wives. One of them, Collatinus, insisting that his wife, Lucretia, is the best, entices the others to strike camp and return to town, where they can secretly observe her. Upon their arrival, several of the princesses are seen feasting and frolicking with their friends, but Lucretia is discovered "bent over her spinning surrounded by her maids as they worked by lamplight" (I.57). Happy with his victory, Collatinus invites his comrades into his home, where one of them, Sextus Tarquinius, the son of the king, develops an insane passion to debauch her. Several days pass, and Tarquin finds a pretext to return to the house of Collatinus, where he is invited in and after dinner is shown to a guest room. After the household is safely asleep, Tarquin enters the room of Lucretia sword in hand and forces her to submit to him. At first Lucretia refuses, but Tarquin threatens to kill her and further disgrace her by leaving the naked body of a murdered slave near her bed as proof that Lucretia had been killed in the act of adultery. "When by this threat his lust vanquished her resolute chastity," Livy writes, "he left the house exulting in his seeming conquest of the woman's honor" (I.58).

The story continues with Lucretia summoning her father and husband back home to bear witness to the crime. Each is instructed to bring a trustworthy companion. Lucretia's father brings with him Publius Valerius—the same Publius whose name would be adopted by the authors of the *Federalist Papers*—and Collatinus brings his friend Junius Brutus. When Lucretia reveals to them that she has been raped by Tarquin, she makes them promise that the outrage will not go unavenged, after which she plunges a dagger in her heart and dies on the spot. It is Brutus—previously believed to be a fool and half-wit—who pulls the bloody knife from her body and declares vengeance on Tarquin and his family (I.56). Those around him were amazed at the "miraculous change" that seemed to have come over Brutus as he made a speech over the body of Lucretia, declaring that the Tarquins had to be driven from power. Livy admits that Brutus had used his reputation for stupidity as a shield, biding his time for the moment when he could emerge as a liberator of the people. "The most spirited young men" were quick to join Brutus, with the result that they marched on Rome and with this act of vengeance established the republic (I.59).

The story of Lucretia became one of the great founding myths of Rome, discussed at some length in Augustine's *City of God*.[13] Augustine was fascinated with the case of Lucretia and used it to raise a problem never asked by Livy, namely, the ethics of suicide. Is it ever morally justified to take one's own life? If Lucretia truly was chaste, what was she guilty of? Augustine considers a thought experiment in which there were two Lucretias, one the victim, the other, the murderer. Why should the Romans extol a murderer who killed an innocent woman? But then Augustine goes on to consider a second possibility. What if Lucretia was not as blameless as Livy's account would suggest? What if she were actually an accomplice in her own victimization? In such a case, it would be criminal to exalt her sacrifice. Lucretia's death was the result of the false esteem that the Romans gave to the concept of honor and to worldly goods. It was "due to the weakness of shame, not to the high value she set upon honor," that led to Lucretia's death. Suicide becomes a form of moral weakness, rather than a mark of courage. Lucretia's suicide was in fact a case of wounded vanity: "Since she could not display her pure conscience to the world she thought she must exhibit her punishment before men's eyes as a proof of her state of mind" (I.19). When Christian women were violated, Augustine claims, they did not respond by taking their lives. Rather than adding crime to crime, they preferred to carry "the glory of chastity within them." It is in "the testimony of conscience," rather than concern for the opinion of others, in which true glory lies (I.19). By the time Augustine gets through undermining the credibility of Lucretia's sacrifice, it might seem that there is little left to say.

Machiavelli addresses the rape of Lucretia on three different occasions in the *Discourses*. Interestingly, he minimizes the incident. He refers to it as an "accident," an "error," and an "excess." In *Discourses* III.2, he uses the story of Lucretia to illustrate the wisdom of Brutus's policy of pretending to play the fool. The chapter begins with an extraordinary sentence: "There was never anyone so prudent (*tanto prudente*) nor so esteemed so wise (*tanto estimato savio*) for any eminent work of his that Junius Brutus deserves to be held in his simulation of stupidity." What most amazes Machiavelli is Brutus's capacity not only for dissimulation, which allowed him to live securely in enjoyment of his patrimony, but also for using the "occasion" of the rape "for crushing the kings and freeing his own fatherland." Rather than expressing outrage at the rape, Machiavelli coolly draws two lessons about how potential usurpers should behave. If they believe themselves sufficiently powerful to overthrow a reigning prince, they should openly make war because this is "less dangerous and more honorable." But if they deem themselves too weak to mount an immediate coup d'état, they should make every effort to befriend the prince "by becoming obsequious to his wishes and by taking pleasure in everything in which they see that he takes pleasure." By adopting this second strategy of playing the fool, it is possible to enjoy the prince's largesse while "providing ample opportunity for fulfilling your intentions."[14]

Three chapters later, Machiavelli draws another lesson. The key to preserving a kingdom is for a prince to respect the ancient institutions and customs that had been established by his predecessors. The true cause of the expulsion of the Tarquins was due not to the rape of Lucretia but to the fact that the monarchs had deprived the Senate of its ancient prerogatives and began to rule tyrannically. Not only had Tarquin lost the support of the Senate, he had alienated the plebs by forcing them to perform menial tasks and thus "aroused in all Romans a spirit of revolt, ready to break out should occasion arise." The term "occasion" here is the giveaway. For Machiavelli, it means something like a cause or a pretext from which to act. "If the accident of Lurcetia had not come," he writes, "as soon as another had arisen it would have brought the same effect. For if Tarquin had lived like the other kings and Sextus his son had made that error, Brutus and Collatinus would have had recourse to Tarquin and not to the Roman people for vengeance against Sextus."[15] Machiavelli claims that the incident was used by Brutus as a pretext for overthrowing the monarchy and establishing a republic; in other words, any other event could have served him just as well. To say the least, Machiavelli is not outraged by the rape.

Finally, in *Discourses* III.26, entitled "How Women Have Brought About the Downfall of States," Machiavelli comes close to blaming the victim for the crime. "Women," he asserts, "have been the cause of many troubles, have done great harm to those who govern cities." The rapes of Lucretia and of Virginia later in the work are simply two instances of a general rule that has led to the downfall of tyrants. Machiavelli even credits Aristotle—Aristotle!— with the insight that among the "primary causes" that lead to political revolution are the injuries that tyrants do to women, whether by rape or the breakup of marriages. His recommendation: "I say here, then, that absolute princes and the rulers of republics should not treat such matters as of small moment, but should bear in mind the disorders that such events may occasion and look to the matter in good time, so that the remedy applied may not be accompanied by damage done to, or revolts against, their state or their republic."[16] Machiavelli here repeats a lesson that he discovered in *The Prince,* namely, for a ruler to stay in power it is important to leave alone the property and the women of his subjects.[17]

What is treated as an accident or a pretext in the *Discourses* is turned into a joke in *Mandragola,* in which the new Lucretia—Lucrezia Calfucci—becomes a willing and able accomplice in the overturning of the old order. Livy's telling of the story is a deeply moral tale of dishonor and revenge. The chastity of the Roman woman was taken very seriously, so seriously in fact that the violation of this taboo led to the founding of a new, republican regime. But if Livy's telling of the story concludes with the birth of the republic, Machiavelli's retelling of it results in the creation of a new order, more by fraud than by force, in which all are able to realize their fondest dreams.

In *Mandragola,* the story of the rape of Lucretia is turned upside down. In the first place, the rape and suicide of the Roman Lucretia is replaced by a conspiracy in which Machiavelli's Lucrezia becomes a willing, even an eager, participant in the deception of her husband. In place of the young Tarquin, a hereditary prince who forces himself on Lucretia, Machiavelli creates Callimico, who we learn has been living abroad as an expatriate for twenty years precisely to escape the wars then plaguing his native land. Callimico refers explicitly to "the march of Charles," meaning King Charles VIII of France and his invasion of Italy in 1494. The action of the play takes place under the shadow of political defeat and the loss of virtue, at least in the political sense. Political life does not seem to be a concern of Callimico's. Private intrigue has become a surrogate for politics. Whatever else you might say about him, Callimico is no patriot.

In *Mandragola,* the stern and unforgiving morality of the ancient Romans is replaced with a modern Epicurean morality that stresses the pursuit of happiness as the only policy. The opening words of the *canzone* that precedes the Prologue succinctly state the play's governing philosophy:

Because life is brief and many are the pains
Which, living and struggling, everyone sustains,

> Let us follow our desires passing and consuming the years,
> Because whoever deprives himself of pleasure
> To live with anguish and with worries, doesn't know the tricks of the world,
> Or by what ills and by what strange happenings all mortals are almost over-
>   whelmed. (Song)

In other words, due to the unpredictability of fortune, let us pursue pleasure wherever it leads. Life is too short to deny ourselves anything we want. Don't worry, be happy.

THE CONSPIRACY

It has often been noted that the centerpiece of *Mandragola* is a conspiracy, a topic close to Machiavelli's heart and the subject of the longest single chapter from the *Discourses*.[18] In the chapter Machiavelli considers a range of different conspiracies, conspiracies undertaken by a single individual, those formed by the weak and by the strong, the dangers to conspiracies by informers, by indiscretion, and by change of plan, conspiracies against a prince and against a republic. Yet nowhere in this lengthy chapter does he discuss the possibility of domestic conspiracies, of husbands against wives, wives against husbands, and mothers against daughters. In the *Discourses,* Machiavelli cites Tacitus's "golden sentence" that men need to respect the past but submit to the present, that one is entitled to wish for good princes but must accept what fate gives one.[19] The chapter as a whole deals with the dangers of conspiracies and the unlikelihood of their success. Yet despite his apparent warnings, Machiavelli constructs a conspiracy of his own. By putting the problem of conspiracy at the center of the play, Machiavelli is inviting the reader to become complicit in his plot.

The main figure of the conspiracy—I am reluctant to call him the hero—is Callimico Guadagni. The action begins with a dinner conversation among some fellow expatriates in Paris who are debating the respective merits of French and Italian women. Callimico admits that he has no way of judging for himself, having been away from Italy for so long. But one of his dinner companions boasts that one of his relatives—Lucrezia Calfucci—is so renowned for her beauty and manners that it leaves the other dinner guests "stupefied," one of Machiavelli's favorite words. Much like young Tarquin in Livy's story of Lucretia, Callimico develops a burning passion to see her for himself, but the problem is that Lucrezia is stuck in a childless marriage with a man who is described as "the simplest and most stupid man in Florence" (I.1).

Callimico returns to Florence in order to expedite his plan. With the help of his servant, he enlists a former marriage broker, Ligurio, who hatches a plot to present Callimico as a famous doctor recently arrived from the court of the French king, who will persuade Nicia that the only way to make his wife pregnant is to have her drink a love potion made from a special root—the mandragola, or mandrake root. The catch is—he tells the gullible Nicia—that the concoction will cause death to the first person to sleep with her after taking the potion. By this time, Ligurio has succeeded in enlisting the help not only of the family priest but also of Lucrezia's mother to be part of the plan. Now disguised as a street singer, Callimico pretends that he needs to be convinced by Nicia to sleep with his wife. In the course of their evening together Callimico reveals the fraud to Lucrezia, who decides to take Callimico as her permanent lover. The play ends with the happy couple agreeing to continue in their deception, leaving the witless Nicia to believe that the love child is in fact his own.

Mandragola inevitably invites comparison to Machiavelli's *Prince*. To what extent is the play an allegory for Machiavelli's Florence? To what extent are the characters in the play representations of actual Florentine political actors? Which character best embodies those characteristic virtues—strength and cunning, the qualities of the lion and the fox—that Machiavelli claims are needed for the true prince? The play reveals a hierarchy of characters fashioned around their different degrees of perception and capacity for manipulation. It is a perfect illustration of Machiavelli's dictum that the great pretenders and dissemblers always get the better of the simple and obedient. The question is, Who is the master conspirator? Who, at the end of the day, will end up on top?[20]

The most obvious choice would seem to be Callimico. One can certainly see him as an example of Machiavelli's "new prince" who overthrows the traditional or hereditary head of the household as represented by Nicia. Like Machiavelli's new prince, Callimico is presented as an outsider to traditional rule and authority. All we know of him is that having lost his parents as a child, he has lived abroad for twenty years with no country or friends. At the outset of the play, he has been living as an exile in Paris managing to make himself "agreeable" to everyone at the French court and is persuaded to return to Florence only to observe for himself the beautiful Lucrezia. He is willing to father a child whose true connection to him can never be revealed. His only companion, Ligurio, is a recent acquaintance and a social inferior. In short, Callimico is a man alone, radically detached from the conventional ties of family, friends, and country. He is a kind of "new man," a potential usurper who seeks to undermine the traditional institution of marriage and the family much as Machiavelli's new prince seeks to undermine the established political order.

And yet, Callimico is an imperfect Machiavellian at best. The problem is that he is weak. He is a creature of his passions. His lust for Lucrezia leaves him completely dependent on *fortuna* and the whims of others. Callimico's greatest talent has been the art of pleasing others, of making himself "agreeable to the middle class, to gentlemen, to the foreigner, to the native, to the poor, to the rich" (I.1). In addition to the desire to please, Machiavelli's description of Callimico as "carrying off the honor and prize for courtesy" points to attributes lesser than the manly virtues necessary for a true prince (Prologue). The true Machiavellian—to use one of Machiavelli's most famous images— knows that he who is dependent upon *fortuna* comes to ruin. This is why "it is better to be impetuous than cautious because fortune is a woman and it is necessary, if one wants to hold her down, to beat her and strike her down."[21] But this image is the very opposite of Callimico, who finds himself paralyzed, torn between hope and fear (IV.1). At a crucial point in the play, he contemplates suicide ("I'll either throw myself from those windows or I'll stab myself with a knife in her doorway" [IV.4]) as a relief from his pains. Can one imagine one of Machiavelli's heroes giving way to such fits of doubt and uncertainty over a woman?

If Callimico is a man who lacks legitimacy in the eyes of the world, Nicia is the very embodiment of traditional authority based on age and convention. Yet it has been suggested that Nicia is really Machiavelli's prince because he so completely plays the fool that he tricks everyone into believing that he really is a fool.[22] After all, at the end of the play Nicia is the one who gets what he most wants: an heir (even if it is not his own). Is this Machiavelli's idea of a joke on his readers? If so, it has been successful. This seems to stretch the theme of deception too far. Almost universally Nicia has been judged a simpleton. "Old Nicias is the glory of the piece," Macaulay wrote. "We cannot call to mind anything that resembles him. The follies which Molière ridicules are those of affectation, not those of fatuity."[23] If Nicia is under cover, his cover is so deep that no one seems to realize it.

Here as in so much else, Machiavelli's choice of names tells us something. To be sure, the choice of Nicia bears a resemblance to Machiavelli's own name,

Niccolò. But it is more likely that Nicia refers back to the Athenian general Nicias, whose procrastination, superstition, and gullibility led to military disaster in the Sicilian campaign in the Peloponnesian War. The Athenian Nicias was a decent man, but slow and cautious. For Thucydides, Nicias was a genuinely tragic hero, who, Thucydides wrote, "of all the Greeks of my time least deserved such a fate seeing that the whole course of his life had been regulated with strict attention to virtue."[24] But if Nicias was a tragic hero for Thucydides, Machiavelli turns his namesake into a dolt. He is easily duped by Callimico, who is encouraged by Ligurio to embellish his speech with some stock Latin phrases and other gibberish that he knows will impress Nicia. Machiavelli's depiction of Nicia's pomposity—a learned *dottore* steeped in the philosophy of Boethius—could also express his jibes against his own contemporaries, the Humanists, whom Machiavelli satirizes in the Preface to the *Discourses* by saying that they would rather have a piece of ancient statuary to adorn their homes than attempt to imitate ancient virtue.[25]

There are two characters who are not movers of the conspiracy but are nonetheless essential to its success: Lucrezia's mother, Sostrata, and the family priest, Fra Timoteo. Sostrata is introduced as someone who used to be "good company"—a woman of easy virtue—whose main task is convincing Lucrezia to submit herself to Callimico. "I believe that you believe" are her first words to her daughter (III.10). The belief in question concerns her daughter's fear of the "error" to which she will be exposed if she follows her husband's design for children. She is being asked not only to consent to an act of adultery but also to become complicit in the death of an innocent man. "If I were the only woman remaining in the world," she laments to her mother, "and if human nature had to rise again from me, I couldn't believe that such a course would be allowed to me" (III.10). For Lucrezia, morality is a matter of all or nothing. Even if the future of the human race depended on her alone, she could not submit to a sin. She seems to admit to Kant's edict *fiat iustitia, et pereat mundus,* let justice prevail even if the world perishes.[26]

It is here that Fra Timoteo steps in. Earlier he has been introduced as one of those "ill-living *frati*," in other words, as thoroughly corrupt (Prologue). Ligurio has him pegged as "cunning" and "astute," one of those who "because they know our sins and their own" are in a position to use them against us (III.2). The terms "cunning" and "astute" suggest that the priest is no stock fool. He is a skillful conman in his own right. He is a shrewd manipulator of people, especially of women, who he believes have "few brains." How like Machiavelli to use the family priest as an instrument of betrayal!

But it is in fact the friar on whom the tables are turned with the abortion ruse. Knowing with Machiavelli that all successful conspiracies must drape themselves in the mantle of religion, Ligurio steps in to snare the priest. He introduces Callimico as a nephew of Nicia, a widower who went to France after leaving his only daughter in the care of a convent. The nuns, Ligurio tells Fra Timoteo, failed in their calling and the girl is now four months pregnant. Ligurio asks the priest to help persuade the abbess of the convent to give the girl a potion to induce an abortion. "Keep in mind," he tells the priest, "in doing this, how many goods will result from it: you maintain the honor of the convent, of the girl, of her relatives," and what is at risk but "a piece of unborn flesh, without sense, which could be dispersed in a thousand ways" (III.4). Ligurio offers—on Nicia's behalf—to pay a handsome sum to the convent, most of which, we suspect, will end up in the pocket of the priest, but before the scene is over Ligurio excuses himself and returns with supposedly the good news that the girl has suffered a miscarriage and the priest will not be needed after all. The alms will still be given, but in the meantime there is something else that needs doing, "less burdensome, less scandalous, more agreeable to us, and more profitable to you" (III. 6). Getting the priest to concede to the first plot makes it all that much easier to gain his consent to the second. Timoteo has been thoroughly co-opted.

We are introduced to Ligurio at the beginning of the play as a former marriage broker who is now managing to earn a living as a kind of "parasite," who has insinuated himself into Nicia's household and is dining at his table. Yet even though Nicia has been supporting him, Ligurio comes to the aid of Callimico. Why?

I think it is clear that Ligurio is Machiavelli's self-image.[27] "A darling of malice" is the way Machiavelli describes him in the Prologue, something akin to a traditional view of Machiavelli as a teacher of evil.[28] He is the brains behind the conspiracy that will bring Nicia down and establish Callimico as the new prince in his place. At one point he says to Callimico: "Don't doubt my faith because even if the profit I hope for were not here, your blood is in accord with mine" (I.3). Ligurio feels a vague sense of kinship with Callimico: they are clearly birds of a feather, except that Ligurio is intrigued by the game itself. It is not, as he says, "profit" that motivates him but the chance to organize the conspiracy, to rule the ruler, as it were. "I desire for you to satisfy this desire of yours almost as much as you do yourself," he tells Callimico (I.3). To take but one example, in chapter 3 of *The Prince* Machiavelli describes the virtue of the Romans as the ability to spot an occasion and see danger at a distance. In the play we see that Nicia is about to take Lucrezia to a spa where he hopes that the waters will improve her chances of conception, but Ligurio immediately sees the danger to the plan. At the spa Lucrezia would be likely to meet several wealthy and eligible young men who would set themselves up as competitors to Callimico. In such a contest, it is by no means clear that Callimico would win out. Better to stay put in Florence and allow Ligurio to put his plan in motion.

Like Machiavelli, Ligurio is a master manipulator. He puts himself on the side of youth and daring, rather than age and tradition. His motto might be, to the young go the spoils. Throughout the play, Ligurio is presented, much in the way that Machiavelli presents himself, as a master of rhetoric and persuasion. We see him speaking to and persuading Nicia, Callimico, Fra Timoteo, and Sostrata. It could even be argued that the main theme of the play is the art of persuasion and its conspiratorial use in the private sphere.[29] The very plot is a testimony to Ligurio's ingenuity. We might ask what Ligurio gets out of the conspiracy in much the way we might ask what Machiavelli expects to get out of advising princes and other potential heads of state. As Ligurio says to Callimico, it is not profit that drives him, nor is it the kind of erotic ambition that clearly drives Callimico. It is the desire to rule. Ligurio will obviously not rule directly, but he hopes to rule behind the scenes, to be the power behind the new throne, to rule the ruler. To rule indirectly is Ligurio's and Machiavelli's dominant passion. This is the passion of the philosopher who governs without being seen.

MACHIAVELLI, FEMINIST?

The central character of the play—the jewel in the crown, as it were—is Lucrezia. We have already learned something of her Roman forebear. Like the Roman Lucretia, Lucrezia is, we are told at the beginning of the play, "extremely honest"—meaning chaste and virtuous in the conventional sexual sense—and is also governed by the conventional religious pieties of the day. Nicia tells the story of how Lucrezia believed one of her neighbors who told her that her supposed sterility could be cured by attending Mass for forty consecutive mornings. But we also learn how her natural piety was undermined by one of the friars, who began making advances, after which she became increasingly suspicious and alert (III.2). She seems ripe for corruption.

Lucrezia is often presented as a largely passive figure, and the only question that remains is who will exercise domestic governance over her. What's more, she seems to recognize this herself. As the play goes on, she allows herself to become a willing partner in her own seduction. First, she permits herself to be convinced by the sophistry of the priest, who has been bribed by Lugurio to become a part of the conspiracy. "There are many things," Fra Timoteo tells her about adultery, "that from far away seem terrible, unbearable, strange, and when you get near them, they turn out to be humane, bearable, and so it is said, that fears are worse than evils themselves" (III.11). The act of adultery may be a sin, but, the priest says, "the will is what sins, not the body. . . . As to the conscience, you have to take this general principle: that where there is a certain good and an uncertain evil, one should never leave that good for fear of that evil. Here is a certain good, that you will become pregnant, will acquire a soul for our Lord. The uncertain evil is that the one who will lie with you after you take the potion may die. . . . As to the act, that it might be a sin, this is a fable, because the will is what sins, not the body" (III.11). The priest goes on to compare Lucrezia's situation to the biblical daughters of Lot, who slept with their father because they thought it was the only way to regenerate the human race. The moral seems to be, go ahead and enjoy yourself, just not *too* much.

Lucrezia allows herself to be convinced not just by the family priest but by the concurrence of her mother and her own husband, who is so anxious for an heir that he aids in the plot against himself. If everyone concurs, she seems to ask, who am I to resist? In her final speech she says the following to her lover:

> Since your astuteness, my husband's stupidity, my mother's simplicity, and my confessor's wickedness have led me to do what I never would have done by myself, I'm determined to judge that it comes from a heavenly disposition which has so willed; and I don't have it in me to reject what Heaven wills me to accept. Therefore I take you for lord, master, and guide; you are my father, my defender, and I want you to be my every good, and what my husband wanted for one evening, I want you to have always. You will, therefore, make yourself his close friend, and you'll go to the church this morning, and you'll come have dinner with us, and your comings and goings will be up to you, and we'll be able to come together at any time and without suspicion. (V.4)

As everyone knows, all comedies end in a marriage with the promise that the protagonists will live happily ever after. Here Machiavelli subverts the genre, noting that it is the lovers who will live happily, allowing Callimico to come and go as he pleases and even dine with the family, while he and

Lucrezia continue their deception of the husband. Here is the new Machiavellian family!

But is this the whole story? Lucrezia is often presented—as I have just done—as a largely passive figure, who in the course of the play comes to consent to or acquiesce in her own seduction. But is this entirely accurate? In fact, Lucrezia shares much in common with the goddess Fortuna, with whom Machiavelli was so intrigued.[30] Like Fortuna, Lucrezia is a friend to the young (Callimico), whom she encourages to approach her boldly. And like Fortuna, Lucrezia has a protean, adaptable quality. She is clearly the most psychologically pliable character in the play. At the beginning we are told that she is chaste and incorruptible, but by the end she has become bold and assertive. She is willing to deceive her husband and do what it takes to get what she wants. "Look how she responds," Nicia says of her. "She looks like a rooster" (V.5).

Lucrezia has many of the qualities necessary for a prince. She has those protean qualities of adaptability and willingness to seize the occasion that are characteristic of Machiavelli's founder princes.[31] Speaking in his own voice, Machiavelli refers to Lucrezia as "a young woman, a shrewd one" (Prologue). In act 1 Callimico remarks: "She has a very rich husband and one that, in all things, lets himself be governed by her," and a few lines later we read, "She has no maid or servant who's not afraid of her" (I.1). This suggests that there is a domineering, even tyrannical, side of Lucrezia for which her reputation for virtue may simply be a mask, as in so many Renaissance comedies. These qualities suggest that it may be Lucrezia, not Ligurio, who is the true manipulator. This is even suggested by Ligurio himself, who describes her as "prudent" and "wise, well-mannered, and *fit to govern a kingdom*" (I.3; emphasis added). What makes her fit to govern? It may well be that she is perfectly constructed to epitomize Machiavelli's advice in chapter 18 of *The Prince* that in politics a *reputation* for virtue is everything, while the reality of it may be most harmful. In that chapter Machiavelli remarks that what is important for a prince is not to have virtue but to *seem* to have it, "to appear merciful, faithful, humane, honest, and religious, and to be so"—but also, he remarks, "to know how to change to the contrary" should this become necessary. "So he needs to have a spirit disposed to change as the winds of fortune and variations of things command him and . . . not to depart from good, when possible, but to know how to enter into evil, when forced by necessity."[32] This passage might well be Lucrezia's motto.

By the end of the play, Lucrezia seems to have been "reborn," the same term that Livy applied to the supposed simpleton Brutus when he organized the people to expel Tarquin and establish the republic. The question is whether she has truly been transformed or if she has been shrewd all along. Has she been transformed from retiring and shy to bold and outspoken or, like Brutus, has she merely been playing the fool? To what extent has she truly been the passive, pious wife? Or is she the embodiment of Machiavellian *virtù?* Has she been in waiting to topple the kingdom—not an actual empire, to be sure, but the household as run by the rather traditional tyranny of Nicia? Her miraculous rebirth merely exhibits the protean nature of her true self. Lucrezia has become, in a word, more virtuous, not in the Christian, but in the Machiavellian sense of the term: audacious, bold, and controlling. She has simply cast off the veil of modesty and revealed herself for who she has been all along. Like Livy's Brutus, she has merely affected playing the fool in order to seize the right time. Although she takes Callimico for her "lord, master, and guide," it is clear that it is she who will be pulling the strings. We know of Callimico's passionate desire for her, but nowhere do we ever see that this desire is reciprocated. Lucrezia simply uses Callimico's passion to further her goals. She seems to be the new kind of prince—or *principessa*—maybe even a new kind of feminist hero for whom Machiavelli's works have been written.

This Lucrezia has learned the lesson of *Discourses* III.5. There Machiavelli argues that if a prince is to gain legitimacy in the eyes of the people, he must respect the ancient customs and ways of a kingdom. This is why the play ends with Callimico agreeing to follow Lucrezia to church to bless their union of sorts. The old forms must be respected even if they are used to sanctify a radically new beginning. Fra Timoteo is there to provide his blessing, and all will live happily ever after in their ménage à trois.

All of this might lead one to conclude that Lucrezia is more (and other) than she first appears. I suggest she is less the passive foil of the conspiracy than the prime mover of it. There is a manipulative side to her that seems to undercut her reputation for piety and passivity. What Lucrezia wants, Lucrezia gets. She shows the promise of modernity in her ability to manipulate persons and situations to achieve her own ends. And while her name points backward to a central figure in Roman history known for her spotless reputation and virtue, it also points forward to a very different figure. Lucrezia Borgia was the sister of Cesare Borgia, one of Machiavelli's heroes in *The Prince*. Even more so than her brother, Lucrezia Borgia has gone down in history as willing to use promiscuity, duplicity, and murder to get her way. Lucrezia Borgia was still alive when Machiavelli's play was first performed, and her reputation was already the stuff of legend. Perhaps it is her character who may well have served as Lucrezia's ambiguous namesake.

CONCLUSION

Let me return to Machiavelli's self-description: *istorico, comico, et tragico.* Who, or better what, is Machiavelli: a historian, a comic, or a tragic writer? He suggests all three, but do these exhaust all the possible categories? Note that he does not say "philosopher," perhaps because he associated philosophy with idle speculation and utopian pie in the sky. Many writers have seen the fate of Italy as the tragic hero—or heroine—at the center of his works. The final chapter of *The Prince* with its call to liberate Italy from the barbarians has been read as Machiavelli's tragic lament over the fate of his homeland.

But Machiavelli also writes with vigor and a prophetic tone about Italy's power to liberate itself. His view is less tragic than edifying and inspirational. He identifies with youth over age, boldness over caution, and novelty over tradition. He writes to inspire his readers with a love of liberty and a love of country that he believes has been lost due to centuries of Christian rule over Italy. He imbues his work with a love of life and a joy in our powers of fantasia to seize events and control them, much like the comic end to the *Mandragola.* The end of the play portends the coming of a new birth, the child of Lucrezia and Callimico, whose true origins can never be revealed. The suggestion is that modernity begins in an act of usurpation—a conspiracy—whose offspring will be unaware of the illegitimacy of their true parentage. Machiavelli points the way to a bold new future whose very legitimacy will be veiled in secrecy and deception, and if we do not see this, then the joke is on us.

Chapter 3 The Exemplary Life of
René Descartes

Remember, if you please, the history of your mind. It is expected from
all your friends.
—Guez de Balzac to Descartes, March 30, 1628

It is a truth universally acknowledged that René Descartes is the
founder of modern philosophy.[1] While political theorists have frequently treated him as the harbinger of a new age, there is widespread disagreement over precisely what his modernity means. The
majority of his readers have focused on the *cogito,* the "I think" that
is the *fons et origo* of all knowledge. The method of doubt and the
famous rules of evidence have played a crucial role in the formation
of a distinctively modern search for foundations of truth.[2] Tocqueville
regarded the Cartesian method as ideally suited to the new democratic age and as a harbinger of the Revolution: "The philosophic
method of the eighteenth century is therefore not only French, but
democratic, which explains why it was so easily accepted in all of
Europe, whose face it has contributed so much to changing. It is not
because the French changed their ancient beliefs and modified their

ancient mores that they turned the world upside down; it is because they were the first to generalize and to bring to light a philosophic method with whose aid one could readily attack all ancient things and open the way to all new ones."[3]

More recently, the influence of Descartes has virtually been turned upside down. Having once been the model for Enlightenment progressivism, he has now become a virtual poster child for every evil, from genetic engineering to environmental devastation. He has become the straw man for postmodernists, who regard his thought as being at the core of two distinctively modern pathologies: subjectivity and aggressiveness. The Cartesian paradigm of the solitary thinker, it is alleged, was said to make the monadic subject the sole basis for truth. Likewise, it was the very rootlessness of the Cartesian subject—unmoored from the restraining bonds of tradition, custom, and history—that established a domineering and controlling posture toward nature and the environment. According to no less an authority than Martin Heidegger, Cartesianism carries the seed of totalitarianism, characterized by the techniques of mastering nature and the full-scale domination of society.[4]

It is not just that the postmodern reading of Descartes borders on caricature (of course it does). Rather, the caricature depends on a specific misreading of Descartes as a thinker concerned with purely metaphysical and epistemological problems (what can I know?) at the expense of moral and ethical ones (what should I do?). A close reading of the *Discourse on Method* shows that the book is not about the creation of some anonymous epistemological subject called *ego cogitans* but is the autobiography of one real, historical individual named René Descartes.[5] The *Discourse* was published in 1637 when Descartes was forty-one years of age. Here he tells the story of his background and education at the Jesuit college of La Flèche ("one of the most famous schools in Europe" [1:113]); his disillusionment with his teachers and the books of ancient and modern philosophy on which he had been brought up; his discovery of his famous rules of method during a daylong confinement in a stove-heated room while still serving as a solider in the war then raging in Germany (the Thirty Years' War); his elucidation of a "provisional moral code" by which to conduct himself during this period of intellectual experimentation; and his continued wanderings that led him finally to settle in Holland ("amidst this great mass of busy people who are more concerned with their own affairs than curious about those of others" [1:126]).

It has become common to view the *Discourse* as a response to the crisis of skepticism provoked by the rehabilitation of ancient Pyrrhonism. Descartes was but the best known of the figures attached to the group around Marin Mersenne that included such luminaries as Pierre Gassendi and Hobbes. The Mersenne Circle was deeply concerned with the creation of a new science that could answer the skeptical challenge of the Pyrrhonists. Descartes's famous method of "hyperbolic doubt" accepted the skepticism of thinkers like Pierre Charron and Montaigne but then added his own escape clause to it. The *cogito ergo sum* was hoped to provide a platform for absolute certainty (I cannot doubt that I doubt without falling into self-contradiction) that could in turn serve as the foundation for the new science of knowledge. This science would lay the foundation for human progress and the increasing betterment of humankind.[6]

Descartes's answer to the problem of skepticism has proven contentious, to say the least, but while the epistemology of the *Discourse* has been the subject of extensive study, what frequently goes unacknowledged is the moral import of the work. While the discussion of Descartes's ethical theory has focused mainly on the *morale par provision* from part 3 of the *Discourse,* this ethic suggests, as the term implies, that it is merely provisional. That it is not Descartes's final word on the subject is clear from the letter to Abbé Claude Picot that prefaces the French edition of the *Principles of Philosophy* (1647), where Descartes uses the metaphor of the tree of knowledge to explicate his moral views: "The whole of philosophy is like a tree," he writes. "The roots are metaphysics, the trunk is physics, and the branches emerging from the trunk are all the other sciences, which may be reduced to three principal ones, namely, medicine, mechanics, and morals." By morality, he understands, "the highest and most perfect moral system, which presupposes a complete knowledge of the other sciences and is *the ultimate level of wisdom*" (1:186; emphasis added).

The program for a completed moral system was never finished, but it is at least arguable that the sketch for such a system is already present in the *Discourse.* The question rarely asked about the book is why Descartes chose to present his work in the form of an autobiography. What is the connection between ethics and autobiography? In choosing to present his ideas in the form of a philosophical autobiography, Descartes produced a modern variant of the genre of exemplary history recently recovered by Renaissance historiographers.[7] But unlike the Plutarchian model of exemplary history from which it is drawn, the life that Descartes sets out to immortalize is his own. It is one of the first great modern autobiographies.

Descartes is the inheritor of the classical formula *historia magistra vitae,* history is a teacher of life.[8] The *Discourse* is offered in the first instance as "a history or, if you prefer, a fable" in which the center of the story is Descartes himself (1:112). He offers his life as both a singular achievement and something supremely "worthy of imitation." At the core of his life story is the quintessentially modern search for a vocation. His quest is not merely epistemological but moral. Descartes asks not just, What can I know? but, What should I do? It is this search for a vocation or something to do with his life that makes him one with the other great adventurers of modern self-discovery.

It is easy to reduce Descartes's story to a few simple clichés about clear and distinct ideas, the dualism between the mind and body, and the myth of the "ghost in the machine."[9] This entirely abstracts from the profound picture of the individual to which Descartes is struggling to give voice. The *Discourse* is, above all, a bildungsroman, a novel of self-discovery. It tells the story of not only the discovery but also the shaping of a life. The story of Descartes's life is not extraneous to his philosophy; it is constitutive of it. In developing the contours of the self, Descartes clearly draws on the personal style of Montaigne's *Essays,* but just as importantly anticipates the great philosophical explorations of the modern self through Don Quixote, Robinson Crusoe, and Emma Bovary.[10]

WHY THE *DISCOURSE*?

At the beginning of part 6, Descartes mentions that it had been three years since he had completed the essays to which the *Discourse* was intended as the introduction.[11] His decision to delay publication is not without importance for an understanding of the theologico-political context in which the work was written. In particular Descartes draws attention to the climate of compulsion and persecution that forced him to defer publication of his work.[12]

Near the end of the *Discourse,* Descartes alludes to, without mentioning explicitly, the name of Galileo, whose essay *The Assayer* (*Il saggiatore*) had influenced the Mersenne Circle. Descartes was especially fascinated by Galileo's view that the "great book of nature" is written in the language of mathematics.[13] The fact that Galileo had been forced to recant his views provided a sobering lesson about the limits of free inquiry. While he claimed to have noticed nothing in Galileo's treatise that could be construed as "prejudicial either to religion or to the state," Descartes nevertheless decided to delay publishing his own work. Under cover of false modesty he claims that he felt forced to withdraw his work lest "there be some mistake in one of my own theories, in spite of the great care I had always taken never to adopt any new opinion for which I had no certain demonstration, and never to write anything that might work to anyone's disadvantage" (1:141–42). The reasons he adduces for changing his mind may, he avers, be of some interest to the public.

For an author who makes "unswerving resolution" a necessary component of his method, Descartes seems curiously irresolute. After initially deciding not to publish his work, he proceeds to give two reasons for now presenting it to the public. In the first place, he worries that if he failed to publish the book, those who knew of its existence "might suppose that my reasons for not doing so were more discreditable to me than they are" (1:149). He professes indifference to fame ("I am not excessively fond of glory") but at the same time is concerned that his reputation will suffer for his reluctance to publish.

The second reason is even more revealing. It is not only for fear of his reputation but also from a desire to benefit the public that he has agreed to publish the *Discourse.* He stresses the active humanitarianism underlying his project. "Every man," he says, "is indeed bound to do what he can to procure the good of others" (1:145). This good does not concern only the present generation but extends to posterity as well. The project is such that it cannot be carried out by Descartes himself alone but requires the help of others over many generations: "Every day I am becoming more and more aware of the delay which my project of self-instruction is suffering because of the need for innumerable observations which I cannot possibly make without the help of others. Although I do not flatter myself with any expectation that the public will share my interests, yet at the same time I am unwilling to be so unfaithful to myself as to give those who come after me cause to reproach me some day on the grounds that I could have left them many far better things if I had not been so remiss in making them understand how they could contribute to my projects" (1:149).

Like Bacon, Descartes is convinced, or wants to convince others, of his essential humanity and generosity.[14] These are the key terms of the new ethic Descartes proposes. There is more than a note of pride or ambition in this ethic when he acknowledges that it will require the work of many future investigators to complete "my projects." But in what does this ethic consist? From what is it derived? What are the benefits that follow from its use? Before attempting to answer these questions, Descartes feels it necessary to tell his story.

THE EDUCATION OF A PHILOSOPHER

Part 1 of the *Discourse* tells the story of the education of a young philosopher. Descartes begins, modestly enough, by informing the reader that "the power of judging well and of distinguishing the true from the false" is more or less equal in all men (1:111). This assertion of intellectual equality dovetails nicely with his claim near the very end of his work that he would prefer to be read not by scholars who judge things by the standards of "the ancients" but by those readers who combine "good sense with application" (*le bon sens avec l'étude*) (1:151).

The author of the work never claims to possess anything more than an ordinary intelligence and in fact developed his method to compensate for the "mediocrity" of his mind. Despite his profession of intellectual modesty, he cannot refrain from boasting of the education he received from the Jesuit priests at La Flèche, where in addition to the regular curriculum, he claims, "I had gone through all the books that fell into my hands concerning the subjects that are considered most abstruse and unusual" (1:113). The result of this education seems to have been a kind of Socratic awareness of the limitations or worthlessness of existing knowledge.

Descartes provides a catalogue of the uselessness of traditional knowledge, especially the value paid to the study of languages and histories. He appears, ironically, not to notice that the same word ("fable") is used to describe both the useless but charming stories he rejects and the *Discourse* that he presents as frank and exemplary. Why refer to his book as "a history or . . . a fable" if such knowledge is considered useless? This must cause the reader to wonder whether the work is being offered as a true account or something like a salutary myth. While recognizing that reading the great books is "like having a conversation with the most distinguished men of past ages," Descartes nevertheless finds this to be little more than a kind of intellectual tourism: "For conversing with those of past centuries is much the same as travelling. It is good to know something of the customs of various peoples, so that we may judge our own more soundly and not think that everything contrary to our ways is ridiculous and irrational. . . . But one who spends too much time travelling eventually becomes a stranger in his own country; and one who is too curious about the practices of past ages usually remains quite ignorant about those of the present" (1:113–14). Descartes's warning about the dangers of spending too much time away from one's own country is ironic in light of the extensive role that travel plays in his own intellectual development.

It is ultimately the failure to achieve any sort of agreement among the greatest minds that led Descartes to despair. Learning that does not result in certainty is not worth having. Despite the fact that philosophy has been cultivated for centuries, there is no single proposition that is not disputable and hence subject to doubt. At best one might expect probable knowledge rather than truth. Even mathematics, which "delighted" Descartes because of "the certainty and self-evidence of its reasonings," had failed to discover its "real use." Deciding to abandon study for "the great book of the world" (*le grand livre du monde*), he resolved to spend his time in travel and "mixing with people of diverse temperaments and ranks, gathering various experiences, and testing [himself] in the situations afforded by fortune" (1:115). The result of this immersion in the world of practical experience was a lesson in skepticism, "not to believe too firmly anything of which I had been persuaded only by example and custom."

It is only at the end of part 1 that Descartes makes a decisive discovery that determines the rest of the *Discourse*. Finding no satisfactory foundation for knowledge in anything outside himself ("example and custom"), he decides that only what is within himself is reliable: "I resolved one day to undertake studies within myself too and to use all the powers of my mind in choosing the paths I should follow" (1:116). The question is, What is the nature of interiority, the inner world of human subjectivity, that provides a better guide to life than all the experiences of travel or study?

THE REFORM OF THE UNDERSTANDING

Descartes's proposals for the reform of the understanding grew out of a daylong confinement in a stove-heated room (*poêle*) while returning to the army after attending the coronation of the emperor of Bavaria. He says nothing about why he, a private citizen, was attending the coronation. And he reports little about what happened during that extraordinary day that led up to his proposals for intellectual reform.[15] His first thoughts focused on the nature of beginnings. Just as a building is more perfect the more it is the design of a single architect, so too is this true for all foundings. The Spartan constitution has been widely praised not because each of its laws is admirable but because they were all the product of a single founder and directed toward the same end (1:117). What is true of buildings and constitutions is also true for knowledge. The existing sciences have often grown up piecemeal with no uniform plan that explains why they are nothing but a patchwork of opinion and mere probable reasoning.

Descartes denies that his plan to undertake the reform of knowledge has a revolutionary design. Unlike Machiavelli, he believes it unwise to undertake the reform of a state or education by undertaking it from the ground up, but regarding his own opinions and beliefs, it would be preferable "to get rid of them, all at one go, in order to replace them afterward with better ones" (1:117). He appears not to notice the improbability of getting rid of all one's opinions at a single stroke. How is this possible? What will Descartes replace his former opinions with? Nonetheless, he insists that his proposals concern himself alone and are not intended as a guide to anyone else ("My plan has never gone beyond trying to reform my own thoughts" [1:118]). He excoriates all reformers ("those meddlesome and restless characters") who undertake to overhaul public institutions.

Descartes situates himself as a mean between two types of person. There are those on whom "God has bestowed more of his favors" and will no doubt see Descartes's plans for self-improvement as too cautious. Then there are others who are content to follow existing opinion and practice as the only reliable guide. Descartes tells the reader that he would have included himself in this second class had he not early on come upon a discovery, namely, that there is no opinion or custom so strange that it has not been held or practiced by someone somewhere. His travels merely confirmed to him that custom is variable and that we hold the opinions we do purely as a matter of chance. "I have recognized through my travels," he writes in a sentence that could have come directly out of Montaigne, "that those with views quite contrary to ours are not on that account barbarians or savages, but that many of them make use of reason as much or more than we do" (1:119).[16] The result is that Descartes has found it necessary to be his own guide.

The enumeration of the four rules of method follows from Descartes's desire to find a secure ground for knowledge. The advantage of these rules is their relative simplicity, provided the user has made "a strong and unswerving resolution never to fail to observe them" (1:120). These rules of method are not themselves a form of knowledge but are a means for determining what is to count as knowledge by winnowing truth from opinion. Because of Descartes's view that all knowledge is interconnected, these rules of method should be potentially applicable to every human endeavor. Descartes's confidence in his method is such that after only "two or three months" problems that had previously seemed difficult had been solved, and for others it was at least possible to determine whether they admit of a solution. Descartes's main fear seems to be that the possession of this method will make him appear "too arrogant," although he boldly asserts that "since there is only one truth concerning any matter, whoever discovers this truth knows as much about it as can be known" (1:121).

MORALE PAR PROVISION

It is in the third part of the *Discourse* that Descartes considers the practical consequences of adopting his rules of method. As the example of Galileo had already demonstrated, the implications of the new science were widely believed to have unsettling implications for the conduct of moral and religious life. Accordingly, Descartes felt compelled to address the concerns of critics (or potential critics) who saw the new method as subversive of existing modes and orders. While he attempted to protect himself from the charges of unbelief by appending an argument for the existence of God along with his rules of *évidence,* he clearly knew he was skating on thin ice and took pains to protect himself from a plunge.

Descartes's answer to these critics is provided in the "provisional moral code" (*morale par provision*) that is adopted as a guide to conduct at least until such time as the fruits of the method have begun to pay off.[17] The question asked by Descartes here is "How can the skeptic live his beliefs?" that is, after submitting all his previous beliefs to systematic doubt how is it possible to live in the world?[18] In answering this question he went out of his way to try to assuage critics by affirming the broadly "conservative" nature of his moral teachings. As we shall see, his avowals of obedience to the established laws and religion are but a thinly veiled disguise to be adopted until the new or definitive moral teaching can be revealed. Descartes is nothing if not a master of the double teaching.[19]

The provisional or exoteric character of Descartes's morality is plainly revealed in his effort to use it as a kind of prophylactic to protect the inquirer from the destabilizing effects of systematic doubt. Imagining himself in the situation of an architect building a new house who must arrange for some temporary accommodations, Descartes elaborates a scheme to "live as happily as [he] could" while waiting for the new dwelling to be constructed. The morale par provision consists of "three or four maxims" which he knows to be "imperfect" but which must be followed until it can be replaced by a definitive or scientific morality. The first maxim is "to obey the laws and customs of my country, holding constantly to the religion in which by God's grace I had been instructed from my childhood, and governing myself in all other matters according to the most moderate and least extreme opinions—the opinions commonly accepted in practice by the most sensible of those with whom I should have to live" (1:122). Having previously repudiated custom and opinion as guides to truth, Descartes here adopts their guidance as authoritative. The decision to live not just according to opinion but according to the "least extreme" and "most moderate" opinions is intended as a hedge against the disorienting effects of radical doubt. The exemption of public institutions from methodical doubt has often made Descartes seem, at least to some, cautious and fearful of change.[20] His statements that "these large bodies are too difficult to raise up once overthrown, or even to hold up once they begin to totter," and "it is almost always easier to put up with their imperfections than to change them" suggest an external conservatism that belies the internal radicalism of Cartesian doubt (1:118). Apparently the rules of method are to be applied only to matters of theory or science rather than practice. The principle of this rule seems to be internal freedom and external conformity.[21]

It is deeply misleading to think of Descartes as a conservative moralist content to live by prevailing laws and customs alone. It may be more accurate to say of him what Macaulay said of Bacon, that his philosophical temperament revealed "a singular union of audacity and sobriety."[22] This becomes especially apparent in the second maxim of the provisional morality that exhorts a kind of single-mindedness and resoluteness. This maxim entails his resolve "to be as firm and decisive in my actions as I could, and to follow even the most doubtful opinions, once I had adopted them, with no less constancy than if they had been quite certain" (1:123). Here Descartes compares himself to a traveler lost in the forest who determines to keep walking straight in one direction to avoid going in circles. This suggests an attitude of firmness or resoluteness that it is important to adopt even in the absence of reliable information. Only by adopting a course of action forcefully and decisively is it possible to avoid "all the regrets and remorse which usually trouble the consciences of those weak and faltering spirits" (1:123). In short, he who hesitates is lost.

Descartes's third maxim provides evidence for the Stoic influences on his thought. "My third maxim," he writes, "was to try always to master myself rather than fortune, and change my desires rather than the order of the world" (1:123). The essence of this third maxim is the virtue of self-control. Although he will later boast that the use of the rules of method will make us "masters and possessors of nature," he here wishes to appear far more modest, asserting only that "nothing lies entirely within our power except our thoughts" (1:123). Powerless to control fortune, we can at least try to control our thoughts and desires. We should learn to desire only what it is in our power to obtain. If we could but teach ourselves to regard all "external goods" as beyond our power, we would be spared frustration and unhappiness. This sounds like generally good advice, although the examples he uses are startling: a person should not desire to be healthy when he is sick or free when imprisoned, although Descartes admits that it takes "long practice and repeated meditation to become accustomed to seeing everything in this light" (1:124).

The adoption of this moral code is only complete with Descartes's decision "to review the various occupations which men have in this life, in order to try to choose the best" (1:124). On the basis of this "comparison of lives," he professes contentment with his own self-chosen occupation as a searcher for knowledge. He affirms this choice again at the end of the *Discourse* when he asserts, "I have resolved to devote the rest of my life to nothing other than trying to acquire some knowledge of nature from which we may derive rules in medicine which are more reliable than those we have had up till now" (1:151). Descartes gives us no reason for claiming that his way is best, only that he could find nothing better left to do. His question seems to be not the ancient one "Which way of life is best?" but the existential one "What should I do with my life?"

It could be wondered whether the rules of Descartes's morale par provision constitute a coherent ethic at all or merely a set of prudential guidelines for action to be adopted as a matter of convenience.[23] If the latter, one might legitimately wonder whether there is anything distinctively ethical about these provisions at all. In point of fact, however, Descartes purposely describes these rules as par provision, thus indicating that they are to be in place only until the rules of his definitive morality can be safely enumerated. Par provision means exactly what the term implies, temporary or opportunistic. Its principles are like ammunition or supplies stockpiled in order to withstand a siege. The morality by provision is, then, to be viewed as a security blanket to be adopted until such time as it can be replaced by the higher or more complete morality, but by no means Descartes's final statement on the subject. The complete or definitive morality will take the form of "the highest and most perfect moral system" that we have seen alluded to in the letter preface to the *Principles of Philosophy* (1:186).

The adoption of this morality par provision, it would seem, is connected not to any Stoic vision of rest or *ataraxia* but to a period of frenzied motion and self-exploration.[24] It was only after his survey of the various occupations, Descartes tells the reader, that he was induced to leave his stove-heated room and set out on a series of adventures that lasted nine years, when, he says, "I did nothing but roam about in the world trying to be a spectator rather than an actor in all the comedies that are played out there" (1:125). While he had earlier complained that too much travel makes one a stranger in one's own country, he here emphasizes his deliberate separation from any of the customs or habits that could properly be called a home, viewing the world through the lenses of a detached ironist. Like the biblical Cain, Descartes seems compelled to roam the earth until finally taking up residence in a modern-day land of Nod.

Descartes's adventures, however, were to lead to a most peculiar, hermetic way of life: "Exactly eight years ago this desire made me resolve to move away from any place where I might have acquaintances and retire to this country [Holland], where the long duration of the war has led to the establishment of such order that the armies maintained here seem to serve only to make the enjoyment of the fruits of peace all the more secure. Living here, amidst this great mass of busy people who are more concerned with their own affairs than curious about those of others, I have been able to lead a life as solitary and withdrawn as if I were in the most remote desert, while lacking none of the comforts found in the most populous cities" (1:126).

It is fitting that Descartes's peregrinations brought him to Holland, the commercial capital par excellence of Europe. It is here that Descartes is able to live as a stranger and private individual, but among all the conveniences of life. "I take a walk each day amid the bustle of the crowd with as much freedom and repose as you could obtain in your leafy groves, and I pay no more attention to the people I meet than I would to the trees in your woods or the animals that browse there," he writes in a letter to Balzac (3:31). A generation after the publication of the *Discourse,* Spinoza could laud this regime as a place where you can think what you like and say what you think. "For in this most flourishing republic," Spinoza wrote, "this most outstanding city, all men of whatever nation or sect, live in the greatest harmony."[25] The toleration of the Dutch Republic extended to men like Descartes and Spinoza at least a temporary place of refuge where they could freely pursue their chosen way of life.

This, of course, raises the profound question about the relation between Descartes's chosen way of life and his adopted home.[26] What is the connection between the commercial republic and the new philosophy? In what respects is the practice of Descartes's method ideally suited to a commercial society like Holland? Does the method of Descartes portend the commercial ethic of Benjamin Franklin and Adam Smith? In what respect is the solitude of Descartes connected to his stated desire to bring aid and comfort to mankind? These questions can only be answered in considering Descartes's definitive morality alluded to in part 6 of the *Discourse*.

"A REAL MAN"

In sections 4 and 5 of the *Discourse,* Descartes takes the reader on a brief tour of his metaphysics and physics, respectively. The picture of the self to emerge here is that of a thinking substance—the famous cogito ergo sum—I think therefore I am. In order to arrive at this conception, however, Descartes feels it necessary to engage in his project of systematic doubt. Because our senses may sometimes deceive us, he goes on to draw the conclusion that "all the things that had ever entered my mind were no more true than the illusions of my dreams" (1:127). The only ground for certainty in a world where everything can be doubted is the experience of thinking itself. The fact that we cannot doubt that we think gives Descartes a platform from which to arrive at truth.

What, then, is the self behind this paranoid vision of a world in which nothing is certain and where everything appears as if in a dream? Descartes answers as follows: "I knew I was a substance whose whole essence or nature is simply to think, and which does not require any place, or depend on any material thing, in order to exist. Accordingly this 'I'—that is, the soul by which I am what I am—is entirely distinct from the body, and indeed is easier to know than the body, and would not fail to be whatever it is, even if the body did not exist" (1:127).

This strange conception of the I "entirely distinct from the body" is joined with a materialistic physics of bodies in motion. It is here that Descartes references his earlier treatise *The World* (*Le monde*), written between 1629 and 1635 but only published posthumously in 1664. In this work, of which he gives only the barest summary, he sets out to rewrite the biblical account of Creation in Genesis, beginning with the problem of light. It was due, however, to the troubles encountered by Galileo that he decided to forgo publication of the work ("I did not want to bring these matters too much into the open" [1:132]) and focus instead on the discussion of human creation.[27] The human world, we are told, consists of various "automatons" and other mechanical bodies. Anticipating later debates over the possibility of artificial intelligence, Descartes even wonders whether there could ever be a human machine and how we could distinguish a robot from a person (1:139).

Whatever similarities there may be between a robot and a person, Descartes maintains that there are "two very certain means" for distinguishing between them. The first derives from the nature of language. Although we can imagine a machine that could make simple preprogrammed responses to particular situations, "it is not conceivable that such a machine should produce different arrangements of words so as to give an appropriately meaningful answer to whatever is said in its presence, as even the dullest of men can do" (1:140). The second characteristic distinctive of human nature is reason that confers a latitude, an openness in our ability to act not open to any machine. Reason is a "universal instrument that can be used in all kinds of situations" that not even the best-made machine can duplicate. It is "for all practical purposes impossible" that a robot could ever achieve the ability "to act in all the contingencies of life in the way in which our reason makes us act" (1:140).

The question is what the connection is between this thinking substance that is the mind and the extended substance that is the body. Descartes seems aware that he has provided an extremely awkward conception of a human being, composed of an interior world of reason, feeling, and belief, and an exterior world of bodies in motion. Having once affirmed the independence of the soul from the body, he now seems concerned to reunite them: "And I showed how it is not sufficient for it [the soul] to be lodged in the human body like a helmsman in his ship, except perhaps to move its limbs, but that it must be more closely joined and united with the body in order to have, besides the power of movements, feelings, and appetites like ours and so constitute a real man" (*un vrai homme*) (1:141).

Descartes's use of the term "a real man" in this passage is not just epistemological but also ethical. He seems intent on putting the *vir* (to say nothing of the *vrai*) back in virtue. Virtue here implies notions of authenticity, individuality, and self-assertion. His conception of the self is that of a sovereign, autonomous, self-legislating agent. The autonomy of reason is expressed not only in the realm of knowledge but also in a new kind of moral idealism and cosmopolitanism found in Descartes's ethic of generosity and humanity. This is an ethic not for citizens but for individuals of a particular kind, those whose very independence from all particular attachments to homeland and country makes it possible for them to consider the well-being of humanity as a whole. It is, above all, *humanité* that Descartes hopes to serve.

"MASTERS AND POSSESSORS"

The final section of the *Discourse* provides an intimation of Descartes's definitive ethic of generosity. Despite his professed aversion to publication, it is an ethic of humanitarianism that compels him to make his work public. "I believed I could not keep them secret without sinning gravely against the law which obliges us to do all in our power to secure the general welfare of mankind" (1:142). Descartes does not indicate the source of this law or explain why, after three years of waiting, he suddenly feels its force. He goes on, like Bacon before him, to distinguish the useful or philanthropic character of his philosophy from the purely "speculative philosophy" of the schools.

It is here that Descartes for the first time spells out the larger aim and purpose of his investigations: "Through this philosophy we could know the power and action of fire, water, air, the stars, the heavens and all the other bodies in our environment, as distinctly as we know the various crafts of our artisans; and we could use this knowledge—as the artisans use theirs—for all the purposes for which it is appropriate, and thus make ourselves, as it were, the masters and possessors of nature" (1:142–43).

The benefits of Descartes's science of mastery will be in the first instance "innumerable devices" that make possible increased comfort and convenience. But Cartesian science is concerned above all with matters of health ("undoubtedly the chief good and the foundation of all the other goods in this life"). Descartes holds out the possibility that future advances in the science of medicine will indefinitely extend the scope of life: "All we know in medicine is almost nothing in comparison with what remains to be known, and that we might free ourselves from innumerable diseases, both of the body and of the mind, and perhaps even from the infirmity of old age, if we had sufficient knowledge of their causes and of all the remedies that nature has provided" (1:143).

Descartes's ethic is intended to enhance and secure health and material well-being, a task that will not be achieved in a day but will require the cooperation and collaboration of generations of research scientists. He presents himself, modestly, as simply adding one block to the edifice of science: "By building upon the work of our predecessors and combining the lives and labors of many, we might make much greater progress working together than any-one could make on his own" (1:143).

It has been common to treat Descartes's reference to the mastery and pos-session of nature as the harbinger of a completely administered technological society and other utopian visions of a rational social order. His hope that we may one day overcome "the infirmity of old age" has suggested to Leon Kass a dangerous attempt to transform the human condition not only through the indefinite prolongation of life but by impiously extending our biblically allot-ted three score years and ten.[28] Descartes appears to Joseph Cropsey like the biblical serpent who holds out the possibility of a "philanthropic Eden" in which humankind will enjoy all things previously prohibited, including the fruit of the tree of knowledge.[29]

The image of Descartes as a serpentine tempter is only a part of the story. Although Descartes makes allusion to the practical benefits to be achieved by science, there is an important moral dimension to this project that is often overlooked by those bedazzled by his promise of material benefits alone. The *Discourse* makes repeated references to the public good and the spirit of gen-erosity that underlies the new science. This is, again, the ethic not of a citizen tied to the good of one's own country but of a benefactor of humanity freed from all particular obligations and attachments. Descartes may have begun his work by enjoining obedience to "the laws and customs" of one's own coun-try, but he ends by assuming the mantle of a spokesman for humanity. His new ethic, like his new science, has as its object not just the technological ad-vancement but also the moral mastery of human nature.

CARTESIAN GENEROSITY

Descartes never wrote a treatise spelling out the ethical implications of his promise to make us the "masters and possessors of nature," but he did briefly touch upon this at the end of the *Discourse*. This phrase appears just once in his entire collected work, although it remains one of his most readily identifi-able themes.[30] Despite Descartes's professed abhorrence of Machiavelli, there are strong Machiavellian overtones to his conception of mastery. His repu-diation of Machiavelli is undertaken on grounds that are prepared by Machia-velli. His conception of un vrai homme suggests Machiavellian qualities of boldness and audacity. While in *The Prince* Machiavelli had suggested that it was possible for a prince to best *fortuna* at most half the time, Descartes implies that with the proper resoluteness of will, we may become the masters of our own fate. His goal seems to be to overcome completely the role of chance as a controlling factor in life. The Cartesian aspiration to autonomy and self-sufficiency is a fitting analogue to the Machiavellian politics of princely self-creation.[31]

The ethic of self-mastery, only briefly suggested at the end of the *Discourse,* represents a prolegomenon to the finished or definitive ethic of generosity announced in Descartes's last work published in his lifetime, *Passions of the Soul* (1649). Here Descartes addresses his readers not as an orator or a moralist but *en physicien,* that is, as a scientist or physiologist of the passions whose aim is to understand their causes and effects (1:327). This work fills out and completes the morale par provision of the *Discourse* by offering its own ethic based on a supposedly scientific or medical understanding of the passions. It is in the area of moral psychology that Descartes claims to depart most dramatically from the work of his predecessors: "The defects of the sciences we have from the ancients are nowhere more apparent than in their writings on the passions. . . . I cannot hope to approach the truth except by departing from the paths they have followed. That is why I shall be obliged to write just as if I were considering a topic that no one had dealt with before me" (1:327). Although he does not mention the Stoics by name, it seems clear that theirs is the ancient doctrine to which he is referring. Rather than trying to repress the passions, the aim of the new science is to redirect them to nobler ends.

The new morality announced at the beginning of *Passions* is only brought to fruition at the end of the work that proposes *générosité* as the crown of the virtues ("the key to all the other virtues and a general remedy for every disorder of the passions" [1:388]).[32] Generosity, Descartes tells the reader, consists of two parts. The first consists in the knowledge that nothing truly belongs to us but the freedom of volition, and that no one should be praised or blamed for anything but using the free will for good or ill. The second consists of "a firm and constant resolution to use it [the will] well—that is, never to lack the will to undertake and carry out whatever he judges to be best." To undertake both of these capacities is "to pursue virtue in a perfect manner" (1:384).

In adopting the term *générosité* Descartes was self-consciously appropriating an aristocratic ideal that had begun to make a reappearance in the second half of the seventeenth century in the dramas of Corneille, such as *Horace* and *Le Cid*.[33] The use of the term, ironically, recalls an ideal that long preceded Descartes's final study of the physiology of the passions. The term itself recalls the exploits of heroes from the past (Cyrus, Alexander, Caesar), the very stuff of history and poetry that Descartes had ostensibly repudiated in the *Discourse*. Yet unlike his contemporaries—Hobbes, La Rochefoucauld, and Pascal—who delighted in showing how the heroic virtues were in reality forms of vanity or the frantic escape from real knowledge, Descartes sought to retain, although in modified form, some of its classical antecedents. The ideal of *l'homme généreux* is tied to the classical ideal of the gentleman, the Aristotelian *megalopsychos,* or great-souled man, who gets much because he deserves much. But Descartes also modifies the heroic ethic of *générosité de l'esprit* in important ways. The Cartesian ethic is readapted less for achieving military and political purposes than for the private ends of self-mastery and control of the passions. He purposefully distinguishes his understanding of generosity from the Roman and Scholastic concept of *magnanimitas* (1:388). Descartes emphasizes that, unlike ancient virtue ethics, his is not an ethic for warriors and statesmen but is intended to be far more egalitarian and inclusive in scope. It can be acquired by anyone with a sufficiently firm and resolute act of will.[34]

Cartesian generosity suggests, then, an ethic of moral inwardness connected to the rational mastery of the passions and strength of will. It is preeminently a private struggle with the individual over himself or herself. It is this mastery of the self that provides the true ground of moral autonomy and individual accountability that would later be given more notable expression by Kant. Thus generous persons never show contempt for others and attribute wrongdoing more to bad judgment than to bad will (1:384). Generosity provides protection against feelings of disdain and inferiority. Generous persons never feel belittled, whatever disadvantages they may suffer in terms of wealth, honor, beauty, and intelligence. Rather they feel a sense of confidence and self-assurance that comes from the knowledge that virtue is dependent on the will alone. What is more, generosity consists in power over the passions of hatred, fear, anger, and envy because such emotions show an unworthy dependence on the opinions of others (1:385).

The science of heroic self-mastery is, however, only half of the story. Cartesian generosity is not just a recipe for the control of the passions, it is harnessed to a powerful philanthropic vision for the relief of man's estate. The ideal of generosity informs Descartes's interest in medicine and the higher mathematics as the branches of knowledge most capable of benefiting humanity. It combines elements of the heroic ideal of greatness of soul with the modern democratic passion to be of service to humankind. Generosity has a public dimension expressed in terms of large-scale actions undertaken for the sake of the public good: "Those who are generous in this way are naturally led to do great deeds, and at the same time not to undertake anything of which they do not feel themselves capable. And because they esteem nothing more highly than doing good to others and disregarding their own self-interest, they are always courteous, gracious, and obliging to everyone" (1:385).

It is impossible to read these references to "great deeds" and "doing good to others" without thinking that they represent Descartes's final reflection on his chosen way of life, his answer to the search for an ethical vocation. Descartes's ethic of generosity is not simply an addendum to the *Discourse*. It is, as one of his principal biographers has put it, the "fruit of his metaphysics."[35] No longer cautious and conservative, his ethic has become bold and assertive. Descartes is the hero of his own story. Cartesian generosity is concerned not so much with the improvement of souls—it is not a form of Christian *caritas*— as with acts of public philanthropy and the worldly betterment of humankind.[36] Descartes clearly regards himself as a benefactor of humanity, and the scope of his benefactions is potentially universal and cosmopolitan. Generosity, understood as the duty to help humankind, is the moral core of Descartes's scientific project.

CONCLUSION

"Descartes has long been celebrated as 'the founder of modern philosophy,' but never of modern political philosophy," Richard Kennington has written.[37] Descartes may have been the least directly political of all the great philosophers, but this has not prevented readers of his work from associating his name with a host of modern ideologies and social movements, from democracy, to technology, to patriarchy. He and his influence have been castigated by critics as the cause of a range of modern ills and pathologies. For some, he has been alleged to stand at the beginning of a peculiarly rootless, deracinated conception of the self said to be characteristic of modern liberal political philosophy; for others, his subjectivism is thought to be responsible for a hubristic attitude toward nature and the desire to extend a kind of technological domination of the earth; while for others still, his ethic of generosity is seen to portend a syrupy morality of compassion and humanitarianism.

I have tried to show that the *Discourse* is not just an epistemological or methodological introduction to the modern sciences, as most readers have interpreted it. Nor is it simply a "post-skeptical" response to the crisis engendered by sixteenth-century Pyrrhonism.[38] Descartes's concerns were as much moral as epistemological. The fact that Descartes refers to morality as "the ultimate level of wisdom" suggests that he regarded his scientific endeavors as being in the service of a moral and political teaching. The *Discourse* is an ethical autobiography concerned, above all, with the question of how one ought to live one's life. It offers a powerful exemplary vision that grew out of its author's highly personal, even existential, search for a vocation or plan of life. The *Discourse* is less a scientific work than a novel of self-discovery, part of the Renaissance literature of exemplarity that puts the creation of the self at the center of the text.

Descartes may not have written a political philosophy, but he understood his philosophy in political terms. Along with Machiavelli, Montaigne, Hobbes, and Spinoza, Descartes helped to provide a sense of idealism and high moral purpose that went together with their constructivist images of politics and the state as the creation of free human will and choice. The aim of this ethic is misunderstood if we read it as concerned only with the technological mastery of external nature. Descartes is as much, if not more, concerned with the ethical mastery of our inner life as with control over the environment. His emphasis on qualities such as firmness and resoluteness of will speaks to the power of individuals to take control over fortune or providence and accept responsibility for their own actions. As much as anything, his work is a tribute to the autonomy and dignity of the individual. Generosity is addressed to strong or great souls who carry something of an aristocratic code of honor into the beginnings of bourgeois modernity.[39]

Most important of all, the vocation of Descartes is connected to his plan for the moral improvement of humanity. This improvement is intended for societies that are open to the possibility of science and hence of public enlightenment. Amsterdam was his model for such a regime, much as it was for Spinoza a generation later, but Descartes clearly intended his method to have broader cosmopolitan purposes. It would be almost exactly two centuries later that Tocqueville would declare America to be the first truly Cartesian nation, and this despite the fact that Descartes had very few readers there. "There is no country in the civilized world," Tocqueville declares, "where they are less occupied with philosophy than in the United States." This has not prevented the Americans from developing a method that is distinctly their own: "To escape from the spirit of system, from the yoke of habits, from family maxims, from class opinions, and, up to a certain point, from national prejudices; to take tradition only as information, and current facts only as a useful study for doing otherwise and better; to seek the reason for things by themselves and in themselves alone, to strive for a result without letting themselves be chained to the means, and to see through the form to the foundation: these are the principal features that characterize what I shall call the philosophic method of the Americans."[40]

So well were Descartes's precepts learned that in the time separating the publication of the *Discourse* from Tocqueville's *Democracy in America* the influence of the teacher had been almost completely erased. "America is the one country in the world where the precepts of Descartes are least studied and best followed." "That," Tocqueville adds, "should not be surprising."[41]

Chapter 4 Was Hobbes a Christian?

Of all Christian authors the philosopher Hobbes is the only one who saw clearly the evil and the remedy, who dared to propose reuniting the two heads of the eagle, and to return everything to political unity without which no state or government will ever be well constituted.
—Jean-Jacques Rousseau

If Descartes was the founder of modern philosophy, Hobbes claimed to be the founder of modern political philosophy. He famously boasted—he was a great boaster—that "civil science" was no older than his book *De Cive*, published in 1642.[1] To be sure, Hobbes had serious rivals for his claim to be the founder of political science in the works of Machiavelli and Bacon. Each of these thinkers claimed to raise politics to the status of a science, but only Hobbes thought through this claim to its fundamental premises. Where does Hobbes's novelty lie?

Few would deny that Hobbes was the first to develop the modern idea of the sovereign state with full vigor and clarity. His term for the state—Leviathan—has been for many sufficient to cover his name in infamy. Hobbes, on this account, is the founder of modern state theory that would be more fully developed in the writings of the great modern realists, from Max Weber and Carl Schmitt to Hans Kelsen and Henry Kissinger. Indeed, the modern concept of the state as the possessor of the means of force within a given territory is the essence of the modern politics and is unthinkable without Hobbes.[2]

But Hobbes was concerned not only with the state as the monopoly of violence but also with what made the use of violence legitimate. He was not so much a realist as a moralist concerned with the legitimate uses of power. Accordingly, he introduced the idiom of the social contract, in which the consent or agreement of each individual formed the basis of all legitimate authority. The contract, or "covenant," as Hobbes called it, deliberately using a biblical concept, is the device by which individuals leave the uncertainty and volatility of the state of nature to enter the peaceable kingdom of civil society. The idea of the contract has itself been a subject of considerable controversy. A contract is an agreement, that is, a moral relationship between people capable of making and keeping promises. But the state of nature is said to be prior to any morality. How is it possible, then, to posit a moral institution like a contract to serve as the foundation of any possible morality? There seems to be a hopeless circularity at the core of the social contract. These kinds of considerations have received renewed attention in recent decades, especially with the revival of social contract theory since the publication of John Rawls's *A Theory of Justice.*

Most readers of Hobbes have focused on the first two parts of *Leviathan,* entitled "On Man" and "On the Commonwealth," in which Hobbes gives his unforgettable account of the state of nature and the social contract, while ignoring the second half of the work containing the parts entitled "Of the Christian Commonwealth" and "Of the Kingdom of Darkness."[3] Yet focusing only on the first half of the work gives an extremely truncated account of Hobbes's book. There has been a tendency to ignore the theological dimension of Hobbes's thought or just to assume that it has nothing to say to the contemporary reader. And while it is possible to consider Hobbes's state of nature along the lines of the famous "prisoner's dilemma," doing so is to abstract it entirely from the deeply embedded Hebraic and eschatological dimensions of his thinking. It has only been recently—very recently—that some readers have begun to take seriously the biblical, even prophetic, aspects of Hobbes's political theory. Indeed, Hobbes's critique of religion has become a topic of controversy in part due to the revival of interest in political theology.[4]

This raises the question of the role of religion in Hobbes's thought. Here too opinions have varied greatly. A traditional view has been that Hobbes was a thoroughgoing materialist whose views on religion, such as they are, were at best a smoke screen to cover a barely concealed atheism. "It is enough to remark," Leslie Stephen (better remembered today as the father of Virginia Woolf) has written, "that his system would clearly be more consistent and intelligible if he simply omitted the theology altogether."[5] On this reading, the attention that Hobbes gives to religion is an accidental feature of his historical situation that obliged him to pay lip service to conventional opinion but that has no essential connection to his utterly secular philosophical principles. As far as Stephen is concerned, Hobbes's materialism is "incompatible with anything that can be called theism."[6]

The atheistic reading of Hobbes was challenged most famously by Howard Warrender, who tried to locate Hobbes within an older tradition of natural law.[7] For Warrender, Hobbes's social contract theory requires a prior account of moral obligation if it is to make sense. If we were simply rational egoists, so the argument goes, wouldn't it be rational for us simply to break our word whenever it seemed in our interest to do so? But Warrender puts the theory of obligation at the center of Hobbes's philosophy. The intellectual coherence of the social contract only makes sense if it is put under a higher obligation to the natural law. It would be difficult, on this reading, to distinguish Hobbes from Aquinas or any of the great medieval defenders of the natural law. Warrender's thesis was more fully developed by F. C. Hood in his book *The Divine Politics of Thomas Hobbes* and more recently by A. P. Martinich in *The Two Gods of Leviathan*. Martinich argues that Hobbes was not only indebted to the tradition of natural law but also a Christian and a religious thinker, even a very devout one.[8] We now seem to have come full circle.

None of these views quite hits the mark. If Hobbes really was a traditional natural law theorist, why does he go out of his way to announce and even to champion his break with the philosophical tradition that he describes with the neologism "Aristotelity," a combination of Aristotle and Christianity (IV.xlvi.13)? The most obvious objection to the Warrender thesis is that if Hobbes really was an orthodox Christian, why did none of his contemporaries perceive this? To the contrary, Hobbes's early readers unanimously thought of him as an iconoclast who attempted to derive all obligations not from any theological authority but from the self-interested calculations of each individual. To regard Hobbes as a theist would be tantamount to suggesting that he was misunderstood by virtually everyone around him and that the true meaning of his thought would not become evident until more than three centuries after his death. A theory of interpretation like the one offered by Warrender and company that stands so far removed from the original reception of Hobbes's thought cannot pass the bar of historical credibility.[9]

What I want to contend is that the core of Hobbes's political philosophy—what makes Hobbes a thoroughgoing modernist—is the critique of religion. Hobbes's goal was the dismantling of the entire theologico-political nexus that he describes as "the kingdom of darkness." The kingdom of darkness, we shall see later, refers to a specific configuration of theological politics in which priests and those claiming to represent God have usurped political authority. The struggle between kings and priests has been the bane of Christian politics, resulting in continual war, conflict, and instability. Hobbes's hope was to put religion on a new foundation and so reunite spiritual and temporal power under a single head. Hobbes stands at the head of the queue of those modern political theologians who recognized that no sovereign can afford to dispense with religion and therefore that religion must serve the ends of supporting the legitimacy of the state. Leo Strauss hit the nail on the head when he remarked that Hobbes's book, no less than Spinoza's, should be thought of as a theologico-political treatise.[10]

This union of spiritual and temporal power is at the basis of the modern reading of Hobbes as an advocate of the total state. In his book *The Leviathan in the State Theory of Thomas Hobbes,* Carl Schmitt agreed with Hobbes about the centrality of political conflict and the need for an absolute sovereign to decide matters of war and peace. "Hobbes' leviathan," Schmitt writes, "a combination of god and man, animal and machine, is the mortal god who brings to man peace and security."[11] Hobbes is the great forerunner of Schmitt's doctrine of political decisionism. This is especially evident in Hobbes's discussion of the biblical doctrine of miracles. A miracle is what a sovereign says it is. It is what people are commanded to believe. The great flaw in Hobbes's system for Schmitt (to be examined more fully below) is his granting of an area of freedom of conscience where state and law are unable to penetrate. The Achilles heel of Hobbes's system, Schmitt asserts, and one later exploited by Spinoza and Moses Mendelssohn, was to grant a distinction between private and public, faith and confession, that would pave the way to the future philosophy of liberalism with its doctrine of the neutral state. This would sound for Schmitt the death knell of the mighty leviathan.[12]

This affiliation of Hobbes with liberalism was stated even more candidly by Leo Strauss and Michael Oakeshott. Already in his 1932 "Comments on Carl Schmitt's *Concept of the Political*" Strauss argued that Schmitt had misunderstood Hobbes by enlisting him in the great line of critics of liberalism, whereas Hobbes in fact stood at the beginning of the liberal tradition.[13] This point was later developed in his classic study *The Political Philosophy of Hobbes: Its Basis and Its Genesis*, in which Strauss credited Hobbes with putting an absolutely unprecedented emphasis on the natural right of the individual—rather than duties or obligations—as the basis of politics. This right—the right to self-preservation—is derived not from any transcendent source but from an analysis of the passions of pride and fear. From the outset, Hobbes attempted to build his new morality not on the desire for honor or glory, which can only lead to conflict, but on mutual fear, which leads us to seek peace. He emphasizes the ever-present danger of violent death as the precondition of bourgeois existence. On Strauss's account, Hobbes gave decisive expression to a new morality that has its home with the modern bourgeois desire to achieve peace, safety, and comfort.[14]

Strauss's argument was adopted with some modifications by Michael Oakeshott in the introduction to his landmark 1946 edition of *Leviathan*.[15] It was Hobbes's combination of nominalism and skepticism that elevated him, in Oakeshott's eyes, to the rank of the defenders of modern liberalism. Central to Hobbes's individualism is his skeptical appreciation of the limits of human reason. "His skepticism about the power of reasoning which applied no less to the 'artificial reason' of the Sovereign than to the reasoning of natural man, together with the rest of his individualism, separate him from the rationalist dictators of his or any age," Oakeshott wrote.[16] Yet Oakeshott also took issue with the "bourgeois" reading of Hobbes that Strauss had advanced. Hobbes's individualism, on Oakeshott's reading, is informed by aristocratic elements of pride, magnanimity, and honor that distinguish it from a low-minded focus on fear and security. "Indeed, Hobbes, without being a liberal himself, had in him more of the philosophy of liberalism than most of its professed defenders," Oakeshott affirmed.[17]

Strauss and Oakeshott agree that Hobbes was essentially a humanist whose teachings depend less on his scientific naturalism than on a new moral attitude toward the individual. This line of interpretation has recently been defended with regard to Hobbes's views on religion in Mark Lilla's book *The Stillborn God*. Here Hobbes is treated, along with Locke, as an advocate of what Lilla calls "the great separation." Hobbes instrumentalized religion, depriving it of the power of truth and revelation, and turning it entirely into a thing of human making. This humanization of religion meant that it could eventually be reduced to a cipher, belonging ultimately to the private precinct of individual conscience and rendered irrelevant to determining the shape of the public good. According to Lilla, "the way modern liberal democracies approach religion and politics today is unimaginable without Hobbes."[18]

THE NATURAL SEED OF RELIGION

Hobbes expected that his views on religion would prove controversial. In *Leviathan*'s dedication to Francis Godolphin (the younger brother of Hobbes's friend Sidney Godolphin, who had been killed in the English Civil War), he writes: "That which perhaps may most offend are certain texts of Holy Scripture alleged by me to other purpose than ordinarily they use to be by others" (Epistle Dedicatory). Hobbes clearly knew that he was treading on thin ice in entering the labyrinth of theology. His goal, broadly stated, was to reform theology in such a way not only that it would not but that it could not conflict with the demands of social order. Hobbes was adopting here an uncompromisingly secular attitude toward Christianity. Religion is to be evaluated exclusively in terms of its service to preserving social peace. In offering this claim, Hobbes was not retreating from Christianity but offering his own conception of the one true faith.

Hobbes actually provides two analyses of religion, one natural and the other prophetic. The locus classicus of Hobbes's natural religion is found in chapter 12 of *Leviathan,* which contains arguably the most important sentence in the entire book: "Seeing there are no signs nor fruit of religion but in man only, there is no cause to doubt that the seed of religion is also only in man" (I.xii.1). What is the "seed" of religion to which this passage refers? One might argue that if this seed had been planted by God, then there would be nothing particularly heterodox or impious about this statement, but this is not what Hobbes affirms.

Hobbes traces the seed of religion back to human curiosity about the causes of things. We all have a desire to know the causes of the good or evil fortunes to which we are subject. We are also inclined to believe that every event must have a cause and to trace this cause back to its beginning. Unlike the beasts, which are content to enjoy the "quotidian," humans have a need to put their experience into some kind of order by arranging it into temporal sequence, traced back to God as the first cause of things. Given that Hobbes adamantly denies our ability to grasp the ultimate foundations of knowledge, it is not immediately evident how postulating God as a first cause can satisfy our curiosity, but be that as it may. Religion is simply the way human beings try to make sense of their situation, at least until it can be replaced by a higher and more adequate form of understanding.

The difficulty arises, according to Hobbes, from the fact that the mind is weak and the causes of things are often difficult to determine. The ignorance of causes becomes the source of anxiety and fear, which are for Hobbes the truth of the human condition (I.xii.5). Man is born weak, ignorant, and beset by a host of uncertainties. As a result of this fearfulness, Hobbes speculates, we create imaginary powers who are believed to be the arbiters of our fates and who, by means of prayers and offerings, can be enjoined to ameliorate our condition. Religion is, therefore, a projection of the imagination, the creation of a fantasy world of ghosts and spirits that are thought to control our lives. At one point Hobbes simply defines religion as fear of "powers invisible" as imagined or "feigned" by the mind (I.vi.36). This superstitious fear is combined with a tendency to defer to others who we think are wiser than ourselves to do our thinking for us. Herein lies the source of priests and other authorities who use our gullibility to gain power and advantage for themselves.

Hobbes gives voice to the classic "fear theory" of religion that found its first and arguably greatest exposition in Lurcetius's famous (or infamous) prose poem *De rerum natura*. The influence of Lucretius on the early moderns—Hobbes, Spinoza, Voltaire—has been well attested.[19] Hobbes and Lucretius agreed on a number of themes. They shared broadly antiteleological and materialist theories of nature; held antipolitical conceptions of human nature and saw human well-being as residing in pleasure and minimizing pain, although they would disagree over what constituted the highest pleasure; and most of all regarded fear as the most fundamental passion that needs to be mastered if we are to live pleasantly in a state of peace and contentment. Lucretius presents his poem as the antidote to fear and the means of achieving tranquility of mind. In images that would be widely adopted by his great Enlightenment popularizers, he uses metaphors of light and darkness to chart the transition from a life based on fear, ignorance, and superstition to one based on reason, science, and a true understanding of nature. It is fear of death that is the origin of all religion. Religions are founded on our need to escape this fear but end up merely reestablishing it. The stories told in all religions about eternal punishments in the afterlife serve as an unending source of anxiety.

The teachings of Lucretius were always too austere to be truly popular. His conception of nature as matter in motion, unformed by purpose or divine ends, was always intended for a philosophical elite rather than the credulous many. Hobbes took Lucretius's ideas about the primacy of fear and gave them a political direction. He could be described as the founder of political Epicureanism.[20] Hobbesian science may not be able to banish fear, but it could redirect it. A well-ordered commonwealth is one in which citizens no longer fear one another but fear the sovereign, who is the worldly locus of all matters governing life and death. The ends of stability, prosperity, and even civil liberty will, it is hoped, come to assuage the kinds of irrational fears to which we are prone in the state of nature. Yet even if fear cannot be banished, it can be managed. By adopting Lucretius's psychological explanation of the birth of the gods, Hobbes hopes to reduce the fears and superstitions that are a direct consequence of our ignorance of nature: "This perpetual fear, always accompanying mankind in the ignorance of causes (as it were in the dark), must needs have for object something. And therefore, when there is nothing to be seen, there is nothing to accuse, either of their good or evil fortune, but some power or agent invisible, in which sense, perhaps, it was that some of the old poets said that the gods were first created by human fear; which spoken of the gods (that is to say, of the many gods of the Gentiles) is very true" (I.xii.6).

Hobbes is careful in this passage to distinguish between the gods of the "Gentiles," or pagans, that grow out of fear and the God of the monotheistic religions that ostensibly grew out of a desire to understand natural causes, although it is hard to see on what basis this distinction can be maintained. Yet on this basis Hobbes goes on to distinguish between two kinds of religion. "For these seeds," he reports, "have received culture from two sorts of men" (I.xii.12). The first were those like Numa who established religion through their own "invention," and the second were those like Abraham, Moses, and "our blessed Saviour" who have done so through "God's commandment and direction." The pagan civil theologies created ceremonies, festivals, and rites that established "human politics," while the founders of Judaism and Christianity created "divine politics" that not only established civil peace but also promised those who followed them a place in the world to come. We shall return later to just exactly what Hobbes meant by this.

Hobbes's reference to "the old poets" in the passage cited above not only points back to Lucretius—the most controversial author of classical antiquity—

but also looks forward to a new attitude that would increasingly characterize modernity. This disposition of fear and anxiety was turned by Hobbes into the virtually universal experience of all mankind—for what is political philosophy but the exploration of the nature and destiny of mankind?—and is the experience that Locke would later call "uneasiness," Rousseau *amour-propre,* and Tocqueville *inquiétude.*[21] This attitude is already nicely summed up in Hobbes's famous statement that there is no summum bonum, or highest good, of life and that all action is simply a means of avoiding pain and violent death. Life becomes the restless pursuit of desire after desire that has no final point of rest (I.xi.1).

The return to Lucretius also suggests a new social and political teaching. It is the continual edginess, restlessness, and unease that would become the hallmark not so much of human nature as of modernity. Hobbes's new morality is essentially bourgeois morality, the morality of striving, self-making, and independence without even the surviving remnant of Descartes's Stoic self-sufficiency. It is the antithesis of the ethic of glory, honor, and magnanimity celebrated by the ancients. Not the desire for fame but the continuous desire to escape fear becomes the primary goad to action. It also marks the rise of a new class to political power. This new class is left to pursue its desires without the resources of tradition and untethered from the trappings of conventional authority. *Leviathan* was a handbook—a long and ambitious handbook, to be sure—for a new class taking its first tentative steps on the road to power. And if the aspirations of this new class were anticipated a century earlier by Machiavelli's new prince, it was only with Hobbes that it received its complete theoretical expression and would find a sympathetic reading in the works of Spinoza, Locke, Hume, Franklin, and the authors of the *Federalist Papers.*

THE LAWS OF NATURE

The implications of this situation are clear. The disposition of radical uncertainty gives rise to a state of war that Hobbes associates with the natural condition of humankind (I.xiii.8). While he notes the ordinary sources of conflict such as the scarcity of material resources and the desire of some for fame and renown, he also acknowledges how religion exacerbates the situation. One can say of religion what Karl Kraus famously said of psychoanalysis: it is the disease that believes itself to be the cure. The problem is that so long as the reason of man remains fallible (to use James Madison's felicitous phrase), how do we know which religion is the true one? Prophets and priests each claim to speak for God, but since no one can know for sure the will or mind of God, whom should we believe? Religion adds an "ideological" component to the war of all against all. The famous Hobbesian account of the sate of nature as "solitary, poor, nasty, brutish, and short" is not merely a struggle for earthly survival and material well-being, it is also a struggle over claims about the right way to live and worship. It is a "theologico-political" conflict. To say that man is the religious animal is, for Hobbes, not to say that we are created in God's image or born with a spark of divine grace but simply provides one more cause over which people can fight and kill one another. It adds an element of what Machiavelli called "pious cruelty" into the already violent world of the state of nature.[22]

If the natural condition of mankind is one of maximum fear and anxiety, a remedy must be found to alleviate the situation. As an escape from fear, Hobbes sets out a series of axioms—he calls them "laws of nature"—that can begin to provide a peaceful transition from the fearful state of nature to the peaceful kingdom of society. These laws provide the general rules or basic framework for organizing and maintaining society. The first and most famous of these laws is the injunction to seek peace wherever and whenever possible (I.xiv.4). This is followed in turn by a number of further laws—nineteen in all—that enjoin such things as sociability, gratitude, equity, and humility and that contribute to the well-being of men in society and are later said to constitute "the true and only moral philosophy" (I.xv.40).

The question that generations of readers of Hobbes have asked is what the status of these laws is. Hobbes sometimes writes as if the laws of nature were merely "theorems" or "conclusions of reason," maxims of practical reason that are determined by prudence and foresight. Such laws seem to be what Kant would have called "hypothetical imperatives," that is, useful rules that help us achieve our desires. Hobbes's laws of nature could be seen as human inventions responding to our experience of the world. But what claim do these laws have to be "the true and only moral philosophy"? Do these laws have any genuine moral force? Why should we not simply choose to disregard these laws when they no longer serve our convenience? Perhaps aware of this problem, Hobbes occasionally refers to these laws as the laws of God, as though to give them additional moral force. He maintains that even in the state of nature the laws of nature are binding *in foro interno* (in conscience), even if there is no way to enforce them *in foro externo* (in actual conduct) (I.xv.36).

Hobbes seems to offer some resolution to this problem in the final two sentences of chapter 15: "These dictates of reason men use to call by the name of laws, but improperly; for they are but conclusions or theorems concerning what conduceth to the conservation and defense of themselves, whereas law properly is the word of him that by right hath command over others. But yet if we consider the same theorems, as delivered in the word of God, that by right commandeth all things, then are they properly called laws" (I.xv.41).

This passage is, to say the least, ambiguous. Hobbes calls these precepts of reason "laws of nature," but he says "improperly so." A law requires a lawgiver, and so far all we can say of Hobbes's God is that he is a first cause of all things, scarcely the kind of being who issues commands or intervenes in human affairs. But if these precepts are not really laws, why does Hobbes continue to use the term? One answer is that he deliberately invoked an older and respectable moral vocabulary going back to Cicero and the Stoics in order to disguise and render palatable a more radical, even atheistic, political teaching. If this reading is true, then Hobbes would seem to have collapsed the distinction, alluded to earlier, between the purely political religions created by the pagans and the "divine politics" associated with the word of Abraham, Moses, and "our blessed Saviour" (I.xii.12).

Yet Hobbes also leaves himself an escape clause. In the second sentence quoted above, he says that these theorems that enjoin us to seek peace can be properly called laws of nature if they are regarded "as delivered in the word of God, that by right commandeth all things." On the basis of this passage, Warrender and Hood regard the laws of nature as genuinely supported by divine sanction. They are not simply prudential rules of thumb but the actual word of God. But Hobbes's language here is deeply ambiguous. He does not exactly say that the laws of nature have been commanded by God; he only says that they are true and proper laws, if we choose to consider them that way. The result proves highly inconclusive.

The problem, of course, is that the laws of nature by themselves are not self-enforcing. Ironically, we cannot rely on the laws of nature alone, because we do not sufficiently fear God. If men could be trusted to fear God as they ought, there would be no necessity for an earthly sovereign to rule over us, but precisely because we are prone to a range of superstitions and other irrationalities, we must find other means to motivate people to respect the laws of nature. This is why a sovereign power—the "mortal God," as Hobbes describes it—needs to be created who can act as God's surrogate on earth. We are, so it seems, more afraid of the lesser power than the greater power! Hobbes's sovereign is charged with the duty of enforcing the laws of nature to which the sovereign himself remains subject. The sovereign may owe nothing to any of his subjects, but he too remains, like everyone else, subject to the laws of nature.

PROPHETIC RELIGION

Only two chapters of *Leviathan* are devoted to natural religion, while twelve chapters deal with the themes of scripture, prophecy, and eschatology. Yet most modern readers have largely passed over this part of the book. Far greater attention is paid to religion in *Leviathan* than in any of Hobbes's earlier political works, but little attention has been paid to why. One possibility is that Hobbes's earlier writings were written under the influence of his discovery of geometry and the geometrical method. Hobbes's discovery of Euclid became the model for his new moral and political science. This discovery ostensibly marked the transition from Hobbes's early "humanist" period, based on his appreciation of history, to his mature "scientific" studies.[23]

Yet this claim for a break between the humanist and scientific periods in Hobbes's writings has difficulty in accounting for *Leviathan,* in which the scientific and theological parts of the book are given virtually equal attention and where history—at least biblical history—is taken with great seriousness. If Hobbes were a consistent scientific naturalist, why should scripture occupy half of his most important work? The reason is that because only in *Leviathan* did Hobbes fully understand that scripture offers the deepest, the most profound, challenge to the claims of a scientific politics. If the possibility of a scientific politics was to be demonstrated, it could only be by showing that religion teaches nothing that runs contrary to reason. Science and religion may have different sources—one based in reason, the other in revelation—but they run on parallel tracks.

Hobbes introduces the concept of revealed religion in chapter 31 of *Leviathan,* entitled "Of the Kingdom of God by Nature," in which he distinguishes between what he calls natural and prophetic religion: "There may be attributed to God a twofold kingdom, *natural* and *prophetic:* natural, wherein he governeth as many of mankind as acknowledge his providence by the natural dictates of right reason; and prophetic, wherein, having chosen out one particular nation (the Jews) for his subjects, he governed them, and none but them, not only by natural reason, but by positive laws, which he gave them by the mouths of his holy prophets" (II.xxxi.4).

Hobbes takes for granted—or appears to take for granted—that scripture is the revealed word of God as handed down and passed on by his prophets.

But how can we be assured of this? This naturally raises the question "What is a prophet?" and Hobbes spends considerable time parsing the distinction between true and false prophets. A prophet is an intermediary between man and God. He notes that among all prophets Moses was unique in that he was the only prophet to whom God spoke directly; all others received their prophecies indirectly through either visions or dreams (III.xxxvi.11). Hobbes realizes that by these criteria most prophets will be false. Prophecy, like all human activities, is a form of power, and he is aware that anyone claiming to have received a divine voice is most likely claiming some form of power over others. It follows that most people claiming to be prophets will be either self-deluded or, as he indelicately puts it, "liars." Ahab apparently interviewed four hundred false prophets before determining that only one, Micaiah, was genuine. In one of his most pointed utterances Hobbes remarks: "To say [that God] hath spoken to him in a dream is no more than to say he dreamed that God spake to him, which is not of force to win belief from any man that knows dreams are for the most part natural and may proceed from former thoughts. . . . To say he speaks by supernatural inspiration is to say he finds an ardent desire to speak, or some strong opinion of himself, for which he can allege no natural and sufficient reason" (III.xxxii.6). In other words, those claiming the mantle of prophecy are usually blowhards who simply don't know when to stop talking.

Hobbes's account of prophetic religion takes the form of a history of scripture. He was a brilliant Hebraicist who delved into the deeper relevance of Hebrew history for the constitution of society, although he did not know Hebrew.[24] To be sure, Hobbes was an ingenious reader of scripture, and his goal was to make his account of prophetic history square with his theoretical account of the foundations of authority developed in parts 1 and 2 of *Leviathan*. His central thesis, repeated over and over, is that the kingdom of God was a genuine political sovereignty rather than a religious spiritual one: "The kingdom of God is a real, not a metaphorical, kingdom; and so taken, not only in the Old Testament, but the New. When we say 'for thine is the kingdom, the power, and glory' it is to be understood of God's kingdom by force of our covenant, not by the right of God's power; for such a kingdom God always hath, so that it were superfluous to say in our prayer, 'Thy kingdom come' unless it be meant of the restoration of that kingdom of God by Christ" (III.xxxv.11).

Hobbes's prophetic history is a play in three acts.[25] In the first act, God had chosen Abraham and his progeny to serve as "a kingdom of priests and a holy nation." This kingdom was established first by God's covenant with

Abraham and was renewed by God's covenant with Moses at Mount Sinai. Under the terms of this covenant, God ruled the Hebrews directly, with Moses and later prophets serving merely as God's "lieutenants" (III.xxxv.7). But after the death of Moses, the covenant at Sinai proved increasingly unstable as different prophets competed with one another for political power. Although theocracy in the original sense meant direct rule by God, this came to mean in effect rule by priests and others claiming to speak for God. Rival voices each claiming divine inspiration led to a condition of anarchy—the prototype of Hobbes's state of nature—in which authority became fragmented among the various tribes, and "there was no sovereign power in Israel" (III.xl.10).

This brings us to act 2. The covenant with Moses was abrogated at the time of Samuel when the sons of Eli caused the people to lose faith in the prophetic succession and to demand a king, so as to be ruled "like all the nations." On Hobbes's reading of the story, this marks a decisive moment in the prophetic narrative. It is one in a series of rebellions against God that had its source in eating from the tree of knowledge in the book of Genesis. Hobbes pays particular attention to the biblical passage in which God tells Samuel to "heed the demand of the people in everything they say to you," but not before Samuel warns the Israelites about the dangers of kingship (I Samuel 8:10). Never has there been a clearer case of the warning to be careful what you wish for.

But the third and final act of Hobbes's drama is the preparation for Christ's restoration of the kingdom of God on earth. Christ promised a restoration of the covenant with God that had existed from the time of Moses to Samuel, and had ceased to exist only with the election of Saul. The crowning of Saul as a flesh-and-blood king was nothing short of a rebellion against God that would not be fully repaired until the Second Coming of Christ. As with the older covenant, the new covenant will be a kingdom of this world ruled from Jerusalem. The difference is that the kingdom of Christ is yet to come: "If then Christ, whilst he was on earth, had no kingdom in this world, to what end was his first coming"? And Hobbes goes on to answer his own question: "It was to restore unto God, by a new covenant, the kingdom which, being his by the old covenant, had been cut off by the rebellion of the Israelites in the election of Saul. . . . So that there are two parts of our Saviour's office during his abode upon the earth: one to proclaim himself the Christ; and another, by teaching and by working of miracles, to persuade and prepare men to live so as to be worthy of the immortality believers were to enjoy" (III.xli.4).

Hobbes's claim that the role of Christ will do no more than restore the ancient Hebraic covenant established between God and Moses has often been advanced as evidence of his philosemitism. Hobbes in effect "Judaicizes" Christianity by making Christ serve as the agent for the restoration of the Mosaic theocracy (III.xli.4). In Gershom Scholem's terms, Hobbes is a restorative, not an apocalyptic, messianist.[26] In traditional Judaism, restorative messianism meant a restoration of political sovereignty, particularly as it was under the Davidic kingdom. It also denied that the world to come would represent any rupture in historical time or bring about some radically new law. The Hobbesian kingdom of Christ—a restored theocracy—would be a return to the moment when God ruled directly over his subjects without the intermediary of the coercive power of political institutions. This kingdom will be, so to speak, a purely "faith-based" community of believers, much like the one that had sustained the Jews in the time of Abraham and Moses.[27]

The idea of a society living directly under the laws of God suggests an antimonarchic, even messianic, dimension in Hobbes's thought far removed from the strained political realism usually associated with him. But—and here is the crucial point—the kingdom of Christ is yet to come. Christ came not as a legislator or political founder but as a teacher. He did no more than announce the coming of the kingdom of God, while leaving the laws of the existing state as well as the practices of the Jews untouched (III.xli.5). It remains a futural condition, and there is no end date in sight. Furthermore, Hobbes was no Sabbatai Zevi, who at the age of twenty-two proclaimed himself the Messiah and declared that the kingdom of God was at hand. Hobbes would have absolutely opposed any human attempt to force the end or bring it about by human means. Until the day when Christ returns, we still remain very much the children of Saul in rebellion against God. The institutions of law and sovereignty remain in full force to compel obedience precisely because faith is lacking. Hobbesian politics remains the politics for a fallen age. Until such time as Christ returns to earth, the rule of kings remains absolutely in place.

THE KINGDOM OF DARKNESS

Hobbes's kingdom of God is a polemical concept intended to oppose the kingdom of darkness (the title of the fourth part of *Leviathan*). By the kingdom of darkness Hobbes means "a confederacy of deceivers that, to obtain dominance over men in this present world, endeavor by dark and erroneous doctrines to extinguish in them the light, both of nature and the gospel, and so to dispreprepare them for the kingdom of God to come" (IV.xliv.1). His reference to a "confederacy" is meant to apply, above all, to the Catholic and Presbyterian clergy, but more generally a conspiracy of priests who claim some special knowledge of the ways of God and set themselves up as authorities to be obeyed.

The basis of this priestly claim to authority derives in the first instance from a faulty metaphysics. This goes back to the belief in an eternal soul that exists independently of the body and consequently to the belief in an afterlife beyond this world. For Hobbes, there is no life beyond this one, and he devotes an entire chapter of *Leviathan* (chapter 38) to showing that what is meant by eternity applies to the life of the state, not the individual. Not only does Hobbes debunk the idea of an eternal felicity after this life, he similarly undermines the idea of eternal torment. The idea of hell is a translation of the Hebrew Gehenna, which actually refers to a garbage dump on the outskirts of Jerusalem where fires continually burned (III.xviii.10)! But this faulty metaphysics has had important political consequences. The priesthood has set itself up as a kind of kingdom within a kingdom, a spiritual kingdom in competition with the temporal power. The result has been an ongoing civil war between kings and priests.

Hobbes's goal, to reiterate, was to reunite the spiritual and temporal powers under one head. This meant attributing to the civil sovereign such powers as the right to establish the forms of public worship, to determine which books of scripture are to be regarded as canonical, and to interpret scripture on behalf of the commonwealth as a whole. Even the churches are nothing but authorized arms of the sovereign. In an extraordinary sentence, Hobbes defines a church as "a company of men professing Christian religion, united in the person of one sovereign at whose command they ought to assemble, and without whose authority they ought not to assemble" (III.xxxix.4). Because the church must be under the control of the civil sovereign, the Christian is duty bound to obey the religion of the sovereign. Temporal and spiritual powers are but two sides of the same coin, a point Hobbes elaborates in the last paragraph of chapter 39: "There is therefore no other government in this life, neither of state nor religion, but temporal; nor teaching of any doctrine, lawful to any subject, which the governor, both of the state and of the religion, forbiddeth to be taught. And that governor must be one, or else there must needs follow faction and civil war in the commonwealth: between the Church and

State; between spiritualists and temporalists; between the sword of justice and the shield of faith: and (which is more) in every Christian man's own breast, between the Christian and the man" (III.xxxix.5). And Hobbes concludes this passage with the claim that the "civil sovereign" is none other than the "chief pastor" because "the Scripture has assigned that office" to him.

A major part of Hobbes's strategy is clearly the disempowerment of the clergy. Hobbes helped to begin the war on what the Enlightenment called "priestcraft," which would reach its height in Voltaire's *écrasez l'infâme*. There is only one source of legitimate power, and that is the sovereign. This position too, so Hobbes maintains, can be construed from scripture. Because the kingdom of Christ is yet to be, it follows that Christ had no political authority and his apostles even less. "The office of Christ's ministers in this world is to make men believe and have faith in Christ," Hobbes writes. "But faith hath no relation to, nor dependence at all, upon compulsion or commandment, but only upon certainty or probability of arguments drawn from reason or something men believe already" (III.xlii.9). The power of the clergy is to be "ministerial," not "magisterial." It follows, further, that persecution for heresy or other forms of unbelief is completely forbidden (III.xlii.25).[28]

All that is needed to ensure salvation, Hobbes assures the reader, is faith in Christ and obedience to the laws of the sovereign (III.xliii.3). These form the basic principles of Hobbes's civil religion. "The *unum necessarium* (the only article of faith which the Scripture maketh simply necessary to salvation) is this: that Jesus is the Christ" (III.xliii.11). This is all that salvation requires. Given that neither the church nor its ministers has any right to coercive power, what if a king is an unbeliever or a heretic who forbids belief in Christ? Here Hobbes answers in a manner that will sound eerily like Locke's later arguments for toleration: "To this I answer," he replies, "that such forbidding is of no effect because belief and unbelief never follow men's commands" (III.xlii.11). Laws can compel actions but not faith. For this reason, even if a person is forced to forswear belief in Christ, Hobbes argues that he commits no sin. "Profession with the tongue," he remarks, "is but an external thing" and can signify obedience, but not belief.

A CHRISTIAN MALGRÉ LUI

So what are we to make of Hobbes's critique of religion? Among his own contemporaries, there was little doubt that Hobbes was an atheist. His materialism, his reduction of the person to matter in motion, his denial of personal immortality, and his attack on the independence of the episcopacy all led those like the Earl of Clarendon—one of his earliest and best readers—to remark "a good Christian can hardly hear of Hobbes' name without saying his prayers."[29] Today opinion has gone full circle. We who often pride ourselves on our skepticism tend to be utterly unskeptical when it comes to Hobbes's professions of religious faith. We are often less skeptical of Hobbes than we are of those doubting his sincerity. Thus in his massive study *The Authority of the Bible and the Rise of the Modern World,* Henning Graf Reventlow concludes his chapter on Hobbes with the observation that he was "completely a child of his time," namely, a Christian humanist in keeping with conventional church politics.[30] Why did Hobbes's contemporaries fail to grasp this? We who claim to know Hobbes so well seem to know him less well than those who burned his books.

The more interesting—and more difficult—question is to assess the sincerity of Hobbes's religious beliefs. For John Pocock, it seems patently inconceivable that a thinker as "notoriously arrogant" and "vehement in his dislike of 'insignificant speech'" as Hobbes could have written what he did not believe.[31] Indeed, for a man who famously said he and fear were born twins, Hobbes was unusually outspoken by the standards of his age.[32] But even Hobbes's boldness had its limits. A major source of evidence for doubting Hobbes's complete sincerity is his remark, reported in John Aubrey's *Brief Lives,* that his reading of Spinoza's *Theologico-Political Treatise* "had cut through him a barre's length, for he durst not write so boldly."[33]

Aubrey's statement could well provide evidence for Strauss's view that Hobbes was reluctant to openly express his religious convictions for fear of persecution. Hobbes's religious views, Strauss alleges, can be tacked to the changing currents of English politics of the day and to Hobbes's desire to survive or at least to die in peace, which he did at the age of eighty-nine. Although Hobbes was "relatively close to Anglican Episcopalianism" in his early writings, appearances can be deceiving: "He was as little a believing Christian then as later," Strauss remarks. "Only political considerations can have induced him to defend the Episcopal constitution of the Church and for this very reason to speak more circumspectly on dogma than during the Civil War and under the Republic and the Protectorate."[34]

Strauss's statement that Hobbes was never a "believing Christian" but a Christian for convenience only forces us to consider not just what Hobbes said but also his sincerity in saying it. Strauss later admitted that he could not prove that Hobbes was an atheist, even according to Hobbes's own views on atheism.[35] Strauss is surely right when he notes than many who write on religious topics today fail to appreciate the degree of "circumspection" and "accommodation" used in earlier generations by writers who wished to avoid persecution. One cannot read Hobbes on religion the same way one reads the works of Bertrand Russell on the same topic. Yet if this were simply true, Hobbes would have failed his own test, as his work caused him endless trouble. He may not have suffered the fate of Socrates, but the frequent attacks on his doctrines and the coinage of a new term, "Hobbism," was more than enough to prevent a serious reckoning with his thought until his rehabilitation in the twentieth century.[36]

The point is not what Hobbes may have believed in his heart of hearts but how he meant to be understood. No one can claim to know Hobbes's mind, only his words. And even if we could know Hobbes's mind, what difference would it make? As noted above, Hobbes was notoriously anticlerical. By the term "kingdom of darkness" he meant not merely the Church of Rome but also the Presbyterian clergy, whom he blamed for lighting the flame that would ignite the Civil War. Yet Hobbes's repeated insistence that the single dogma of the Christian faith is that "Jesus is the Christ," whether intended or not as a prophylactic against the charge of atheism, is enough to label him a Christian. Hobbes may have been an idiosyncratic Christian, a member of a sect of one, but he was a Christian nonetheless.

The question is, If Hobbes was indeed a Christian, albeit an eccentric one, what kind of Christian was he? One answer is that he was a theological skeptic. This does not mean that he was skeptical of religion as such, only of the arguments that have been used in its defense. This is especially true, as we have seen, of those claiming to speak for God. Hobbes does not deny that a person may receive a genuine communication from God. He only denies that this entitles any person to impose his or her views on others. Since no one is in a position to confirm someone else's claim to divine communication, it follows that no one is under any obligation to anyone claiming to have heard the voice of God (III.xxxii.9). All we are entitled to say with any degree of certainty is that God exists and that his ways are unknowable (I.xi.25). Anything we attempt to allege beyond this is a form of impiety.

Hobbes could deny that this kind of skepticism was a cover for atheism. Atheism is a kind of vulgar skepticism. It claims to know something that cannot be known, like the fool who says in his heart that God does not exist (I.xv.4). For Hobbes, by contrast, faith is inseparable from skepticism, from what we cannot know. The essence of Hobbes's skeptical religion, as Shirley

Letwin has argued, is what Keats described as a "negative capability," that is, "the ability to live with uncertainties, mysteries, doubts, without any irritable reaching after fact and reason." Hobbes's goal was to limit reason to make room for faith.[37]

Connected to the debate over Hobbes's sincerity is the question of his relation to liberalism. If we focus on his attempt to put the churches and all other forms of civil association under sovereign control, Hobbes seems to be flirting with a dangerous form of caesaro-papism. It is indisputable that Hobbes gave the sovereign extraordinary powers in determining such matters as the right of scriptural interpretation (III.xxxiii.25), of declaring which books of the Bible are to be regarded as authoritative (III.xxxiii.1), to censor or forbid publication of books deemed dangerous to public safety, to excommunicate subjects (III.xlii.29), and to compel worship even if it contradicts conscience. It is hardly surprising that twentieth-century thinkers like Carl Schmitt have turned to Hobbes's doctrine of the sovereign as illustrating a form of political "decisionism."

Recently, a number of revisionist interpreters have argued for a more tolerationist understanding of Hobbes.[38] On this reading, he may have ascribed unlimited de jure authority to the sovereign, but he also believed that it should be used as sparingly as possible. Hobbes, it is argued, put limits on what sovereigns can reasonably demand of their subjects. His arguments for imposing religious uniformity are less principled than pragmatic and political. In *Behemoth,* his history of the English Civil War, he repeatedly showed how attempts to impose religious uniformity backfired and produced conflict and resistance.[39] The sovereign should be able to control ideas that genuinely *are* dangerous to peace and order, but still leave ample room for what people are allowed to think and do in their private lives. Religion, Hobbes maintains, is a matter of faith—and faith, and unlike behavior, cannot be coerced. The combination of outward compliance and inner freedom is the key to Hobbes's worship. Hobbes's reduction of Christianity to one single maxim—"Jesus is the Christ"—leaves a great deal of latitude for what people may do and believe.

The strongest evidence for the tolerationist Hobbes comes in a passage near the end of *Leviathan* (IV.xlvii.19). Here Hobbes gives a brief and necessarily truncated history of Christianity as a story of growing ecclesiastical encroachment over the liberty of conscience. Under primitive Christianity, conscience was deemed free, while words and actions were subject to the civil authorities. Soon enough, the "presbyters" determined what they deemed was appropriate doctrine, and all who disagreed were subject to excommunication. "And this," Hobbes writes, "was the first knot upon their liberty." The second knot appeared with the appointment of bishops to oversee the provincial presbyters. And the final knot was the appointment of the bishop of Rome as Pontifex Maximus to oversee all the bishops of the empire.

One might have thought the Catholic image of a unified Christendom would have appealed to Hobbes's desire to unite the two heads of the eagle as Rousseau had claimed, but he goes on to present the situation of Christian Europe since the Reformation as a return to the condition of early Christianity before the rise of the power of the priests to control people's beliefs: "First, the power of the Popes was dissolved totally by Queen Elizabeth. . . . And so was untied the first knot. After this the Presbyterians lately in England obtained the putting down of the episcopacy. And so was the second knot dissolved. And almost at the same time the power was taken also from the presbyterians. And so we are reduced to the independency of the primitive Christians, to follow Paul, or Cephas, or Apollos, every man as he liketh best" (IV.xlvii.20).

Hobbes then goes on to consider this new ecclesiastical commonwealth as "perhaps the best" that has existed: "First, because, there ought to be no power over the consciences of men but the Word itself, working faith in everyone one, not always according to the purpose of them that plant and water, but of God himself, that giveth the increase. And secondly, because it is unreasonable (in them who teach that there is such danger in ever little error) to require of a man endued with reason of his own, to follow the reason of any other man, or of the most voices of many other men (which is little better than to venture his salvation at cross and pile)" (III.xlvii.20).

It is clear that Hobbes is speaking here of the situation of Christian Europe since the Reformation. The end of the great wars of religion and the Treaty of Westphalia have undercut the claims of a universal church and have opened the door, at least a crack, to the possibility of religious pluralism. We are in a situation in which all people can think and believe what they will, and it is contrary to reason to coerce people to believe what others tell them to believe. Hobbes seems to be suggesting here a kind of religious toleration as the best arrangement for a civil society. We are now, in short, coming within hailing distance of Spinoza's territory.

Chapter 5 What Kind of Jew Was Spinoza?

"[Hobbes] told me that [Spinoza] had cut through him a barre's length, for he durst not write so boldly."
—John Aubrey

Spinoza occupies a central place in the development of modernity. He exemplified the first modern Jew, coming to typify a distinctly modern form of Jewish identity. Yet even today, more than three hundred years after his death, the question remains: "What kind of Jew was Spinoza?" What was the relation between Spinoza and Judaism, and how did he transform the Jewish tradition? And perhaps most important, how did his transformation of Judaism bear on the development of modernity? Spinoza was without doubt the first to put what later became known as the Jewish Question—*der Judenfrage*—at the center of modern philosophy.[1]

Spinoza's relation to Judaism is by no means an incidental or peripheral aspect of his thought. It is not simply a contingent feature of his biography, as it is sometimes portrayed, or a matter of only psychological curiosity. Due to the research of great Spinoza scholars like Harry Wolfson and Shlomo Pines, we know that Spinoza lived in virtually continual conversation with the great themes and texts of the medieval Jewish philosophers and exegetes like Maimonides, Hasdai Crescas, Gersonides, Rashi, Ibn Ezra, and Leone Ebreo.[2] Yet at the same time, Spinoza, more than any other Jewish thinker, has been vilified at the hands of the Jewish tradition. Spinoza was not a faithful mediator and loyal transmitter of his tradition; he was its most profound and far-reaching critic, whose criticism was made all the more hurtful by the fact that it was carried out by someone steeped in and deeply conversant with the texts and sources of classical Judaism.

Let us begin with what is always taken as Exhibit A in the case against Spinoza. On July 27, 1656 (6 Av 5416), the elders of the synagogue of Amsterdam pronounced on the twenty-four-year-old Baruch de Espinosa the following *Herem,* or edict of excommunication: "By the decrees of the Angels and the words of the Saints we ban, cut off, curse, and anathemize Baruch de Spinoza . . . with all the curses written in the Torah. Cursed be he by day and cursed by night, cursed in his lying down and cursed in his waking up, cursed in his going forth, and cursed in his coming in; and may the Lord not want his pardon, and may the Lord's wrath and zeal burn upon him . . . and ye that did cleave unto the Lord your God are all alive today."[3]

The text of the Herem is short on the details that led the rabbis to cut off Spinoza from the Amsterdam Jewish community. There are some vague references to certain "horrible heresies," "awful deeds," and "evil opinions" said to be practiced or held by Spinoza. Indeed, the Herem concludes with the ominous warning that anyone who seeks to aid, comfort, or abet Spinoza or "read anything composed or written by him" will suffer the same fate.

The reasons for Spinoza's excommunication are obscure or even lost to history. But fourteen years after the Herem was issued, Spinoza published an anonymous work under a fictitious imprimatur that constituted his settling of accounts with Judaism and the Jewish people. The *Tractatus Theologico-Politicus*—henceforth cited as *TTP*—provides all the evidence necessary for a judgment on the justice of Spinoza's excommunication.[4] For some, this work more than fully justifies the ban on Spinoza, which has not been lifted to this day. For others, the treatment of Spinoza puts him in a long line of martyrs from Socrates to Jesus to Galileo who suffered persecution for the cause of freedom of thought and opinion. The legacy of Spinoza, even today, remains a hotly contested one.

The image of Spinoza throughout much of Jewish thought has been deeply divided. Some of the most powerful voices within modern Judaism have agreed that Spinoza fully warranted the ban against him. Hermann Cohen, one of the great founders of the neo-Kantian movement in Germany, denounced him as a "renegade to his people" and an "apostate" who slandered Judaism before an anti-Jewish world. Spinoza was depicted by Cohen as a traitor to the Jews, guilty of a "humanly incomprehensible betrayal."[5] The French philosopher and Talmudist Emmanuel Levinas has been no less severe in his judgment. "Spinoza," Levinas writes, "was guilty of betrayal. . . . Thanks to the rationalism patronized by Spinoza, Christianity is surreptitiously triumphing, bringing conversion without the scandal of apostasy."[6]

At the same time that Spinoza was being anathematized by some, he was being lionized by others. In *Rome and Jerusalem,* Moses Hess signed his name "a young Spinozist" and treated Spinoza as a prophet of Jewish national aspirations for a homeland in Palestine.[7] George Eliot began a translation of the *TTP,* and in her novel *Daniel Deronda* the character of Mordecai regards Spinoza as a proto-Zionist who "saw not why Israel should not again be a chosen nation": "Who says that the history and literature of our race are dead? Are they not as living as the history and literature of Greece and Rome, which have inspired revolutions, enkindled the thought of Europe, and made the unrighteous powers tremble? These were an inheritance dug from the tomb. Ours is an inheritance that has never ceased to quiver in millions of human frames."[8]

From time to time, petitions have been made to rescind the ban on Spinoza. At the Hebrew University in Jerusalem in 1925, the Hebraicist and historian Joseph Klausner denounced the ban on Spinoza as a historical anachronism. Spinoza may have been expelled from the Jewish community, but he did not cease to be a Jew (I shall return to this later). Spinoza showed what it was to be a new kind of Jew. "The ban is revoked," Klausner declared—on whose authority, no one knew—and then proceeded to proclaim three times, "Baruch Spinoza, you are our brother."[9] A similar call was repeated, equally unsuccessfully, by David Ben-Gurion.

How did Spinoza's views on Judaism help to shape our conception of modernity? Are these views justified, and what can explain them? What led to such radically different responses to Spinoza's work? And finally, what kind of Jew was Spinoza, and what has been his influence—for better or worse—on modern Judaism?

THE PSYCHOLOGICAL SOURCES OF
RELIGIOUS BELIEF

The first sentence of the *TTP* reads as follows: "If men were able to exercise complete control over all their circumstances, or if continuous good fortune were always their lot, they would never be prey to superstition" (Pref/1). The key word here is *superstition*. Spinoza proposes a far-ranging statement about human psychology and the origins of our beliefs that sets the stage for everything that follows. He here helps to launch the Enlightenment's war on superstition or what would later become Voltaire's famous rallying cry, *écrasez l'infâme*. The aim of the book is to explain the origins of superstitious beliefs and therefore to liberate the reader from them. Its task is both diagnostic and emancipatory. But what is a superstition, a term that Spinoza nowhere exactly defines?

A superstition is a species of false belief. I say a *species* because it is obvious that not all false beliefs are superstitions. Many false beliefs are based simply on factual misinformation or faulty perception. Such beliefs are those subject to falsification in the light of empirical evidence. Superstitions, by contrast, are beliefs that defy evidentiary claims. Spinoza offers a psychological analysis of why superstitions have such a lasting hold on the mind. Superstitions are for Spinoza rooted in the passions. As human beings, we are prone to diverse passions—hope and fear being the two most powerful—depending on our condition of life. We are said to "waver" between these passions and let them—not reason—determine our beliefs. The passions are sources not of intellectual creativity but of error and confusion. It is ultimately fear of the unknown—fear being the dominant passion—brought about by ignorance of causes that leads some to believe that the future can be determined, not through the study of nature, but by consulting shamans, fortune-tellers, and other charlatans who prey on human gullibility (Pref/1).

Based on Spinoza's psychology of the passions, there may be any number of superstitions, but the greatest one—the mother of all superstitions, as it were—is the belief that God is an intending agent, a being such as ourselves but infinitely more powerful, who can be influenced to act on our behalf or to benefit our situation through prayers and supplications. This belief has created an immense superstructure of habits, institutions, and rituals—the totality of organized religion—that has led in turn to the enslavement of the human mind: "The supreme mystery of despotism, its prop and stay, is to keep men in a state of deception, and with the specious title of religion to cloak the fear by which they must be held in check, so that they will fight for their servitude as if for salvation, and to count it no shame, but the highest honor, to spend their blood and their lives for the glorification of one man" (Pref/3).

But superstitions are not simply forms of deception and false belief, although they are surely that; they are tools of political control and persecution. By persecution, Spinoza means the use of force or coercive power to control the mind. A central paradox that the *TTP* seeks to unwrap is how Christianity that began as a religion of love and peace became a religion of persecution and intolerance. Spinoza traces the source of intolerance back to the weakness and gullibility of human beings who are willing to cede their powers of reason and self-legislation to power-hungry priests and kings. As a consequence of human gullibility, faith has become "identical with credulity and dogma" and religion a "form of ridiculous mysteries" (Pref/4).

Most dangerously, the church in alliance with the state has made use of popular credulity to control not only the actions but also the minds of their subjects. It is because of his opposition to all forms of censorship and mind control that Spinoza has entered the liberal tradition as one of the great champions of freedom of thought and opinion: "To invest with prejudice or in any way coerce the citizen's free judgment is altogether incompatible with the freedom of the people. As for those persecutions that are incited under the cloak of religion, they surely have their only source in this, that law intrudes into the realm of speculative thought, and that beliefs are put on trial and condemned as crimes. The adherents and followers of these beliefs are sacrificed, not to the public weal, but to the hatred and savagery of their opponents" (Pref/3).

The intention of the *TTP* is to liberate the mind from scriptural and ecclesiastical supervision. Like Hobbes, Spinoza is careful to say that it is not religion as such that he opposes but priestcraft, that is, the willful deception of human beings by clerics and other religious authorities who use their power to achieve dominance over them. He proposes what would become a classic liberal move, separating the spheres of reason and revelation. Reason pertains to the operations of the mind and its ability to grasp factual and necessary truths, while revelation pertains to right conduct and acts of piety and obedience. The question for Spinoza is not the medieval one of how to reconcile faith and reason but the preeminently modern one of how to separate them. Spinoza stands at the forefront of what has been called the "Great Separation"— the separation of philosophy and religion—upon which the entire architecture of modernity has been built.[10] Reason and revelation are not so much in competition as they are simply incommensurable. They are not in conflict with one another because they speak different languages, operate on completely different assumptions, and therefore occupy their own distinct spheres of operation (Pref/6).

To whom is this argument addressed? Near the end of the Preface to the *TTP*, Spinoza acknowledges the "learned reader" as his addressee (Pref/7). It would seem that the book is primarily a philosophical work intended for the enlightened few who have managed to escape the shackles of prejudice and superstition. But on closer inspection, this turns out to be not quite true. In virtually the same breath, he acknowledges that the "main points" of his work will already be "familiar to philosophers" (Pref/7). It seems hardly likely that Spinoza would have written a book to tell his audience what they already know. At the same time, he says that he does not recommend the work for "the common people" and those "who are victims of the same emotional attitudes" (Pref/8). These are the people who are under the influence of the preachers and clerics and who include the actual or potential persecutors of Spinoza. For readers such as these, the book will prove useless or worse than useless and may even expose its author to harm and abuse. But here too it seems unlikely that Spinoza would need to warn the lay reader against a book written in an erudite language—Latin—that most will not have access to in any case. So to whom is the book really addressed?

The ideal reader is neither the tiny and politically insignificant class of philosophers nor the larger and more dangerous multitude. Instead, Spinoza appeals to those of a more "liberal" persuasion for whom such events as the wars of religion and the Inquisition have led to a desire to achieve some kind of peaceful accommodation, a modus vivendi, which might put an end to religious persecution. Such "liberal" readers were, for historically contingent reasons, most likely to be drawn from the dissenting sects of Protestant Holland who were influential in the struggle to achieve Dutch independence from Hapsburg Spain (XVIII/210–11). The *TTP*, to some degree like Machiavelli's *Prince*, is a patriotic work designed to achieve national liberation. Those to whom the book is actually addressed—the "left-leaning" dissenters, like the Menonites and Collegiants—represented a new party in Dutch and European politics: the party of liberty.

Politically, these dissenting sects were the main supporters of the republican faction in Dutch politics, who stood in opposition to the monarchist House of Orange and the Calvinist clergy.[11] These sects were by no means free of prejudice themselves, but Spinoza hopes they will have an interest in turning toleration from a philosophical ideal into a matter of public policy. These sects, he confidently muses, "will derive great profit from this work." He even appeals to their sense of civic patriotism by praising "the rare good fortune" to live in a republic "where nothing is esteemed dearer and more precious than freedom" (Pref/3). The model of Amsterdam's commercial republic was the "European miracle" of the seventeenth century that Spinoza hoped to promote and export. Such a regime, he reasoned, would be of great benefit to the Jews.

SPINOZA'S CRITIQUE OF RELIGION

Every reader of the *TTP* is confronted with the question of Spinoza's religion and its relation to the work as a whole. The preponderance of the work deals with Jewish materials and sources; it cites almost exclusively Jewish authorities and predecessors. Some readers have concluded that Spinoza's biblical criticism is a criticism of the Hebrew Bible only, while others have argued that he criticizes the Hebrew Bible in order to launch a more far-ranging attack on the power of revealed religion in general. In any case, Spinoza sets out to undermine systematically the three pillars of Jewish faith and life: the revealed character of the Torah, the status of the prophets, and the divine "election" of the Jewish people. I want to consider each of these in turn.

The fundamental principle of Spinoza's biblical criticism can be summed up as a variation of the Protestant principle of *sola Scriptura,* namely, that the Bible should be read by itself alone without the use of historical commentaries or the intervention of priestly or rabbinic authorities.[12] The central principle of this method is that "the method of interpreting Scripture is no different from the method of interpreting Nature": "For the method of interpreting Nature consists essentially in composing a detailed study of Nature from which, as being the source of our assured data, we can deduce the definitions of the things of Nature. Now in exactly the same way the task of Scriptural interpretation requires us to make a straightforward study of Scripture, and from this, as the source of our fixed data and principles, to deduce by logical inference the meaning of the authors of Scripture" (VII/87). Much like Descartes's method for arriving at clear and distinct knowledge, Spinoza confidently asserts that by following his reconstructive procedure "steady progress can be made without any danger of error" (VII/87).

The student of the Bible must approach his work in the same manner as a naturalist seeking the explanation of any physical phenomenon. The "book of nature" and the "book of books" are subject to the same causal laws and processes. Rather than being approached as a repository of revealed truth, the Bible must be viewed in the same value-neutral manner as a scientist would investigate the natural causes of things. For Spinoza, this means undertaking a kind of natural history of scripture, reasoning about the Bible solely in terms of the time, place, and circumstance in which the text was written. The biblical scholar must have a thorough knowledge of the Hebrew language, note down all passages that seem obscure or inconsistent with one another, and relate the contents of each book to its subsequent reception. Spinoza initiates a method that would today be called "canon formation," showing how the many diverse works that make up scripture came to be unified in a single body and accepted as a sacred text (VII/88–90).

Spinoza's method of reading is a seventeenth-century precursor of what became known as the "higher criticism." The purpose of this criticism was clearly to undermine the authority of the Bible by historicizing it, showing it to be a purely historical book, much like any other work of ancient literature. Thus Spinoza distinguishes between "hieroglyphic" works, like the Bible, that require elaborate and painstaking methods of historical reconstruction and "intelligible" works, like Euclid's *Elements*, whose meaning is self-evident to anyone capable of following a chain of reasoning from premise to conclusion (VII/note 232). No one needs to be a learned student of the Greek language or ancient history to grasp the properties of a triangle. But the content of biblical narrative is something entirely different. It needs the formidable skills of the philologist, the archaeologist, and even the social psychologist if one is to make sense of the bizarre and often inexplicable happenings recorded there. When suitably reconstructed, the Bible presents itself as a work of imaginative literature no different from that found among many ancient peoples. Spinoza even sets the stage for studying the Bible as literature by comparing the story of Elijah to the goings-on he claims to recall from the works of Ovid and the tales of Orlando Furioso (VII/97).

Spinoza uses this method of sola Scriptura to cast doubt on the literal truth of scripture because it contains a host of fallacies and historical anachronisms. For example, he takes elaborate pains to deny the Mosaic authorship of the Pentateuch. He makes much of the fact that Moses could not be the sole author of the work, for the reason that the last chapters of Deuteronomy record his death and funeral (VIII/108). He points to repeated references to Moses written in the third person as sufficient evidence to conclude that the work must have been written by someone else. And he concludes that the work could only have been compiled by later redactors several centuries after the events it is relating, most likely the scribe Ezra (VIII/113).

In addition to the problems of disputed authorship, the Bible is a text that contains outright contradictions. Spinoza's proof text here is Samuel's denial and Jeremiah's affirmation that God repents of his decisions (1 Sam. 15:29; Jer. 18:8–10). Spinoza attributes these contradictions not to any attributes of God but to the different psychological states and dispositions of the prophets whose judgments they express. Prophets are people not with gifted intellects but with vivid imaginative powers (II/21). Here Spinoza takes particular exception to Maimonides, the greatest philosophical figure in the Jewish tradition, who regarded prophecy as an "overflow" emanating from the "active intellect." In a remarkable piece of philosophical chutzpah, Spinoza accuses Maimonides of introducing foreign Aristotelianisms into Judaism and making the words of scripture conform to the speculations of Gentiles (Pref/5).

The power of prophecy, he concludes, implies not "a more perfect mind but only a more vivid imagination" (II/21). There is no reason to believe that prophets who claim to speak for God had great speculative powers or were bearers of profound philosophical truths. To the contrary, they were simple men with powerful imaginations whose prophecies varied according to their individual temperaments and prejudices, who otherwise maintained "quite ordinary opinions about God." The biblical texts provide ample evidence that the prophets were ignorant of the causal mechanisms of nature. A crucial instance is the miracle recorded in Joshua 10:11, in which it appears that the earth stood still in the heavens, to which Spinoza rhetorically asks, "Are we to believe that Joshua, a solider, was also skilled in astronomy?" (II/26).

The most durable illusion of scripture, however, is the belief in the divine election of the Jews. In the third chapter of the *TTP*, Spinoza argues that the category of divine election or chosenness is not a theological but a political designation. Chosenness, he argues, applied only to the period of the ancient Jewish commonwealth and then only so long as it maintained its national sovereignty. The entire Torah—the law of Moses—was nothing more than a political legislation of the Hebrew state that ceased to be binding with the destruction of the Temple. Taking a cue from Machiavelli, Spinoza maintains that the ancient Hebrews were chosen only with respect to their mode of social organization and military success.

In suggesting that the belief in divine election applies only to the limited period of national sovereignty, Spinoza does much to undermine the traditional belief that the Jewish people have a special mission to live as "a king-dom of priests and a holy nation" (Exod. 19:6). Spinoza is a moral universalist. He maintains that there is simply no such thing as a people chosen in respect of their moral and intellectual qualities. These qualities are more or less ran-domly distributed among the human race, and it is sheer arrogance to believe that they reside in one people. In respect to their moral and intellectual qual-ities, Spinoza avers, the Jews were on a par with other nations, for "God is equally gracious to all" (III/40). To say that one nation is chosen over others is simply a way of expressing the desire for that nation to be superior to or rule over others. The belief in divine election is nothing more than a mark of vanity or national superstition.

Spinoza ridicules the idea that Jewish survival over the centuries of the Dia-spora had anything to do with God's favor. The fact that the Jews have re-mained a nation despite the absence of a state can be explained by purely human causes. The adoption of certain ritual practices and ceremonies like circumcision served to separate the Jews from other peoples, but at the same time it has been the cause of much anti-Jewish animus (III/45–46). The rea-sons for Jewish survival had less to do with divine providence than with the hatred of the Gentiles, which, more than anything else, preserved the Jewish people intact. Indeed, so effective have been these ritual forms in inciting the hatred of the nations that Spinoza suggests—with deliberate hyperbole—that they will cause the Jews to exist in perpetuity. The conclusion to which the *TTP* leads—to be reconsidered later on—is that the category of election is not a metaphysical privilege but a political curse. Spinoza's advice is that the Jews should abandon this dogma as quickly and as painlessly as possible. If anti-Judaism is the result of religious arrogance and aloofness, then the Jews should abandon this belief in order to avoid what would today be called "dis-crimination."

SPINOZA'S DOUBLE STANDARD

Of the twenty chapters that make up the *TTP*, the first fifteen—a full three-quarters of the work—are devoted to strictly theological concerns. Of these fifteen, only one—chapter 11—is devoted to problems specific to the New Testa-ment. It is clearly for this reason that many readers have regarded the *TTP* as an attack on the Hebrew Bible alone. Spinoza explains this disparity in his treatment of Judaism and Christianity on the spurious grounds that his knowl-edge of Greek is not adequate and that criticism of the Christian Bible has already been carried out by other, unnamed authorities (X/137). Yet Spinoza's apparent philological modesty did not prevent him from systematically presenting the New Testament as morally superior to the Old and the Christian apostles as superior to the Hebrew prophets. Most notably, he presents Jesus— invariably referred to as "Christ"—as the Messiah and, as such, the successor to Moses. Let us consider some further features of Spinoza's dual treatment of the two scriptures.

First, Spinoza continually asserts that the Mosaic prophecy was a purely political legislation. Moses appears in the *TTP* as the bringer of a new *nomos,* but scarcely a divine dispensation. He denies that the Mosaic law promised anything more than security and its attendant advantages, such as military and political hegemony. Moses is the model for the legislative founder. "The task of establishing a wise system of laws and of keeping the government in the hands of the whole community was quite beyond them," Spinoza writes, "for they were in general inexperienced in such matters and exhausted by the wretched conditions of slavery" (V/64). The sovereignty of Moses was thus accomplished because "he surpassed all others in divine power which he convinced the people he possessed." Accordingly, Moses is said to have brought only a legal code, which he instilled not through reason and argument like a philosopher but through compulsion and command (II/31).

Second, Spinoza not only politicizes Judaism, he materializes it. He plays dangerously to certain anti-Jewish stereotypes, especially the one that suggests that Jews are only concerned with material well-being and success. The carnal character of Judaism is revealed in the fact that Moses was said to have spoken with God "face to face," while Jesus communed "mind to mind" (I/13– 14). The sole ends of the Mosaic legislation were "security and comfort," which were held as the only conceivable reward for obedience to the law. Likewise, the "Pharisees"—a long-standing term of Christian opprobrium for Jews— taught that the laws of the Jewish state constituted the sole ground of morality (V/60, 62).

Finally, Spinoza treats the Mosaic prophecy as coercive and paternalistic. Moses is said to have treated his fellow Jews "the same way as parents teach children who have not reached the age of reason" (II/31). The commandments are presented as given by a "law giver and judge" with penalties established for nonobservance. Even the image of God as a "law giver and prince," who is alternately harsh and merciful, represents a concession to popular understanding that was unable to develop any elevated sense of the deity. The various ceremonies and ritual practices of Judaism had no other function than reinforcing coercive authority. The entire sum and purpose of the ceremonial law is that "men should never act of their own volition but always through another's behest" (V/65). Moreover, these ceremonies were said to be of no aid to "blessedness" and contributed only to "the temporal prosperity of the state" (V/60).

One might expect Spinoza's excoriating attack on Judaism to be complemented by an equally vitriolic assault on Christianity. It is not, to say the least, self-evident that Judaism is more particularistic or parochial than Christianity. Spinoza's own approving references to the universalism of Isaiah would seem to indicate this (V/59). Nor is it obvious that Christian ethics appeal to love while Judaism rests on law and coercion. Although Spinoza says that the Jews "despised" philosophy, he refers to Solomon, "who possessed the natural light of reason beyond all men of his time," by the term "philosopher" (II/31). Despite these crucial admissions and in full awareness of what he is doing, Spinoza goes on to depict the prophecy of Jesus as the virtual antithesis of Moses, and Christianity as the successor to Judaism. Just consider some of the following contrasts.

The prophecy of Jesus is presented not as political but as moral. Unlike Moses, Jesus prophesied without the aid of the imagination. "God revealed himself to Christ, or to Christ's mind, directly, and not through words and images" (IV/54). Christ was not so much a prophet as the veritable "mouthpiece of God" (IV/54). He came not as a legislator but as a teacher concerned with purifying morality. Thus while Moses was concerned with founding a commonwealth, Jesus is said to have expounded his views as a "teacher" because "he was intent on improving men's minds rather than their external actions" (VII/91).

The teachings of Jesus are presented as universal—addressed to all—rather than parochial or exclusionary. While the Mosaic prophecy was intended for the Jews alone, "God sent his Christ to free all men from bondage to the law" so that they would act righteously, not "from the law's command, but from the unwavering resolution of the heart" (III/44). The Hebrew prophets operated under a "specific mandate" to preach only to a specified nation, but the apostles "were called to preach to all men without restriction and to convert all men to religion" (XI/141). While in the time of the prophets the words of God needed to be set down in stone, the apostles were able to find the spirit of God in the heart (XVIII/205).

Finally, the preaching of Jesus and the apostles appealed to reason rather than fear and coercion. The prophets presented God's commands as issuing from "dogmas and decrees," while the apostles "seem to be conducting a discussion rather than prophesying" (XI/139). The books of Moses are to be understood simply as "figures of speech" expressed to make God's commands effective, while the apostles appealed to "their own natural faculty of judgment," and their teachings consist of "brotherly admonitions mingled with courteous expressions very different, indeed, from prophetic authoritativeness" (XI/140). Thus Jesus and Paul "philosophized" when speaking to the Gentiles, but they had to change their tactics when speaking to the Jews, to which Spinoza has the temerity to add: "Happy indeed would be our age, if we were to see religion freed again from all superstition" (XI/144).

THE HEBREW THEOCRACY

Despite his often-unconscionable denigration of Judaism, Spinoza argues that the Hebrew scriptures contain important political teachings that remain applicable to his time. The teachings of the Tenakh are not exactly as archaic as Spinoza would sometimes have us believe. Beginning in chapter 17 of the *TTP*, he presents the biblical account of the exodus from Egypt as the archetypal story of political founding, making use of the modern Hobbesian conceptions of the state of nature and the social contract. Contrary to what we have been led to believe, the covenant in Sinai between God and his chosen people is now taken to be the paradigm case of the creation of political legitimacy.

Spinoza begins his case by arguing that after Moses led the Jews out of slavery in Egypt, they found themselves in both a literal and a figurative state of nature. Being under no obligations to any human ruler, they were free to establish new laws and institutions of their own. The crucial passage reads as follows:

> For after their liberation from the intolerable oppression of the Egyptians, being bound by no covenant to any mortal man they regained their natural right over everything that lay within their power, and every man could decide afresh whether to retain it or to surrender it and transfer it to another. Finding themselves thus placed in this state of nature, they hearkened to Moses, in whom they all placed the greatest confidence, and resolved to transfer their right not to any mortal man, but to God alone. Without much hesitation they all promised, equally and with one voice, to obey God absolutely in all his commands and to acknowledge no other law but that which he should proclaim as such by prophetic revelation. (XVII/189)

Spinoza treats the covenant between God and the Hebrews as the creation of a new form of government: theocracy. Theocracy—a term coined by the Romanized Jew Josephus—is perhaps the most distinctive Hebrew contribution to political theory.[13] What distinguished the theocracy from all other regimes was the aspiration to be ruled directly by God, with no human intermediaries. By giving themselves over to God alone, the theocracy was also the most democratic form of government that ever existed, "for in reality the Hebrews retained their sovereign right completely" (XVII/190). Most important of all, no individual or group was authorized to speak for God, though each retained the right to interpret God's law and share equally in the powers of the state. What was a de jure theocracy was a de facto democracy.

Yet no sooner had the original contract between God and the Hebrews been established then it was almost immediately abrogated. Finding the voice of God too threatening, the Hebrews declared "all that the Lord hath spoken we will do" (Exodus 19:8) and consequently handed their rights of sovereignty over to Moses. The transfer of rights to Moses effectively turned the original theocracy from a democracy to a monarchy: "They clearly abrogated the first covenant, making an absolute transfer to Moses of their right to consult God and to interpret his decrees. . . . Therefore Moses was left as the sole lawgiver and interpreter of God's laws and thus also the supreme judge, whom no one could judge, and who alone acted on God's behalf among the Hebrews, that is, held the supreme kingship since he alone had the right to consult God, to give God's answers to the people and to compel them to obey" (XVII/190).

The transfer of rights to Moses reads like a conventional account of the origins of political authority. Spinoza opines that the Hebrew commonwealth may still have lasted "indefinitely" had it not been for certain fatal steps set in motion with the election of Moses. No sooner had the Hebrews transferred their rights to Moses than they lost the right to choose his successors. The subsequent failure of Moses to appoint a successor resulted in a division of power between Aaron, the high priest, and Joshua, the commander in chief. This left a period of weakened authority that was the first step toward the degeneration of the state into rule by priests (XVII/191). The establishment of a dual sovereignty between the priests and the military commanders created a dangerous precedent that would have far-reaching consequences.

The most significant post-Mosaic development was the creation of a priestly caste, the Levites, who assumed the right of interpreting the laws and of rebuking kings. This division of temporal and spiritual power would prove fatal.

The priestly caste set about usurping power by impinging on the right of kings to conduct matters of war and foreign policy. The continuous struggle between kings and priests would lead the commonwealth to ruin. "For what can be more intolerable to kings," Spinoza asserts, "than to rule by sufferance and to allow a dominion within a dominion?" (XVII/202). The eventual demise of the Hebrew polity was due not to external causes but to what Hobbes called "intestine disorder."[14]

The degeneration of the Hebrew polity from a theocracy to a monarchy to a loose federation in which power was divided among the various tribes is described as swift and irreversible. The fundamental feature of the post-Mosaic constitution was the separation of authority between kings and priests. One might think that this divided authority would be welcomed, but Spinoza regards it as the source of instability and civil war. It is the unity of politics and religion in the theocracy that gave the ancient Hebrews their political strength and military greatness. Spinoza follows tradition in holding up the Davidic monarchy as the time when the Hebrews were governed best. Under David's kingship, nothing could be considered more abhorrent than to swear allegiance to another nation or even to contemplate emigration. "The patriotism of the Hebrews was not simply patriotism but piety," Spinoza observes, "and this, together with hatred for other nations, was so fostered and nourished by their daily ritual that it inevitably became part of their nature" (XVII/197). It was only later during the period of the Judges that this happy unity of politics and religion fell apart, when there was no king in Israel and "everyone did as he pleased" (Judg. 21:25). This seems to describe a return to the state of nature endured after the flight from Egypt.

Spinoza's interpretation of biblical history is too detailed to detain us here, but he was clearly drawing lessons that had immediate application to the politics of the Dutch Republic. First, Spinoza followed the "Erastian" doctrine—so named after the Swiss theologian Thomas Erastus—that the sovereign should have supreme power over matters of religion.[15] Spinoza opposed the idea of splitting religion off from the state in large part because he distrusted the ambitions of clerics, especially the Calvinists in his own time. Since religion is crucial to the peace and well-being of the commonwealth, it is simply too important to be given over to the priests; only religious laws promulgated by the sovereign should be valid. Spinoza even accuses anyone who would deny this power to the sovereign of attempting to foment civil war. The development of an autonomous priestly class has been a recipe for civil conflict ever since the Levites claimed for themselves the sole privilege of performing the sacred rites (XVII/201).

The second lesson drawn by Spinoza is that religion pertains only to practice and outward behavior. Here is the core of Spinoza's claims for the freedom of thought and conscience. The nineteenth chapter of the *TTP* revealingly proclaims that "the external forms of worship should be such as accord with the peace of the commonwealth," suggesting that religion applies to action and not beliefs (XIX/212). The task of religion, as Spinoza sees it, is to reform character and not to compel conscience. Spinoza's conception of religion remains deeply Hebraicized. The danger with turning religion into a creed or doctrine—something that Spinoza dates back to Paul—is always the tendency toward persecution or apostasy. Spinoza condemns any law that would criminalize belief rather than reform conduct. Religion remains a matter of laws, which by their nature cannot affect the inner chamber of the mind. It remains best "to grant freedom of judgment and to govern men in such a way that the different and conflicting views they openly proclaim do not debar them from living together in peace" (XX/227).

THE NEW JERUSALEM

The question for any reader of the *TTP* is how to explain these evident disparities in Spinoza's treatment of Judaism and Christianity. What is he up to? As Emil Fackenheim observed: "Why does the author of the *TTP* resort to distortions and discrimination against the minority religion which he has forsaken, especially and above all when compared to the majority religion he has yet refused to embrace?"[16] In other words, is the best strategy for promoting toleration to knowingly and misleadingly appeal to bigotry? For many readers, Spinoza's strategy of knowingly demeaning Judaism has been an unforgiveable sin. His appeal to certain anti-Jewish prejudices and stereotypes has been marked down to political sycophancy and a desire to curry favor with the Christian authorities whose approval he sought. If this were Spinoza's strategy, it must be said that it backfired. The *TTP* was greeted with equal hostility from Jews and non-Jews alike.

And yet it is possible that Spinoza's manner of writing was not grounded in any anti-Jewish animus but was rather part of a rhetorical strategy of "accommodating" his rhetoric to the understanding of his audience. This project of accommodation was intended to gain a hearing for his larger project of promoting a liberal state and a policy of religious toleration. Leo Strauss has gone so far as to suggest that Spinoza was animated by a profound sense of "sympathy" for his people, even though it is a sympathy that is well hidden.

"Spinoza may have hated Judaism," Strauss avers, "but he did not hate the Jewish people. However bad a Jew he may have been in all other respects, he thought of the liberation of the Jews in the only way in which he could think of it, given his philosophy."[17] This is not to mitigate the dangers of appealing to the prejudices of his audience, a strategy that Strauss admits was "Machiavellian" in the extreme. Spinoza plays in Strauss's words "a most dangerous game," even an "amazingly unscrupulous" one, but one that was "humanly comprehensible" nonetheless.[18]

The purpose of Spinoza's double standard was to prepare the way for a new kind of scripture—a universal religion (*fides universalis*)—that would be, strictly speaking, neither Jewish nor Christian but an amalgam of both. This new dispensation is presented in the *TTP* as a democratic civil creed composed of seven tenets or dogmas to which all citizens must adhere. These seven dogmas are as follows:

1. God, the Supreme Being, exists.
2. God is one.
3. God is omnipresent.
4. God has supreme right and dominion over all things.
5. Worship of God consists entirely of acts of justice and charity or love of one's neighbor.
6. All who obey God are saved.
7. God forgives repentant sinners. (XIV/162)

This new theology was intended not only to lay the basis for civil peace but also to foster a new regime of toleration that would gain the assent of both Jews and Gentiles. Thus Spinoza can confidently aver that there are no dogmas of this new universal faith that can give rise to conflict among "honest men," since it contains "only those dogmas to which obedience to God absolutely demands, and without which such obedience is absolutely impossible" (XIV/161).

Spinoza represents his universal or "catholic" religion as nothing less than a new theology for a new age that would supersede the earlier dispensations of Moses and Jesus. The essence of this new moral theology is an unprecedented teaching of toleration and noninterference with the beliefs of others. This new liberal theology would be tolerant of the varieties of religious experience so long as they accepted the norm of toleration in return. This means, among other things, the right of the individual to think and judge for himself or herself in matters ecclesiastical. One reason for Spinoza's attack on "Pharisaic" authority—there had not been Pharisees for centuries—was in part to deny the Calvinist clergy of its authority. Spinoza offers the following formula as his principle of religious liberty: "As the sovereign right to free opinion belongs to every man even in matters of religion, and it is inconceivable that any man can surrender this right, there also belongs to every man the sovereign right and supreme authority to judge freely with regard to religion, and consequently to explain it and interpret it for himself. . . . For since the supreme authority for the interpretation of Scripture is vested in each individual, the rule that governs interpretation must be nothing other than the natural light that is common to all, and not any supernatural light, nor any external authority" (VII/103–4).

The liberal society for the sake of which Spinoza has composed his new religion is to be neither specifically Jewish nor specifically Christian but presumably neutral to any specific faith. The idea of a state that was neutral with respect to the historically revealed religions, while a staple of legal theory today, was virtually unprecedented in Spinoza's time. The *TTP* sets out to demonstrate that "not only can freedom be granted without endangering piety and the peace of the commonwealth" but "the peace of the commonwealth and piety depend on this freedom" (Pref/3). This regime would be neither the virtuous city of classical antiquity nor the holy city of the Bible but the commercial metropolis of modernity.

Spinoza concludes the *TTP* with a glowing tribute to Amsterdam, where, he had said earlier, "nothing is esteemed dearer and more precious than freedom" (Pref/3): "Take the city of Amsterdam, which enjoys the fruits of this freedom, to its own considerable prosperity and the admiration of the world. In this flourishing state, a city of the highest renown, men of every race and sect live in complete harmony; and before entrusting their property to some person they will want to know no more than this, whether he is rich or poor and whether he has been honest or dishonest in his dealings. As for religion and sect, that is no account because such considerations are regarded as irrelevant in a court of law" (XX/228). One can say with only slight exaggeration that Amsterdam represents for Spinoza the new Jerusalem, a commercial republic based upon freedom of trade, freedom of religion, and freedom of opinion.

SPINOZA'S BARGAIN

To return to our question: What kind of Jew was Spinoza? Despite his attack on the Hebrew scriptures as a collection of ancient prejudices, despite his denigration of Moses and the prophets in comparison to Jesus and the apostles, and despite his attacks on the ceremonial laws of Judaism as an instrument of worldly well-being, Spinoza remains a recognizably and unmistakably Jewish thinker. To put the matter a different way: the entire structure of modern Judaism would be unthinkable without him. He is the founder of two of the most distinctive forms of modern Judaism.

Spinoza has entered the history of Jewish thought as the spiritual ancestor of Zionism and the modern state of Israel. He was the first modern thinker to advocate the restitution of Jewish sovereignty and a Jewish state. Shortly after the passage cited earlier in which he offers a purely secular explanation for Jewish survival based on the hatred of the nations, we come across the following sentence: "Indeed, were it not that the fundamental principles of their religion had effeminated their minds, I would not hesitate to believe that they will one day, given the opportunity—such is the mutability of human affairs— establish once more their independent state, and that God will again choose them" (III/46; translation modified).

On the basis of this statement, the *TTP* was read as a work of proto-Zionism in the nineteenth century by Moses Hess and Leon Pinsker and in the twentieth by David Ben-Gurion, who even sought to have the ban on Spinoza officially lifted (he was unsuccessful). Note that the foundations for any future Jewish state would no longer be placed in God's providence but would be in one's own arms and actions. Spinoza does not even say that such a state would have to be founded in the historical land of Israel. He attaches no particular significance to the land or language of Israel, although he was working on a Hebrew grammar at the time of his death. A Jewish state could, from his point of view, just as easily be located in Canada or Katmandu.[19]

This is by no means to absolve Spinoza or to canonize him as a secular saint. To the contrary, this passage in many respects confirms the negative judgments on Spinoza held by his critics. It confirms the view that it is not the corruption of Judaism but its very foundations that are the cause of Jewish passivity and weakness. These fundamentals have caused the Jews to be "effeminated" such that they lost their taste for political freedom and consigned themselves to an impotent longing for a messianic world to come. Spinoza's advice is, then, to cease passive waiting for a messiah to deliver them from their woes and to take affairs into their own hands. Only then might the Jews merit election a second time (de novo).[20]

But if Spinoza was the first Zionist, this by no means exhausts his Jewishness. He helped to shape a new kind of psychological Jew who seeks liberation from tradition and dependence on external authority, wishes to think for himself or herself, and values independence, self-mastery, and courage as the highest human virtues. Long before Freud or even Marx, Spinoza was the virtual prototype of this kind of Jew. Indeed, the idea of the emancipated Jew turned Spinoza into a philosophical, even a literary, hero from Isaac Bashevis Singer's Nachum Fischelson, "the Spinoza of Market Street," to Bernard Malamud's protagonist in *The Fixer,* who leaves his shtetl not with the Torah but with a copy of Spinoza's *Ethics,* to Paul Auster's novel *Mr. Vertigo,* whose mysterious character Master Yehudi is never without his edition of Spinoza.

Spinoza's model of the modern emancipated Jew does not entail conversion. Unlike Heinrich Heine two centuries later, Spinoza did not believe the baptismal certificate to be the "passport" to Western civilization. The *TTP* promises liberation from an ancient tradition that has been the cause of Jewish passivity and weakness; it offers a new, rational theology that provides for civil equality in place of the Mosaic law with its promise of special providence; it proffers a new promised land, as it were, based on freedom of religion, commerce, and inquiry. The new type of Jew who is to inhabit this land can be said not only to value his or her own freedom but also to identify with certain liberal values, such as love of social justice, a support for the underdog, and an insistence on the universality of human rights. These are the values, as one modern observer has noted, of a new kind of individual, "the non-Jewish Jew."[21]

Spinoza's critical analysis of Judaism grew not out of self-hatred or anti-Judaism but as a part of a project of liberalizing reform. His defense of the liberal state requires a religion that is itself quite liberal. Spinoza believed that the price of admission to this state entailed a radical secularization of Judaism both as a body of revealed law and as a distinctive way of life. His purpose was to strip all religion—both Judaism and Christianity—of its claims to exclusivity and reduce it to a handful or so of tenets that could provide the moral foundation of the modern state. Spinoza's religion of reason would be stripped of all metaphysical claims that might give rise to controversy or could be used as a pretext for persecution. His fides universalis would be used to support adherence to the modern liberal state.

The cost of admission to Spinoza's state has been high. There is, as an economist said, no such thing as a free lunch. The chief cost of Spinoza's bargain has been the assimilation of Judaism, not to Christianity, but to liberalism. Indeed, for many Jews, Judaism has become virtually synonymous with support for liberal social causes. Even the expression "Jewish liberalism," rather than a paradox, has become a commonplace. The result of this identification of Judaism with liberal values like autonomy and emancipation has been the loss of both religious identity and fidelity to an ancient way of life. The *TTP*, it seems, may have eloquently defended freedom for Jews, but at the cost of what was specific to Judaism.

The idea of an emancipated or "worldly Jew" has struck many people, both Jew and Gentile, as a contradiction, an enigma, and a paradox. How does one account for Jewish survival outside the context of authoritative Jewish texts and traditions? What becomes of Jewish continuity when ritual practices cease to have the force of law and are confined to the precinct of private conscience? What kind of Judaism is it that would be willing to readmit an avowed heretic like Spinoza? Is the offer to exchange an ancient heritage for a modern secular identity a real bargain or something like an offer to buy the Brooklyn Bridge? To recognize a paradox is not to resolve it. The persistence of a recognizable Jewish identity, even apart from the authority and institutions of traditional Judaism, remains one of the great paradoxes of modernity. It would take another Spinoza to do it justice.

Chapter 6 Benjamin Franklin's American Enlightenment

For generations, Benjamin Franklin's *Autobiography* has been considered a classic of American literature.[1] It is the first and remains the classic American success story. It is the story of a poor boy, coerced into indentured servitude, who eventually becomes the most famous American of his age. Along the way, we learn how Franklin became a successful printer, the publisher of *Poor Richard's Almanack,* the organizer of a volunteer fire company, the founder of the American Philosophical Society (which still exists today), the organizer of a militia, and the inventor of the Franklin stove. We learn how he was honored by the leading men of his era and how he met five kings and had dinner with one of them (the king of Denmark). A reader of the book might come away thinking "only in America."

Although Franklin was a voluminous writer, the *Autobiography* was his only book, and even then was left incomplete. The *Autobiography* begins with Franklin's birth in Boston in 1706 and breaks off around the year 1757. We do not even learn of his experiments with electricity that brought him honorary degrees and that allowed him to be addressed (at least in England) as "Dr. Franklin."

Missing also is any account of Franklin's diplomatic work abroad or his involvement in the Constitutional Convention. During his years in London, he hobnobbed with the likes of Jeremy Bentham, Edmund Burke, and David Hume, but it was in France that he became a celebrity. Franklin became a cult figure in Paris, where his image was reproduced on cameos, fans, handkerchiefs, and prints. When he appeared in Louis's court without a wig, he instantly became lionized as the figure of the common man. He proposed to Madame Helvétius (but was rejected). He was a friend of Turgot and Condorcet, who would come to see the American Revolution as an anticipation of the French.

The *Autobiography* was the product of Franklin's maturity, begun in 1771 at the age of sixty-five and then continued again in France in the 1780s. It was unfinished at the time of Franklin's death and not even published until 1818, when it was given the title *The Autobiography of Benjamin Franklin*. As he says at the beginning, the book was started during a week's leisure in the country. It is addressed to his son, William, but is also intended for posterity: "Having emerg'd from the Poverty & Obscurity in which I was born & bred, to a State of Affluence & some Degree of Reputation in the World, and having gone so far thro' Life with a considerable Share of Felicity, the conducing Means I made use of, which, with the Blessing of God, so well succeeded, my Posterity may like to know, as they may find some of them suitable to their own Situations, & therefore fit to be imitated" (1307).

Most of all, Franklin says he wrote the book for his own pleasure, simply retelling the story of a remarkable life: "That Felicity, when I reflected on it, has induc'd me sometimes to say, that were it offer'd to my Choice, I should have no Objection to a Repetition of the same Life from its Beginning, only asking the Advantage Authors have in a second Edition to correct some Faults of the first. So would I, if I might, besides corr[ecting] the Faults, change some sinister Accidents & Events of it for others more favorable, but tho' this were deny'd, I should still accept the Offer. However, since such a Repetition is not to be expected, the Thing most like living one's Life over again, seems to be a *Recollection* of that Life; and to make that Recollection as durable as possible, the putting it down in Writing" (1307). It is clear that Franklin takes pride in his rags-to-riches story and his astonishing rise from poverty to the status of America's first international celebrity.

To be sure, not everyone has enjoyed Franklin's life as much as the author himself did. Practically no sooner had the ink dried on Franklin's *Autobiography* than his critics began to line up against him. Romantics like the nineteenth-century French journalist and critic Charles Augustin Sainte-Beuve called him (in a memorable phrase) one of the *grands simplificateurs* of the Enlightenment for failing to grasp the inner world of spirit, passion, and eros. The problem with Franklin's practical attitude toward life is its failure to plumb or even to imagine the deeper, more mysterious, regions of the soul. "An ideal is lacking," Sainte-Beuve writes, "in this healthy, upright, able, frugal, laborious character of Franklin—a flower of enthusiasm, tenderness, sacrifice—all that is the dream, and also the charm and the honor of poetic natures. . . . Also there is a flower, a bloom, of religion, of honor, of chivalry, that we must not ask of Franklin. . . . He applies to the examination of chivalry a method of moral arithmetic that he is fond of using."[2]

Franklin's very simplicity, Sainte-Beuve complains, prevented him from imparting to his French compatriots any of the dangers of attempting the experiment in revolution on French soil. Franklin's attitude—that of the political empiricist—did not envision the hazards that the reform of an ancient society might encounter: "If all those who conversed with Franklin at Passy had truly understood his precepts and his measures, they would have thought twice before undertaking in the Old World a universal recasting. . . . This optimistic man had nothing in him that discouraged utopia; on the contrary, he rather invited it by the novelties and inventions that seemed to open onto the future."[3] Sainte-Beuve concludes by noting that providence had mercifully spared Franklin—who died in 1790—the pain of witnessing the violent deaths of those very men who went to the guillotine "in the name of the principles he had so long approved and cherished."

If Sainte-Beuve saw Franklin's philosophy behind the French Revolution, he also came to be seen as the epitome of the new capitalist order and its gospel of wealth. Typical is Marx's pithy observation in *Capital:* "Strictly," he wrote, "Aristotle's definition is that man is by nature a citizen. This is quite as characteristic of ancient classical society as Franklin's definition of man as a tool-making animal is characteristic of Yankeedom."[4] What Marx here calls "Yankeedom" was to become for Max Weber the model for his book *The Protestant Ethic and the Spirit of Capitalism*. Franklin's mind-set is taken to be the perfect representation of the "Protestant ethic" in its secular form, which Weber thought to be the driving force of capitalism.

Weber virtually begins his book with three pages of quotations from Franklin to illustrate his thesis. His reading of Franklin starts from the observation that everything Franklin says is focused around the centrality of work, or what might be called the work ethic. Work, like everything else that Weber notes about Franklin, is valuable only insofar as it leads to worldly success. Consider the following: "In fact, the *summum bonum* of this ethic, the earning of more and more money, combined with the strict avoidance of all spontaneous enjoyment of life, is above all completely devoid of any eudaimonistic, not to say, hedonistic admixture. It is thought of so purely as an end in itself, that from the point of view of happiness of, or utility to the single individual, it appears entirely transcendental and absolutely irrational. Man is dominated by the making of money, by acquisition as the ultimate purpose of life."[5]

If asked why the making of money should be the central focus of life, Weber answers as follows: "At the same time it expresses a type of feeling which is closely connected with certain religious ideas. If we thus ask *why* should 'money be made out of men,' Benjamin Franklin himself, although he was a colorless deist, answers in his autobiography with a quotation from the Bible, which his strict Calvinistic father drummed into him again and again in his youth: 'Seest thou a man diligent in his business? He shall stand before kings' (Prov xxii, 29). The earning of money within the modern economic order is, so long as it is done legally, the result and the expression of virtue and proficiency in a calling."[6]

Perhaps what Weber despised most in Franklin is what he believed was the absence of any sense of moral duty. Weber was a strict Kantian in ethics and held that all notions of duty, morality, and obligation must be kept rigorously distinct from notions of utility, pleasure, and happiness. He believed it impossible—even a contradiction—that a duty could be something profitable or useful to the moral actor or that duty could lead to happiness. Duty is an end in itself, and whatever departs from this view is not morality. For this reason Weber could write: "Now, all of Franklin's moral attitudes are colored with utilitarianism. Honesty is useful because it assures credit; so are punctuality, industry, frugality, and that is the reason they are virtues. A logical deduction from this would be that where, for instance, the appearance of honesty serves the same purpose that would suffice, and an unnecessary surplus of this virtue would evidently appear to Franklin's eyes as unproductive waste. . . . The impressions of many Germans that the virtues professed by Americanism are pure hypocrisy seems to have been confirmed by this striking case."[7]

Weber was by no means the only writer to see in Franklin an anticipation of all of his worst fears about modernity. In his *Studies in Classic American Literature,* D. H. Lawrence finds in Franklin the model of unfeeling, mechanical self-control. "The idea of the perfectibility of man," Lawrence writes, "which was such an inspiration in Europe, to Rousseau and Godwin and Shelley, all those idealists of the eighteenth and early nineteenth century, was actually fulfilled in America."[8] It is in Franklin's *Autobiography* that we find the fulfillment of the Enlightenment's image of the "Perfect Man," a "supreme monster" of human contrivance, the counterpart to Mary Shelley's *Frankenstein*. "Franklin proceeded to automatize himself, to subdue life so that it should work automatically to his will," Lawrence continues. "This deliberate entity, this self-determined man is the very Son of Man, man made by the power of the human will, a virtuous Frankenstein's monster."[9]

What enrages—and this is not too strong a word—Lawrence is what he calls Franklin's belief in "perfectibility," that is, the view that we can make or remake our lives through a concerted act of the will. The moral perfectionist believes that life is only good when it is ordered, controlled, or subject to a plan. While Weber saw in Franklin the forerunner of the "iron cage" of capitalism and instrumental rationality, Lawrence finds in Weber's plan of moral reform everything that opposes his own romantic conception of passion and spontaneity. As we shall see later, this completely misunderstands Franklin. One thing that distinguishes Franklin's American Enlightenment from some of its French and German variants is an awareness and even appreciation of human fallibility and the ultimate failure of all perfectionist plans of reform.

Both Weber and Lawrence completely fail to see the irony, the humor, and the sheer joie de vivre that permeates Franklin's *Autobiography*. As is now common knowledge, Franklin's life was anything but ascetic; he had a powerful sexual appetite and had, on the whole, far fewer hang-ups than either Weber or Lawrence, who were tortured by their own sexuality. There is little dry or "colorless" Puritanism in Franklin. The book itself is a testimony to one of the most remarkable public and private lives ever. How can any serious reader of Franklin fail to see his immense playfulness and enjoyment of life's pleasures?

EDUCATION AND ENLIGHTENMENT

A major theme—perhaps the central theme—of the *Autobiography* is Franklin's education. The book could just as easily have been called *The Education of Benjamin Franklin* or *The Education of a Young American*. It was modeled on the Puritan confession, although without any of the Puritan sense of guilt or sinfulness. To the contrary, the book is a testimony to the power of the individual to become whoever or whatever he or she wants to be. Education was always, for Franklin, the key to self-improvement. He was not the type to lose sleep over wrongs committed. What regrets he did harbor were described simply as "errata"—printer's errors—that presumably could be corrected in an improved second edition. "Thus," he remarks after agreeing to marry Deborah Reed in Philadelphia and then virtually forgetting about her in London, "I corrected that great *Erratum* as well as I could" (1371). His lesson: no one is perfect. These errata were not simply regrettable acts of omission or commission but necessary steps on the path to Franklin's achievement of good moral character. His capacity to learn from his mistakes without assigning blame or feeling guilt over what he has done is one of the great themes of the *Autobiography*. In fact, the book is a testimony to its author's belief in the power of education, especially education's ability to achieve three goals most characteristic of the American experiment in self-making: material success, moral improvement, and social progress.[10]

Franklin's theory of education falls under the category of "utility" broadly understood, if by that term is meant not the narrow Benthamite calculus of pleasures and pains but something closer to John Stuart Mill's famous definition of utility as "the permanent interests of mankind as a progressive being" or what Tocqueville referred to as an ethic of self-interest well-understood."[11] Under this category, Franklin would certainly have included such ends as prosperity (to be sure), reasonableness, and public-spiritedness. It was less a system than a way of life. Franklin's utility was a practical doctrine aimed at reform in its many dimensions. But Franklin's reformism had none of the zeal that Michael Oakeshott would characterize by the term "rationalism in politics." Franklin did not set out to remake the world according to a blueprint or a plan. His temperament was empirical rather than dogmatic, always a matter of trial and error. His reformism was optimistic but tempered by moderation, a strong sense of human imperfectability, and most of all, a sense of humor. His attitude toward human nature was closer to what Kant—and later Isaiah Berlin—would call "the crooked timber of humanity."[12]

Franklin regarded his own life as an object lesson in the power of education to achieve almost limitless goals. He was a man with virtually no formal education and endowed with little more than "a tolerable Character to begin the World" (1360). He attended one year at the Boston Latin School but was withdrawn by his father for lack of funds. And yet, Franklin remarks that he cannot remember when he could not read (1313). His father brought him into his candle- and soap-making business, but shortly afterward indentured him to his older brother's printing shop. It was during his years of involuntary indenture—not far removed from slavery—that Franklin mentions reading Bunyan's *Pilgrim's Progress,* Plutarch's *Lives,* Locke's *Essay Concerning Human Understanding,* and Xenophon's *Memorabilia.* It was also during this period that he said he became a "real Doubter" regarding religion (1321).

Early in the *Autobiography,* Franklin realizes that education will be the key to upward mobility in the new American society. All of his friends were "Lovers of Reading" (1340). Upon moving to Philadelphia, he found work as a printer's apprentice and later, after being abandoned in London by his patron Sir William Keith, found himself working in a famous printing house. It was here that he published a philosophical pamphlet entitled *A Dissertation on Liberty and Necessity, Pleasure and Pain* purporting to prove that pleasure and pain are the determining drives of human nature and that our categories of virtue and vice are arbitrary distinctions. The mature Franklin described publishing this work as another of the various "errata" of his life and came to agree with his employer's judgment of him as "a young Man of some Ingenuity," though his principles "appear'd abominable" (1346).

Franklin does not explicitly acknowledge why publication of the *Dissertation* was such a great mistake. In a letter to Benjamin Vaughn, Franklin excused the work as a piece of youthful indiscretion ("I was not nineteen years of age when it was written" [1016]). Beyond that, he acknowledged that he published one hundred copies of the work and afterward, "conceiving it might have an ill tendency," went on to burn all but one highly annotated copy. From the context, it is not clear whether Franklin meant that printing the work would have some ill consequences for him or whether the *Dissertation*'s teachings on morality would have ill consequences for society. Upon mature reflection he came to see this work as "not so clever a Performance as I once thought of it" and regretted the influence it seems to have had (1359). In any case, the pamphlet achieved some notice and led to an introduction to the Dutch philosopher Bernard de Mandeville, whom Franklin describes as "a most facetious, entertaining Companion" (1346).

Franklin's was an intensely practical life, but it was a life never without books. These remained his constant companions. After moving to Philadelphia, Franklin describes the absence of a decent bookstore. "Those who lov'd Reading," he remarked, "were oblig'd to send for their Books from England" (1379). To alleviate this problem, he set out his "first project of a public nature" and became the founder of the first public library in America. He loved books most of all as a spur to conversation, sociability, general enlightenment, and the defense of liberty. "These Libraries," he wrote, "have improv'd the general Conversation of the Americans, made the common Tradesmen & Farmers as intelligent as most Gentlemen from other Countries, and perhaps have contributed in some degree to the Stand so generally made throughout the Colonies in Defense of their Privileges" (1372).

RELIGIOUS REFORM

The theme of religious reform is one that Franklin returns to several times in the *Autobiography*. He recalls that he was brought up "piously in the dissenting way," but that when he was "scarce fifteen," he came upon some antideist tracts that had on him precisely the opposite effect from what was intended. He became a "thorough Deist" (1359). The young Franklin describes his reputation as that of "a young Genius that had a Turn for Libelling & Satyr" (1324). He recalls later that his father reproached him for "lampooning & libelling," for which he had "too much inclination" (1335). Deism fitted in nicely with the young Franklin's "disputatious" character, which he soon discovered had the very bad effect of "making people often extremely disagreeable in Company" (1318). This led in turn to a falling out with the governing party in Boston, which came to regard him as "an Infidel or Atheist" for his "indiscrete Disputations about Religion" (1325).

The young Franklin's penchant for libeling and satire is fully on display in his "Silence Dogood" letters. In one letter, Franklin recounts a dream in which Mrs. Dogood comes across a famous "Temple of LEARNING" where "Every Peasant who had wherewithal was preparing to send one of his Children," who for the most part "were little better than Dunces and Blockheads" (11). Most who were admitted to this academy found the work too difficult and therefore "contented themselves to sit at the foot, with Madam *Idleness* and her Maid *Ignorance*" (12). While many of the graduates took to trade and travel, Franklin maliciously notes that most of the crowd gathered around "*The Temple of Theology*," about which he notes he found nothing of value except "ambitious and fraudulent Contrivances" (13). Even as a young man, Franklin is carrying on the Enlightenment's war against priestcraft and superstition through the medium of mockery and ridicule. But it is not theology alone that is the subject of Franklin's jests. It is also the great seats of academic learning that teach little more "than how to carry themselves handsomely, and enter a Room genteely (which might as well be acquir'd at a Dancing School)." It is only at the end of the letter that Franklin shows his hand: "While I was in the midst of these unpleasant Reflections, *Clericus* (who with a Book in his

Hand was walking under the Trees) accidentally awak'd me; to him I related my Dream with all its Particulars, and he, without much Study, presently interpreted it, assuring me, *That it was a lively Representation of* HARVARD COLLEGE" (13).

The *Autobiography* as a whole can be read as Franklin's never fully successful effort to wean himself away from his tendency toward satire and mockery and adopt an attitude of tolerance and moderation in all things. A turning point comes with the young Franklin's exposure to the example of Socrates. Franklin admits that he was "charmed" by the Socratic method that led him to drop the manner of "abrupt Contradiction and positive Argumentation" and adopt an attitude of "the humble Enquirer & Doubter" (1321). This experiment—so he claims—met with great success and proved of "great advantage" to its author (1322). The best test of a doctrine, he began to realize, was its effect on character, whether it helped one become agreeable with those around one. Of his early deism he wrote: "I began to suspect that this doctrine though it might be true, was not very useful" (1359). He became convinced that it was not "metaphysical Reasonings" but "*Truth, Sincerity & Integrity* in Dealings between Man & Man" that was the best test of religious doctrine (1359). Franklin's attitude toward religion here is entirely pragmatic, that is, the test of a belief is its effect on practice. Actions were to be followed or avoided, not because they were commanded, but because they were deemed useful in the conduct of life.

The generally nondoctrinal character of Franklin's religious views was expressed in his attitude of tolerance toward all sects that have as their goal the promotion of our worldly well-being. "I had been religiously educated as a Presbyterian," he wrote, and was never "without some religious Principles" (1382). Though he admits that he "seldom attended any Public Worship," this did not bar him from appreciating the general utility of religion "when rightly conducted" (1383). This led him to believe that every religion, however bad, must have some good consequences, with the result that he sought to "avoid all Discourse that might tend to lessen the good Opinion another might have of his own Religion" (1382). Even the worst religion, he claimed, might produce some social good, with the result that when new places of worship were constructed by voluntary contribution "my Mite for such purpose, whatever might be the Sect, was never refused" (1382–83).

Despite his many years spent in France, Franklin never adopted Voltaire's attitude of *écrasez l'infâme* or the d'Holbach circle's fashionable materialism. Franklin's Enlightenment was always of the moderate sort.[13] Gerald Stourzh, one of Franklin's most perceptive readers, likens his views on religion to Gibbon's description of the Rome of the Antonines, where all religions were regarded as equally false to the philosophers, equally true to the believers, and equally useful to the magistrates.[14] This is probably too cynical. Rather than regarding religion simply as a tool for social control, Franklin believed that all religions contained some core of moral truth that was usually mixed with purely superfluous beliefs and practices. He recalls his attempt to develop "the substance of an intended creed" that would contain "the essentials of every known religion," among which were the following:

> That there is one God, who made all things.
> That he governs the World by his Providence.
> That he ought to be worshipped by Adoration, Prayer & Thanksgiving.
> But that the most acceptable Service of God is doing Good to Man.
> That the Soul is immortal.
> And that God will certainly reward Virtue and punish Vice, either here or
>   hereafter. (1396)

These tenets form the core of Franklin's civil theology that he believed could be found—more or less—in all existing creeds. It is a list notably similar to Spinoza's seven dogmas of his "universal faith" in the *Theologico-Political Treatise* and to Rousseau's catechism of the Savoyard Vicar in his *Emile*. It is also a list notably silent on the question of divine revelation. In a letter to Ezra Stiles written shortly before his death, Franklin responded to Stiles's question concerning his opinion on the divinity of Christ. Franklin claimed that he had "some Doubts as to his Divinity," adding, "It is a question I do not dogmatize upon, having never studied it," but that he believed Jesus taught a "System of Morals" that was "the best the World ever saw or is likely to see" (1179).

Yet Franklin's attitude of genial acceptance did not result in moral complacency. Franklin could be withering in his description of the Quakers, whom he regarded as hypocritical for adopting pacifism while simultaneously being "unwilling to offend Government" by supporting the common defense (1415). But it was with his own sect that he found the most reason for complaint. Many of the Calvinist doctrines of predestination, election, and reprobation Franklin calls "doubtful" and "unintelligible" (1382). He tells the story of how he was once prevailed upon to attend Philadelphia's only Presbyterian congregation for five consecutive Sundays even though the practice interfered with his use of the Sabbath as a day for study. He quit the church not just because the sermons were "dry, uninteresting, and unedifying" but because they were designed more "to make us Presbyterians than good Citizens" (1383).

The one sect that elicits Franklin's greatest esteem is an obscure group called the Dunkers. What Franklin admires is their application of the Baconian method of experimentation—of trial and error—to matters of religious belief. This sect refused to publish a statement of its articles of faith on the grounds that further experience might lead them to revise their principles and they did not want to be bound to a previous doctrine. "This Modesty in a Sect," Franklin concludes, "is perhaps a *singular Instance* in the History of Mankind, every other Sect supposing itself in Possession of all Truth" (1417; emphasis added). Typically, Franklin draws a general lesson from this singular case. Every sect is like a man traveling in foggy weather who can only see that those in front of him and those behind him are engulfed in fog, while the truth is that "he is as much in the Fog as any of them" (1417). This kind of doctrinal antidoctrinalism forms the core of Franklin's American Enlightenment.

MORAL REFORM

The most memorable part of Franklin's *Autobiography* is certainly his project for moral reform. This is the part of the book that has achieved the most bemused response from its readers. His plan for the achievement of moral perfection follows the same kind of clear and orderly method that Descartes had proposed for examining knowledge. It would be almost impossible to exaggerate the importance that method plays in Franklin's program for reform. It is in the midst of recounting his various public plans and business dealings that Franklin announces, virtually out of the blue, his proposal for achieving moral perfection:

> It was about this time I conceiv'd the bold and arduous Project of arriving at moral Perfection. I wish'd to live without committing any Fault at any time; I would conquer all that either Natural inclination, Custom, or Company might lead me into. As I knew, or thought I knew, what was right and wrong, I did not see why I might not *always* do the one and avoid the other. But I soon found I had undertaken a Task of more Difficulty than I had imagined. While my Care was employ'd in guarding against one Fault, I was often surpriz'd by another. Habit took the Advantage of Inattention. Inclination was sometimes too strong for Reason. I

concluded at length, that the mere speculative Conviction that it was our Interest to be compleatly virtuous, was not sufficient to prevent our Slipping, and that the contrary Habits must be broken, and good Ones acquired and established, before we can have any Dependence on a steady uniform Rectitude of Conduct. For this purpose I therefore contriv'd the following Method. (1383–84)

Franklin's method here was to take one virtue at a time, work on it systematically until it had been mastered, and then move on to the next. With his list of thirteen virtues and by focusing on each virtue for one week, Franklin figured he could complete the cycle four times in the space of one year—more than enough time to achieve moral perfection! Even here, Franklin is subtler than the caricature of him would have us believe. He admits that his plan proved more difficult than he first believed, that inclinations and habit sometimes overcame reason, and perhaps most revealingly that utility alone ("the mere speculative conviction") was not a sufficient motive.

Franklin lists his virtues with a short definition or clarification following each:

1. TEMPERANCE. Eat not to Dullness; Drink not to Elevation.
2. SILENCE. Speak not but what may benefit others or your self. Avoid trifling Conversation.
3. ORDER. Let all your Things have their Places. Let each Part of your Business have its Time.
4. RESOLUTION. Resolve to perform what you ought. Perform without fail what you resolve.
5. FRUGALITY. Make no Expence but to do good to others or yourself: i.e. Waste nothing.
6. INDUSTRY. Lose no Time. Be always employ'd in something useful. Cut off all unnecessary Actions.
7. SINCERITY. Use no hurtful Deceit. Think innocently and justly, and if you speak, speak accordingly.
8. JUSTICE. Wrong none, by doing Injuries, or omitting the Benefits that are your Duty.
9. MODERATION. Avoid Extreams. Forbear resenting Injuries so much as you think they deserve.
10. CLEANLINESS. Tolerate no Uncleanness in Body, Cloaths, or Habitation.
11. TRANQUILITY. Be not disturbed at Trifles or at Accidents common or unavoidable.

12. CHASTITY. Rarely use Venery but for Health or Offspring; Never to Dullness, Weakness, or the Injury of your own or another's Peace or Reputation.

13. HUMILITY. Imitate Jesus and Socrates. (1384–85)

Franklin's list of virtues perfectly fits what Marx called "Yankeedom." It is an impressively bourgeois recasting of the virtues to fit Franklin's own model of the ideal American. Notable is not only what is included but also what is left out. Franklin includes homely virtues like cleanliness, silence, and industry that formed no part of the classical or Renaissance conception of an ethic of glory. There is no entry for courage, and the Aristotelian virtue of liberality is replaced by the emphasis on frugality. His novel definition of chastity—"*rarely* use venery but for health or offspring"—is surely not what earlier writers meant by that term, as Alasdair MacIntyre has sardonically noted, apparently missing the joke.[15] Yet while these may be put down as merely "bourgeois" virtues, they are virtues nevertheless. They may not aspire to glory or nobility or saintliness, but they do seek order, decency, and stability. Such virtues may lack a vision of moral perfection that is beyond the reach of all but a few, but they do have the advantage of validating the useful and mundane professions that are within the grasp of most people's normal capacities. In a quiet and understated way, Franklin is engaged in a piece of spiritual warfare with the heroic virtues associated with the aspiration to fame, glory, and immortality.[16]

Readers have long noted Franklin's explicit omission of the Christian virtues of faith, hope, and charity. Franklin even anticipates this objection noting that while his plan "was not wholly without Religion," there was "no Mark of any of the distinguishing Tenets of any particular Sect" (1391). Instead, he hoped to write a book in which the general utility of the method would provide something of value for members of all persuasions. In contrast to Christian preaching about the duty of charity—about which Franklin says nothing—he will show the actual method for how people can begin to provide for themselves. Although Franklin referred to Bunyan's *Pilgrim's Progress* as an influence, there is little of the Puritan sense of sin or guilt on his journey through life (1317, 1326). His invocations of God seem more like rhetorical devices, as his goals are always this-worldly and depend on himself alone.[17] Long before Emerson, Franklin taught an ethic of self-reliance: "I should have called my Book the ART *of Virtue,* because it would have shown the

Means & Manner of obtaining Virtue, which would have distinguish'd it from the mere Exhortation to be good, that does not instruct & indicate the Means, but is like the Apostle's Man of verbal Charity, who only, without showing to the Naked & the Hungry *how* or where they might get Cloaths or Victuals, exhorted them to be fed & clothed" (1392).

Yet for all of his confidence in the utility and certainty of his plan, Franklin discovers that the path to moral perfection is a bumpy one. If anything, it leads him to a cheerful recognition of human imperfection. Franklin admits that he was "incorrigible" when it came to the virtue of order and that "I never arrived at the perfection I had been so ambitious of obtaining but *fell far short of it*" (1391; emphasis added). The effort, though unsuccessful, still left him "a better and happier man" than he would have been otherwise. Franklin makes fun of his own search for perfection by telling the following anecdote. He was, he says, "Like the Man who in buying an Ax of a Smith my Neighbour, desired to have the whole of its Surface as bright as the Edge; the Smith consented to grind it bright for him if he would turn the Wheel. He turn'd while the Smith press'd the broad Face of the Ax hard & heavily on the Stone, which made the Turning of it very fatiguing. The Man came every now & then from the Wheel to see how the Work went on; and at length would take his Ax as it was without further Grinding. No, said the Smith, Turn on, turn on; we shall have it bright by and by; as yet 'tis only speckled. Yes, says the Man, but *I think I like a speckled Ax best*" (1390).

The image of the "speckled ax"—something like Kant's better-known image of "the crooked timber of humanity"—is Franklin's image of the moral life. We may struggle to present a bright shiny figure to the public, but at best we know that our efforts will fall short of perfection. We are all speckled axes.

THE LIMITS OF REFORM

Franklin's awareness of his own imperfections did not lead to a gloomy acquiescence to the sinful nature of man. Rather it cheered him to take a moderate, tolerant, and easygoing attitude toward the flaws of others. His book is full of stories of those who cheated or betrayed his trust—think of the way he was lied to by Governor Keith, who essentially left him high and dry in London—and those whom Franklin himself misused. He is not sparing of himself. He recalls the breach of contract of indenture to his brother, his misuse of funds that had been placed in his trust, and his betrayal of his fiancée, Deborah Reed, once he reached London. Franklin admits his faults, but he is not a man tortured by past mistakes. More than anything, Franklin is struck by human malleability and our capacity to learn from our missteps. Most revealing is an amusing anecdote he tells of a failed experiment with vegetarianism. He describes a mighty struggle between "principle and inclination" until he noticed that because larger fish ate the smaller ones, there was no reason he should not indulge his taste for fish. From this he drew the wonderful maxim: "So convenient a thing it is to be a *reasonable Creature,* since it enables one to find or make a Reason for every thing one has a mind to do" (1339).

Franklin's antiperfectionism is further revealed in another story, about his thirteenth virtue, humility. Originally, Franklin tells us, he had only twelve virtues on his list, but a "Quaker friend" told him that he was generally considered proud and that he should add humility to his list, defining it as the imitation of Jesus and Socrates. Franklin admits that he was never able to acquire more than the appearance of humility. It is a vice, he admits, that dogged him from his youth. Early in the *Autobiography,* he tells the story of how he and his friend John Collins developed a taste for debate, which often leads to pride in one's own rhetorical and logical skills: "We sometimes disputed, and very fond we were of Argument & very desirous of confuting one another. Which disputacious Turn, by the way, is apt to become a very bad Habit, making People often extreamly disagreeable in Company, by the Contradiction that is necessary to bring it into Practice & thence, besides souring & spoiling the Conversation, is productive of Disgusts & perhaps Enmities where you may have occasion for Friendship. I had caught it by reading my Father's Books of Dispute about Religion. Persons of good Sense, I have since observ'd, seldom fall into it, except Lawyers, University Men, and Men of all Sorts that have been bred at Edinburgh" (1318–19).

Like Hobbes, Franklin regarded the disagreement over opinion as a source of pride, vanity, and conflict. He took particular pleasure in scolding clerics, professors—especially Harvard professors—and even himself for our tendency toward pride and domination. Franklin's solution was the use of coded speech as a way of offsetting the tendency to dominate. Rather than using words like "certainly" and "undoubtedly" and "surely," it is better to say "it seems" or "it appears to me." Franklin claims this method of circumlocution best for persuading people who are more likely to be convinced when the speaker appears less certain or dogmatic in his convictions (1321–22).

Franklin finally congratulates himself for making some efforts to subdue his natural pride, but he admits that after fifty years of struggle he has been at best only partially successful: "In reality, there is perhaps no one of our natural Passions so hard to subdue as *Pride*. Disguise it, struggle with it, beat it down, stifle it, mortify it as much as one pleases, it is still alive, and will every now and then peep out and show itself. You will see it, perhaps, often in this History. For even if I could conceive that I had compleatly overcome it, I should probably be proud of my Humility" (1393–94).

POLITICAL REFORM

Franklin's *Autobiography* is not primarily a political work. Readers seeking out Franklin's views on rights, justice, or property will be disappointed. Its focus is mainly on the development of certain traits of individual character that will prove most useful for the attainment of moral improvement. We hear, for example, nothing about Franklin's early support of the British monarchy and his later turn to the cause of colonial independence, nor do we hear about his support for a unicameral legislature in Pennsylvania or about his later support of abolitionism. And yet the *Autobiography* is not as completely apolitical as it appears. Franklin advocated a conception of politics based on the ideas of progress and civic improvement. His politics were progressive in a Baconian register, that is, a process of experimentation, subject to continual self-correction. On the whole, his attitude toward politics follows the same nondoctrinaire style Franklin adopted toward religion. He seems to have agreed with Pope's famous couplet from the *Essay on Man:* "For forms of government let fools contest / What'er is best administered is best." "There is no *Form* of Government," he told the delegates at the Constitutional Convention, "but what may be a Blessing to the People, if well administered" (1140).

Franklin's most ambitious plan for political reform was the creation of the aptly named Junto, a kind of philosophy club created for the purpose of fostering conversation and debate (1361). The club met on Friday evenings, and each member was required to introduce a topic "on any point of morals, politics, or natural philosophy." Once every three months, each member was required to read a paper on any topic, which would be followed by discussion and debate. The purpose of the club, Franklin avers, was to foster "the sincere spirit of Enquiry after Truth," with the result that "all Expressions of Positiveness in Opinion or of direct Contradiction" were prohibited under penalty of a small fine (1361).

So successful did the club prove that some hoped to expand its membership beyond the original twelve members. Franklin opposed this plan because he believed it would compromise the *secrecy* of the proceedings, on which he insisted: "I was one of those," he wrote, "who were against any Addition to our Number, but instead of it made in Writing a Proposal, that every Member separately should endeavour to form a subordinate Club, with the same Rules, respecting Queries, &c. and without informing them of the Connexion with the Junto" (1402). Franklin regarded the Junto as his own academy providing camaraderie and intellectual companionship. His insistence on secrecy was important to his conception of the Junto as the cell for a new kind of party or sect. Franklin says initially that secrecy was important for keeping out "improper Persons for Admittance" but later acknowledges he feared that expanding membership would compromise the club's ability to influence public opinion (1402–3). What kind of influence was Franklin hoping to exert, and why insist on these conspiratorial methods?

Franklin's ambitious plans for "a great & extensive Project" were set out in a few "observations" that he says were "accidentally preserved" from his readings set on May 19, 1731. Among these observations were the following:

> That the great Affairs of the World, the Wars, Revolutions, &c. are carried on and effected by Parties.
>
> That the View of these Parties is their present general Interest, or what they take to be such.
>
> That the different Views of these different Parties, occasion all Confusion.
>
> That while a Party is carrying on a general Design, each Man has his particular private Interest in View.
>
> That as soon as a Party has gain'd its general Point, each Member becomes intent upon his particular Interest, which thwarting others, breaks that Party into Divisions, and occasions more Confusion.
>
> That few in Public Affairs act from a mere View of the Good of their Country, whatever they may pretend.
>
> That fewer still, in Public Affairs, act with a View to the Good of Mankind. (1395)

Here Franklin allowed himself to speculate on what he hoped would become the model for a new kind of reform party that would set its sights on the great issues of the day. This party, as he explains it, would be called a United Party for Virtue and would bring together "the Virtuous and good Men of all Nations into a regular Body" (1395). It would be set in opposition to all the other parties of his time, which were activated by self-interest, pride, and ambition. Franklin's comments are a model of what Enlightenment thinkers often called the "Republic of Letters" or the "Party of Humanity."[18] The goal of this party was not simply the protection of rights but also the achievement of civic progress. The means to its ends would be achieved largely through the bloodless means of persuasion and negotiation. The members of this new party for virtue would be organized as a "sect" composed of young single men from different walks of life who would be chosen after thirteen weeks of initiation into the party's principles, including the principles of "every known Religion":

> The Existence of such a Society should be kept a Secret till it was become considerable, to prevent Solicitations for the Admission of improper Persons; but that the Members should each of them search among his Acquaintance for ingenuous, well-disposed Youths, to whom, with prudent Caution, the Scheme should be gradually communicated; that the Members should engage to afford their Advice, Assistance, and Support to each other in promoting one another's Interest, Business, and Advancement in Life: That for distinction we should be call'd The Society of the *Free and Easy:* Free, as being by the general Practice and Habit of the Virtues, free from the Dominion of Vice, and particularly by the Practice of Industry & Frugality, free from Debt which exposes a Man to Confinement and a Species of Slavery to his Creditors. (1396)

Franklin's hope for an international society devoted to the progress of humankind sounds strangely utopian for a man generally known for his hardheaded utilitarianism and ethic of self-interest. His claim that his plans for a party of virtue came to naught should be considered in light of Franklin's demand that such a society operate behind a veil of secrecy. Can we simply take at face value his claim that his plans for the club were derailed due to "narrow circumstances"?

Franklin's hope for a new party of virtue would come to fruition in the form of various secret societies and clubs like the Masons and the Illuminati that developed in Europe throughout the eighteenth century. These lodges with their secret rituals and mysterious rites seem the opposite of Franklin's plans for the dissemination of knowledge, but the members saw themselves as part of a covert effort to spread enlightenment in a world where the free exchange of ideas was still too dangerous to practice publicly. These clubs and salons served as the basis of a new civil society or public space outside court culture in which political ideas could be freely debated and out of which political parties later arose. They did much to create a climate for the free exchange of ideas that Locke would characterize by the term "law of opinion," independent of the great institutions of church and state.[19] In England the idea of a political opposition was created by disaffected Tories under the leadership of Viscount Bolingbroke and his circle, who published their satires and parodies in journals like the *Craftsman* and the *Gentleman's Magazine.* The emergence of the first modern political parties—Whigs and Tories—grew out of this attempt to legitimize and lend respectability to the idea of a formed opposition not as a necessary evil but as a permanent feature of government as such.[20]

In France and elsewhere on the Continent similar groups worked under conditions of greater secrecy due to the absolutist state. The political function of these secret societies as "indirect countervailing powers" has been richly described by Reinhart Koselleck in his book *Critique and Crisis.* Here Koselleck makes the very secrecy of these lodges the key to their success: "In advance of its content, the mystery of the lodges lay in the aura it radiated. In secrecy lay the pledge of sharing in a new and better life not known before. The initiation meant 'the discovery of a new world hidden amidst the old.' . . . To the initiated, secrecy brought a new kind of communion. The royal temple was built and held together by the secret; the Arcanum acted as the 'glue' of brotherhood. . . . The secret linked all the initiates, no matter what they were initiated in; regardless of their position in the existing hierarchy they were now united on a new plane."[21]

The Junto was the model for the kind of secret organization responsible for the spread of Enlightenment propaganda throughout Europe and America. Although the *Autobiography* mentions nothing of his involvement with Freemasonry, during his years in France Franklin became the center of Masonic activities. Secrecy was of the essence of these organizations. "Secrecy," Joseph de Maistre wrote of the lodges, "is the natural law, the basis of mutual trust that unites society at large."[22] Franklin would serve as the Grand Master of the French Masonic lodge called the Loge des Neuf Soeurs (Lodge of the Nine Sisters) founded by the Encyclopedists in 1769, which would do much to spread republican ideas in prerevolutionary France. Franklin even helped to initiate Voltaire into membership in the lodge. Several of the leading actors in the early years of the Revolution—Brissot, Condorcet, Danton, Sieyès, although not Robespierre—were members of Paris lodges that helped to support the later revolutionary command structure. It was these literary and philosophical societies that would nurture the seedbed of the revolutionary politics a generation later.

The activities of the lodges were political, literary, and moral, but they also imparted a theological aura to their members. It was Franklin's activity in the Neuf Soeurs, as Bernard Faÿ has written, "that made him the 'holy philosopher and saint' that he so long remained in the eyes of France. The Lodge of the Nine Sisters, with its great religious and symbolic ceremonies in which Supreme Being and Wisdom were worshiped, was a forerunner of things to come."[23] An ardent anti-Masonic polemicist, Faÿ nevertheless maintained a strong sense of the importance of the secret societies, not only in the world of prerevolutionary France, but also for their role in canonizing Franklin as a new kind of secular saint. The entire revolutionary generation, Faÿ remarks with only some exaggeration, joined in their worship at the shrine of Franklin: "They were drawn to him as the annunciator of a new faith that they were seeking and that bore in their hearts. It is no exaggeration to consider him as the prophet and saint of a new religion; for all the mystic elements ordinarily attributed to a saint are found in his legend—humility, an almost supernatural power capable of performing miracles and of controlling the forces of nature, goodness, suffering, and piety. He points the way to all the eager and restless souls who feel the need of a new faith, rational and, at the same time, practical."[24]

Franklin's involvement with these revolutionary societies expresses a visionary and utopian aspect to his thought that moves far beyond the pedestrian gospel of work and success attributed to him by Weber and his other critics. Franklin was not only a revolutionary but also a "thoughtful revolutionary," who understood that changes in government depended upon changes in manners, customs, and moral habits.[25] Even the failure of the Society of the Free and Easy allowed Franklin to enunciate one of his great principles of political organization. "I have always thought that one Man of tolerable Abilities may work great Changes & accomplish great Affairs among Mankind, if he first forms a good Plan, and cutting off all Amusements or other Employments that would divert his Attention, makes the Execution of that same Plan his sole Study and Business" (1397).

OUR "HAPPY MEDIOCRITY"

Franklin is read by many today as the first preacher of the gospel of success. Certainly he had some role in fashioning this image. He presents himself as the original American success story, a rags-to-riches tale, in which hard work, diligence, and industry are sufficient to overcome all obstacles. This is the image of the famous Protestant work ethic that has driven readers like Weber into paroxysms of rage.

Yet a close reading of the *Autobiography* shows that there is much more to Franklin than this. Franklin's is not the vulgar worship of success. He praises reason, sociability, public service, and philanthropy. He supported lending libraries and colleges. His philosophy could be thought of as Baconianism for the people. It is empirical, experimental, practical, and—to use one of Bacon's favorite terms—productive of "fruit." Franklin was a printer and inventor, to say nothing of his place as an experimental scientist, one of the most famous of the age. None of these can be explained in terms of the doctrine of self-interest or utility alone. Even Franklin's moralizing was infused with humor, wit, and a certain self-parody. The subtext of the book could almost read, "Never take yourself too seriously."

Franklin is the face not so much of the "Protestant ethic" or "the spirit of capitalism" as of the American Enlightenment. Perhaps what bothers Weber and others most is that Franklin's Enlightenment is rigorously egalitarian. It really is the Enlightenment for the common man. It shows how a person with no outward advantages, completely self-taught, can rise to the highest levels of national and international fame. Franklin's is an expressly middle-class Enlightenment conceived along democratic lines. In one of his last works, entitled *Information for Those Who Would Remove to America,* Franklin spoke of the "happy Mediocrity" that prevailed in America, "where the cultivator works for himself and supports his family in decent plenty" (975). He knew, of course, that he was a person of exceptional qualities, but he took pains to hide those qualities, making himself out to be a kind of democratic everyman. This is the spirit that Tocqueville would praise half a century later when he described the American desire to rise, excel, and succeed.

Franklin included in the *Autobiography* a letter from Benjamin Vaughn received in 1783 urging him to write the story of his life. "Sir," Vaughn wrote, "I *solicit* the history of your life from the following motives: Your history is so remarkable, that if you do not give it, somebody else will. . . . All that has happened to you is also connected with the detail of the manners and situation of a *rising* people; and in this respect I do not think that the writings of Caesar and Tacitus can be more interesting to a true judge of human nature and society" (1374). Vaughn goes on to assert that an autobiography "will not merely teach self-education, but the education of a wise man"; it will be worth "all of Plutarch's *Lives* put together" (1375, 1377).

Vaughn's treatment of Franklin as a kind of American Socrates is poles apart from the negative assessments of his life and influence cited earlier. What happened? "Franklin is the only American revolutionary to have won world fame before 1776," Douglass Adair has written.[26] Franklin's fame, as Adair continues, was not like Washington's or Hamilton's, based on traditional military and political exploits; it was largely the product of his contributions to science, diplomacy, and journalism. Franklin was a new kind of Enlightenment hero. While extolling the practical virtues of industry and thrift, his was also a life uniquely devoted to the pleasures of the mind. The irony is that while Franklin was idealized in his own time as representative of a "rising people," it was precisely this representativeness that made him seem to a later age insufferably complacent, "colorless," and bourgeois. His story was the victim of its own success. Franklin's story will not be to everyone's taste, but it is a very modern story of self-making and self-becoming. Franklin offered his story not as the example of the singular genius that could not be replicated but as that of a modern man who, from unlikely beginnings, achieved not just great things but also everyday comfortable things that make life enjoyable. His would become the model for all future American success stories, from Emerson's *American Scholar* to Whitman's *Song of Myself* to Saul Bellow's *Adventures of Augie March*. It is a story worth remembering.

Chapter 7 Kant's Liberal Internationalism

Kant brought about this great intellectual movement [the Enlightenment] less by the content of his writings than by the critical spirit that pervaded them and now made its way into all branches of knowledge. . . . Fortunately, it did not interfere with the art of cooking.
—Heinrich Heine

Today it is said that we live in an age of globalization. What this means has many different dimensions, but one implication is certainly the eclipse of the sovereign state as the basic unit of government. A new global political order, similar to the European Union, is often conceived of as characterized by open boundaries and governed by international parliaments and courts of law. Yet the idea of globalization is not just a current artifact. Its inspiration goes back to the time of the French Revolution, which had the same kind of intoxicating effect on many Europeans as the collapse of the Communist regimes after 1989 had on a later generation. Old barriers began to crumble, and people began to think in terms of very different possibilities. One such person who began to think of politics in this new international vein was Immanuel Kant.

Kant was not the first, but he has proven to be the most powerful, theorist of liberal internationalism. In opposition to writers like Machiavelli, Jean Bodin, and Hobbes, who considered the necessities of political order within a single sovereign territory, Kant considered each state to be part of an international federation of states. While Hobbes, Locke, and Rousseau saw the state as the product of a social contract among its members, Kant regarded the new international order as the outcome of a contract between free and independent states that might agree to be governed by international law. Kant is unique among political philosophers for stressing the global dimension of politics and investing international relations with a moral status that it had never previously possessed. He stands at the cusp between early and late modernity, between a modernity that regards the sovereign state as the supreme locus of political authority and a modernity that regards the demands of international justice as taking priority over the state.

Kant is uniquely responsible for giving the Enlightenment tradition of reason, individual rights, and the moral sanctity of the individual its highest expression, but he is also responsible for introducing a new kind of historicism into the understanding of international relations that would ultimately come to fruition in the Marxian theory of revolution. This was a historicism born out of the experience of the French Revolution and its Napoleonic aftermath with its desire to export the principles of republican government and the rights of man—by gunpoint and cannon if necessary—throughout Europe and beyond. To be sure, Kant experienced the Revolution from the far coast of Prussia, but the Revolution awakened in him the belief that the principles of republican government and the rights of man carried the seeds of a new moral order that would gradually work its magic abroad. Inspired by Rousseau, Kant greeted the Revolution with unmatched enthusiasm, as is evidenced from his last political writing, *The Contest of the Faculties,* written in 1798. Here he remarks about the Revolution as follows: "The revolution which we have seen taking place in our own times in a nation of gifted people may succeed, or it may fail. It may be so filled with misery and atrocities that no right-thinking person would ever decide to make the same experiment again at such a price, even if he could hope to carry it out successfully at the second attempt. But I maintain that this revolution has aroused in the hearts and desires of all spectators who are not themselves caught up in it a *sympathy* which borders almost on enthusiasm, although the very utterance of this sympathy was fraught with danger. It cannot therefore have been caused by anything other than a moral disposition within the human race."[1] Kant's statement that the Revolution testifies to the presence of a moral impulse in history places him at the forefront of those thinkers who saw in the Revolution the dawn of a new epoch in human history. I would go so far as to say that Kant's philosophy *is* the philosophy of revolution.

But how will this new international order come about? Kant is at the forefront of those thinkers who believed that this new order would be the product of history as a process or, better, a progress leading humanity to a higher and more elevated conception of its rights and duties. Over the course of human history, as men and women have imperfectly groped their way to an understanding of their rights and the institutions that best secure them, they have also been awakened to a deeper reverence for the individual as a being endowed with dignity and worthy of respect. While earlier thinkers may have attached rights to such tangible goods as life, liberty, and property, Kant turned the aims and purpose of government into securing the basic conditions of human dignity and respect. This is a right—the right to be treated with equal concern and respect—that precedes all other rights. And what is more, our dignity will only be realized when the rights and duties of each individual and each nation are attached to the rights and duties of humanity as a whole. No one's rights will be secure until all people's rights are secure. In order to better secure these rights, Kant worked out a philosophy of history whose aim was nothing less than the achievement of "perpetual peace" among the nations. The idea of peace as a good to be secured not just within states but between them became something like a sacred moral duty if a human rights regime was to be achieved.

THE HUMAN RIGHTS REVOLUTION

Kant's *Perpetual Peace: A Philosophical Sketch* was written in 1796 when its author was already seventy-two years old, a decade or so after the publication of his great critical treatises *Critique of Pure Reason, Critique of Practical Reason,* and *Critique of Judgment.* The repetition of this word "critique" in the titles of his three greatest books is revealing of Kant's aim. His age, he believed, was an age of Enlightenment or criticism, a point that he made clear in a note to the Preface of the first edition of *Pure Reason:* "Our age is in especial degree the age of *Kritik,* and to criticism everything must submit. Religion through its sanctity and law-giving through its majesty may seek to exempt themselves from it. But they then awaken just suspicion and cannot claim the sincere respect which reason accords only to that which has been able to sustain the test of free and open examination."[2] Or consider the following, even better known, passage from his essay *What Is Enlightenment? "Enlightenment is man's emergence from his self-incurred immaturity. Immaturity* is the inability to use one's own understanding without the guidance of another. This immaturity is *self-incurred* if its cause is not lack of understanding, but lack of resolution and courage to use it without the guidance of another. The motto of enlightenment is therefore: *Sapere Aude!* Have courage to use your own understanding."[3]

Kant helped to shape the conviction that he lived at the dawn of a new age, of a final political metamorphosis in which at last the truth of the human situation would be revealed. Like other pioneers of modernity, he wanted to set both science and morality on a new and presumably firmer philosophic foundation. His aim was to propose not so much a new morality as a new "formula" for morality. This new formula consisted in a proper understanding of ourselves as self-legislating or self-determining agents.

Earlier modern philosophers, indeed all philosophers from Aristotle onward, had sought a ground for morality in human nature, especially in certain wants and desires. Aristotle saw the moral life as the achievement of *eudaimonia,* or happiness; Hobbes had derived our obligations from the imperative of survival; Locke had enlarged this imperative to include the desire for liberty and property. For Kant, these formulae were all inadequate to account for the full meaning and scope of duty. A teaching that reduced man to a bundle of desires or a seeker after pleasure cannot possibly account for the sublimity of morality.

Kant regarded morality as an extension of rationality. Insofar as we are rational agents, we act according to certain rules or maxims. We are the rule-following animals. Most of theses maxims—get enough sleep every night, don't drink too much on weekdays, find some time for exercise—are what Kant called "hypothetical imperatives," that is, they take the form "if you want *x,* do *y.*" Hypothetical imperatives have their ends outside themselves. They are useful if we want to achieve something beyond the rule itself. Morality is something entirely different. A moral rule—what Kant calls a "categorical imperative"—is one in which the duty to perform the action has no end other than the fulfillment of the duty itself. If, for example, I ask myself why should I repay my debts, the answer that honesty is the best policy or honesty assuages the wrath of the gods is not a moral answer. The only possible moral answer has nothing to do with the favorable consequences that may follow from an action. Morality concerns only the form in which our maxims are put. Only if my action—or the principle informing my action—can be universalized so that it applies to anyone in similar circumstances can an action be said to conform to the moral law. Universalization is Kant's famous formula for a moral law.

Kant sometimes writes as if his moral doctrine were simply a purification of Protestant theology, with its emphasis on inward grace or a reformulation of the Golden Rule, of not doing to others what you would not have done to you. But this is not the case. It was Rousseau who, Kant himself claims, taught him about the majesty of the moral law. The story of how Kant missed his famous afternoon constitutional because of his immersion in Rousseau's *Emile* is almost too well known to bear mention.[4] More to the point, Kant saw Rousseau as the Newton of the moral universe. While Newton had taught us to think of nature as governed by its own system of internal self-regulating laws, Rousseau saw morality as a similarly autonomous domain of laws governing moral behavior. "Newton saw for the very first time order and regularity combined with great simplicity," Kant wrote in his *Observations on the Feeling of the Beautiful and Sublime.* "Rousseau discovered for the very first time beneath the manifold of forms adopted by the human being the deeply hidden nature of the same and the hidden law."[5]

Kant may have said that Hume awakened him from his "dogmatic slumber," but it was Rousseau who showed him his way. In a rare and revealing personal aside, Kant notes that upon reading Rousseau his first impression was that of "an uncommon acuity of the mind, a noble impetus of genius, and a sensitive soul in such a high degree as has perhaps never before been possessed by a writer of any age or any people." He admits to a feeling of "bewilderment" at Rousseau's seemingly "strange and absurd opinions" and suspects that the author is simply seeking "to prove the magical power of [his own] eloquence and play the eccentric who stands out among all rivals in wit because of a disarming novelty."[6] Yet on closer examination, Kant acknowledges that it is on behalf of human dignity and the rights of man that Rousseau set him straight. "I myself am a researcher by inclination," Kant writes, where the term "research" suggests the quest for theoretical knowledge. Yet it was Rousseau who taught him to value the moral above the philosophical life. "Rousseau has set me right," Kant admits. "This blinding prejudice vanishes,

I learn to honor human beings, and I would feel by far less useful than the common laborer if I did not believe that this consideration could impart a value to all others in order to establish the rights of humanity."[7]

The categorical imperative is not a divine command emanating from the voice of God but a law that wells up from within ourselves, obedience to which makes us free. For Kant, obedience to the will of God is obedience to an externally imposed command and hence cannot be moral. Traditional theistic morality is rendered meaningless, on Kant's account, for only the will that legislates the law is said to be good in itself. As Kant wrote in the famous opening sentence of the *Groundwork of the Metaphysics of Morals:* "It is impossible to conceive anything at all in the world, or even out of it, which can be taken as good without qualification, except a good will."[8] The formula for this universalization of the law demands only one thing, that we treat people as ends and never as a means. Humanity as such is worthy of virtually limitless esteem and respect, or what Kant calls "dignity."

This immediately raises a question. Why is it that human beings—even the worst murderers and sociopaths—are deemed worthy of respect? Kant's answer that has proved endlessly controversial is that we alone have the capacity to prescribe laws to ourselves. Man alone is (or at least can be) the self-legislating animal. All other creatures obey the laws to which their natures submit them; we alone have the ability to give law to ourselves, to act in such a way that genuinely respects this quality of free agency. It is this capacity for self-legislation that elevates us beyond mere "empirical" desires and inclinations and that Kant says fills him with a feeling of awe, bordering on reverence. "Two things fill my mind with new and ever increasing admiration," he wrote near the end of *Practical Reason,* "the starry heavens above me and the moral law within me."[9]

It is this sense of dignity—that we alone are the authors of the laws that we obey—that is the true ground of human rights. Kant's doctrine of the rights of man is a deepened or radicalized version of Rousseau's conception of the general will. Rousseau had said that the general will made us free because in obeying its laws we were only obeying ourselves.[10] But unlike Rousseau, who had limited the application of rights to fellow citizens with whom we have explicitly contracted, Kant proposes the way for a vast expansion of the domain of rights. Earlier thinkers had thought about rights only within the setting of their distinct national polities. A necessary consequence of Kant's newfound awareness of human dignity is an attention to the international dimension of rights. It is impossible to think about the Kantian revolution in rights without considering Kant's influence on such weighty documents as Woodrow Wilson's Fourteen Points or the charter of the United Nations. Kant's doctrine of rights kindles not only the desire for the end of war but also a belief that an era of peace—perhaps perpetual peace—may be for the first time at hand.

THE KANTIAN REPUBLIC

It is not immediately evident that Kant's theory of morality would bear political fruit. The formula for morality is to treat every individual as an end in himself or herself as part of an ideal "kingdom of ends." This applies only to individuals. Kant left it tantalizingly vague as to whether this also applies to collective beings like states that seem to operate by their own imperatives of *raison d'état*. But Kant did not, nor could not, entirely ignore the political dimension of his moral revolution. He recognized from the outset that there is a connection between the moral will and the public context of Enlightenment—the public sphere—in which the will develops. Kant made clear that a good will is entirely the work of the individual. No one can coerce a good will, suggesting a strict separation between the moral realm and the legal realm. But government can nonetheless work to eliminate obstacles to the exercise of moral goodness. Here is where the Kantian rubber meets the road.

Kant is certainly aware of the tension—the necessary and fruitful tension—between means and ends, politics and morality. He realizes that the cosmopolitan condition and a federation of states cannot be achieved by moral means alone. It is not even clear whether the moral enlightenment of mankind can lead to institutional change. In a famous aside from *Perpetual Peace,* he suggests that political change might even be able to dispense with morality altogether. "The problem of setting up a state," he opines, "can be solved even by a nation of devils (so long as they possess understanding)."[11] By a rational devil Kant means someone who is "secretly inclined" to exempt himself or herself from the rules of morality. A rational devil is what we might call an enlightened egoist, that is, someone who obeys the laws or keeps promises because it is in his or her interest to do so, rather than as a requirement of moral duty. If a republican order can be established on the basis of rational self-interest alone, what need is there for morality? The problem of the rational or intelligent devil simply illustrates the gulf between institutional progress and moral progress, between legality and morality, or put otherwise, obeying the law because of its coercive force and obeying it because it is the right thing to do.

Kant makes abundantly clear that the only government capable of respecting rights is a republic. A republic is able not only to respect the rights of its citizens at home but also to pursue a policy of peaceful relations abroad. In the "First Definitive Article of Perpetual Peace" Kant defines a republic as follows: "A *republican constitution* is founded upon three principles: firstly, the principle of *freedom* for all members of society (as men); secondly, the principle of the *dependence* of everyone upon a single common legislation (as subjects); and thirdly, the principle of legal *equality* for everyone (as citizens). It is the only constitution which can be derived from the idea of an original contract upon which all rightful legislation of a people must be founded. Thus as far as right is concerned, republicanism is in itself the original basis of every kind of civil constitution, and it only remains to ask whether it is the only constitution which can lead to a perpetual peace."[12]

Even before defining a republic, Kant has already laid down six "preliminary articles" that he claims are morally obligatory on all states even in an international state of nature. These are:

1. No conclusion of peace shall be considered valid if it was made with a secret reservation for a future war;
2. No independently existing state may be acquired by another whether by inheritance, exchange, purchase, or gift;
3. Standing armies will be gradually abolished altogether;
4. No national debt will be contracted in connection with the external affairs of the state;
5. No state shall forcibly interfere in the constitution and government of another state;
6. No state at war with another shall permit such acts of hostility as would make mutual confidence between them impossible during a future time of peace. Such acts would include assassins or poisoners, breaches of agreements, the instigation of treason within the enemy state, and so on.[13]

The most distinctive aspect of Kant's plan for perpetual peace is the idea of an international league of states, something like a United Nations. Here Kant speaks the language of an international lawyer. His idea seems to be that states would voluntarily enter an international peace treaty, a *foedus pacificum,* to lay down their arms if others agree to do so too. This treaty "would seek to end all wars for good."[14] Kant speculates further that this agreement might eventually lead to an international state, a *civitas gentium,* although he admits that at this time a world republic is not conceivable and that we may have to settle for a world federation of states organized in pursuit of international peace.

Kant's idea of a league of republican states is intended as more than a juridical arrangement. It is a moral goal that carries the promise of world citizenship. In the "Third Definitive Article of Perpetual Peace," Kant defines the law of world citizenship as a right of "universal hospitality" or "the right of a stranger not to be treated with hostility." By hospitality, Kant means the right of all men "to present themselves in the society of others by virtue of their right to communal possession of the earth's surface."[15] No longer will national boundaries and barriers serve as an obstacle to free association. Neither the laws of national citizenship nor private property can trump the right to hospitality. The right to be treated with hospitality extends to all strangers whether they are simply travelers or political refugees, so long as they behave peacefully. Indeed, Kant could hardly have realized that the problem of displaced persons without home or citizenship would become what Hannah Arendt has called "the newest mass phenomenon in contemporary history" and refugees would become "the most symptomatic group in contemporary politics."[16]

Kant invokes the right of hospitality against the growing tendency toward European imperialism. The most notorious violators of this right to hospitality have been the European states ("the civilized countries of our continent") that have engaged in the conquest and exploitation of native peoples around the earth. Kant notes that the British presence in the East Indies has created famine and oppression and that the Sugar Islands have become a "stronghold of the cruelest and most calculated slavery."[17] Yet even here, Kant holds out the belief that increased contact between peoples will eventually be regulated by international law and bring humanity closer to a "cosmopolitan constitution" that is its right: "The peoples of the earth have thus entered in varying degrees into a universal community, and it has developed to the point where a violation of rights in *one* part of the world is felt *everywhere*. The idea of a cosmopolitan right is therefore not fantastic or overstrained; it is a necessary complement to the unwritten code of political and international right, transforming it into a universal right of humanity."[18]

We might wonder why Kant's hope for a new cosmopolitan right does not culminate in a demand for a world government. There is an ambivalence on precisely this issue. At one point, Kant suggests that an international state would simply extend the conditions of the domestic social contract until it embraced all the peoples of the earth. Such a possibility, he acknowledges, is too remote from the "present conception of international right" to be practical. This being the case, an international federation of republics would be a next best alternative.[19] Later in the same text, however, Kant appears to recognize that the legitimacy of republican government cannot be extended indefinitely ("the laws progressively lose their impact as the government increases its range"). He rejects the idea of a world state as little more than a universal monarchy that has succeeded in subduing all the rest. A universal state would produce a "soulless despotism" that "ends in the graveyard of freedom."[20] Kant's acceptance of the impracticality of a world state represents a rare concession to the limits of practical reason and a prudential acknowledgment of the persistence of individual sovereign states.

Kant's plan for a world federation rests upon two highly controversial assumptions. The first is that republicanism is the basis of every constitution. One cannot help but notice a tension between the fifth preliminary article that no state shall interfere with the domestic affairs of another and Kant's demand that every state become a part of this world federation of states. What if some states refuse this offer of membership in an international organization and prefer, for their own reasons, to value their own independence? Is coercion ever permissible for the sake of cosmopolitan goals? This can cut both ways. Can peaceful states launch preemptive attacks to prevent a hostile enemy from gaining an advantage or must democratic regimes stand idly by while others seek to destroy the basis of their existence? Kant may have believed in perpetual peace, but he was no pacifist.[21]

Second, Kant believes that republics are inherently peace seeking, and a world of republics would have peace as their goal. He does not deduce this from historical evidence; in fact, the histories of ancient republics—Sparta, Athens, Rome, Florence—were anything but peaceful! Rather it is derived from the terms of the original contract: "The republican constitution is not only pure in its origins; it also offers a prospect of attaining the desired result, i.e, perpetual peace, and the reason for this is as follows: If, as is inevitably the case under this constitution, the consent of the citizens is required to decide whether or not war is to be declared, it is very natural that they will have great hesitation in embarking on so dangerous an enterprise. For this would mean calling down on themselves all the miseries of war such as doing the fighting themselves."[22]

Kant seems to believe, almost as a first principle, that the people in their collective capacity seek peace and that war is due entirely to the existence of monarchies and autocracies that pursue policies of conquest and ambition. Is this even true? Most of the wars of the twentieth century very successfully mobilized mass opinion and would not have been possible had the nations on all sides not received the full support of their respective populations. Democracies seem to wage war with a ferocity unmatched in previous ages. The interesting question is what sustains Kant's optimism about a world in which peace has yet to be achieved. What mechanism can guarantee peace? To understand this, one has to turn to Kant's conception of world history.

THE IDEA OF REASON

Kant not only idealizes rights—gives them a ground in something higher than a calculating desire for self-preservation—he is the first writer to give our rights an explicitly historical dimension. For Kant, the philosophy of history was a pendant to his moral and political philosophy. Morality, he feared, would lose its meaning unless it could be shown that humankind is moving progressively toward a condition of world peace. "Perpetual peace is *guaranteed*," he assures his readers, "by no less an authority than the great artist Nature herself."[23] But here we already encounter a paradox. If peace is literally "guaranteed" by nature, it seems to be accomplished despite our moral efforts. And if no moral effort is required to achieve peace, then history is at odds with the moral law, that is, never to treat individuals as means but always as ends. The end point of history—cosmopolitan right and international law—would be achieved through a quasi-natural process that leaves no room for the assertion of human dignity.

Kant attempted to resolve this paradox in his *Idea for a Universal History with a Cosmopolitan Purpose* (1784).[24] The *Idea* takes the form of nine numbered propositions the aim of which is to sketch the broad lineaments of world history. Kant's aim is to understand not the history of this or that people or nation but nothing short of the dynamic structure that underlies history as a whole. The term "cosmopolitan," or "weltbürgerlicher," in the title suggests Kant's identification with the Enlightenment and his membership in a world Republic of Letters. When taken piecemeal, history seems nothing more than a dismal and chaotic spectacle—a tale told by an idiot—but when it is seen from an enlightened cosmopolitan standpoint we can regard it as a rational process leading toward progressively higher states of humanity.

The term "idea" in the title of Kant's essay has a technical meaning for him. Ideas are suppositions of reason. This is not the same as the Platonic theory of Ideas that indicate an actual reality behind or beyond the physical world. The function of reason is not to supply us with knowledge about the world—Kant would agree with Hume that this is the job of the senses—but rather to put our knowledge in some sort of order. Reason moves on a higher level, ensuring that our knowledge is not a mere aggregation of facts but takes the form of a system or a self-differentiating whole. The task of reason is to supply moral goals that cannot be provided by dependence on experience alone: "For whereas, so far as nature is concerned, experience supplies the rules and is the source of truth, in respect of the moral laws it is, alas, the mother of illusion! Nothing is more reprehensible than to deprive the laws prescribing what *ought to be done* from what *is done,* or to impose upon them the limits by which the latter is circumscribed."[25]

Kant insists that the idea of reason adds nothing to our knowledge of either nature or history; it operates solely in conformity to the demand for order and meaning, to serve as ideal standards that can guide the course of inquiry. We may never be sure whether the unity we impart to our knowledge is true, but we must nevertheless act as if it is. It makes sense to treat history as a rational whole in the same way it makes sense for a biologist to treat organisms as if they were purposive self-regulating systems. This "as-if" quality suggests that the ideas of reason cannot validate truth so much as meaning. The ideas of reason are not found in experience—they are not "constitutive"—but are connected to a deep-seated need for order and coherence. They are said to perform a "regulative" function.[26]

Kant's view is nothing if not optimistic, probably the high-water mark of Enlightenment optimism. One might wonder how Kant can maintain this optimism about history in the face of the obvious cruelties and inhumanities that must strike any impartial observer. What could possibly justify Kant in his faith? To this it can only be said that Kant's optimism is not empirical but moral. Near the end of *Pure Reason* Kant reduces the basic questions of philosophy to three: "What can I know?" "What ought I to do?" and "What can I hope for?"[27] The idea of history belongs to the third question. It is an aspiration of hope, something to be wished for, even if it cannot be empirically validated. Progress is something like a heuristic—what we have seen above called a "regulative idea"—that we use to make sense of history. It is used not so much to explain or predict historical events as to give them meaning. Kant's goal throughout his philosophy of history is "to keep hope alive."

In the introduction to the *Idea,* Kant begins by expressing disgust, even a sense of nausea, at the apparently random and senseless course of human events. "We can scarcely help feeling a certain distaste on observing their activities as enacted in the great world-drama," he writes, "for we find that, despite the apparent wisdom of individual actions here and there, everything as a whole is made up of folly and childish vanity, and often of childish malice and destructiveness" (42). Despite the appearance of utter randomness, when actions are considered "on a large scale" certain patterns and regularities can be discerned. Speaking like a modern actuarial accountant, Kant notes that marriages, births, and deaths do not follow any pattern when viewed individually, but when considered en masse they seem to follow the same general laws as the weather or any other natural phenomenon. The same is true for intentional human actions. Even though our ends and purposes may be in conflict with one another, in which each person and even each nation may pursue its own self-interest, none may realize that it is "unconsciously promoting" an end set by history itself. It becomes the philosopher's task to discern a rational pattern in history that may not be evident to the historical agents themselves: "The only way out for the philosopher, since he cannot assume that mankind follows any rational *purpose of its own* in its collective actions, is for him to attempt to discover a *purpose in nature* behind this senseless course of human events, and decide whether it is after all possible to formulate in terms of a definite plan of nature a history of creatures who act without a plan of their own" (42).

Kant's conception of history can be seen as following a dual track. The first is the plan of nature. He associates nature with a quasi-teleological order that operates independently of human will or purpose. While individuals may be driven by greed and ambition, their actions ultimately contribute, unbeknownst to themselves, to a historical end state that Kant associates with republican constitutions at home and international peace abroad. Yet, the second track of history depends on human beings coming to an understanding of history and their place within it. This is the plan of morality. The moral track begins with our awareness of ourselves as free moral agents who express our freedom in our capacity to generate moral rules unencumbered by natural causality. We can now see why the Enlightenment—"man's emergence from his self-incurred immaturity"—becomes a central moment in this process of moral self-awareness. Kant's hope for international peace is less a prediction about what will happen than a prophecy about what must happen if we view ourselves not as individuals but as members of the species, who must sacrifice our private inclinations and interests for the benefit of humanity. For the first time, the two tracks of history—the natural and the moral—have joined hands to ensure a rational future.

REASON AND HISTORY

In propositions 1–3 of the *Idea,* Kant proposes the thesis that man is the progressive or historical being. He begins with the observation that it is our destiny sooner or later to live in conformity with our end. The end of mankind is to live freely in accordance with self-created rules, but—and here is the problem—we, alone among the species, confront various obstacles in the achievement of our destiny. Our capacities for freedom and reason can only be developed over time. A cat or a dog will be at the end of its lifetime what cats and dogs will always be. Human capacities, however, cannot be achieved in the life of a single individual or even over the lifetime of an entire generation. The individual cannot achieve his perfection without the aid of the species, and the species can only arrive at its end through the entire course of history. Man is, in short, condemned to become the historical animal.

Kant finds in history not a Polybian cycle of birth, growth, and inevitable decay but a linear process of moral self-discovery where each generation builds on and contributes to the collective well-being of all. What from the point of view of the individual appears random and senseless may turn out to serve a wider purpose when viewed from the standpoint of the species. This idea of history is based on an appreciation of the role of enlightenment. Unless each generation could pass on its discoveries to the next, history would be nothing more than a vast wasteland, and nature "would incur the suspicion of indulging in childish play in the case of man alone" (43). Unlike the other species, which are fully equipped by nature to achieve their ends, we remain the only beings who must discover what our ends are. This discovery is not the work of a day but requires "a long, perhaps incalculable series of generations," with each passing its experience down to the next in a cumulative process of education (*Bildung*).

Kant recognizes a paradox at the heart of his theory. If history is a process of mankind's collective enlightenment, does this not condemn previous generations to be used as means to the achievement of this end? How can nature or history compel us to be what we ought to be? How can nature force us to be free? It is in the third proposition that Kant identifies this problem as the relation between means and ends in history: "What remains disconcerting about all this is firstly, that the earlier generations seem to perform their laborious tasks only for the sake of the later ones, so as to prepare for them a further stage from which they can raise still higher the structure intended by nature; and secondly, that only the later generations will in fact have the good fortune to inhabit the building on which a whole series of their forefathers (admittedly, without any conscious intention) had worked without themselves being able to share in the happiness they were preparing" (44).

The engine of history, the cause of the development of our faculties, is described in the fourth proposition as our "unsocial sociability" (44). We are apparently neither fully social nor fully antisocial beings. We are caught in between. Our reason may lead us to cooperation, but our passions and interests lead us into conflict. It is precisely this antagonism between cooperation and conflict that is, paradoxically, the chief cause of progress. What Kant terms "unsocial sociability" is the same kind of phenomenon his contemporary Adam Smith called the "invisible hand" to account for market transactions or what Hegel would later refer to as the "cunning of reason." Without these inclinations toward evil, our capacities would remain latent. It is this conflict between our selfish ends that leads us, unwittingly, to be sure, to seek out a condition of peaceful cooperation. The human condition is akin to that described by Schopenhauer of a colony of porcupines who were wont to huddle together on a cold winter's night to escape being frozen, but the closer they pulled together the more the pricks of their quills forced them to draw apart. The human condition is much like that: we are neither able entirely to tolerate nor able to do without one another.[28]

This quality of unsocial sociability is the key to the transition from nature to culture. By means of this mechanism, Kant shows how history has gradually evolved from barbarism to civilization, from a condition of ignorance and isolation to one of greater communication and civil order:

> Without these asocial qualities (far from admirable in themselves) which cause the resistance inevitably encountered by each individual as he furthers his self-seeking pretensions, man would live an Arcadian, pastoral existence of perfect concord, self-sufficiency, and mutual love. But all human talents would remain hidden forever in a dormant state, and men, as good-natured as the sheep they tended, would scarcely render their existence more valuable than that of their animals. The end for which they were created, their rational nature, would be an unfulfilled void. Nature should thus be thanked for fostering social incompatibility, enviously competitive vanity, and insatiable desires for possession or even power (45).

Through a variety of means, peoples from the most disparate parts of the globe are brought into contact and communication with one another. "In seeing that men *could* live everywhere on earth, nature has at the same time despotically willed that they *should* live everywhere, even against their own inclinations," Kant wrote in *Perpetual Peace.*[29] The development of commerce, economy, and technology makes it possible for the species to inhabit even the most inhospitable places on earth, from Finland to Tierra del Fuego. Kant depicts the process of globalization as spurred on by often immoral, if not violent, means. Commerce is an artifact of self-interest that leads us to seek out new markets, and markets lead to empires. But unknown to us, the spirit of trade and commerce tends toward peace: "For the spirit of commerce," he writes, "sooner or later takes hold of every people and it cannot exist side by side with war."[30] The kind of republic Kant envisages is a trading or commercial republic. Warlike sentiments will be gradually replaced by those favoring peace, trade, and commerce.

The fifth through eighth propositions sketch Kant's views on the end state toward which history is tending. "The highest task which nature has set for mankind," he writes, "must therefore be that of establishing a society in which *freedom under external laws* would be combined to the greatest possible extent with irresistible force, in other words of establishing a perfectly *just civil constitution*" (45–46). Kant declares the attainment of justice to be "the most difficult and the last [problem] to be solved by the human race" (46). Why is this so? The disposition toward justice—respect for the dignity of man—is not natural to us. It can only be achieved through a long and painful process of self-discipline. It is precisely the difficulty in imparting to the human race a respect for justice that leads Kant almost to the brink of despair: "If he lives among others of his own species, man is *an animal who needs a master.* For he certainly abuses his freedom in relation to others of his own kind. And even although, as a rational creature, he desires a law to impose limits on the freedom of all, he is still misled by his self-seeking animal inclinations into exempting himself from the law where he can. He thus requires a *master* to break his self-will and force him to obey a universally valid will under which everyone can be free. But where is he to find such a master?" (46). If we require a master, it is not clear that human beings can ever be free. Where is such a master to be found? Kant leaves this question unanswered, perhaps because it is unanswerable. It is at this point that Kant utters the most famous sentence in the *Idea:* "Out of timber so crooked as that from which man is made, nothing straight can be built" (46; translation modified).

The greatest irony of history to which Kant calls attention concerns the role of war. War is the most violent expression of human conflict. So long as war between states remains a fact, Kant believes, neither individuals nor peoples can be truly free. The constant preparation for war leads to a condition of perpetual uncertainty and the most extreme violation of rights. Yet at the same time, war has been the most powerful vehicle of historical progress. It is a spur of technological innovation, and technology ultimately favors communication and commerce. Most important of all, in proposition seven, Kant argues that war leads to its own cancellation. "That war (and its growing threat) ultimately leads to a stable peace" is what Susan Shell has called "the lynchpin of Kant's hope."[31]

Kant wonders how it is possible that a state of war can give rise to a condition of peace. Will it be produced through an "Epicurean concourse of efficient causes," which he says would be merely a "lucky accident" unlikely to occur? Or should we assume that nothing rational will ever occur from our various actions and we should expect "a hell of evils to overtake us, however civilized our condition" (48)? Yet Kant considers a third possibility, namely, that through the development of our various capacities we are "forced" to leave the state of war and discover the rationality of peace: "For while the full development of our natural capacities is here likewise held up by the expenditure of each commonwealth's whole resources on armaments against the others, and by the depredations caused by war . . . the resultant evils still have a beneficial effect. For they *compel* our species to discover a law of equilibrium to regulate the essentially healthy hostility which prevails among the states and is produced by their freedom. Men are *compelled* to reinforce this law by introducing a system of united power, hence a cosmopolitan system of general political security" (49; emphasis added).

Kant's repeated references to terms like force and compulsion suggest that the attainment of peace is something other than a moral desire, that it is the result of causes that take place out of grim political necessity. Long before the onset of mass armies, Kant realizes that wars are becoming not only more expensive but more catastrophic. As a consequence of the increasingly destructive power of military hardware, mankind will be forced to change direction. The turn from war, as the grounding principle of political life, to peace will be aided by the creation of certain international agencies and institutions designed to police the actions between states.

The *Idea* culminates in Kant's soul-swelling vision of a new era in human history bringing about perpetual peace. The risks of war and the creation of a vast national debt will gradually be seen to outweigh the advantages of national glory and prestige. States will learn to police one another's activities so as not to hamper the progress of commerce. Kant even hints at the beginnings of a new kind of international authority "without precedent in the past" that could supervene over the individual sovereign states: "Although this political body exists for the present only in the roughest of outlines, it nonetheless seems as if a feeling is beginning to stir in all its members, each of which has an interest in maintaining the whole. And this encourages the hope that, after many revolutions, with all their transforming effects, the highest purpose of nature, a universal *cosmopolitan existence,* will at last be realized as the matrix within which all the original capacities of the human race may develop" (51).

Kant believes that up to his day progress has been achieved largely haphazardly or without a conscious plan or purpose. But nature or history cannot entirely compel men to be free; if we were compelled, what we would have would not be freedom. Despite what he had said in *Perpetual Peace,* nature cannot "guarantee" peace. History can at most provide a direction; it is up to us to do the rest. So far, providence or nature working through our unsocial sociability has been the agent of progress, but the present seems to offer new possibilities. Kant regards his age—the age of Enlightenment—as a turning point in history. Henceforth, we shall hasten the arrival of an enlightened age by direct appeal to the moral power of reason. The watchword of this new age is, of course, *Kritik.* All existing ideas and institutions will be submitted to the force of rational criticism. What cannot stand up to the force of critique does not deserve to exist. Thus, in the future we shall achieve by means of rational planning what previously had been accomplished haphazardly without choice or deliberation.

The age of criticism—which has now replaced the age of miracles—takes the form of a demand that the legal and political orders conform to the moral order. Rejecting the claims of Machiavelli that public and private morality are incommensurable, Kant demanded that the politician subordinate reason of state to the commands of morality. "Politics," Kant maintains in the second appendix to *Perpetual Peace,* "must always bend its knee to morality. The rights of man must be held sacred however great a sacrifice the ruling power may have to make."[32] Unlike the great realists for whom politics is always a matter of choosing the lesser evil, Kant demands that the national interest, or raison d'état, take a back seat to the universal interests of humanity as such, no matter what the consequences. *Fiat iustitia, et pereat mundus,* Kant declared.[33] Let justice prevail though the world may perish for it. It was this stern and uncompromising demand, insistence on principle over prudence, and morality over statecraft, that gives to Kant's thought its unique tenor.

THE LIMITS OF THE KANTIAN PROJECT

Kant is the greatest defender of what later came to be called liberal internationalism. He is the father of the idea—widely shared today by students of international politics—that democracies, or what Kant called republics, do not fight each other. The spread of democratic theory and institutions is the best way to ensure global peace. No one can doubt the practical moral force that Kant's ideas have had in the construction of international peace-keeping institutions.[34]

This being said, there are several deeply problematic aspects to Kant's philosophy of international relations that bear comment. The first and most obvious is the tension between Kant's view that every human being is an end in himself, deserving of dignity and worth, and his teaching about history that treats not only individuals but entire generations as means to the achievement of moral progress. If history is a quasi-naturalistic process operating independently of the plans and intentions of individuals, how is this consistent with the idea that human beings are moral agents whose free will is the ground of their dignity? How can history lead to morally desirable results if it demands the slaughter of millions of innocent victims to achieve those ends?

Kant would no doubt counter that his plan of philosophical history is, as we have seen, merely a regulative idea or a heuristic device. If it is to make moral sense, it is not meant to be an actual account of the way history works, only a way of looking at history. To argue otherwise would be to commit some version of the "naturalistic fallacy," of deriving an "ought" from an "is." Kant's philosophical history, then, would have to be seen as contrary to any claim of the Hegelian-Marxist kind that views progress as natural or even inevitable. Kant's belief in progress was a moral, not an empirical, one. Kant holds on to it not because of but despite the flow of evidence pointing in the opposite direction. It is precisely his willingness to hold on to this idea, despite its many empirical failures, that testifies to a distinctive kind of Kantian heroism.

In the ninth and final proposition of the *Idea*, Kant admits that it seems "absurd" to write a history not of what has been but of what must be. It is material better fit for a novel than a work of philosophy. Yet Kant responds that teleology is needed in history not to explain events but to show that they have value. His job is not to usurp that of the historian but to provide a "guide" for action by describing "an otherwise planless *aggregate* of human actions as conforming, at least when considered as a whole, to a *system*": "But if we assume a plan of nature, we have grounds for greater hopes. For such a plan opens up the comforting prospect of a future in which we are shown from afar how the human race eventually works its way upward to a situation in which all the germs implanted by nature can be developed fully, and in which man's destiny can be fulfilled here on earth. . . . For what is the use of lauding and holding up for contemplation the glory and wisdom of creation in the non-rational sphere of nature, if the history of mankind, the very part of this great display of supreme wisdom which contains the purpose of all the rest, is to remain a constant reproach to everything else" (52–53)?

Even if we were to accept this account of Kant's philosophical history merely as a "just-so" story intended to provide rational hope for the future, his attempt to enlist a theory of history in support of human rights no longer seems remotely sustainable. History is simply too unstable a foundation on which to guarantee rights. Having played the trump card of history against the monarchies and aristocracies of the ancien régime, it was only a matter of time until the same ploy was used against Kantian ideals. In the past century, a variety of both left-wing and right-wing despotisms claimed to represent the rising tide of history and to use this against the bourgeois democracy advocated by Kant. The appeal to history has been used to underwrite some of the worst despotisms known to humanity, each one claiming to represent the wave of the future. Kant seems to have initiated a way of thinking that, rather than lending support to liberal institutions, may have unintentionally helped to undermine them.[35]

Kant's philosophical history is underwritten by a moral optimism that can simply no longer be sustained in the wake of the experiences of the twentieth century. The worst things Kant experienced were the monarchies and autocracies of the eighteenth century. Living long before the tyrannies of Hitler's Germany and Stalin's Russia, he had greater faith in the progress of Western civilization than seems warranted now. How can such monstrosities be explained in terms of his philosophy of progress? Kant hoped, as we all do, that increased communication between peoples will dampen the flames of nationalist, religious, and other vainglorious enthusiasms, but history has shown the opposite is just as likely to occur. Increase of acquaintance does not seem to improve feeling. Familiarity may breed contempt, if not hatred. This became clear especially during World War I when even the socialist workers supported their own countries in opposition to the call for proletarian internationalism. Kant dramatically underestimated the pull of forces like nationalism and ethnicity that have remained vital powers in both the past and the present.

Finally, not only does history treat past generations as means to a superior present, it also treats those of the present generation with a moral entitlement that they may not deserve. What makes the present moment worthy of its superiority, we who are mere epigones? As a moralist, Kant valued strenuousness as a mark of virtue. An action could not be deemed good unless it was the result of deep moral struggle. Struggle must accompany all attempts to realize virtue both in society and within ourselves. There is a romantic strain to Kantian ethics that sees the tortured soul as the mark of virtuous action. But Kant does not adequately consider what value our actions will have once the struggle for rights has been substantially won. The present generation will be left as little more than the beneficiary of the centuries of heroic struggle by its ancestors. The end of history does not seem as morally praiseworthy as the progress toward it.

Kant did not adequately consider the possibility that an era of universal peace may lead not to the ennobling but to the demoralization of humanity. In the past, what lent dignity to human action was the struggle to achieve the mutual recognition of rights. What will become of us once these rights have been achieved? Hegel was perhaps the first to see the dangers to which an era of unqualified peace might lead. In the addition to paragraph 324 of the *Philosophy of Right,* Hegel wrote: "In peace the bounds of civil life are extended, all its spheres become firmly established and in the long run people become stuck in their ways. . . . Perpetual peace is often demanded as an ideal to which mankind should approximate. Thus Kant proposed a league of sovereigns to settle disputes between states. . . . But the state is an individual and negation is an essential component of individuality. Thus even if a number of states join together as a family, this league, in its individuality, must generate opposition and create an enemy."[36] Obviously, that last word—enemy—invokes the future specter of Carl Schmitt.

Schmitt developed the point that Hegel had only hinted at, namely, that all politics is part of an endless struggle between friend and enemy. The Kantian dream of a world federation of republics united in peace is a wish for a world without politics, a postpolitical world. The distinction between friend and enemy is basic and cannot be resolved or transcended in some kind of higher synthesis. Although a man of the extreme right, Schmitt brought an almost Marxian sense of the way in which terms like "rights," "humanity," and "dignity" serve as ideological placeholders in the contest for power. "All political concepts, images, and terms," Schmitt wrote, "have a polemical meaning . . . and they turn into empty and ghostlike abstractions when this situation disappears."[37] Schmitt taught his readers to think of even the most inclusive political vocabulary as creating distinctions between in and out, us and them. The attempt to abolish these distinctions would simply create new distinctions and hierarchies. "Above all the polemical character determines the use of the word," he declared.[38]

Schmitt is merely the best known of those critics who found in Kant's rhetoric of universalism a new tool of war and empire. "The concept of humanity," he wrote, "is an especially useful ideological instrument of imperialist expansion."[39] Schmitt's point is that the term "humanity" is not literally meant to be all-inclusive. It is simply a way of denying the legitimacy of one's opponents. The appeal to a league of nations and the idea of perpetual peace may have had purchase when the enemy was the league of monarchs and the entrenched autocracies of the eighteenth century, but writing in the wake of the German defeat in World War I, Schmitt believed that the appeal to humanitarianism has a new meaning. The belief in a cosmopolitan world state or the Wilsonian vision of a "war to end all war" is itself an invitation to continual warfare.

Furthermore, Schmitt believed that a world without war, a pacified world, would be a world without nobility. Such a world would not be worth fighting for. "What remains," Schmitt noted, "is neither politics nor state, but culture, civilization, economics, morality, law, art, and entertainment."[40] The last word—entertainment—was clearly carefully chosen. It signifies a world of frivolity, fun, and shopping and thus a world without the possibility of heroism, courage, and sacrifice. It points to a kind of technological civilization full of curiosities and inventions that force us to become ever more narrow and specialized. We are all familiar with this world because it is ours.

Kant is held in a position of high esteem today, perhaps higher than virtually any thinker of his age. He is, if anyone is, a candidate for liberal sainthood. He brought the Enlightenment to a pitch of perfection by investing it with moral ideals and purposes that it previously lacked. He is not only the perfection of the liberal theories of the Enlightenment, he is also the profound source for the historicist theories of Hegel and Marx. Kant stood at that golden moment in modern history when reason, history, and the rights of man all seemed to be converging on the present, on an absolute moment when the truth or meaning of history would at last be revealed to all. That present has proved more elusive than he or the Enlightenment believed. But since the influence of Kant has remained such an enduring part of our thinking about ethics, politics, and history, our judgment on his strengths and weaknesses will be also a judgment on ourselves.

Chapter 8 Hegel and the

"Bourgeois-Christian World"

The renaissance of interest in Hegel is due in large part to the prestige accorded to the concept of civil society. Hegel did not coin this term, but his treatment of civil society gave the term its indelible usage. Indeed, his exploration of this concept coupled with the distinction he drew between civil society and the state remains one of the most distinctive and influential characteristics of modern politics.[1]

The concept of civil society has taken on almost talismanic qualities in some quarters. It is regarded as the cure to the ills of centralized state control. Civil society has been identified with a dense network of associations—churches, synagogues, trade unions, ethnic organizations, bowling leagues, PTAs, and voluntary societies of all sorts. These organizations, it is alleged, function as the chief medium through which modern citizens learn the virtues of cooperation, civility, self-restraint, and toleration, necessary for the survival of a healthy democratic polity. It is through membership in voluntary associations that the norms of democratic citizenship are not only preserved but enhanced. "Join the association of your choice," a leading civil society theorist has mused, "is not a slogan to rally political militants, and yet that is what civil society requires."[2]

Hegel's account of civil society differs in important respects from this contemporary version. In the first place, unlike contemporary civil society theorists, Hegel does not regard civil society as a training ground for democracy or political participation. The principal benefit of civil society is its relative independence from the state and its tendency to foster a zone of individual freedom or "subjectivity" apart from politics. The distinction between civil society and the state is Hegel's version of the liberal distinction between the public and private spheres. He is more concerned with maintaining the relative autonomy of the two, rather than regarding civil society as instrumental to the achievement of political goals.

Second, Hegel identifies civil society with the practices and institutions of the new economic order—the modern market economy—then coming into being. It is well to recall that the term "civil society" is the English translation of the German *bürgerliche Gesellschaft,* which has the twofold connotation of civil and bourgeois society. But civil society is more than a set of institutions. It is the home of a distinctive kind of human being with a particular set of habits and manners, namely, the burgher, or bourgeois. For Hegel, the modern world with only slight exaggeration could be called the bourgeois world. Modern art is bourgeois art, modern literature is bourgeois literature, and, of course, modern society is bourgeois society.

Hegel's claim to our attention is as the preeminent analyst of the modern bourgeois world. Hegel's relation to this world was complex. Hegel regarded his philosophy as the completion and perfection of the bourgeois experience in all of its manifold aspects—political, moral, theological, and aesthetic. Yet at the same time, he did as much as anyone to prepare the ground for the radical critique of the very world his philosophy sought to characterize and defend. "Philosophy," he famously pronounced, "is its own time comprehended in thoughts," but where the thought of the future will lead, no one can predict.[3] It is well known that Marx was able to arrive at his views on the alienating and exploitative features of modern civil society largely through an internal criticism of Hegelian texts. It is, then, as both the greatest defender and as one of the greatest critics of the bourgeois experience that Hegel stands at the crossroads of modernity between celebration and discontent.

FROM POLITICAL TO CIVIL SOCIETY

The term "civil society" was taken over by Hegel from his immediate eighteenth-century predecessors, who endowed the term with much of its modern significance. The term derives from the Latin *civitas,* which meant the relations of *cives,* or citizens. Civil society was the Latinized translation of Aristotle's *koinonia politike* and Cicero's *societas civilis.*[4] In Aristotle's sense, a civil society was a political association based upon the rule of law, which governed only the transactions between free individuals and not, for example, those between free men and slaves or between members of rival societies. The rule of law guaranteed that no one would be forced to suffer the self-interested rule of the few over the many, or the many over the few.

The traditional employment of civil society as synonymous with the public realm, or *res publica,* was carried over into the beginning of the modern era. The seventh chapter of John Locke's *Second Treatise of Government* is called simply "Of Political or Civil Society," using the two terms in their traditional sense. But at the same time, a new meaning of the term "civil society" began to crystallize to mean a sphere of human interactions distinct from and prior to the state, which governments are created to protect. Thus in the eighteenth century, a group of Scottish economic and social theorists came to use civil society as encompassing all those factors, not merely the political, but also the social, economic, and cultural factors that constitute a "civilized" way of life.

In *An Essay on the History of Civil Society,* Adam Ferguson uses the concept of civil socity in the broadest sense to mean "polished" and "refined," as contrasted with a "rude" or "savage" state of society. Ferguson paid special attention to the rise of the division of labor and the consequent specialization of functions as the distinguishing feature between economically primitive and refined or civilized societies.[5] Ferguson's countryman David Hume in his essay "Of Refinement in the Arts" regarded the chief aim of civil society as enlarging our common sense of humanity, a kind of cosmopolitan spirit that makes peoples less cruel and barbarous. "When the tempers of men are softened as well as their knowledge improved," Hume writes, "this humanity appears still more conspicuous, and is the chief characteristic which distinguishes a civilized age from times of barbarity and ignorance."[6]

The principal marker distinguishing a civil from an uncivil society is the role accorded to commerce. In his essay "Of Civil Liberty," Hume notes that "the world is still too young to fix many general truths in politics," but one such truth that recommends itself is the role of trade in advancing civility. "Trade," he writes, "was never esteemed an affair of state till the last century; and there scarcely is any ancient writer on politics, who has made mention of it."[7] Even Machiavelli ("a great genius") was too focused on "the furious and tyrannical governments of ancient times, or the little disorderly principalities of Italy," to understand the importance of economics for modern reality. Among the moderns, only the English and the Dutch have fully absorbed this lesson. Most important of all, Hume notes a connection, a kind of elective affinity, between commercial societies and moderate government. "It has become an established opinion" he notes, "that commerce can never flourish but in a free government."[8] While the arts and sciences have reached a state of perfection in absolutist France, commerce requires the rule of law and protection of property.

For Hume, as for his French contemporary Montesquieu, the great distinction is no longer between republican and monarchical governments but between moderate and absolute governments. Hume even wonders whether the moderate monarchies of contemporary Europe may better protect life and property than republics. Moderate monarchies have become what republics once were, government of law, not men: "Property is there secure; industry encouraged; the arts flourish; and the prince lives secure among his subjects."[9] Perhaps expressing Montesquieu's judgment that the English constitution is a republic disguised as a monarchy, Hume predicts that in time, monarchies and republics will become virtually indistinguishable from one another.[10]

The debates about the role of commerce and civil society had a profound effect on the young Hegel. We know that he read Adam Smith's *Wealth of Nations* in Christian Garve's German translation between 1794 and 1796 and around the same time took extensive notes on Sir James Steuart's *Inquiry into the Principles of Political Economy.* So important was the influence of Steuart's book that Hegel gathered his notes on it into a commentary, which was subsequently lost. According to Hegel's earliest biographer, who apparently had access to this commentary as late as 1844, the work contained "a number of magnificent insights into politics and history and many subtle observations."[11] Sadly, we will never know what these observations were, but a good guess might be the Scottish theory of civil society and historical progress.

"THE *BÜRGER* IN THE SENSE OF THE *BOURGEOIS*"

The idea of civil society received its most complete expression in Hegel's *Philosophy of Right* of 1821. Here the term is presented as one of the three "moments" of the "ethical life" (*Sittlichkeit*) of modernity. Civil society is sandwiched in between Hegel's treatment of the individual as a family member and as a citizen of the state (¶157). Civil society is presented as a new form of human association in history that Hegel identifies as a "system of needs" whose organizing principle is individual self-interest: "The concrete person who, as a *particular* person, as a totality of needs and a mixture of natural necessity and arbitrariness, is his own end, is *one principle* of civil society. . . . Civil society is the [stage of] differences which intervenes between the family and the state. . . . The creation of civil society belongs to the modern world, which for the first time allows all determinations of the Idea to attain their rights. . . . In civil society, each individual is his own end, and all else means nothing to him" (¶¶182/182R).

Civil society, in Hegel's idiom, constitutes the sphere of "difference." Difference from what? Civil society is different from the bonds of love and intimacy that constitute the family and different from the ties of duty and obligation that constitute the state. Difference suggests the untrammeled pursuit of individuality and self-interest that are constitutive features of the modern world. The ancient world, Hegel avers, knew nothing of the division between state and society. The civil sphere of family and economic activity were simply swallowed up by the all-encompassing unity of the polis. The separation of spheres is a uniquely modern discovery that presupposed the liberation of the individual from the previous ties of family, guild, church, and community. "The whole of civil society," Hegel writes, "is the sphere . . . in which all individual characteristics, all aptitudes, and all accidents of birth and fortune are liberated, and where the waves of all passions surge forth governed only by the reason which still shines through them" (¶182A).

This new form of association also has as its end the satisfaction of needs through work and labor (¶188). Civil society represents a "system of needs" that operates much along the lines of Kant's doctrine of unsocial sociability. The pursuit of individual interest is the source of both competition and cooperation. It is the task of political economy to discover the rationality inherent in the apparent cacophony of interactions. Political economy is the science of civil society, whose task is "to explain mass relationships and mass movements in their qualitative and quantitative determinacy and complexity" (¶189R). Hegel credits economists like Smith, Jean-Baptiste Say, and David Ricardo for determining the laws ("the necessity at work") governing civil society from among "the endless multitude of details" and "mass of contingent occurrences." He even compares the motions of civil society to the planetary system that "presents only irregular movements to the eye, yet whose laws can nevertheless be recognized" (¶189A).

The science of political economy takes as its object the new socially emancipated individual, whom Hegel was among the first to recognize and describe as "the burgher in the sense of the bourgeois": "In [abstract] right, the object is the *person;* at the level of morality, it is the *subject,* in the family, the *family member,* and in civil society in general the *Bürger* (in the sense of the *bourgeois*). Here at the level of needs, it is that concretum of representational thought which we call *the human being,* this is the first, and in fact the only occasion on which we shall refer to the *human being* in this sense" (¶190R; translation slightly modified).

It is here, in his capacity as bourgeois, that is, as one of the "private persons who have their own interest as their end" (¶187R), that the individual becomes a true "son of civil society" (¶238). To unlock or understand this new kind of human association requires us to regard it as the home of a new, unprecedented kind of human being, "the *Bürger* in the sense of the *bourgeois*."

For reasons connected to the distinctive arc of German history, the concept of the Bürger never carried the negative connotations of the French word "bourgeois." In fact, quite the opposite is the case. Germans belonging to this stratum of society saw themselves as bearers of a distinctive culture and way of life possessed by neither the nobility nor the common people. Civil society was regarded as performing a socially educative function, including political representation and membership in professional organizations (*Stände*). This way of life was the product of another German concept—*Bildung*—which means not just education but something like the process of moral and intellectual maturation. As a notable student of German history has written:

> *Bildung* achieves its aim when the point is reached where the individual—the universe of the *Bürger* consists of individuals, a concept wholly meaningless to the landed gentry or the proletariat—is able not merely to stand on his or her own two feet economically, but has acquired secure possession of the values that make up the *Bürgertum's* way of life. The ultimate refinement of these values is to be found in the classical Weimar culture associated with the magic names of Goethe and Schiller, but it also includes the poetry and philosophy of their Romantic critics

and opponents. . . . Anyone not conversant with this universe of discourse is by definition *ungebildet* (uncultivated) and thus has no claim to being called a *Bürger,* even though he may possess the requisite socioeconomic standing.[12]

The ideal of the burgher was notable above all for its degree of independence, both intellectually and socially. Hegel and his contemporaries—Schelling and Hölderlin—were members of an urban patriciate conscious of their rights and privileges, who sought to give philosophical expression to the values of their class. They believed it was the role of a spiritual elite to be the vanguard of a new class of freemen responsible for the redemption of society through education.[13] A member of the Bürgertum was typically a civil servant from Hegel's "universal class," a university professor, a clergyman, or a member of any of the other liberal professions. In his essay "Theory and Practice," Kant emphasizes the role of independence by distinguishing the citizen of a state (*Staatsbürger*) from the citizen of a town (*Stadtbürger*).[14] This distinction is not between those who look after the public interest in contradistinction to those who attend to their own private affairs. Rather the difference is between someone who is his own master by virtue of having a marketable skill or trade and those who are mere laborers and thus dependent upon the will of others. Only those with a certain degree of property and economic independence can be citizens in the full sense of the term, thus blurring the lines between the civil and political orders.[15]

Hegel's major innovation was to take the concept of the burgher and to turn it into an object of world-historical importance. Hegel is the first German writer to take Rousseau's distinction between bourgeois and citizen and turn it into the defining principle of a new form of civilization. In his lectures on Aristotle's *Politics* from his *History of Philosophy,* he explicitly uses the French terms to make his point about the separation of private and public liberty: "The Greeks were still unacquainted with the abstract right of our modern state, that isolates the individual, allows of his acting as such. . . . It is free nations alone that have the consciousness of and activity for the whole; in modern times the individual is only free for himself as such, and enjoys citizen freedom alone—in the sense of that of a *bourgeois* and not of a *citoyen.* We do not possess two separate words to mark this distinction."[16]

In this remarkable passage, Hegel makes the separation between bourgeois and citizen into a kind of litmus test for modern civil society. Note that unlike Rousseau, who turned to Sparta and republican Rome as the paradigms of moral wholeness and coherence, Hegel makes the emergence of "abstract right"—the right to private property—the mark of a civil or civilized society. In an unmistakable reference to the Scottish Enlightenment's theory of conjectural history, Hegel makes the appearance of social differentiation and the particularization of tasks as the defining feature of civilization over barbarism. He makes clear that modern freedom consists in the enjoyment of one's own individuality even at the expense of the universal. He even suggests that in working for one's own interest one inadvertently advances the interests of humanity. Not the freedom of the citizen to participate in government but the freedom of the individual not to do so becomes the hallmark of modern liberty. Like his Swiss contemporary Benjamin Constant, Hegel celebrates civil or bourgeois freedom as institutionalized in civil society.

"THE BOURGEOIS-CHRISTIAN WORLD"

In what still remains one of the finest analyses of Hegel ever written, Jürgen Habermas appreciates the role of civil society in the creation of a new form of civilization: "Up to the essay on *Natural Law,* Hegel had conceived the domain of formal legal relations as the result of the decay of free morality, basing himself in this on Gibbon's depiction of the Roman Empire. . . . Hegel can replace the negative definition of Abstract Right by a positive one because meanwhile he has come to know the economic interrelation of private law with modern bourgeois society and has seen that these legal categories also incorporate the result of liberation through social labor."[17]

Habermas is correct to view Hegel's appreciation of law—the sphere of Abstract Right—as constituting the zone of modern liberty rather than the decay of morality. While the young Hegel had applauded the French Revolution's experiment with radical republicanism, the mature thinker came to regard the culture of separation as the form of ethical life most appropriate to the modern world. It is this culture of separation, most importantly between civil society and the state, that Marx saw as the secularization of an earlier theological split between the heavenly and earthly cities. This split vision—this *Doppelgestalt,* as Marx revealingly called it—was simply Hegel's attempt to provide philosophical legitimacy for this new distinction between the bourgeois and the citizen. Indeed, Marx found this social division to be the basis for a psychological schism within the individual. "Civil society and the state are separated," he observed. "Consequently the citizen of the state and the member of civil society are also separated. The individual must thus undertake an essential schism within himself."[18] This schism requires us to perform a further separation between ourselves as members of civil society and as members of the state. "Thus in order to behave as actual citizen of the state, to acquire political significance and efficacy," Marx suggests, "he [the individual] must abandon his civil actuality, abstract from it, and retire from this entire organization into his individuality."[19]

In *On the Jewish Question,* Marx disparages as "egoistic" the individual rights and liberties praised by liberal theorists of civil society. Civil rights are simply the freedoms of "egoistic man, of man separated from other men and from the community."[20] Marx complains that Hegel's distinction between civil society and the state, rather than the mark of civilization, has become a new source of conflict that has simply reproduced the theological antagonism between this world and the other: "The political state, in relation to civil society, is just as spiritual as is heaven in relation to earth. It stands in the same opposition to civil society, and overcomes it in the same manner as religion overcomes the narrowness of the profane world."[21] Marx approvingly quotes Rousseau's *Social Contract* to the effect that in civil society one lacks an authentically "human" (that is, social) existence. One is split between the earthly, material interests of civil society and the heavenly, idealized world of citizenship and the state.[22] Our social emancipation lies in overcoming divisions, not in accepting them.

Marx's use of theological language to describe the distinction between civil society and the state grasped a distinctive feature of Hegel's conception of modernity. It was not enough for Hegel to characterize the bourgeois as a distinctively modern phenomenon. The bourgeois was also in large part the product of Christianity. The idea that the individual as such is an object of inestimable dignity and moral worth is almost wholly a product of the Christian revelation. To be sure, while the ideas of *dignitas* and *humanitas* go back to the Romans, these invariably attach to the fulfillment of the duties of some particular office or function. It was Christianity that announced the universal salvation of all humankind by means of faith alone. Furthermore, while ancient moralists frequently condemned *inhumanitas* or needless cruelty, it was also the case that humanity as such did not count for very much. The idea of extending moral dignity to all sentient beings on the basis of their humanitas alone was only possible within what the German historian Karl Löwith has felicitously called "the Bourgeois-Christian world."[23]

Hegel takes up and embellishes upon this great theme, but he regards the advent of the bourgeois-Christian world as a decisive advance over the narrow and crabbed parochialism of antiquity. According to his *Philosophy of*

History, while the Asian world knew only that one man—the oriental despot—was free, and while the Greek and Roman world knew that only some men—the classical citizens—were free, it was the unique contribution of Christianity to recognize that all are free.[24] It is due to Christianity, Hegel avers, that we have acquired the belief that freedom is "the very essence of mind": "Whole continents, Africa and the East have never had this Idea and are without it still. The Greeks and Romans, Plato and Aristotle, even the Stoics, did not have it. On the contrary, they saw that it is only by birth . . . or by strength of character, education or philosophy . . . that the human being is actually free. It was through Christianity that this Idea came into the world. According to Christianity, the individual *as such* has an infinite value as the object and aim of divine love, destined as mind to live in absolute relationship with God himself, and have God's mind dwelling in him: i.e. man is implicitly destined to supreme freedom."[25]

Hegel makes the emergence of free subjectivity the dividing line between the states of Greek and Roman antiquity and those of the modern world. Plato's *Republic* grasped "the substance of ethical life in its ideal beauty and truth" but could still not contain the principle of the freedom of the will that was the specific contribution of Christianity: "This deficiency also explains why the great substantial truth of [Plato's] *Republic* is imperfectly understood and why it is usually regarded as a dream of abstract thought, as what is often called an ideal. The principle of the *self-sufficient and inherently infinite personality* of the individual, the principle of subjective freedom, which arose in an inward form in the Christian religion . . . is denied its right in that merely substantial form of the actual spirit [in the *Republic*]" (¶185R).

Hegel is responsible here for standing the paradigm of classical republicanism on its head. Throughout the *Philosophy of Right,* he defends the presence of individual freedom, not as a cause of weakness or moral corruption, but as the unique source of the strength of modernity by linking it specifically to Christianity. "The principle of modern states," he writes, "has enormous strength and depth because it allows the principle of subjectivity to attain fulfillment in the self-sufficient extreme of personal particularity" (¶260). And in the Addition to the above remark he contrasts "the states of classical antiquity" in which individual "particularity has not yet been released" to the "essence of the modern state" in which "the universal should be linked with the complete freedom of particularity and the well-being of individuals" (¶260A).

The difference between Rousseau and Hegel, then, is that while the one makes the appearance of the bourgeois a symptom of the ethical decay and corruption of the ancient republic, the other regards it as a cause of moral self-development. "The right of the subject's particularity to find satisfaction, or to put it differently, the right of subjective freedom, is the pivotal and focal point in the difference between antiquity and the modern age," Hegel writes (¶124R). This right of subjective freedom was given its initial expression by Christianity but today has become "the universal and actual principle of a new form of the world." Among the "specific shapes" assumed by this civilization are such things as romantic love and the quest for personal salvation, but also "the principle of civil society as moments of the political constitution," which include such typically modern disciplines as "the history of art, the sciences, and philosophy" (¶124R).

LABOR, MORAL SELF-DEVELOPMENT, AND EDUCATION

From what has just been said, it should be clear that Hegel seeks to comprehend and conceptualize the phenomenon of civil society as a response to some of the deepest and most powerful metaphysical imperatives of modernity. Civil society and the new set of social and economic arrangements that sustain it are expressions of the mind's aspiration to freedom. This conception of freedom is intrinsically tied to some idea of individual self-determination, or what Hegel calls "subjectivity."

The idea of subjective or individual freedom emerged philosophically in the famous Cartesian *cogito,* or the "I think," which is the ultimate arbiter of truth. It emerged theologically in the Reformation with the Protestant conception of justification through faith alone without the mediating institution of the clergy. And it emerged politically in the new legal conceptions of the rights to such things as life, liberty, and property that were secured in the American and French Revolutions. Finally, the idea of subjectivity was developed in the institution of the modern market economy, in which such things as the freedom to buy and sell the products of one's labor, to enter freely into contract, to exchange property, and to enter careers based on talent are among the most profound features (¶¶206/299).

Hegel's primary contribution to the civil society debate consists of his conception of the marketplace as an ethical, or *sittlich,* institution. He recognizes the controversial nature of this claim. Civil society represents the stage of "difference," that is, individual free self-expression that juxtaposes itself both to the moral intimacy of the family and to the ethical responsibilities of citizenship (¶182A). For this very reason, the emergence of the modern liberated individual was seen by many as a symptom of the "ethical corruption" responsible for the decline of the civic spirit (¶185). Yet Hegel insists that a political constitution is mature only to the extent that it not only permits but also encourages the widest degree of freedom for its individual members (¶260A).

Civil society is a form of ethical freedom because it allows the maximum scope for the free self-determination of the will. The suggestion here is that freedom is the property of the will alone (¶4A). Even if human beings may be *in* nature, we are not entirely *of* nature. Hegel credits Rousseau with the discovery that the origin of right is found not in nature but in the will. "It was the achievement of Rousseau," he writes, "to put forward the will as the principle of the state, a principle which has thought not only as its form (as with the social instinct, for example, or divine authority) but also as its content" (¶258R). The freedom of the will refers to the ability that allows us to escape or transcend the determined order of nature and obey the laws of our own making. Liberty means for Hegel something like the capacity for self-determination. Liberty is achieved not by obedience to the laws of nature ("natural liberty") but precisely by our ability to transcend and transform them in accordance with the laws of freedom. It is in this sense that Hegel can refer to the institutions of civil society and the state as a kind of "second nature" (¶4).

Civil freedom—the freedom appropriate to civil society—is identified with such "formal" liberties as the right to own property, to choose a marriage partner, and to pursue a career (¶¶75/262A). These become important parts of modern bürgerliche freedom insofar as only in civil society are individuals recognized as moral agents responsible for the choices they make. Indeed, it is only within civil society that individuals are recognized, not on the basis of their inherited social status or ethnic identity, but simply as human beings with common moral needs. Civil society is the great teacher of moral egalitarianism, for only here does "a human being count as such because he is a human being, not because he is a Jew, Catholic, Protestant, German, Italian, etc." (¶209R).

A crucial—perhaps *the* crucial—liberty provided by civil society is the right to own and exchange property. Every bit as much as Locke, Hegel makes private property a central feature of his social theory, except that until now, he believes, the grounds for property have been inadequately understood. Private property is frequently made a litmus test for modern freedom. Thus, while Plato's *Republic* is said to display "the substance of ethical life in its ideal beauty and truth," it failed to understand "the self-sufficient and inherently infinite personality of the individual" in all of its richness and variety (¶185R). While this principle of the infinite value of the moral personality dawned in an "inward" form with the appearance of Christianity, the most important outward manifestation of this freedom is the institution of private property.

Hegel was by no means the first person to identify private property with civil liberty. In the *Second Treatise,* Locke attempted to ground property in the fundamental desire for self-preservation. The fact that everybody has a property in his or her own person is for Locke sufficient to establish a natural right to what is acquired through "the Labor of his Body and the Work of his Hands."[26] Locke here appears to formulate a rudimentary version of the labor theory of value. It is labor that confers value on a thing by adding something more than nature, "the common Mother of all," had done. But while property may grow out of the need for self-preservation, it ultimately answers the human need for liberty by establishing a "fence" between ourselves and our dependence on the will of others. Property fulfills an important political function. It encourages the virtues of rationality and industriousness required to affirm a sense of active citizenship.[27]

Hegel does not so much disagree with Locke's conclusions as with his method of deriving them. The attempt to derive property from the right to our bodies is characteristic of what Hegel thought of as Locke's naturalistic premises. Whatever the origins of property might be, its justification cannot be derived from the needs of the body, only from the claims of moral personality. Property is ultimately derived from the free will and not from its serving bodily needs. Locke mistook the origins of property for its end. The needs of moral personality are not something given by nature but are created through an ongoing process of struggle with certain natural and historical restrictions. Hegel reveals a romantic dimension in presenting personality as fashioned through an ongoing process of struggle and the need to overcome whatever is merely given. "Personality," he writes, "is that which acts to overcome this limitation and give itself reality or, what amounts to the same thing, to posit that existence as its own" (¶39).

Hegel agrees with Locke that our title to a thing is conferred through labor, even if that labor—to use Locke's homely example—is no more than picking an apple from a tree. But Hegel goes beyond Locke in suggesting that labor is more than a means to an end, for example, the enjoyment of the apple. Labor is an expression of the will and as such an expression of who and what we essentially are (¶45). Locke was profoundly correct in seeing labor—a subjective human activity—as the source of value; what he missed was the way in which labor shapes and affects not only external nature but the moral and psychological needs of the personality as well.

To put the matter "dialectically," our labor not only helps to create a world of objects that can be possessed and exchanged for other objects. Labor also shapes the moral personality of the laborer. Work shapes not only the world; it shapes the worker too. Through work, the world ceases to be something "other" or "alien" to us. Rather, the world becomes an expression of who we are. We see ourselves reflected back in the objects that we in turn create. Work is no longer considered the biblically condemned curse of Adam or the classically despised realm of slaves, it has become a crucial factor in our moral self-realization. Private property is, then, an expression of the personality and is necessary for the full self-realization of the moral will. Thus, when Hegel remarks that property has no objective end or purpose of its own but derives "its determination and its soul" from the will alone, he is noting the profoundly transformative character of the labor process (¶44).

Private property, like the institutions of civil society in which it is embedded, performs a deeply moral function in Hegel's philosophy. Property is not just a means to security, comfort, and survival, nor is it primarily a defense against the arbitrary rule by others, although it may be both these things as well. Property and the work that goes into it are primarily forms of Bildung, or education. "Education in its absolute determination," Hegel writes, "is therefore liberation and work towards a higher liberation" (¶187R). Work is a form of liberation in two senses of the word. Through labor, we transform the world into a domain of usable objects, but we also transform ourselves by shaping and refining our skills, abilities, and talents. We take a set of naturally given capacities and shape them into something concrete—a craftsman, an artist, a computer programmer—a being with a specific moral identity (¶207).

Membership in civil society is primarily a form of moral education. Unlike Rousseau and Marx, Hegel does not identify the bourgeois with low-minded materialist egoism. It is only through the crucible of civil society that the bourgeois learns the cardinal virtues of restraint, self-discipline, and respect for others. "Be a person and respect others as persons" is the highest commandment of justice (¶36). Hegel distinguishes a kind of crude "practical education" acquired through work from Bildung in the strict sense as the acquisition of moral personality. "Education," he writes at one point, "is the art of making human beings ethical; it considers them as natural beings and shows them how they can be reborn, and how their original nature can be transformed into a second, spiritual nature so that this spirituality becomes habitual to them" (¶151A).

"The problem of *Bildung*," the great Hegel scholar George Armstrong Kelly once wrote, "is an aspect of the problem of authority."[28] Hegel was here following the model of Rousseau's *Emile*, the greatest modern text linking education with the problem of authority. The purpose of education for both Rousseau and Hegel was to liberate us from the authority of nature, but also to prepare us to accept the authority of civil society. "Education in its absolute determination," Hegel writes, "is therefore liberation and work towards a higher liberation": "Within the subject, this liberation is the hard work of opposing mere subjectivity of conduct, of opposing the immediacy of desire as well as the subjective vanity of feeling and the arbitrariness of caprice. The fact that it is such hard work accounts for some of the disfavor it incurs. But it is through this work of education that the subjective will attains objectivity even within itself, that objectivity in which alone it is for its part worthy and capable" (¶187R).

The idea of education has mainly to do with preparation for participation in the world of work and the marketplace. This is accomplished through membership in one of the authorized "corporations," or professional associations, that make up civil society (¶¶250–56). The corporations are not exactly like modern firms but are more like Tocquevillian civic associations that prevent excessive centralization from the state above and excessive atomization from the market below. Hegel's corporate doctrine and the idea of Bildung that goes with it seek to instill sentiments of pride and integrity that come with the exercise of a recognized profession. The corporations function as a kind of "second family" in which the individual is able to develop an identity and personality of his or her own. This may seem unduly restrictive, but for Hegel a person *ohne Korporation* is a kind of nonperson, without status or honor. Only through membership in one of the basic estates of society does the individual become a "somebody" (¶¶207A/253).

Bildung in the German sense means more than the acquisition of technical skills, it means the cultivation of sense of inner discipline and self-restraint. A *Grammatical-Critical Dictionary of High German Vernacular* of the period defines Bildung as related to the "molding" or "depicting" of the form of an object, especially the face. "A person possessed of fine *Bildung*," the entry says, "is one whose face has fine features."[29] Yet a *gebilditer Mensch* cannot be read from physiognomy alone. "By educated people," Hegel writes, "we may understand in the first place those who do everything as others do it and do not flaunt their particular characteristics" (¶187A). It is a part of education not to offend the feelings of others ("the uneducated man can easily cause offense"). "Thus education irons out particularity to make it act in accordance with the nature of the thing," he says (¶187A). This willingness to do what others do, to blanch out anything that might smack of spontaneity and willfulness, and in general to accept "my station and its duties" is also a part of the education of the bourgeois.

THE FUTURE OF CIVIL SOCIETY

Hegel's defense of civil society is more than an analysis of certain social and economic institutions that mediate between the individual and the state. It is also a defense of the civilizing and educational mission of these institutions. Civil society is inseparable from its moral claims and aspirations. Does this mean that Hegel was uncritical of every aspect of modern economic life and committed to defending even its failures? Can he be accused of producing a bourgeois ideology in the precise Marxian sense of that phrase, a rationalization for existing practices? Certainly not.

There are two respects in which Hegel begins to call into question the moral viability of the market and thus open up room for critique. The first concerns the moral and psychological consequences of the division of labor on the individual worker. This critique was pioneered by the Scots, especially Ferguson and Smith. In the *Wealth of Nations,* Smith deplores how the division of labor leads to the confinement of human activities to one or two simple operations. The result of the constant repetition of the same tasks is the general loss of the moral and intellectual virtues necessary for active citizenship. In a passage that could almost be mistaken for Rousseau, Smith contrasts the situation that obtains in civilized or "improved" societies to that in primitive societies of hunters and gatherers where everyone is called upon to be both soldier and statesman and all "can form a tolerable judgment concerning the interests of society and the conduct of those who govern it."[30] While Smith regards the division of labor as the great engine of social progress, he cannot help but worry about its moral and political effects on "the great body of people," which he believes must necessarily fall "unless government takes some pains to prevent it."[31]

Similarly, Ferguson in *An Essay on the History of Civil Society* reflected on the consequences attendant upon what he called "the separation of arts and professions."[32] In general, he expresses a sense of wonder at the great variety and multiplicity of professions as evidence of the sheer ingenuity of nature. But while the art of separation is at the basis of social progress, he also notes the price that civilization pays for the gains in efficiency and affluence ("every generation, compared to its predecessors, may have appeared to be ingenious; compared to its followers, may have appeared to be dull").[33]

Like Smith and Ferguson, Hegel understood the important respects in which the division of labor increases the overall social product, or what Smith called "the wealth of nations." What was not lost on Hegel was the consequences on the individual whose activities were reduced to an area of mind-numbing narrowness. The process of the ever-increasing "abstractness" of work, he predicts, will end up making the individual worker redundant: "Through this division, the work of the individual becomes *simpler*, so that his skill at his abstract work becomes greater, as does the volume of his output. At the same time . . . the abstraction of production makes work increasingly *mechanical*, so that the human being is eventually able to step aside and let a *machine* take his place" (¶198). Hegel's reference here to the mechanization of skills and the substitution of machines for living labor could almost have served as a template for Marx's thoughts on the alienation of labor in his *1844 Manuscripts*.[34]

In the *Philosophy of Right,* the problem of the division of labor was to some degree eclipsed by a concern for a new and potentially even more ominous problem. Hegel was deeply aware that civil society and the marketplace were inseparable from the creation of poverty. What he recognizes is not, of course, the presence of the poor. There have always been poor people in every society, and it would have been quite surprising had he not recognized this. What makes his analysis stand out is his identification of the moral and spiritual effects of a new kind of poverty that has begun to appear alongside the emergence of civil society. It is not poverty as such, but a new type of poverty that Hegel seeks to describe when he speaks of the creation of a "rabble": "Poverty in itself does not reduce people to a rabble; a rabble is created only by the disposition associated with poverty, by inward rebellion against the rich, against society, the government, etc. . . . . This in turn gives rise to the evil that the rabble do not have sufficient honor to gain their livelihood through their own work, yet claim that they have a right to receive their livelihood" (¶244A).

This is, to my knowledge, the first and still the best description of what sociologists call the "underclass." Hegel is describing not simply the working poor but a kind of distinctively modern pathology with which we are now only too familiar. He observes the emergence of this class but admits to be at a loss about what to do about it. In what must be one of the most prescient understatements in the history of modern social thought, he writes that the abolition of poverty remains "one which agitates and torments modern societies" (¶244A).

Hegel's solution to the social problem is decent and humane but not necessarily satisfactory. Hegel suggests in the first place that both private charity and the state should attempt to correct occasional market failures (¶¶241/242). But he also recognizes the ways in which public welfare prevents the poor from gaining the self-respect that comes from earning a living. In this respect, he anticipates all the later debates about a "culture of poverty" and the unintended consequences that flow from welfare policies.[35] The result is inevitably a class within civil society which is either unable or unwilling to work for a living and which demands to receive subsistence as its right. Hegel suggests that the creation of international markets for domestic products may do much to relieve the domestic poverty created by civil society. Yet even here, he recognizes that this is but a halfway measure, since productivity will continue to increase, and international competition is bound to become tight (¶246).

Hegel's admission that he is unable to solve the problems of civil society puts him in good company. Those who have offered solutions have generally failed or produced unintended consequences worse than the problems they set out to remedy. Hegel did, however, allow us to see with unrivaled clarity the issues and problems presented by civil society. He was, as I have tried to argue, a defender, although not an uncritical one, of the modern market economy and the kind of high bourgeois culture in which the market was enmeshed. Bourgeois society was for him more than a vehicle for producing goods and services. It was a network of moral relations aimed at producing a certain kind of educated or civilized individual.

CONCLUSION

It would be a profound mistake to view Hegel's contributions simply as a precursor of the Marxist state or some variant of the welfare state as has so often been said to be the case. Hegel wrote to establish the accomplishments of modernity in the wake of the Protestant Reformation, the French Revolution, and the new social or civil order represented by bürgerliche Gesellschaft. It was to record the accomplishments of the burgher, or bourgeois, that he devoted his talents. No doubt, there are, and will always be, those like Marx who found Hegel's solutions to the social problem too timid and piecemeal to be fully satisfactory. For such critics, nothing short of a total revolutionizing of society would be adequate to address the issues of poverty and inequality. For others, like Flaubert and Nietzsche, Hegel's celebration of the bourgeois world would seem too prosaic, too unerotic, too lacking in poetry, and frankly too boring to satisfy the deeper longings of the human spirit. For Nietzsche and his heirs, it is not the problem of inequality and exploitation but the reigning drabness, conformity, and philistinism of the new bourgeois order that needs to be transformed to escape the sheer tedium of the last man.

It was in large part in opposition to Hegel's apotheosis of the bourgeois experience that Marx and Nietzsche reacted with such furious hostility, but in the *Philosophy of Right,* the bourgeois appears as both the creator and the creation of a new form of civilization that was by no means an object of contempt. Bourgeois civilization, far from representing the triumph of egoism, greed, and materialism, presents a veritable pantheon of social, cultural, and artistic achievements. Hegel represented both all previous philosophies and all previous forms of society as approximations of the modern mind. In this sense he could rightly be said to have idealized the phenomenon of bourgeois society, viewing it not as something base, ugly, and ignoble but as the highest expression of a new and even heroic aspect of the "world spirit" whose outlines were now being fully realized, especially in the states of northern Europe. Hegel was certainly not the last, but he was the greatest, thinker to devote his efforts to elucidating the virtues of this new bourgeois world.

Part Three **Our Discontents**

Chapter 9 Rousseau's Counter-Enlightenment:
Letter to d'Alembert on the Theater

The Counter-Enlightenment begins with Rousseau. This is not to say that Rousseau opposed modernity. The Counter-Enlightenment, as I have tried to show, is not so much antimodern as it is a higher or more advanced form of modernity. Attacks on the Enlightenment are as much a part of the modern world as the Enlightenment itself. Nor was Rousseau the first to voice discontent with the Century of Light—*l'Âge des Lumières,* as the French *philosophes* pretentiously described their era. Warnings of decadence and decline were almost as constant throughout the eighteenth century as predictions of progress and the advancement of knowledge. Some of these warnings took the form of satirical works, such as Swift's *Gulliver's Travels* and Burke's *Vindication of Natural Society.* Others took the form of a more militant defense of the regime of throne and altar. Yet it was only Rousseau who gave the Counter-Enlightenment its voice. His was the voice of radical discontent with the three great pillars of Enlightenment civilization: science, progress, and commerce. His attack on privilege and inequality did much to create the language of Marxism and the European Left. Moreover, his defense of unique individual cultures and his rejection of cosmopolitanism did much to prepare the language of nationalism and the European Right. Rousseau was at once both and neither. He is virtually impossible to classify under any label. His name has never given rise to an "ism."

Rousseau's discontent with the Enlightenment took the form of a critique of the proudest achievement of the modern age, its development of a sophisticated culture of the arts and letters. The ground of Rousseau's critique of the arts was laid, above all, by Plato's expulsion of poets in the *Republic*. In returning to Plato, Rousseau was returning to the classical conception of the arts, in particular the classical conception of the relation of the arts to society. What is—or should be—the role of literature and the arts in modern society? Plato is often said to be, or more often accused of, lacking in an "aesthetic sense" and therefore regarding the arts as useful only as a tool of moral education. "Tolstoy exaggerates only slightly," Iris Murdoch has written, "when he says (in *What is Art?*), 'the Greeks (just like everybody else always and everywhere) simply considered art (like everything else) good only when it served goodness.'"[1]

Today, Plato is often taken as the model of illiberal education, akin to the totalitarians of the modern age with their efforts at thought control and turning the arts into instruments of propaganda. A different, though only slightly less extreme, approach was taken by Aristotle in the *Poetics*. Like Plato, Aristotle was mainly interested in poetry as a form of moral education. It would be a mistake to view him as if he were the founder of an academic discipline called "literary criticism" as a distinct and autonomous field. For Aristotle, and the classics generally, literature and the arts were designed to form the taste, character, and judgment of a free citizen.[2]

Rousseau's conception of the role of the arts does not fall within any of our standard parameters. Our views of the arts tend to vacillate between two conflicting extremes. The first, more apt to be endorsed by liberals, regards the arts and the whole domain of modern culture as distinct from politics, much like the domains of morality, religion, and the economy. The works of painters, novelists, and playwrights belong to the realm of "civil society" and as such fall outside the scope and limits of politics. Liberals are likely to favor the widest latitude for artistic self-expression. The second, more likely to be endorsed by conservatives, regards the world of culture—of arts and entertainment—as having a profound moral effect on society. The arts are often believed to shape character (often for the worse), and no regime, not even a liberal one, can afford to be entirely indifferent or neutral to the character of its citizens. Conservatives are more likely than liberals to concern themselves with the music people listen to and the television shows and movies they watch.

The importance of literature and the arts, at least as a philosophical problem, has all but disappeared for us. There is, of course, a subfield of philosophy called "aesthetics," or the philosophy of art, but this is a far cry from the study of politics and the arts that might ask such questions as "What is the social function of art?" "What is the responsibility of the artist to society?" "Does art serve to educate judgment and the public mind?" With only a few notable exceptions, the whole topic of politics and the arts has ceased to be of interest to modern philosophers. Among the very few works on this topic still worth reading are Georg Lukács's *Ästhetik* and Allan Bloom's penetrating account in *The Closing of the American Mind*.[3]

Rousseau was the last great thinker to have put these questions at the forefront of his thought. The question of politics and the arts was the theme of Rousseau's first major essay, *The Discourse on the Sciences and Arts*—the *First Discourse*—published in 1750, was reprised in the *Preface to Narcisse* in 1752, and was most fully developed in the *Letter to d'Alembert on the Theatre* in 1758. By the time Rousseau engaged in his exchange with d'Alembert over the theater, he had not only won literary fame on the basis of his *First Discourse* but was also the author of a play, *Narcisse,* and the composer of a highly successful opera, *Le devin du village,* which had been warmly received when it was performed at the court of Louis XV.[4] Rousseau had originally come to Paris with the hope of making his name as the inventor of a new system of musical notation, and he contributed vigorously to the pamphlet war between the partisans of French and Italian opera. He was himself an artistic and literary celebrity and knew of what he spoke.

THE REPUBLIC OF LETTERS

Rousseau's critique of the Enlightenment was given its initial expression in the *First Discourse*. He may not have been the first, but he was the greatest, thinker to signal a discontent with the Enlightenment and the century of taste that it promised to create. This critique was made all the more powerful because it was carried out by someone working within the culture of the Enlightenment, using the Enlightenment against itself, so to speak. The *First Discourse* was submitted as a response to an essay competition sponsored by the Academy of Dijon on the topic of whether the progress of the arts and sciences had led to the refinement of morals. While it was an increasingly widespread belief that scientific and literary development would lead to moral and political progress, Rousseau answered with a decisive no. There was, he argued, an inverse relation between enlightenment and moral virtue.

Rousseau began his broadside against the Enlightenment with an extraordinary tribute to his age as an era of unprecedented emancipation from prejudice and superstition: "It is a grand and fine spectacle to see man go forth as it were out of nothing by his own efforts; to dispel by the lights of his reason the darkness in which nature had enveloped him, to raise himself above himself; to soar by the mind to the celestial realms, to traverse the vast expanse of the universe with giant strides, like to the sun; and, what is grander and more difficult still, to return into himself, there to study man and to know his nature, his duties, and his end. All of these wonders have occurred anew in the past few generations."[5] Rousseau's praise here sets the stage for Kant who, later in the century, would describe the Enlightenment as "man's emergence from self-incurred immaturity" and declare its motto to be "sapere aude," have the courage to think for yourself.[6] But unlike Kant, Rousseau discovered a dark side to the Enlightenment, an underside, which he was the first to identify and exploit.

In the *First Discourse,* Rousseau took aim at what was a cardinal assumption of the Enlightenment, namely, that moral and political progress is fundamentally compatible with, if it does not actually presuppose, the free development of the arts and letters. Rousseau's essay returns instead to the classical skepticism about the role of the arts. Rather than serving as an agent of freedom, the arts and sciences have everywhere served the cause of despotism. "The sciences, letters, and the arts," he writes, "less despotic and more powerful, spread garlands of flowers over the iron chains."[7] The sciences and the arts progress at the expense of morality, by which Rousseau means citizen morality, the virtues of patriotism and love of country. Drawing on the experiences of ancient history, he argues that everywhere the sciences and arts have prospered, societies have become weak and enervated, men have forgotten their public duties, and women have neglected their tasks as the guardians of hearth and home. "We have physicists, geometers, chemists, astronomers, poets, musicians, and painters," he charged with characteristic overstatement, but "we no longer have citizens."[8]

Rousseau's *First Discourse* may be the first full-scale attack on the Enlightenment, but the work should not be read simply as praise of ignorance. Rousseau was concerned not only with the influence of the arts and sciences on society but also with the effects of society on the arts and sciences. It is not science and philosophy as such that he opposes but the popularization—the cheapening—of these supremely valuable activities. He remains something of a Platonist in his desire to protect philosophy from the allures of the cave. In particular he opposes the *philosophes,* the intellectuals, the "theoreticians" who regard themselves as agents of popular enlightenment. "What are we to think of that crowd of popularizers," he asks with evident reference to his colleagues at the *Encyclopédie,* "who have removed the difficulties which guarded the access to the Temple?"[9] Philosophy or science in the wrong hands is a loaded weapon. It all depends on who has access to it. Rousseau heaps praise on Newton, Bacon, and Descartes as the "preceptors of mankind" who "raise monuments to the glory of the human mind." "What guides," he asks, "could have led them as far as their own vast genius carried them?"[10] Science or philosophy is not bad for the individual—it may even be our highest perfection—but it is corrupting to society and should be treated as such. Rousseau's goal is not to banish philosophy from the cities but to create a kind of cordon sanitaire around it that will return it to a place of true honor. Rousseau wrote the *First Discourse* in praise of virtue, but what the essay principally exposes is a new conception of philosophy, or what the eighteenth century called the Republic of Letters, a term we have already seen in regard to Franklin.

The Republic of Letters was the creation of the French Huguenot philosopher and critic Pierre Bayle. Bayle's idea was that of an international society of scholars and researchers who would contribute to the dissemination of ideas across national boundaries. In the *Nouvelles de la Republique des Lettres* published in 1684, Bayle began with the promise that his journal would review the books of both Protestant and Catholic authors with impartiality and would include *éloges,* or encomiums, for illustrious scholars after their deaths. The members of this literary society might be philosophers, theologians, doctors, and poets, anyone who desired to create and contribute to a society of scholars. Accordingly, the Republic of Letters occupied no space or territory but was an ideal network that found its home in the salons, coffeehouses—today we might add the Internet—or anywhere opinion could be freely expressed. The only criterion for membership in this society was a commitment to reason and a willingness to put aside all prejudice as inimical to toleration and civility. "We must therefore lay aside all those terms that divide men into factions," Bayle wrote, "and consider that point that unites them, which is the quality of being an illustrious man in the Republic of Letters."[11]

The Republic of Letters was to be an ideal fraternity (with women also included) based on the equality of all participants and distinguished by merit alone. There they would have complete freedom to exchange ideas wherever they might lead.[12] At the center of this republic was what Bayle called "the regime of critique"—the weighing of "for and against" by a disinterested public reason—which would be applied to all existing opinions and institutions. The reality of this imaginary society was intensely polemical, a kind of intellectual Hobbesian state of nature where freedom to criticize became a blood sport and members were encouraged to make war on one another in a world of endless spiritual combat. In this bloodless war of criticism in which Protestants could attack the pope as the Antichrist and Catholics attack Protestants as heretics, members of the Republic of Letters were encouraged to repeat in unison, "We are all equal, we are all related as children of Apollo," while friends were urged to make war on friends, fathers on sons, all for the greater glory of "the empire of truth and reason."[13]

The institutionalization of the Republic of Letters often took the form of lodges and clubs like the Masons or learned societies, including the famous Academy of Dijon, to which Rousseau submitted his *First Discourse*. The Academy's goal was to "enlighten" opinion by contributing to a society that would be increasingly open to development of the arts and letters. These clubs constituted the birthplace of modern democracy, not because they endorsed the principle of popular election or the ideal of equality, but because they recognized no authority higher than the common will of their members. Originating in Freemasonry, an attitude of *esprit de société* came to replace the older esprit de corps that had been the bond of the old society. It introduced an oppositional principle into the heart of the ancien régime that can be traced directly from the Masonic lodges to the revolutionary clubs of the 1790s.[14]

The Republic of Letters performed the critical, but also destructive, function of delegitimizing whatever could not stand the test of public reason. "Public reason"—a term first used by Hobbes, which has been resurrected in our day by John Rawls and Jürgen Habermas—refers to an artificially created opinion that can serve as the basis for political legitimacy.[15] Henceforth the terms "reason" and "critique" would become inseparable. Reason was no longer considered a neutral term but regarded as a partisan in the struggle against religion and later the state itself. While Bayle had initially thought (or appeared to think) of the Republic of Letters as an apolitical body standing outside the political realm, under the influence of Voltaire and the Encyclopedists, critique quickly became a partisan force in the politics of the ancien régime. What began as an apolitical quest for truth became a morality play in which the members of the Republic of Letters served as a kind of vanguard Party of Humanity, enforcing its own standards of truth and justice.

The Republic of Letters has often been regarded as one of the proudest legacies of the Enlightenment. It shaped the background to Kant's philosophy that declared neither religion nor politics to be exempt from the test of critical reason. But it has also been seen as introducing a profound principle of disorder into political life. In *Critique and Crisis,* Reinhart Koselleck assigned to the Republic of Letters a pivotal role in creating the ambience of restlessness, dissatisfaction, and ultimately revolution characterizing eighteenth-century France. In its struggle against the state, the Republic of Letters became la Règne de la Critique, setting itself up in opposition to the political sovereign. It was the importance given to this new word—critique—that set in motion a process of usurpation and ultimately destruction: "In this trial the critic was simultaneously prosecutor, supreme judge, and interested party. By appealing to the non-partisan sovereignty of criticism but at the same time involving politics in the proceedings, the critics stood above the parties by virtue of their criticism, but as critics of the state they became partisan. . . . Criticism set itself apart from the state as non-political yet subjected it to its judgment. Therein lay the root of the ambivalence of criticism, an ambivalence that after Voltaire became its historical bench mark: ostensibly non-political and above politics, it was in fact political."[16]

Koselleck treated the Republic of Letters as fostering a dangerous utopianism in which literary men with no public experience or responsibility took upon themselves the ability to judge the sovereign. In a remarkable sentence, he even elevates this new imaginary republic to the status of a new religion: "The King as ruler by divine right appears almost modest alongside the judge of mankind who replaced him, the critic who believed that, like God on Judgment Day, he had the right to subject the universe to his verdict."[17]

Nowhere was this new idea of the Republic of Letters more forcefully asserted than in the great collective project known as the *Encyclopédie.*[18] In the *Preliminary Discourse* that would serve as a general introduction to the project, d'Alembert presented the *Encyclopédie* as an effort to shape the taste of the new age. Writing not as an individual but as a spokesman for "a society of men of letters," d'Alembert offered nothing less than a philosophy of history in which the human mind developed over cumulative stages until at last arriving at the age of light. In the second, and central, section of the *Preliminary Discourse,* he singled out four figures—Descartes, Bacon, Locke, and

Newton—as having done the most to contribute to the new age of progress. D'Alembert describes Bacon, "the immortal Chancellor of England," as "the greatest, the most universal, and the most eloquent of the philosophers." Above all, Bacon taught that philosophy should contribute to human happiness and therefore confine itself within "the limits of the science of useful things."[19] Although the Republic of Letters was ostensibly beyond national prejudice and parochialism, you can sense d'Alembert's particular pride in the role played by Descartes, who "dared to show intelligent minds how to throw off the yoke of scholasticism, of opinion, of authority—in a word, of prejudices and barbarism."[20] Descartes was "a leader of conspirators" who "had the courage to arise against a despotic and arbitrary power and who, in preparing a resounding revolution, laid the foundations of a more just and happier government, which he himself was not able to see established."[21]

A central idea of the *Encyclopédie* was the role that the arts play in society. The very idea of the aesthetic standpoint was itself a product of the Enlightenment. Poetry, painting, music, and literature came to be regarded as the "fine arts" that provided adornment to the century of progress. Burke's *Philosophical Inquiry into the Origin of Our Ideas of the Sublime and the Beautiful*, Hume's essay "On the Standard of Taste," and Kant's *Critique of Judgment* all attempted to establish an area of aesthetic experience that followed its own distinctive canons of taste and judgment. Yet in the same text, d'Alembert was already forced to acknowledge Rousseau's charge against this new consensus: "This would perhaps be the place to parry the recent thrusts of an eloquent and philosophical writer [Rousseau] who accused the sciences and the arts of corrupting human mores. It would hardly be appropriate for us to concur with this opinion at the head of a work such as this and, indeed, the worthy man of whom we speak seems himself to have given suffrage to our work by the zeal and the success of his collaboration on it."[22]

Rousseau's case against the arts, as noted before, bears certain resemblances to Plato's case against poetry. The arts—theater, poetry, the whole domain of representation—was corrupt. And what Rousseau was worried about was not lowbrow entertainment but the masterpieces of the French theater of the classical age, much as Plato was concerned with Homer and Sophocles. Rousseau's case against the arts, we shall see, is not that of a Puritan or Calvinist as he is often interpreted to be, the kind of person who, as H. L. Menken once said, lives in constant fear that someone, somewhere is having fun. Rousseau is concerned not only to protect society from the corrupting influences of the arts but also to protect the true artist from the pressures and the bewitchments of society.

THE EMPIRE OF OPINION

Rousseau's *Letter to d'Alembert* is his fullest statement on the role of the arts in society.[23] The context of Rousseau's *Letter* is familiar. It was a public response (and rebuke) to his erstwhile colleague d'Alembert, who in his article on the Calvinist and republican city Geneva for the *Encyclopédie* had proposed the establishment of a theater. Rousseau's argument is that every society is based on a delicate network of opinions, morals, habits, and customs and that any alteration in one aspect of society is bound to have consequences—often dangerous and unforeseen consequences—in others. D'Alembert, Rousseau argues, is unaware of or worse indifferent to the role of unintended consequences in his proposal for a theater. The *Letter* is one of the first great attacks on the arrogance of the Enlightenment. It also signaled once and for all Rousseau's break with the Enlightenment project of social reform.

Rousseau's statecraft begins with him taking the side of the Genevan clergy. D'Alembert's text had begun by praising the liberalism and toleration of the clerics and claimed that they subscribed to a complete Socinianism. Socinianism was an extreme form of theological liberalism often associated with Spinoza, and in this context Rousseau complained that d'Alembert's praise could do nothing more than stir up theological conflict for the very pastors he hoped to praise (258–59). Even if such praise were warranted, it should be left unsaid. In politics, it is a sound rule to let sleeping dogs lie. The theoretical claim Rousseau seems to be advancing is that every society rests on a tacit moral consensus in which it is best to leave matters of fundamental principle alone.

The term that Rousseau uses to describe this consensus is "opinion." By opinion he did not mean the kind of information elicited through polling data or focus groups. Nor did he mean the kind of intellectually purified opinion that made its appearance in the Enlightenment idea of public reason. Rather opinion referred to the entire range of morals, habits, manners, and sentiments that constitutes a people's way of life. Rousseau contrasts the unity of reason with the diversity of opinion that gives to each society its particular taste, tone, and identity: "The theatre is made for the people, and it is only by its effects on the people that one can determine its absolute qualities. There can be all sorts of entertainment. There is, from people to people, a prodigious diversity of morals, temperaments, and characters. Man is one; I admit it! But man modified by religions, governments, laws, customs, prejudices, and climates becomes so different from himself that one ought not to seek among us for what is good for men in general, but only what is good for them in this time or that country" (262–63). From the diversity of opinion derives the diversity of tastes that in turn shapes the diversity of peoples and nations.

Rousseau sometimes refers to these opinions as "sentiments" to indicate their affective character. In every society these common sentiments will determine what a people look up to, what they find worthy of honor. This is markedly different from what he had written in the *Second Discourse*—completed three years before the *Letter*. Here the reign of opinion had meant a desire to live "outside oneself," to appear as better than one is. Opinion was associated with *amour-propre,* a form of vanity that he once criticized as false, duplicitous, and hypocritical, but in the *Letter* he praises common sentiments as the only source of public well-being: "If our habits in retirement are born of our own sentiments, in society they are born of others' opinions. When we do not live in ourselves but in others, it is their judgments which guide everything. Nothing appears good or desirable to individuals which the public has not judged to be such, and the only happiness which most men know is to be esteemed happy" (300).

Philosophers of sentiment—one thinks of Hume, Francis Hutcheson, and Burke—are frequently criticized for being political conservatives, that is, the appeal to sentiments provides no independent standard from which to judge practices and institutions. Moral sentimentalists are often seen as simply re-endorsing patterns of feeling and behavior that merely happen to exist. Rousseau would disagree. While his Enlightenment colleagues looked at the world and saw only entrenched hierarchies of power and privilege that needed to be torn down, Rousseau was inclined to regard society as consisting of a delicate balance of habits and manners that have developed over long stretches of time. He was more likely to stress the extreme fragility of institutions that can easily be disrupted and once disrupted cannot so easily be repaired. Social reform must always be attentive to context, and in politics context is everything. Although the introduction of a theater may be carried out from the best of intentions, there is no way of predicting the consequences that this or any other innovation might have: "Public opinions, although so difficult to govern, are nevertheless in themselves very mobile and changing. Chance, countless accidental causes, countless unforeseen circumstances, do what force and reason could not; or, rather, it is precisely because chance directs them that force can do nothing; like the dice which leave the hand, whatever impulsion is given them does not bring up the desired point any more easily" (305). As Rousseau's reference to dice and gaming suggests, life is a crapshoot.

The task of the legislator is, therefore, not to act as a social reformer but to act as a public-minded custodian of opinion, to know what practices and institutions will preserve or destroy prevailing sentiment. In this context, Rousseau celebrates the *cercles,* the small clubs and civic associations where Genevans gather to eat, discuss politics, drink, gossip, and play cards (323–32). In the *Social Contract,* he had famously deplored the influence of intermediary associations and other organizations that might frustrate the emergence of the general will, but in the *Letter* he praises these public-spirited groups whose aim is to promote cooperation and sociability. Such groups composed of simple citizens remain the most reliable custodians of public morals. Perhaps in the best regime of the *Social Contract,* citizens would have no need of such groups to police their behavior, but in the real world, we are heavily dependent on the opinions of others to enforce good habits and prevent others. The Genevan circles serve the same function as what Burke called "the little platoon" of the family or Tocqueville's civic associations, without which society could not function.[24]

Rousseau praised these circles as serving the same function as the ancient Roman censorship because no one was ever entirely free of its gaze. "How many scandals are prevented for fear of these severe observers?" Rousseau asks (329). In a passage that speaks to his sense of political realism, he shows that all institutions are subject to abuse, but that politics is a question of weighing not absolute right against absolute wrong but relative goods over relative evils: "Let us then preserve the circles, even with their faults. For these faults are not in the circles but in the men who compose them; and there is no imaginable form of social life in which the same faults do not produce more harmful effects. Again, let us not seek for the chimera of perfection but for the best possible according to the nature of man and the constitution of society" (332).

MORALITY AND THE ARTS

The most memorable parts of the *Letter* are those devoted to Rousseau's analysis of the moral effects of the theater. Rousseau is concerned not with the effects of the theater and the arts in the abstract but specifically with the effects on the city of Geneva. This is a point that he had underscored in the *First*

Discourse. The arts and sciences will have different effects depending on the type of society in which they are considered. What might be beneficial in capital cities like London and Paris may have the opposite effect in provincial Geneva. In short, it all depends on the context and character of the people. The *Letter* is nothing if not a study of the danger of unintended consequences in politics.

Rousseau agrees that the theater in itself may be nothing more than a form of harmless entertainment. All peoples require amusement, and the Genevans are no different from others. But have the possible consequences been adequately considered? A theater adds new expenses to a people's budget, and these expenses, Rousseau complains, will fall disproportionately on the poor. Building a theater will have some of the same economic consequences as the arguments about casinos do today. Theaters become magnets, especially for those people who can least afford them, and as a result deepen inequality (297, 334–35). Once again, in some contexts these inequalities will hardly be felt, while in others they can have corrosive consequences. Furthermore, time spent in the theater is time spent away from work. An increase in luxury will mean a decline in trade. As if this were not enough, theaters will require a host of other support services. To keep a theater open during bad weather will require roads to be made passable at all times of year and as a result will entail an increase in taxes.

Here, Rousseau shows himself especially sensitive to the effects of the theater on different peoples with different manners and customs. There is no institution that is right for all people at all times. Under certain circumstances the presence of a theater may have tolerable, even beneficial, effects: "In certain places [theater] will be useful for attracting foreigners; for increasing the circulation of money; for stimulating artists; for varying the fashions; for occupying those who are too rich or aspire to be so; for making them less mischievous; for distracting the people from its miseries; for making it forget its leaders in seeing its buffoons; for maintaining and perfecting taste when decency is lost; for covering the ugliness of vice with the polish of forms; in a word, for preventing bad morals from degenerating into brigandage" (298).

Elsewhere—in Geneva, for example—the same institution may have completely different consequences: "In other places [theater] would only serve to destroy the love of work; to discourage industry; to ruin individuals; to inspire them with the taste for idleness; to make them seek for the means of subsistence without doing anything; to render a people inactive and slack; to prevent it from seeing the public and private goals with which it ought to busy itself; to turn prudence to ridicule; to substitute a theatrical jargon for the practice of the virtues; to make metaphysic of all morality; to turn citizens into wits, housewives into bluestockings, and daughters into sweethearts out of the drama" (298).

Some of his strongest words are directed against what Rousseau regards as the self-delusions fostered by the arts. Theaters affect our capacity for fellow feeling and expressing an active sympathy for others. We often regard attending a theater as a social event, but the opposite is actually the case. "People think they come together in the theater and it is there that they are isolated," Rousseau writes. "It is there that they go to forget their friends, neighbors, and relations in order to concern themselves with fables" (262). Theatrical productions are often praised for their capacity to extend our range of imaginative sympathies. Defenders of the theater claim that plays and other spectacles make better persons of us. We learn to sympathize with people we never knew by imaginatively putting ourselves in their shoes. In fact, the opposite is more likely the case. Rousseau is the first analyst of what is called compassion fatigue. Theatrical productions deplete our capacity for fellow feeling. The more sympathy we invest in a person on stage or on a movie screen, the less we have for those that are actually around us. Our very capacity to identify with a tragic hero on stage produces a smugness and self-satisfaction in the spectator that excuses him from fulfilling his duties to others. Rather than leading the spectator to do good, the effect is to wall us off into our own private narcissisms. "In the final accounting," Rousseau asks, "when a man has gone to admire fine actions in stories and to cry for imaginary miseries, what more can be asked of him? Is he not satisfied with himself? Does he not applaud his fine soul?" (269). Rather than teaching us to sympathize with others, the theater ends up teaching us to congratulate ourselves.

What seems to bother Rousseau most about the theater is that it is a form of falsehood and deception. Here he continues Plato's critique of poetry as mimesis, or imitation, in the *Republic*. Imitation is a form of deceit. Actors are adept at producing passions they do not feel. "What is the talent of the actor?" he asks. "It is the art of counterfeiting himself, or putting on another character than his own, of appearing different than he is, of becoming passionate in cold blood, of saying what he does not think as naturally as if he really did think it, and finally, of forgetting his own place by dint of taking another's" (309).

The problem with the theater is that it encourages a culture of deception, duplicity, and dishonesty, of pretending to be something we are not and furthering the gulf between "seeming" and "being." Our emotions cease to be our own and instead become filtered through the experience of certain theatrical or literary role models. The result is a loss of originality and hardy independence. At the core of Rousseau's critique is the belief that people are best when they have fewer distractions that agitate their imaginations. To make his point, Rousseau creates an imaginary comparison between the hustle and bustle of Parisian life and "the apparent inactivity and listlessness" of a provincial town. While in the capital cities "everything is judged by appearances because there is no leisure to examine anything," it is in the towns where true originality and even genius can emerge. Most inventions and discoveries come from the provinces, and because people are less dependent on each other there, all have the opportunity to develop their own endowments: "In a little town, proportionately less activity is unquestionably to be found than in a capital because the passions are less intense and the needs less pressing, but more original spirits, more inventive industry, more really new things are found there because the people are less imitative; having few models, each draws more from himself and puts more of his own into everything he does; because the human mind, less spread out, less drowned in vulgar opinions, elaborates itself and ferments better in tranquil solitude; because, in seeing less, more is imagined; finally, because less pressed for time, there is more leisure to extend and digest one's ideas" (295).

Most important of all, Rousseau warns against the effects of the theater on the relation between the sexes. "Do you want to know men?" Rousseau asks. "Study women" (311). No woman, he opines, will want to go to the theater without jewelry, designer clothing, wigs, and other luxury items. Theaters, art galleries, and other such places are designed for people who want to distinguish themselves, to stand out from the crowd, and who are willing to pay to do so, and this is especially true for women. The theater in large capital cities may be a harmless mode of distraction, but in small towns like Geneva it is an avatar of inequality and corruption. The corruption of women is probably the most dangerous consequence of a theater.

The theater imposes an intimacy on men and women—sitting together in the dark—that contributes to the breakdown of healthy gender differentiation. Rousseau praises the Genevan habit of maintaining men and women on what might be called a "separate but equal" footing. In Geneva as in Sparta, women rule, albeit indirectly, by setting examples of chastity, modesty, and care for their husbands and children. The result of prolonged intimacy is that men and women become more alike, more functionally interchangeable. This is especially true in the Parisian salons run by women. Here men and women have actually come to take on one another's habits: "As for us," Rousseau remarks of men, "we have taken on entirely contrary ways; meanly devoted to the wills of the sex which we ought to protect and not serve, we have learned to despise it in obeying it, to insult it by our derisive attentions; and every woman at Paris gathers in her apartment a harem of men more womanish than she" (326).

Not only have men become more feminine, women have become more masculine. The natural virtue of the woman, Rousseau speculates, is modesty. The ancients paid tribute to this virtue by maintaining a respectful silence about women in their theater and public oratory. Thucydides captured some of this when he put in the mouth of Pericles his advice to the war widows at the very end of his famous Funeral Oration. "Great will be your glory," he said, "in not falling short of your natural character and greatest will be hers who is least talked of among men whether for good or for bad."[25] For we moderns, however, it is the opposite that has become the case: "The most esteemed woman is the one who has the greatest renown, about whom the most is said, who is the most often seen in society, at whose home one dines the most, who most imperiously sets the tone, who judges, resolves, decides, pronounces, assigns talents, merit, and virtues their degrees and places, and whose favor is most ignominiously begged for by humble, learned men. . . . Actually, in society they do not know anything, although they judge everything" (286).

Rousseau's concerns about the moral effects of the theater and actors were by no means simply a peculiarity. Half a century after the *Letter* was written, Jane Austen wrote a novel, *Mansfield Park,* in which the theme of theatricals is central. Mansfield Park is a perfectly self-contained community—much like Clarens in Rousseau's *La nouvelle Héloïse*—and the introduction of theatricals is a portent of disharmony and decay. With Sir Thomas Bertram, the head of the household, away, his wife, children, and some newly imported London visitors introduce these theatricals as a way of relieving the boredom of country life. The play in question is *Lover's Vows,* based on the work of the German playwright August von Kutzeube's work dealing with extramarital sex and illegitimate birth. Only Edmund and Fanny Price (Sir Thomas's niece and the heroine of the book) resist, but eventually even Edmund is overcome, and this represents an abdication of his true self in order to become a role player. Only Fanny is left as the exponent of true judgment and clear-sightedness, until Sir Thomas reappears and is able to reassert patriarchal authority over

the estate. Fanny Price may not be one of Jane Austen's most popular hero-
ines, but she was surely a woman after Rousseau's own heart—modest, quiet,
reticent to the point of immobility, and a defender of traditional values. I think
she is the character in any of Austen's novels that Rousseau would have most
admired.

ROUSSEAU AS LEGISLATOR

In a classic article entitled "Rousseau's Images of Authority," Judith Shklar
discusses Rousseau's great authority figures.[26] The first and most obvious is
the Legislator in the *Social Contract*. Rousseau describes this figure as "a superior intelligence who saw all of man's passions and experienced none of
them." Such a person is able to give shape to the general will by force of personality alone. In a famous passage Rousseau describes him as able "to persuade without convincing" and capable of "changing human nature" by
fashioning a people.[27] The second figure is the tutor in *Emile*. Emile's tutor is
a figure who guides his student's life from earliest childhood to the birth of
his first child. He is the deus ex machina who is able to arrange every aspect
of Emile's life without appearing to do so. And finally there is the figure of
the Baron Wolmar in *La nouvelle Héloïse*. Wolmar is the perfect godlike figure who is the hidden hand behind the vast estate at Clarens where Julie and
Saint-Preux are able to carry out their innocent pastimes. Like the Legislator,
Wolmar is distinguished by an absence of all passion—he is a bloodless
atheist—except the desire for order, regularity, security, and fairness.

There is, of course, one more authority figure in Rousseau's writings, namely,
Rousseau himself. Rousseau not only exercised authority over his own works,
he also served as a practical legislator. He was approached by members of the
Polish nobility to write a constitution for their country. He also wrote a constitutional project for Corsica, which in the *Social Contract* he had called "the
one country left in Europe capable of receiving legislation."[28] And he served
as a legislator for his own city of Geneva most directly in the Dedicatory Letter to the *Second Discourse* and in the *Letter to d'Alembert*. He wrote the *Letter*
not as a contributor to the European Republic of Letters but as the Citoyen
de Genève. It is his most public-spirited book.

Rousseau always takes as his model for statecraft the small, free city-states
of Greece and the Roman Republic. His one positive example of the theater
comes from the Greeks. Rousseau contrasts the dark and exclusive character
of modern theaters with the open-air festivals of the ancients. For the Greeks,

theater was a form of public celebration: "These great and proud entertainments, given under the sky before a whole nation, presented on all sides only combats, victories, prizes, objects capable of inspiring the Greeks with an ardent emulation of warming their hearts with sentiments of honor and glory" (308).

The theater in Greece could be salutary because it celebrated the most solemn, the most sacred, moments of the people's history. The theater was an expression of the patriotic sentiment; its purpose was not to mock but to educate: "The example of ancient Athens, a city incomparably more populous than Geneva, presents us with a striking lesson; it was in the theater that the exile of many great men and the death of Socrates was prepared for; it was by the violence of the theater that Athens was lost, and its disasters justified only too well the chagrin to which Solon gave witness at the first performances of Thespis. What is quite certain for us is that it will be an ill omen for the Republic when we see the citizens, disguised as wits, setting themselves to composing French verses and theatrical plays, talents which are not ours and which we will never possess" (340).

The difference between the ancient and the modern theater is that for the ancients, the entire people were engaged, while for the moderns the theater and the arts have become elite activities that further exacerbate inequalities. Theaters in Greece were communal festivals much like the grape harvest Rousseau describes in *La nouvelle Héloïse*.[29] "Ought there to be no entertainments in a Republic?" he asks, to which he answers: "On the contrary, there ought to be many. It is in republics that they were born, it is in their bosom that they are seen to flourish with a truly festive air. . . . It is in the open air, under the sky, that you ought to gather and give yourselves to the sweet sentiment of your happiness. Let your pleasure not be effeminate or mercenary; let nothing that has an odor of constraint and selfishness poison them; let them be free and generous like you are, let the sun illuminate your innocent entertainments; you will constitute one yourselves, the worthiest it can illuminate" (343–44). Rousseau would like to see such indigenous Genevan activities as horseback riding, rowing, and swordplay turned into public spectacles and citizens turned into active participants rather than passive spectators.

Rousseau's plans to establish public festivals—which figure prominently in his constitution for Poland—were among his most influential ideas. Recall the role of such festivals during the French Revolution. In the *Considerations on the Government of Poland,* Rousseau gives advice on how lawgivers today might establish the reign of opinion on which any nation is based. In the second section of the *Considerations,* he begins by contrasting ancient and modern systems of legislation, noting that in modern nations there are "many lawmakers but not a single lawgiver." Among the ancient lawgivers, he distinguishes three—Moses, Lycurgus, and Numa—from which the moderns have most to learn. His remarks on Moses are especially noteworthy. Rousseau's Moses, like Machiavelli's and Spinoza's, is almost entirely a secular figure who created a people out of sheer dint of will. Here, Rousseau observes how Moses dared to make a "national body" from a people who "had not an inch of territory of their own" and who were "a troop of strangers on the face of the earth." Moses succeeded by giving a set of laws and ritual practices that set the Jews apart from all other peoples and that created ritual bonds that continued to exist even after centuries of exile: "That is how this singular nation, so often subjugated, so often scattered and apparently destroyed, yet ever idolizing its rule, has nevertheless maintained itself down to our days, scattered among the other nations without ever merging with them, and how its morals, its laws, its rites subsist and will endure as long as the world itself does, in spite of the hatred and persecution by the rest of mankind."[30]

Rousseau believes that the Jewish example can serve as a model for the Poles. The Poles may not be scattered, but they live under the hegemony of Russia, their powerful neighbor to the east. How is it, Rousseau asks, that the Poles can remain free, even if they find themselves unable to exert political sovereignty? "It is national institutions," he writes, "which form the genius, the character, the tastes, and the morals of a people, which make it be itself and not another."[31] Only by giving a people their own national institutions can a lawgiver "raise their souls to the level of the souls of the ancients." Among the practices that Rousseau recommends is, first of all, providing for a common mode of education. All activities, crucially including play, should be carried out in public and under the eye of watchful guardians. A distinctive mode of national dress should be adopted to foster a spirit of independence ("let no Pole dare show himself at court dressed in the French fashion"). Ceremonies should be created replete with honors and public rewards to Poles—like those at the Confederation of Bar—who sacrificed in the cause of national independence. National sports and games must be championed and courtly entertainments like the theater and opera discouraged. Horsemanship and the use of firearms, Rousseau argues, suit the Polish character and make for "dazzling spectacle." All of these are necessary for the legislator to create the "national physiognomy" that will distinguish the Poles from all other peoples.[32]

The ideal form of such public spectacles is treated in a lengthy footnote near the very end of the *Letter* in which Rousseau recalls an incident—whether apocryphal or not—from his childhood. Here, he remembers how what began as a drunken soldiers' brawl turned into a festival celebrating the virtues of community and the patriotic spirit:

> I remember having been struck in my childhood by a rather simple entertainment, the impression of which has nevertheless always stayed with me in spite of time and variety of experience. The regiment of Saint-Gervais had done its exercises, and according to the custom, they had supped by companies; most of those who formed them gathered after supper in the St. Gervais square and started dancing all together, officers and soldiers, around the fountain, to the basin of which the drummers, the fifers and the torch bearers had mounted. A dance of men, cheered by a long meal, would seem to present nothing very interesting to see; however, the harmony of five or six hundred men in uniform, holding one another by the hand and forming a long ribbon which wound around, serpent-like, in cadence and without confusion, with countless turns and returns, countless sorts of figured evolutions, the excellence of the tunes which animated them, the sound of the drums, the glare of the torches, a certain military pomp in the midst of the pleasure, all this created a very lively sensation that could not be experienced coldly. . . . My father, embracing me, was seized with trembling which I think I still feel and share. "Jean-Jacques," he said to me, "love your country. Do you see these good Genevans? They are all friends, they are all brothers; joy and concord reign in their midst. You are a Genevan; one day you will see other peoples; but even if you should travel as much as your father, you will not find their likes." (351)

Here, we find all of Rousseau's favorite themes condensed in a single image: the military character of the event, the initial meal followed by music and dance, the patriotic presence of men in uniform, the presence of the father figure, and the temporary sense of equality created by the celebration. Who, Rousseau seems to say, could ask for more?

ANCIENT OR MODERN?

Rousseau's critique of the theater may seem quaint, even laughable, today, but it portends a vital current of modern thought—the national idea—that deeply shaped the Counter-Enlightenment. In attacking the theater, Rousseau was attacking the cosmopolitanism of the Enlightenment as represented by the free development of the arts and letters. Rousseau saw in the development of this Republic of Letters a new kind of cosmopolitanism hostile to the exclusive and particularistic spirit of the nation. His assault on the cosmopolitan civilization of his age prepared the way for the nineteenth and twentieth centuries' religion of the nation. His appeal to the indigenous cultures of distinct peoples—Poles, Swiss, Corsicans—based on their diverse languages, manners, habits, and customs made him a prophet of the ideal of national self-determination that would come to occupy so much of modern thought.

It is often said that Rousseau's appeal to nationalist and patriotic sentiment represents a rejection of modernity in the name of the small city-state of antiquity. This is the basis of the liberal critique of Rousseau, from Benjamin Constant to Isaiah Berlin, namely, that he endorsed a new kind of tribalism that was ultimately responsible for the collectivist tyrannies of the twentieth century.[33] There is little evidence to support this claim, but what is more important, it fails to grasp Rousseau's intention. Rousseau's critique of the modern Republic of Letters was undertaken in the name of the nation. Nationalism is a distinctively modern phenomenon and no older than the late eighteenth century. There had, of course, always been peoples divided by language, ancestry, and territory, but never in the past did these divisions coincide with political ones. Empires and states were not homogenous linguistic or cultural groupings but juristic or territorial ones. Political units were often smaller than national units, as in the case of the Greek city-states, or were often larger than national units, as in the case of the large multinational empires like that of the Hapsburgs or the Holy Roman Empire. The new idea of the nation changed all of this. Rousseau made it possible to believe that the national grouping and the political grouping should be one and the same.[34]

Rousseau is the theoretician of this bizarre hybrid—a first in political history—called the nation-state. The nation-state was conceived as an acceptable middle ground between the polis and the empire, the two previously dominant forms of political organization. How to combine a nation, or people, with a state, or a political apparatus? To complete this act of unification, the people would have to be shorn of their previous theological, ethnic, and tribal identities and transformed into a nation exercising the right of legislation. Only the people in their collective capacity—not kings or legislatures—are sovereign, Rousseau argued in the *Social Contract*. The nation would cease to be simply a collection of people who over time had acquired certain common characteristics; it would be a body of persons in whom sovereignty resided. It was not enough to be a citizen of Languedoc or Picardy or Provence; one had to be a citizen of France. "What is a nation?" asked the Abbé Sieyès. "It is a body of associates living under a common law, represented by the same legislature."[35] This definition successfully combined the nation's claim to be self-determining along with the political unity of the state. A nation was that body that could represent or elect representatives for the state. "With some notable exceptions," Robert Wokler has written, "the modern state is of its essence a nation-state, in which nationality is defined politically and political power is held to express the national will."[36] The political form that has appeared since the eighteenth century—with some notable prodding from the French Revolution—has been known as the democratic republic.

Rousseau might be called the creator of the nation-state, and yet his creation of something new began with a return to something old, to the spirit if not the letter of antiquity. His models of patriotism and love of country are drawn exclusively from the world of Greece and Rome. What he admired—or said he admired—was the spirit of self-sacrifice found in the devotion to law, constitution, and military victory characteristic of ancient Sparta. His paradigm of the citizen is drawn from the famous story of the Spartan mother as told by Plutarch: "A Spartan woman had five sons in the army and was awaiting news of the battle. A Helot arrives; trembling she asks him for news. 'Your five sons were killed.' 'Base slave, did I ask you that?' 'We won the victory.' The mother runs to the temple and gives thanks to the gods."[37]

Rousseau's use of the Spartan mother would seem to support the contention of Constant and Berlin that Rousseau's politics were antimodern in the extreme. Yet for Rousseau, this kind of Spartan self-renunciation may be heroic, though no longer fitting for modern times, where he believes manners have become milder and gentler, where man is no longer simply a citoyen but a bourgeois. Sparta may be an ideal, but it is irretrievably lost. It is important to remember it as an example of what people once were, but it is no longer practically realizable, or even desirable, as a goal toward which to aspire. It is simply beyond our grasp.

Rousseau protested the Enlightenment in the name of the national idea that he conceived along the lines of a wide diversity of cultures, each with its own unique spirit. He helped to plant the seed of the idea that a nation's spirit is the product of its history, of the social, economic, and political factors that combine to make a people what they are. According to this view, man is a being that has no nature, only a history, that humanity is whatever it makes of itself or might become. It is the very plasticity of human nature that accounts for our moral and political diversity. Here as in so much else, Rousseau's true forerunner was Montesquieu, whose *l'esprit générale d'une nation* is at the basis of what is often thought of as liberal pluralism.[38]

Rousseau thought of nationalism as having a higher dignity than the cosmopolitanism of the Enlightenment. What he protested was not true cosmopolitanism, which he thought was a rare and precious thing, but a kind of sham universalism that, he warned, portended a new kind of individual, really a new kind of human being, that he was the first to isolate and define as the bourgeois.[39] Rousseau may not have coined the term "bourgeois," but he brought it into prominence. Although he did not exactly define the term, it would not be long until the bourgeois came to be viewed as a social climber, a hypocrite, and a philistine, the kind of person who wants to be seen at the theater but who falls asleep promptly after the curtain has gone up. The bourgeois, as Rousseau understands the term, is a product of the Enlightenment and, despite national differences, will be the same whether speaking of France, England, Germany, or America. We shall all come to have common tastes, common amusements, and common sentiments. "There are no more Frenchmen, Germans, Spaniards, even Englishmen nowadays," Rousseau wrote, "regardless of what people may say; there are only Europeans. All have the same tastes, the same passions, the same morals because none has been given a national form by a distinctive institution."[40]

Rousseau typically contrasts the cosmopolitanism of the bourgeois to the exclusiveness of the citizen. The citizen is animated by a powerful sense of membership and belonging to a people; the bourgeois can be at home anywhere. The ethic of citizenship is the love of country, while the ethic of the bourgeois is love of humanity. "The patriotic spirit is an exclusive spirit," Rousseau wrote in a letter to Leonhard Usteri, "which makes us look on everyone but our fellow citizens as strangers, and almost as enemies."[41] The very language of citizenship—of loyalty, self-sacrifice, and virtue—is foreign to his ears. Rousseau knew that the modern era would be the bourgeois era; the only question was what form this era would take. The dissatisfaction with this particular form of individual would form the basis of European social and political thought for the next century. All of the great thinkers who come after Rousseau, from Kant and Hegel to Tocqueville and Marx to Mill and Nietzsche, would grapple with this problem, the problem that Rousseau bequeathed.

Chapter 10 Tocqueville's America

If we could first know *where* we are, and *whither* we are tending, we could then better judge *what* to do, and *how* to do it.
—Abraham Lincoln

Tocqueville was the first great thinker of the postrevolutionary period to apply Rousseau's critique of the Enlightenment to the conditions of modern democracy. Rousseau was, on Tocqueville's own account, one of the three writers—the others being Pascal and Montesquieu—who most decisively shaped his thinking.[1] At first glance, the pairing is not obvious: Rousseau, the writer who foretold an age of revolution, and Tocqueville, the man who hoped to put an end to it. Rousseau, we have seen, wrote in praise of small republics, both ancient and modern, Sparta, early Rome, and modern Geneva. Tocqueville focused his attention on modern America, a large, diffuse, middle-class democracy. Rousseau extolled the republic as the site of the self-sacrificing subordination of the interests of the individual to the public good of the community. Tocqueville emphasizes the individualism, materialism, and ethic of "self-interest well understood" as the characteristic features of modern bourgeois democracy. Rousseau—at least the Rousseau of the *Social Contract*—excoriates the "intermediary bodies" that separate the individual from the general will, while Tocqueville has become the great apostle of "civil associations" as the key to modern democracy, the germ cell out of which public-spiritedness develops.[2]

Despite their evident differences, Rousseau and Tocqueville were prophets of a new age. As Françoise Mélonio has argued, Tocqueville is above all a prophet of democracy in "the very French prophetic line that began with Rousseau."[3] When Tocqueville wrote in the Introduction to *Democracy in America* that "a new political science is needed for a world altogether new," he may well have been reflecting upon Rousseau's comment in the *Social Contract* that "every legitimate government is republican."[4] Tocqueville recognized that modern political science would necessarily be the science of democracy. The question he posed with unremitting clarity is what would the democracy of the future look like? Would it be peaceful and moderate as it had been in America or would it be disorderly and chaotic as in Europe? Would it provide for liberty and an equality open to talents or would it become tyrannical and suspicious of all differences? These were the questions left unresolved by the great revolutions of the modern age, to which Tocqueville hoped to provide answers.

TOCQUEVILLE'S *IDÉE MÈRE*

What kind of book is *Democracy in America?* Is it even accurate to call it a book at all? Was its author, in the famous phrase of Isaiah Berlin, a hedgehog or a fox, a man with one big idea or many small ones? This simple question conceals a host of problems. As is well known, the book was written in two large installments five years apart. There is scarcely a page that does not bring forth some startling generalization or revealing aperçu. Despite the fact that Tocqueville used the same title for both books and that they now appear, at least in English-language editions, within a single volume, Tocqueville scholars have often referred to the books as *Democracy I* and *Democracy II,* published respectively in 1835 and 1840.[5]

Further complicating the difficulties is the vast range of topics treated in both volumes, ranging from historical themes such as the Puritan origins of American democracy, the federal structure of the Constitution, and the three races that inhabit the continent in the first volume to the influence of democracy on the intellectual, moral, and psychological lives of its citizens in the second volume. Briefly summarized, one could say that *Democracy I* deals with the social structure and political institutions of American democracy, while *Democracy II* deals with the cultural life of democracy and the general differences between democracy and aristocracy understood as two fundamentally different regime types.

There is in the United States a textbook image of Tocqueville as a young French aristocrat who came to America with his friend Gustave de Beaumont to study the prison system and found himself utterly transformed by his ten-month contact with the New World. Nothing could be farther from the truth. The idea for the *Democracy,* the germ cell of the book, as it were, had already been hatched long before Tocqueville even stepped off the boat. In a letter to Louis de Kergolay written on the eve of the publication of *Democracy I,* Tocqueville wrote:

> It is not without having carefully reflected that I decided to write the book I am just now publishing. I do not hide from myself what is annoying in my position: it is bound to attract active sympathy from no one. Some will find that at bottom I do not like democracy and that I am severe toward it; others will think that I favor its development imprudently. It would be most fortunate for me if the book were not read, and that is a piece of good fortune that may come to pass. I know all that, but this is my response: nearly ten years ago I was already thinking about part of the things I have just now set forth. I was in America only to become clear on this point. The penitentiary system was just a pretext.[6]

If one does the math, it would appear that Tocqueville's idea for the book—in fact the idea that would become Tocqueville's life work—was conceived as early as 1825 when its author was only around twenty years old, the same age as a college undergraduate. Far from being transformed by his contact with democracy, Tocqueville came to America to see confirmed what he had already suspected. This suspicion is confirmed in a letter to John Stuart Mill in which he said: "America was only the frame; my picture was Democracy."[7]

Tocqueville returns to this theme in his Introduction to the *Democracy,* in which he apologizes for the apparently random and haphazard appearance of the book and the lack of documentary evidence to support his claims. Appearances to the contrary, he assures the reader, the book has been organized around a single *idée mère:* "I think those who want to regard it closely will find, in the entire work, a mother thought that so to speak links all its parts. But the diversity of the objects I had to treat is very great, and whoever undertakes to oppose an isolated fact to the sum of facts I cite or a detached idea to the sum of ideas will succeed without difficulty. I should therefore wish that one do me the favor of reading me in the same spirit that presided over my work, and that one judge this book, by the general impression it leaves, just as I myself decided, not by such and such a reason, but by the mass of reasons" (Intro., 14–15).

Just what was Tocqueville's idée mère, and how did it structure the *Democracy* as a whole? Perhaps the simplest answer is contained in the book's opening sentence: "Among the new objects that attracted my attention during my stay in the United States, none struck my eye more vividly than the equality of conditions" (Intro., 3). It is the equality of social conditions that Tocqueville refers to as a "generative fact" from which everything else arises. He treats equality not simply as an isolated phenomenon or one fact among others but as nothing less than the root cause of an entire way of life, a new form of civilization.

It is in the United States, Tocqueville opines, that the fact of equality has at present reached its outer limits. This is not to say that the form of democracy in America is somehow complete. Far from it. Democracy is not a condition but a process. It has the quality that Rousseau described as *perfectibilité,* namely, an almost infinite elasticity and openness to change. It is less a determinate way of life than a perpetual work in progress. We do not yet know where the process of democratization will end or what shape it will take elsewhere. It is revealing that Tocqueville called his book *Democracy in America,* perhaps recalling Burke's *Reflection on the Revolution in France.* His point is not that democracy is a peculiarly American phenomenon, just as Burke's was not that the revolution is peculiarly French, but rather that this is the form that the democratic revolution has taken in America. What form it will take elsewhere will be dependent on time, circumstance, and statesmanship.

Nowhere are Tocqueville's concerns with the future shape of democracy more in evidence that in his analysis of the dangers posed to human liberty by the rise of a new kind of administrative despotism. In *Democracy I* Tocqueville treated the problem of the "tyranny of the majority" largely in terms inherited from Aristotle and the *Federalist Papers.* The danger to be confronted was of a mobilized majority faction able to ignore the rights of the minority. This image was inseparable from the threats of revolutionary or "charismatic" military leaders like Andrew Jackson and Napoleon capable of mobilizing the masses in fits of patriotic zeal.

In *Democracy II,* however, the very terms of Tocqueville's analysis have changed. Tocqueville no longer even uses the term "tyranny of the majority," speaking instead of a new kind of soft, or mild, "administrative despotism." The very language of a soft despotism—redolent of Montesquieu's *doux commerce*—is intended to shock. How can despotism be mild? How can it soften? The fear is not of a Neronian tyrant or a mobilized and intolerant majority but of a passive and apathetic population who no longer even think of themselves as citizens. The change of terminology indicates the awareness of an entirely new problem. Tocqueville himself indicated awareness of this change of perspective. "In this painting lies all the originality and profundity of my idea," he wrote in a marginal note near the end of *Democracy II.* "What I wrote at the end of my first work was trite and superficial."[8]

THE TYRANNY OF THE MAJORITY

Tocqueville's first analysis of tyranny is contained principally in part 2, chapter 7, of *Democracy I.* To be sure, the concept of democratic tyranny is hardly new. In the *Politics,* Aristotle associated democracy with rule of the many, generally the poor, for their own interests. The danger of democracy was precisely that it represented the self-interested rule of one class of the community, the majority, over the minority. Democracy was thus always potentially a form of class rule of the poor over the rich, often egged on by populist demagogues.

The dangers of the tyranny of the majority were also considered by the *Federalist* authors, for whom democracy was always associated with the unstable polities of ancient Greece and Rome. While the *Federalist Papers* often invoked classical precedent and even invoked the pseudonym "Publius," for one of the founders of the Roman Republic, its authors were more impressed with what distinguished the modern American experiment from its ancient predecessors. "It is impossible to read the history of the petty republics of Greece and Italy without feeling sensations of horror and disgust at the distractions with which they were continually agitated," Hamilton wrote, "and at the rapid succession of revolutions by which they were kept in a state of perpetual vibration between the extremes of tyranny and anarchy."[9] The *Federalist*'s solution to the problem of majority faction was to "enlarge the orbit" of popular government in order to prevent the creation of a permanent and intractable majority opinion. The greater the number of factions, the less likely any one of them would be able to exercise despotic control over national politics.

Tocqueville's chapter "On the Omnipotence of the Majority in the United States and Its Effects" should be read as a direct reply to *Federalist* No. 10. The U.S. Constitution had enshrined the majority ("We the People") even as it sought to limit its power through institutions like the Electoral College and the indirect election of senators. Although Tocqueville had devoted a lengthy chapter to the federal structure of the Constitution (I.i.8 [105–61]), he is clearly less confident than the *Federalist* authors that the problem of majority faction has been solved. While the *Federalist* believed that institutional means could be found that would limit the power of majorities, Tocqueville was much less sanguine that constitutional means alone would be sufficient. In particular, he was skeptical of the efficacy of constitutional checks and balances to constrain the "restlessness" (*inquiétude*) of democratic majorities.[10] Rather than regarding majorities in Madisonian terms as shifting coalitions of interest groups, he tended to identify the power of the majority with the theory of unlimited popular sovereignty. Legal guarantees of minority rights were not likely to be effective in the face of mobilized mass opinion.

The omnipotence of the majority—a term with clear theological overtones intended to convey the doctrine of divine omnipotence—is a direct consequence of the democratic doctrine of the sovereignty of the people (I.i.4 [53–55]). This principle, which Tocqueville admits is "always more or less at the foundation of almost all human institutions," only comes into its own in democratic times. What in other societies "lies buried" or remains hidden in "the darkness of the sanctuary" here becomes sanctified in law and established in mores. Tocqueville offers the following as a definition: "In America, the principle of the sovereignty of the people is not hidden or sterile as in certain nations; it is recognized by mores, proclaimed by the laws; it spreads with freedom and reaches its final consequences without obstacle. If there is a single country in the world where one can hope to appreciate the dogma of the sovereignty of the people at its just value, to study it in its application to the affairs of society, and to judge its advantages and its dangers, that country is surely America" (I.i.4 [53]).

The idea of popular sovereignty that in France had been, at most, a rallying cry of radicals or a dream of visionaries like Rousseau had become an almost commonplace reality in the United States. It was not until the rise of Jacksonian democracy, however, that the fear of majority tyranny began to be heard. Jackson was the American equivalent of Bonaparte, a military conqueror riding to power on the wings of popular support. More than anything, Tocqueville feared militarism combined with a kind of unlimited patriotic zeal. It was only in America that one could begin to see not only the enno-bling qualities of equality and popular sovereignty but also the more ominous possibilities contained within the concept.

It is the "dogma" of popular sovereignty that is the true cause of the "em-pire of the majority" (I.ii.7 [235]). The phrase suggests that not only does the majority carry strength of numbers, it also accrues moral authority to itself. It is the moral authority of majoritarianism that Tocqueville finds so troubling. "I regard as impious and detestable the maxim that in matters of government the majority of a people has the right to do absolutely everything," he declares (I.ii.7 [240]). The empire of the majority makes itself felt first of all through the dominance of the legislature. "Of all political powers," Tocqueville writes, "the legislature is the one that obeys the majority most willingly" (I.ii.7 [236]). Contrary to the *Federalist*'s conception of checks and balances that would keep any one branch of government from dominating the others, Tocqueville re-gards the legislative branch as exercising a despotic supremacy over the others that has the force of numbers behind it.

Tocqueville is overall less impressed than Madison with the distinction be-tween democracies that are ruled directly by the people and republics that are ruled indirectly through the people's representatives. Americans keep their rep-resentatives on a very short leash by insisting on short terms and precise man-dates. "It is as if, except for the tumult, the majority were deliberating in the public square" (I.ii.7 [236]). In a dramatic moment in the text, Tocqueville cites Jefferson's warning in a letter to Madison that "the tyranny of the legislatures is the most formidable dread at present and will be for long years." Tocqueville regards this warning as especially perspicuous because in Jefferson one finds "the most powerful apostle that democracy has ever had" (I.ii.7 [249]).

The moral authority of the majority asserts its dominance on the basis of two alleged facts. The first is "the idea that there is more enlightenment and wisdom in many men united than in one alone." This is, of course, a variant of Aristotle's claim about the "wisdom of the crowd." In matters of public de-liberation, just as in a potluck dinner, many chefs with a range of culinary skills may be superior to the meal created by one chef alone.[11] Tocqueville re-gards this as "the theory of equality applied to intellects" (I.ii.7 [236]). There may be strength in numbers, but not necessarily truth. The second is the idea that in matters effecting public policy the interests of the many should always take priority over those of the few. It is precisely the "omnipotence" of the majority, not any particular public policy, that Tocqueville finds "dire and dangerous for the future" (I.ii.7 [237]).

What precisely are the dangers that Tocqueville fears? As the title of his chapter indicates, Tocqueville's main interest is not with the causes of tyranny but with its effects. In the classical analysis of tyranny from Aristotle to Montesquieu, tyrannical government was invariably identified with arbitrary rule, being under the arbitrary whim of a person or body of persons, whether they be one, few, or many. The antidote to tyranny was the rule of law, which implies some idea of impartiality or fair treatment under known rules. But Tocqueville notes here a peculiar feature of democratic institutions. "One must distinguish well arbitrariness from tyranny," he writes. "Tyranny can be exercised by means of law itself, and then it is not arbitrariness; arbitrariness can be exercised in the interest of the governed, and then it is not tyrannical" (I.ii.7 [242]). It is at the moment when the majority translates its will into law that the formula for tyranny is defined.

Tocqueville is aware that the effects of majority rule are more likely to be felt at the local rather than the national level. Although early in *Democracy I* he praised local self-government and the New England *communes* as the seedbed of freedom, he is also deeply aware of how intolerant local majorities can violate rights. He illustrates this point by means of a pair of examples. The first concerns two antiwar journalists in Baltimore during the War of 1812 when pro-war opinion was running high. The two journalists were arrested for their opposition to the war, taken to prison, and under the cover of darkness murdered by a mob. Those who participated in the crime were subsequently exonerated by a jury of their peers (I.ii.7 [241–42]). Tocqueville tells another story, of how even in Quaker Pennsylvania freed Negroes were unable to vote because of popular prejudice against them. He sums up this situation with the following barb: "What! The majority that has the privilege of making the law still wants to have that of disobeying the law!" (I.ii.7 [242]). No more chilling story could be told of the dangers of the omnipotence of the majority.

It is, however, in the realm of thought and opinion that the majority exercises its greatest control. In an always-startling passage, Tocqueville asserts: "I do not know any country where, in general, less independence of mind and genuine freedom of discussion reign than in America" (I.ii.7 [244]). The dangers to freedom of thought come not from the fear of an Inquisition or the auto-da-fé but in the more subtle forms of exclusion and social ostracism. Tocqueville is perhaps the first and still one of the most perceptive analysts of what today would be called the power of "political correctness."

Tocqueville's statement that there is less freedom of discussion in America than in any other country known to him is clearly an overstatement intended to shock the complacent. Tocqueville's point is that persecution can take many forms from the cruelest as exemplified by the Spanish Inquisition to the most mild. It is the very mildness—a term that Tocqueville uses throughout the *Democracy*—of democratic exclusion that he regards as exercising a profoundly chilling effect on the free expression of unpopular beliefs: "Chains and executioners are the coarse instruments that tyranny formerly employed; but in our day civilization has perfected even despotism itself, which seemed, indeed, to have nothing more to learn. Princes had so to speak made violence material; democratic republics in our day have rendered it just as intellectual as the human will that it wants to constrain. Under the absolute government of one alone, despotism struck the body crudely, so as to reach the soul, and the soul, escaping from those blows, rose gloriously above it; but in democratic republics, tyranny does not proceed in this way; it leaves the body and goes straight for the soul" (I.ii.7 [244]).

Like other liberals of his era such as Lord Macaulay and John Stuart Mill, Tocqueville believes that democracy and the freedom of the press can actually exert a perversely chastening effect on the free expression of beliefs. Fiery individualism and love of truth, as Isaiah Berlin once wrote, grow at least as often in illiberal societies—the Puritan communities of Scotland and New England and even under conditions of military discipline—as they do in more tolerant or indifferent ages.[12] Moreover, societies with aristocratic traditions and privileges are often more hospitable to forms of satire and mockery than democratic populations that live in a state of "perpetual adoration" (I.ii.7 [245]). Thinking no doubt of himself, Tocqueville writes that "only foreigners or experience" will be able to bring home certain uncomfortable truths to the Americans.

THE DANGERS OF CENTRALIZATION

The difference between the accounts of tyranny in *Democracy I* and *Democracy II* could not be more striking. "Fear of despotism was Tocqueville's own earliest and most powerful political passion," Jean-Claude Lamberti has written, but the locus of despotic power changed dramatically in the five years separating the publication of the two *Democracies*.[13]

Tocqueville's 1835 account of the tyranny of the majority remained tied to a fear of mobocracy, or mob rule. The danger of the "mobocratic spirit," as

Abraham Lincoln called it, was certainly a theme of the *Federalist*'s legacy, with its fear of the direct participation of the people in legislation. The dangers of mob psychology were never far from the *Federalist*'s mind. "Had every Athenian been a Socrates," James Madison warned, "every Athenian assembly would still have been a mob."[14] More to the point, the fear of tyranny was a consequence of the memory of the National Convention during the French Revolution. Revolution and tyranny were virtually synonymous with each other for the first generation of postrevolutionary writers like Constant, François Guizot, and Pierre Paul Royer-Collard.[15] But by the time Tocqueville wrote his 1840 account of tyranny, either the memory or the fear of revolution (or both) had begun to wane. An important chapter from *Democracy II* was called "Why Great Revolutions Will Become Rare" (II.iii.21 [606–17]). It is doubtful that Tocqueville would have written that five years earlier.

What accounts for Tocqueville's change of mind? As the dangers of revolutionary violence and mob rule began to wane in Tocqueville's mind, a new threat gradually arose to take its place. This was the danger of the centralization of power. Tocqueville is often read as a critic of centralization and a defender of local self-government. To be sure, this is not incorrect, although it grasps only a part of the picture. Tocqueville did not, as did Montesquieu, eulogize the place of the provincial parlements and other intermediary institutions as the basis of political liberty. He was deeply aware of the injustice of this system and saw many benefits in having a unified center of law. It is not the growth of state power per se that bothers Tocqueville but the rise of bureaucracy and with it the growth of the centralizing spirit. Exactly what Hegel, almost twenty years before, had seen as a professional class educated to take over the care and administration of the state, Tocqueville came to regard as the most serious threat to political liberty.

The theme of centralization is a constant in Tocqueville's thought, not only linking the two volumes of the *Democracy* but also providing the connection between the *Democracy* and his other great work, *The Old Regime and the Revolution*. The issue of centralization emerges early in *Democracy I* with Tocqueville's distinction between political centralization and administrative centralization (I.i.5 [82–93]). Tocqueville regarded political or governmental centralization as a good thing. The idea of a uniform center of legislation was greatly to be preferred to any system of competing or overlapping sovereignties. Governmental centralization took hold in France under the rule of Louis XIV, and in England one sees it brought to a very high degree (I.i.5 [83]).

It is in America, however, that this process has been brought to its "highest point," eclipsing even the monarchies of Europe. Political centralization is a consequence of legislative supremacy such that "no state legislature has to contend with any power capable of resisting it." State legislatures continually accrue power to themselves, just as the French revolutionary assemblies did earlier. Yet far from decrying this fact, Tocqueville applauds it. "For my part," he contends, "I cannot conceive that a nation can live or above all prosper without strong governmental centralization" (I.i.5 [83]).

The danger is not with centralization as such but with a particular species of centralization, namely, administrative centralization. In both England and America, Tocqueville writes, political centralization may exist to the highest degree, but a centralized administrative structure is more or less unknown. What does this distinction amount to? Tocqueville regards a centralized sovereign as necessary for the promulgation of common laws that pertain equally and equitably to all ("the government called mixed has always seemed to me to be a chimera" [I.ii.7 (240)]). Governmental centralization is necessary to ensure that equal justice is afforded to every citizen. Administrative centralization is another matter. The science of administration concerns not the establishment of common rules but the oversight of the details of conduct and the direction of the everyday affairs of citizens. It represents the slow penetration by the bureaucracy into every aspect of daily affairs. While governmental centralization is necessary for the purposes of lawmaking and national defense, centralized administration is mainly preventative and produces nothing but languid and apathetic citizens.

Administrative centralization carries with it the germ of what today we would call the regulatory state. It is the spirit of regulation that Tocqueville regards as enervating the initiative of citizens to do anything for themselves and act on their own initiative. This kind of centralization, he writes, "succeeds without difficulty in impressing a regular style on current affairs; in skillfully regimenting the details of social orderliness; in repressing slight disorders and small offenses; in maintaining society in a status quo that is properly neither decadence nor progress; in keeping in the social body a sort of administrative somnolence that administrators are accustomed to calling good order and public tranquility" (I.i.5 [86]). Tocqueville then goes on to give a striking description of the dangers of administrative centralization: "Then sometimes it happens that centralization tries, in desperation, to call citizens to its aid; but it says to them: 'You shall act as I wish, as long as I wish, and precisely in the direction that I wish. You shall take charge of these details without aspiring to direct the sum; you shall work in the darkness, and later you shall judge my work by its results.' It is not under such conditions that one obtains the concurrence of the human will. It must have freedom in its style, responsibility in its actions. Man is so made that he prefers standing still to marching without independence toward a goal of which he is ignorant" (I.i.5 [86–87]).

What led to Tocqueville's focus on administrative centralization? One would have to say that, writing in the first third of the nineteenth century, Tocqueville had a peculiarly Francocentric view of the world. "Centralization was a topic that seems, at first glance, yet another example of Tocqueville discovering America only to find France," Sheldon Wolin has written.[16] In England the modernization of public administration would not even get under way for another generation. In America the issues of civil service reform, the elimination of the grossest abuses of patronage (Tammany Hall's "honest graft"), and creation of any of the national regulatory commissions would not appear until the emergence of the progressive movement at least half a century after the publication of *Democracy II*.[17] Only in France did the centralization of administrative power go back deep into the heart of the ancien régime.

Tocqueville's interest in the theory and history of the administrative state grew out of his reading of the dynamics of European history. The tendency toward administrative centralization is not simply a feature of postrevolutionary Europe but can be traced back to the heart of the ancien régime. It was the administrative conquests of the kings of France that did the most to prepare the age of equality and the democratic revolution. The principal characteristic of administrative centralization was always its antipathy to provincial or intermediary institutions, the *pouvoirs intermédiaires,* which had been the power base of the aristocracy. Tocqueville regarded the concentration of power in the office of the *conseil du roi,* or Royal Council, as doing more to hasten the Revolution than did all the writings of Voltaire and Rousseau. "The formation of the centralized democratic state, which for Tocqueville is the very meaning of the Revolution, was also the meaning of the Ancien Regime," François Furet has written.[18] Rather than creating a break with the old aristocratic order, as the revolutionaries had believed, the Revolution merely exacerbated the tendency toward centralization that had been the administrative legacy of the French monarchy.

The process of administrative centralization created a bureaucracy—the most bourgeois of institutions—that became "the aristocracy of the new society." Not content to tear down the old intermediary associations, the bureaucracy set about rebuilding society anew. It was the Enlightenment ideas of progress and reform that had been given heroic expression in the writings of the *Encyclopédie* and Condorcet that were now given institutional form in the bourgeois state. "When the long malaise that preceded the Revolution began to make itself felt," Tocqueville wrote, "all kinds of new social and political theories blossomed": "The purposes of the reformers varied, but their means were always the same. They wanted to borrow the strength of the central power and use it to destroy and rebuild everything according to the new plans they thought up; only the state appeared to be sufficient to accomplish such a task. . . . These ideas did not stay in books; they penetrated all minds, were mingled with mores, infused habits, and spread everywhere, even into everyday life. No one thought that any important business could be well managed without the involvement of the state."[19] In a passage that uncannily anticipates Flaubert's description of the agricultural fair in *Madame Bovary,* Tocqueville even contemplates the possibility of awarding government honors and certificates to farmers who have produced the best crops and livestock. "Inspectors and medals!" Tocqueville exclaims. "This is an idea that would never occur to a Suffolk farmer."[20]

DEMOCRATIC DESPOTISM

It is only at the very end of *Democracy II* that Tocqueville provides his final reflection on the administrative state, in a chapter ominously entitled "What Kind of Despotism Democratic Nations Have to Fear" (II.iv.6 [661–65]). It is here that we see him abandon his earlier concerns with the tyranny of the majority and the danger of mob rule for a new kind of power, the outlines of which are only now becoming legible. Tocqueville gives some indication of his change of perspective when he remarks near the outset of the chapter that "five years of new meditations have not diminished my fears but they have changed their object" (II.iv.6 [661]).

At first, Tocqueville seems reluctant to define this new power. "I think therefore that the kind of oppression with which democratic peoples are threatened," he writes, "will resemble nothing that has preceded it in the world." No longer is he concerned with the emergence of a revolutionary charismatic leader, the prototype of the military despot. Rather there is no image for this new despotism in our memories. Even our language is inadequate to define it ("the old words 'despotism' and 'tyranny' are not suitable" [II.iv.6 (662)]). What, then, is it?

One feature of Tocqueville's new despotism that distinguishes it from tyrannies of the past is its very mildness, or "sweetness" (*douceur*) (II.iii.1 [535–39]). The mildness of democratic habits and manners is a theme that runs throughout both volumes of the *Democracy*. The equality of conditions has rendered men gentler and more considerate with respect to one another. Being more alike, we have, as Bill Clinton famously said, an ability to feel one another's pain. "Do we have more sensitivity than our fathers?" Tocqueville asks with apparent incredulity. "I do not know, but surely our sensitivity bears on more objects" (II.iii.1 [538]).

The word "douceur" is, of course, a term that Tocqueville's readers would have associated with Montesquieu's description of commerce. The idea of moneymaking as a soft or innocent pastime is one that ran throughout the eighteenth century. The qualities associated with trade—thrift, honesty, moderation, deferred gratification—were presented as an antidote to the destructive virtues associated with the older aristocratic ethic of honor and glory. The heroic ethic received its canonical expression in the great ethical treatises of Greek and Roman antiquity, although it remained with some modification the ideal of the Latin West. In a Christianized form it became the basis for the famous medieval chivalric code of honor. This code was given expression in such medieval romances as the *Chanson de Roland* and the *Song of El Cid*. These were great epic poems—*chansons de geste*—stories of heroic deeds, and they were the first to appear in the West after Virgil's *Aeneid*.

These epics expressed a code of honor that would later come to be parodied in the first great novel of European literature—one familiar to all—Cervantes's *Don Quixote*. Marx, whose skill as a literary critic has often been noted, wrote: "Don Quixote long ago paid the penalty for wrongly imagining that knight errantry was compatible with all economic forms of society."[21] In other words, Marx understood the book less as a satire on the medieval code of chivalric honor than as a statement of its obsolescence; ideas of chivalry and honor were appropriate for certain kinds of society with certain kinds of economic relations, but these ideas were being made redundant by a new kind of society that he called capitalist society or that we might call market society.

The transition from a medieval world based on hierarchy, status, and honor to a new bourgeois or commercial world based on equality, contract, and interest has been described in a number of ways. Marx called it the transition from feudalism to capitalism; Henry Maine called it the transition from status to contract; Tocqueville called it the transition from the age of aristocracy to the age of democracy. But no one provided a more powerful description than the economist and intellectual historian Albert O. Hirschman in *The Passions and the Interests: Arguments for Capitalism before Its Triumph.*[22]

In this brilliant book, Hirschman shows how the arguments for the commercial society were first made possible only after the destruction of the heroic ideal that had made a return during the Renaissance with its rediscovery of the Greek and Roman celebration of glory. A whole series of writers beginning with Hobbes, but including Montaigne, Bacon, Mandeville, Hume, and Montesquieu, turned their collective eye on discrediting the idea of the hero as a species of vanity and the product of an overheated imagination. In place of the heroic ideal, these writers posited an alternative conception of human nature based on the benefits of interest and self-interested behavior. Self-interest, as Hirschman writes, "was by no means limited to the material aspects of a person's welfare; rather it comprised the totality of human aspirations but denoted an element of reflection and calculation with respect to the manner in which these aspirations were pursued."[23]

Hirschman made two important points. The first, as the subtitle of the book indicates, is that the transition to capitalism was only made possible due to the prior emergence of certain ideas and arguments. Markets are not simply a natural form of human organization but are embedded in a dense web of moral argumentation in which the pursuit of interest—so long considered a deadly sin within the Christian moral universe—came to be seen as a virtue for constraining the destructive passions for fame and honor. The market society was an idea before it became a reality.

The second discovery was to show that the concept of self-interest is not a universal key for understanding all human behavior as this is so often claimed by economists and social scientists today. Rather the idea of self-interest emerged as a strategy to counteract the dominance of certain passions, especially the kinds of desires associated with fame, honor, and heroic immortality. The pursuit of interest was deemed to exercise a tranquilizing effect on society and on human behavior generally. The passions were seen as wild and irrational, while interests were calm, gentle, even placid. A society devoted to moneymaking, as opposed to aristocratic practices like war, was described by such metaphors as "polishing," "refining," and "softening" morals. A society dominated by the pursuit of interest could be counted upon to be less grand, noble, and heroic but more peaceful, prosperous, and secure.

The idea that commerce "softens" or "polishes" manners is a theme that runs throughout *The Spirit of the Laws* and found its way into Tocqueville's account of democracy.[24] Montesquieu put his thesis about the softening effects of commerce in the form of a general law of social development: "Commerce cures destructive prejudices and it is an *almost general rule* that everywhere there are gentle mores there is commerce and that everywhere there is commerce, there are gentle mores."[25] Commerce was seen as exercising a pacifying and purifying effect on fierce and warlike peoples. It makes people less harsh toward one another, which is not incompatible with a decline of certain primitive virtues that Montesquieu associates with hospitality and a generosity of spirit: "The spirit of commerce produces in men a certain feeling for exact justice, opposed on the one hand to banditry and on the other to those moral virtues that make it so that one does not always discuss one's interests alone. . . . By contrast, total absence of commerce produces the banditry that Aristotle puts among the ways of acquiring. Its spirit is not contrary to certain moral virtues; for example, hospitality, so rare among commercial countries, is notable among bandit people."[26]

The effect of commerce is to produce a new ethic of *l'humanité*. This is what could be called a law of peoples. "The natural effect of commerce is to lead to peace. Two nations that trade with each other become reciprocally dependent; if one has an interest in buying, the other has an interest in selling, and all unions are founded on mutual needs," Montesquieu notes.[27] People who trade with one another, who are constantly forced into one another's company, develop habits of tolerance and an enlargement of their moral horizons. They are much less likely to be motivated by an ethic of glory and honor and are therefore less likely to seek salvation in devotion to *la patrie*. By looking to their material affairs rather than to grandiose political ambitions, commercial nations instill habits of "frugality, economy, moderation, work, wisdom, tranquility, order, and rule."[28]

Montesquieu regarded the transition from the feudal warrior ethic to the modern bourgeois commercial ethic as a marker of progress. One sees this especially in the effect that commerce has had on government. It is especially in England where the spirit of commerce has made the deepest inroads. "Other nations," Montesquieu writes, "have made commercial interests give way to political interests; England has always made its political interests give way to the interests of its commerce."[29] This is not to say that the progress of commerce has been benign in all respects. Montesquieu notes that a certain kind of sameness and uniformity is to be found among commercial nations. In a passage that clearly resonates with us today, he observes: "This commerce is a kind of lottery and each one is seduced by the hope of a lucky number."[30]

Tocqueville had less confidence in the effects of doux commerce for the attainment of political liberty. To be sure, he believed that liberty of commerce and the rights of property stood as formidable checks to despotism, even while decrying the mediocrity of commercial republics. He is frequently contrasted with Marx, who believed that modern industrial capitalism simply created new hierarchies of wealth and inequality. Tocqueville doubted that without a rigid system of primogeniture modern commerce could ever establish an aristocracy as in the past in part because of the mobility of modern capital (II.ii.20 [530–32]).[31] Wealth does not become crystallized in the great families as it had in aristocratic times, when it was passed down from generation to generation. Furthermore, Tocqueville believed that the relations between labor and capital did not create the same relations of hierarchy and dependence characteristic of an aristocratic order.[32]

Yet if Tocqueville did not accept Marx's apocalyptic vision of the development of capitalism and the inevitability of revolutionary struggle, he regarded Guizot's passion for the policy of *enrichissez-vous* as far too complacent and materialist. The great danger was to accept the belief that material progress was a guarantee of liberty. There may come a time, Tocqueville warns, when "the taste for material enjoyments develops . . . more rapidly than enlightenment and the habits of freedom." When this comes—and Tocqueville writes as if this is well under way—people come to neglect their political responsibilities for the sake of their private fortunes: "Preoccupied with the sole care of making a fortune, they no longer perceive the tight bond that unites the particular fortune of each of them to the prosperity of all. There is no need to tear from such citizens the rights they possess; they themselves willingly allow them to escape. The exercise of the political duties appears to them a distressing contretemps that distracts them from their industry" (II.ii.14 [515]).

Tocqueville writes with uncanny clarity about how a certain kind of people can become so absorbed in the pursuit of wealth and similarly become so fearful of the rough-and-tumble of political life that they take refuge in a new form of despotism, which the twentieth century described as fascism. The love of tranquility for the sake of a favorable business environment can easily encourage "an ambitious able man [who] comes to take possession of power" and who will find "the way open to every usurpation." The love of order is admirable, but not when it has the effect of killing the civic spirit. "A nation that demands of its government only the maintenance of order is already a slave at the bottom of its heart," Tocqueville writes, "it is a slave to its well-being and the man who is to put it in chains can appear" (II.ii.14 [516]).[33]

The fact the democracy has rendered people gentler in their habits and practices is no doubt preferable to the kind of deliberate cruelty and indifference to human suffering described in the letters of Madame de Sévigné to her daughter (II.iii.1 [537]). It has also, so Tocqueville believes, rendered us more pliant and subject to manipulation. It is here that he coins the term "democratic despotism" to describe this new species of power that has so far defied definition. He describes this despotism as "an immense tutelary power" (*un pouvoir immense et tutélaire*) that keeps its subjects in a state of perpetual political adolescence (II.iv.6 [663]). It is, above all, the paternalism of the new administrative state that elicits his strongest reaction. "It was not tyranny, but rather being held in tutelage by government that has made us what we are," Tocqueville writes in a marginal comment to volume 2 of the *Old Regime*. "Under tyranny, liberty can take root and grow; under administrative despotism liberty cannot be born, much less develop. Tyranny can create liberal nations; administrative despotism, only revolutionary and servile peoples."[34]

INDIVIDUALISM AND SOFT DESPOTISM

Tocqueville is clearly concerned with the effects of this new kind of soft despotism on the lives of its citizens. It is not revolutionary outbreaks of uncontrollable passion that will characterize the democratic social order but rather an extreme form of docility and apathy, a quality that he calls *individualisme* (II.ii.2 [482–84]). Individualism is a term associated with the French Revolution and its aftermath. Burke feared, for example, that without the restraining effects of tradition men would become "flies of a summer" and that after a few generations "the commonwealth itself would . . . crumble away, be disconnected into the dust and powder of individuality."[35]

The first use of the term "individualism" in France has been attributed to the Catholic reactionary thinker Joseph de Maistre, who condemned the experiment with democracy for producing a "deep and frightening division of minds, this infinite fragmentation of all doctrines, political protestantism carried to the utmost individualism."[36] The attack on individualism was not the exclusive property of those on the political right. Socialist writers found this liberation of the individual as simply another term for selfishness and egoism. Marx attacked the idea of the stand-alone individual as one of "the unimaginative conceits" of eighteenth-century political economy. "As little as Rousseau's *contract social* which brings naturally independent, autonomous subjects into relation and connection by contract, rests on such naturalism" Marx wrote.

"This is the semblance, the merely aesthetic semblance, of the Robinsinades great and small."[37] Even an arch-liberal like John Stuart Mill could complain about our "miserable individuality" to describe people who cared only for pleasure at the expense of all higher feelings and motivations.[38]

Tocqueville drew on some of these negative connotations, not of the individual, but of individualism, as the name for a pathology unique to democratic times. "Our ancestors," he wrote in the *Old Regime*, "lacked the word 'individualism' which we have created for our use because in their era there were, in fact, no individuals who did not belong to a group."[39] In *Democracy II*, Tocqueville attempted to distinguish between individualism and egoism. The latter, he believed, was a natural instinct, while the former was born out of modern conditions. "Individualism is a recent expression arising from a new idea," he wrote. "Our fathers knew only egoism. Egoism is a passionate and exaggerated love of self that brings man to relate everything to himself alone and to prefer himself to everything. Individualism is a reflective and peaceable disposition (*un sentiment reflechi et paisible*) that disposes each citizen to isolate himself from the mass of those like him and to withdraw to one side with his family and his friends, so that after having thus created a little society for his own use, he willingly abandons society at large to itself" (II.ii.2 [482]; translation modified). The isolated individual was not the village eccentric or nonconformist—someone whom Tocqueville might have admired—but the eremite, the solitary, cut off from society altogether. Unlike the egoist who is fixated on the self, the individual stimulated the creation of a narrow circle of family and associates who remain, in Tocqueville's chilling phrase, confined "in the solitude of his own heart (*la solitude de son propre coeur*)" (II.ii.2 [484]).

The fact that equality renders us alike also renders us indifferent to one another and our common fate. Unlike Montesquieu, who had located the principle of despotism in fear, Tocqueville regards it as a product of modern individualism. In crucial respects, as we shall see, he anticipates later fears about "mass society" with its tendency to eliminate all social ties and connections. Mass society is not a quantitative determination; it is not defined in terms of the numbers of people entering political life. It defines a social relationship, or rather the lack of one. It describes a disposition that substitutes for the experience of free individuality the experience of dependence, uniformity, and social isolation: "Despotism, which in its nature is fearful, sees the most certain guarantee of its own duration in the isolation of men, and it ordinarily puts all its care into isolating them . . . a despot readily pardons

the governed for not loving him, provided that they do not love each other"
(II.ii.4 [485]).

Tocqueville seems less concerned with the effects of despotism on the true
genius, who is capable of looking after himself, than on society as a whole or
on those who are without great gifts. The democracy of the future is less likely
to be a land of rugged individualists and freethinkers than of couch potatoes.
Individualism is associated with passivity and apathy. It becomes the precondition for a new kind of tyranny:

> Thus, after taking each individual by turns in its powerful hands and kneading
> him as it likes, the sovereign extends its arms over society as a whole; it covers its
> surface with a network of small, complicated painstaking uniform rules through
> which the most original minds and the most vigorous souls cannot clear a way to
> surpass the crowd; it does not break wills, but it softens them, bends them, and
> directs them; it rarely forces one to act, but it constantly opposes itself to one's
> acting; it does not destroy, it prevents things from being born; it does not tyran-
> nize, it hinders, compromises, enervates, extinguishes, dazes, and finally reduces
> each nation to being nothing more than a herd of timid and industrious animals
> of which the government is the shepherd. (II.iv.6 [663])

Has there even been a more powerful and prescient description of the modern administrative state?

Tocqueville came to regard the rise of this soft despotism as ultimately more
dangerous to liberty than his early concerns with majority tyranny. To be sure,
his democratic despotism was an imaginary condition ("I want to imagine
with what new features despotism could be produced in the world" (II.iv.6
[663]). Tocqueville was by no means a determinist. He was not predicting the
future course of history in the manner of either a social scientist or a dooms-
day prophet. Such a future was not inevitable, even though it was possible.
His book was written as a warning to his contemporaries not about what must
happen but about what might happen unless they acted to resist. He was describing one possible tendency of modern history, but one that has become all
too familiar in the ensuing centuries. With all countervailing powers under
the administrative control of the state, citizens have no choice but to become
wards of the state. "They console themselves for being in tutelage (*en tutelle*)
by thinking that they themselves have chosen their schoolmasters (*tuteurs*),"
Tocqueville writes (II.iv.6 [664]).

It is important to bear in mind that Tocqueville's description of democratic
despotism was written for the benefit not so much of Americans as of French-

men. To some degree Tocqueville believed that the Anglo-Americans were partially exempted from the dangers of democratic despotism because of long-standing habits of civic association, trial by jury, and freedom of the press. His concerns about the growth of administrative centralization grew out of his readings in French history and municipal archives that increasingly dominated his thought in the last twenty years of his life. The story of European history has been the story of the slow but steady concentration of state power. It would not have surprised, but would have deeply saddened, Tocqueville to see the European Union today as the successor state to Rome.

TOCQUEVILLE'S CHILDREN

Tocqueville's fears about democratic despotism—its soft tutelary power, the trend toward social isolation and atomization, the tendency to foster apathy and conformism—remain the most powerful aspect of his work. These are the parts of the *Democracy* that bore fruit in the following century with the rise of fascism and mass society in Europe and its American offshoots in the form of parochialism and isolationism.

Tocqueville is widely regarded today as the teacher of American exceptionalism. Although Tocqueville never actually used this term, it has become associated with him, largely through Louis Hartz's classic study *The Liberal Tradition in America*.[40] The genius of Hartz's book was to use Tocqueville as a template for understanding American political development. Accordingly, Hartz began his study with an epigraph from Tocqueville: "The great advantage of the Americans is to have arrived at democracy without having to suffer democratic revolutions, and to be born equal instead of becoming so" (II.ii.3 [485]). For Hartz, the key to America's exceptional development was found in the condition of absence, namely, the lack of a feudal or aristocratic tradition against which the experience of democracy could develop. Lacking a feudal past, American democracy was achieved without the kind of violent, wrenching break from the past that characterized the birth of democracy in France. From the beginning, Americans enjoyed a bourgeois "Lockean" middle-class liberty as a birthright and therefore avoided the implacable hatreds and class struggle that accompanied European democratic movements. Without an aristocratic tradition against which to contend, America never developed a reactionary Right that looked to the restoration of an ancien régime. Even the antebellum slave-owning planters lacked a true aristocratic order of privilege and hierarchy. Hartz's book has often been read as a celebration of American uniqueness, its moderation and sobriety, but this was hardly its intention. Rather than celebrating America's unique path, Hartz regarded it as a major source of dissatisfaction.

The question posed by Hartz was in fact why America has never produced a truly progressivist socialist movement, a class-based politics like the British Labour Party. His thesis was that, absent a feudal past, America also lacked a socialist future. As a result, he believed, America remained in a permanent condition of arrested development. What began with Locke stayed with him. Hartz never embarked on a serious engagement with Locke's philosophy but used it as a cover-all term to describe the "ideology" of middle-class laissez-faire individualism. It was precisely the dominance of this ideology that was the key to America's liberal consensus. By virtue of "an absolute and irrational attachment" to Lockean liberalism, America remained as uniquely impervious to the challenge of socialism as it had been unfamiliar with the tradition of feudalism. "The hidden origin of socialist thought everywhere in the West," Hartz wrote, "is to be found in the feudal ethos. The *ancien régime* inspires Rousseau; both inspire Marx."[41]

At the core of Hartz's reflections on America is the problem that Tocqueville had identified, namely, its tendency toward a new kind of soft tyranny. If Lockeanism had originally been a doctrine of individual liberty and revolution, in America it has become a nationalist creed with coercive power that has "posed a threat to liberty itself." "I believe," Hartz contended, "that this is the basic ethical problem of a liberal society: not the danger of the majority which has been its conscious fear, but the danger of unanimity, which has slumbered unconsciously behind it: the 'tyranny of opinion' that Tocqueville saw unfolding," even in his own era.[42] It was precisely this form of tyranny that Hartz believed was crystallized in the phenomena of the American Legion, McCarthyism, and the doctrine of the "American Way of Life."

Another original and far-seeing use of Tocqueville's account of democratic despotism can be found in Hannah Arendt's acute analysis of mass society in *The Origins of Totalitarianism*.[43] To be sure, Tocqueville hardly predicted the rise of communism and National Socialism in the twentieth century, but he foresaw the conditions that would make them possible. Totalitarianism, Arendt argued, was a new type of political regime that grew out of the collapse of the traditional class structure and party government that had formed the backbone of the nation-state system and gave birth to a new phenomenon, previously unknown to history. Totalitarianism presupposes a society where the old classes and parties have given way to a mass population. Mass society is not the same as totalitarianism but is the precondition for it. The emergence of mass society is not a quantitative designation applied just to large-scale populations, it applies also to peoples who have become an atomized and individualized mass, who no longer share in the communal ties and connections that form the basis of what Hegel had called *bürgerliche Gesellschaft.*

Arendt's analysis of the social basis of mass society closely follows Tocqueville's account of the dangers of *individualisme.* She found the basis for mass society to be in a degenerated form of bourgeois life. The typical recruits of the totalitarian party were not social outcasts and moral fanatics but "first and foremost job holders and good family men." Arendt's term for this kind of "single-minded devotion to matters of family and career" is severe: philistine. The term "philistine" was a virtual curse word of German romanticism used to designate the most cowardly and despicable form of bourgeois life. "The philistine," she writes, "is the bourgeois isolated from his own class, the atomized individual who is produced by the breakdown of the bourgeois class itself."[44] It was this new kind of "atomized individual" who could be easily molded and manipulated into being a member of a mass movement.

A central feature of Arendt's mass man is the feeling of extreme atomism and social isolation that comes from the breakdown of traditional classes and hierarchies, which leads people to seek comfort, solace, and relief in the hands of mass organizations like the totalitarian party. The totalitarian party, unlike the bourgeois parties of both the traditional Right and Left, is conceived not as an organization of class interests but as the locus of a new kind of identity politics that can completely remake the individual in the light of the party's reigning ideology. "The truth is," Arendt avers, "that the masses grew out of the fragments of a highly atomized society whose competitive structure and concomitant loneliness of the individual had been held in check only through membership in a class. The chief characteristic of the mass man is not brutality and backwardness, but his isolation and lack of normal social relationships."[45] It is the experience of loneliness, she explains later on, and the feeling of uprootedness, of having no place in the world, that forms the backdrop for the emergence of totalitarianism. Like Tocqueville, she regards the experience of extreme isolation as increasingly the defining feature of the modern age. "What prepares men for totalitarian domination in the non-totalitarian world," she writes in a passage that is both warning and prediction, "is the fact that loneliness, once a borderline experience, usually suffered in certain marginal social conditions like old age, has become an everyday experience of the ever growing masses of our century."[46]

Arendt's analysis of mass society has been further amplified by Michael Oakeshott. In his seminal essay "The Masses in Representative Democracy," Oakeshott traces the emergence of modern society to a new kind of individualism, but one to which he offers a distinctive twist.[47] Like Tocqueville with his conception of equality, Oakeshott did not regard the experience of individuality as constituting a fundamental rupture with the past but saw it as a slow and gradual modification of the conditions of medieval life. The emergence of this new "disposition" toward individuality appeared initially in the thirteenth century in Italy with the breakup of the older communal structure of civic life. North of the Alps, it was given early expression by Montaigne and more systematically by Hobbes ("the first moralist of the modern world to take candid account of the current experience of individuality") and later by Kant and was finally given political expression in the institutions of modern representative democracy.[48]

The problem is that this newly empowered sense of individuality also nourished a counterimage, which Oakeshott describes as the "individual *manqué*." In this type of anti-individual is found the locus of modern mass society and the rise of the new tutelary state. For the individual manqué, freedom is less a condition to be explored than a burden to be escaped. Although the basis for this new anti-individual could be found in the newly emancipated laboring classes, Oakeshott describes the phenomenon less in sociological than in moral and psychological terms. At the core of this disposition are the feelings of envy, jealousy, anger, and resentment. "The 'masses' as they appear in modern European society," Oakehsott writes, "are not composed of individuals: they are composed of 'anti-individuals' united in a revulsion from individuality . . . the 'anti-individual' had feelings rather than thoughts, impulses rather than opinions, inabilities rather than passions, and was only dimly aware of his power. . . . The 'anti-individual' needed to be told what to think: his impulses had to be transformed into desires, and these desires into projects: he had to be made aware of his power; and these were the tasks of his leaders."[49]

The modern anti-individual also needed new forms of political organization to provide, not for liberty, but for security and protection. Oakeshott traces the modern tutelary state back to the "godly princes" of the Reformation and the "enlightened despots" of the eighteenth century, but it was the socialist movement that offered a new vision of social solidarity as an antidote to the conditions of modern freedom. Governments henceforth came to be seen not as providing the formal guarantees against the arbitrary encroachment upon individual liberties but as the engine for satisfying "substantive" wants and desires. Its role was that of the architect or custodian of the public good. Parliament was no longer considered a debating assembly but regarded as a "workshop" in which political rule became "management" and "leadership."[50] In one particularly extreme version of this image, Oakeshott compares the modern managerial state to a hospital and its citizens to patients in need of continual care and attention.

The image of the therapeutic state similarly has a long lineage rooted in the idea of human nature, variously described by terms like mortality, sin, guilt, and pride. The modern therapeutic state is closely connected to the rise of modern science and especially the social sciences, which present themselves as uniquely capable of curing society of the diseases to which it has been prone: "The therapists are distinguished from their patients in virtue of their skill; they are currently sociologists, social psychologists, psychiatrists, group therapists, and what are called 'trained social workers,' and their engagement is 'counseling,' 'behavioral engineering,' and 'behavioral modification.' . . . In short, whereas the subjects of 'enlightened' government were identified as somewhat doltish children, sunk in ignorance, prone to idleness and folly, and in need of instruction, discipline, and management, here they are understood to be 'disturbed' patients in need of 'treatment.' "[51] Oakehsott's image of this new kind of tutelary state that may have been influenced by Anthony Burgess's *Clockwork Orange* provides frightening testimony to the kind of soft despotism that Tocqueville was the first to uncover.

CONCLUSION

The question posed by *Democracy in America* is "What form will the democracy of the future take?" Will democracy be relatively open and liberal or will it be centralized and despotic? Will it be libertarian or egalitarian? These two images of democracy represent two conflicting tendencies within modern history, even within human nature itself, the one favoring liberty and pluralism, the other equality and uniformity. Which will be the dominant trend? Tocqueville cannot say with certainty, but the tendency toward administrative centralization seems to be the more powerful of the two. The manifest and deliberate centralization of all power has proceeded in a number of ways. It is the result of a centuries-long process that began in the heart of the ancien régime, but more recently it has gained strength from certain currents of modern philosophy, beginning with Descartes, and its attempt to gain mastery and control over every aspect of life.

Tocqueville's two democracies are really less sociological than psychological studies of two very distinctive types of human being, almost two different species of humanity (II.iv.7 [675]). Tocqueville was one of the great moral psychologists who analyzed political institutions for what they did to individuals and what effect they had on human character. What kind of human being will the democracies of the future produce? These two conflicting democratic tendencies also express two contrary dispositions of the soul, one that seeks to be strong, proud, and independent, the other that seeks protection from harms, real or perceived, and for whom the small seed of *ressentiment* carries with it intolerance, not only of superiority, but also of diversity: "One must not dissimulate the fact that the social state I have just described lends itself almost as readily to the one as to the other of its two consequences. There is in fact a manly and legitimate passion for equality that incites men to want all to be strong and esteemed. This passion tends to elevate the small to the rank of the great; but one also encounters a depraved taste for equality in the human heart that brings the weak to want to draw the strong to their level and that reduces men to preferring equality in servitude to inequality in freedom" (I.i.3 [52]).

Tocqueville's fear—like that of Hartz, Arendt, and Oakeshott—is that democracy has not yet found a defense against the spirit of conformism and the dangers of democratic despotism. Yet Tocqueville did not give up on democracy, precisely because, like Churchill, he knew it was preferable to the alternatives. In writing as he did, Tocqueville hoped to rescue democracy from its own worst tendencies. He refused to be a flatterer of democracy precisely because he was a friend.[52]

Chapter 11 Flaubert and the Aesthetics of the Antibourgeois

The psychologists of France—and where else are any psychologists left today?—still have not exhausted their bitter and manifold delight in the *bêtise bourgeoise*. . . . Flaubert, for example, that solid citizen of Rouen, in the end no longer saw, heard, or tasted anything else any more.
—Friedrich Nietzsche

Madame Bovary is not, in any obvious sense of the term, a political novel.[1] Unlike *A Sentimental Education,* which unfolds during the great revolutionary upheavals of 1848–1851, *Madame Bovary* never even alludes to the political events of the day. It is a novel about adultery in a small, mid-nineteenth-century French town.

The plot of the story could not be simpler. Emma Rouault is the daughter of a well-to-do farmer from Normandy in the northern part of France. Soon after the novel begins, she marries Charles Bovary, a medical practitioner, who has come to attend to her father's broken leg. Marriage to a provincial physician proves not to be to Emma's taste, and she soon becomes bored with Charles and resentful of the child they have together. Emma begins two adulterous affairs, one with Rodolphe Boulanger and the second with Léon

Dupuis. She has expensive tastes and soon finds herself in debt far beyond her husband's meager ability to pay. Desperate, she commits suicide by swallowing arsenic. End of story.

Despite the banality—the quite deliberate banality—of the plot, *Madame Bovary* is a book that deals at a profound level with the era that had been anticipated by Rousseau and analyzed by Tocqueville, the era following the great bourgeois revolutions. *Madame Bovary* is a novel focused on the aftereffects of the Enlightenment and of the French Revolution with its promise to put an end to the old regime based upon throne and altar and install a new kind of society centered around the ideas of progress, science, and the rights of man. The result, Flaubert believed, was an age of ugliness, shallowness, and stupidity. Flaubert's, as we shall see, was not so much a political as an aesthetic response to the Enlightenment. The novel is Flaubert's cri de coeur against the mediocrity of the new bourgeois age.[2]

Like Tocqueville, Flaubert was a Norman, born in the town of Rouen in 1821. But while Tocqueville had come from an ancient aristocratic house—in one letter he claims he could trace his ancestors back to the Norman conquest—Flaubert was the son of a physician, Achille-Cléophas Flaubert, director of a hospital in Rouen, who may have served as a model for Dr. Larivière, who attends to Emma at the very end of her life. Flaubert was an indifferent student who briefly studied law in Paris before turning to literature. He began work on *Madame Bovary* in 1851 when he was thirty years old, and the book was published in 1856. At the core of the novel was the story of adultery, which immediately embroiled him in a national scandal. The reception of the work is something that Flaubert anticipated, and it confirmed his beliefs about the narrow-mindedness and philistinism of his contemporaries.

Flaubert's own life was neither a romantic nor an exciting one. He developed a long-standing affair with the poet Louise Colet, whom he referred to as his muse. For years, they met periodically for trysts in a hotel in Rouen that may have been an inspiration for the description of Emma's meetings with Léon. Flaubert spent eighteen months in Egypt and North Africa, where he was a frequent visitor to brothels, and returned to France disfigured by syphilis. He was never married except to his art.

Madame Bovary was Flaubert's greatest achievement and is characterized by a profound sense of disgust at the age in which Flaubert was brought up. This was the age of the bourgeois, a term he used to characterize not only the smug and prosperous middle classes—represented in the book by the apothecary Homais—but everything that struck him as narrow and vulgar. When his friend the art critic Théophile Gautier died at the age of sixty-one, Flaubert remarked that it was caused by an overexposure to modern stupidity.[3] Only Marx and later Nietzsche could rival Flaubert for the sheer contempt he was able to heap on the bourgeoisie. But his attack on the bourgeoisie was less social or political than aesthetic. What most appalled Flaubert was the sheer banality of the age. "I feel waves of hatred for the stupidity of my age," he wrote in a letter. "They choke me. Shit keeps coming into my mouth, as from a strangulated hernia. I want to make a paste of it and daub it over the nineteenth century, the way they coat Indian pagodas with cow dung."[4] Flaubert's only escape would come through his art. *Madame Bovary* was both an expression of his era and Flaubert's attempt to escape from it.

Madame Bovary was Flaubert's attempt to give expression to the age of the bourgeois that he believed was becoming—or had become—the dominant character of his time. He was a notorious perfectionist and took days, sometimes weeks, to work on even the smallest scenes to capture the rhythm of bourgeois life and speech. Here is what he wrote to Louise Colet on the difficulty of writing the book:

> What trouble my *Bovary* is giving me! Still, I am beginning to see my way a little. Never in my life have I written anything more difficult than what I am doing now—trivial dialogue. . . . There are moments when I want to weep; I feel so powerless. But I'll die rather than botch it. I have to portray simultaneously and in the same conversation five or six characters (who speak), several others (who are spoken about), the setting itself, the entire town, giving physical descriptions of peoples and objects, and in the midst of all that I have to show a man and a woman who are beginning (through a similarity in tastes) to be a little taken with each other. If only I had space. . . . I am going to put everything down quickly, proceeding by a series of sketches of the ensemble. By repeated revision I can perhaps pull it together. The language itself is a great stumbling block. My characters are completely commonplace, but they have to speak in a literary style and politeness of the language takes away so much picturesqueness from their way of expressing themselves![5]

What was Flaubert's relation to his most famous protagonist? It is common to read the story of Emma as that of a dupe and a victim. Flaubert is merciless in his unmasking of Emma's romantic illusions and her failed attempts to find romance in a loveless world. She is the quintessential victim of her own self-deceptions. Yet, there is also a strong sense of personal identification between the author and his creation: an almost Pygmalion-like transfer. Perhaps

Flaubert's most memorable pronouncement on his book was his famous "Madame Bovary, c'est moi" (302). Emma's faults are those of Flaubert's in his attempt to find some escape, some small voice of protest, against what he believed was the stifling conformity of the age.

The idea that Emma is not a victim but a hero, even a kind of proto-feminist hero, has been suggested in Tom Perrotta's novel *Little Children*.[6] Here is a book that retells the story of Emma Bovary set in a middle-class Boston suburb. The heroine of the story, Sarah Pierce—played by Kate Winslet in the film—is trapped in a loveless marriage and has a child she does not understand. Her husband is not a doctor but a computer analyst who is addicted to an Internet porn site called "Slutty Kay." Sarah is carrying on an affair with a neighborhood hunk whom she has met at the community swimming pool. She is intimidated by one of the neighborhood women, named Mary Ann, who is the symbol of bourgeois respectability—smug, confident, sure of her opinions, which are all filtered through listening to the Rush Limbaugh radio program. In a marvelous moment of self-referentiality, both Sarah and Mary Ann are invited to participate in a neighborhood book group in which several older women are reading *Madame Bovary*. Sarah, who has an M.A. in English literature, is dreading the meeting, especially when she finds out that her nemesis, Mary Ann, will also be present. Mary Ann immediately voices outrage at Emma's infidelities, and it is only then that Sarah suddenly finds the courage to speak:

"I think I understand your feelings about this book. I used to feel the same way myself." She shifted her gaze around the circle, making eye contact with each of the older women. It was okay being the center of attention; it was even kind of fun. "When I read this book back in college, Madame Bovary just seemed like a fool. She marries the wrong man, makes one stupid mistake after another, and pretty much gets what she deserves. But when I read it this time, I just fell in love with her."

Mary Ann scoffed, but the ladies seemed intrigued. Jean smiled proudly, as if to remind everyone who was responsible for Sarah's presence at the meeting.

"My professors would kill me," she continued, "but I'm tempted to go as far as to say that, in her own strange way, Emma Bovary is a feminist."

"Really?" Bridget sounded skeptical, but open to persuasion.

"She's trapped. She can either accept a life of misery or struggle against it. She chooses to struggle."

"Some struggle," said Mary Ann. "Jump in bed with every guy who says hello."

"She fails in the end," Sarah conceded. "But there's something beautiful and heroic in her rebellion."

"How convenient," observed Mary Ann. "So now cheating on your husband makes you a feminist."

"It's not the cheating. It's the hunger for an alternative. The refusal to accept unhappiness."

"I guess I just didn't understand the book," Mary Ann said, adopting a tone of mock humility.[7]

Let us now turn to the novel.

THE ILLUSIONS OF ROMANTICISM

Can a person's life be formed by the books he or she reads? Flaubert clearly believes so, which is why he begins *Madame Bovary*—not quite literally—with the education of Emma. Few authors are as precise as Flaubert in describing the literary tastes of their characters. Emma's education begins in the convent school where she has been sent by her father. Perhaps the first thing we learn about her is that she is a reader. All of Emma's later troubles are prefigured in her initial choice of books and the vast discrepancy she observes between the erotic and sexualized world she imagines and the reality that she actually experiences.

Emma's taste in literature runs to the high romanticism of the era. She reads *Paul and Virginia,* a popular novel by a disciple of Rousseau about two children who grow up marooned on a desert island away from the corrupting influences of society (24). At first Emma dreams about possibly joining the convent. She is attracted to the mysticism of the church, but she finds herself even more attracted to the historical novels of Sir Walter Scott and his stories of gothic romance. She devours novels, poems, sentimental songs, and love stories. She loves "illustrious or unhappy women" like Joan of Arc, Héloïse, and Agnès Sorel. After the death of her mother, she imagines herself a tragic heroine from Lamartine. The nuns ply her with attention, but they soon feel she is slipping away from them. By the time she is ready to leave the convent, she has experienced her first disillusionment, her first crisis of faith, so to speak. The mother superior even believes that she had been less than respectful to the community. Something in her "rebelled against the mysteries of faith, as it had rebelled against discipline as something alien to her constitution" (28). Emma is perhaps the first rebel without a cause.

Emma next hopes that marriage might produce for her what the church and religion had failed to provide. She wants to discover what words like "bliss, passion, ecstasy" mean in life, which up to this point she has only read about in books. Her marriage to the bumbling Charles Bovary is one of the great mismatches in all of literary history. Even his name, Bovary—like the word "bovine"—suggests dullness and stupidity.

Charles is an *officier de santé*—not exactly a real doctor, more like a physician's assistant—who is called to the Rouault farm to set the broken leg of Emma's father. Charles is a bumbler, although the break is quite simple to fix, and he ingratiates himself into the family. The first thing he notices about Emma is the whiteness of her nails, and he begins to make frequent visits to the house. It turns out, however, that Charles is less the predator than the prey. On one of his visits, Emma creates a beautifully elaborate seduction scene: "After the fashion of country folk she asked him to have something to drink. He said no; she insisted, and at last laughingly offered to have a glass of liqueur with him. So she went to fetch a bottle of curaçao from the cupboard, reached down two small glasses, filled one to the brim, poured scarcely anything into the other, and having clinked glasses, carried hers to her mouth. As it was almost empty she bent back to drink, her head thrown back, her lips pouting, her neck straining. She laughed at getting none, while with the tip of her tongue passing between her small teeth she licked drop by drop the bottom of her glass" (16). Needless to say, Charles is hooked.

Emma dreams of a magnificent midnight wedding with torchbearers but gets a country wedding instead, with forty-three guests and a meal that lasts for sixteen hours. On the day after the wedding, Flaubert notes maliciously, "it was [Charles] who might have been taken for the virgin of the evening before while the bride gave no sign that revealed anything" (21). It is not long before Emma becomes bored. Charles's utter obliviousness to his wife's needs soon begins to irritate her. He is completely happy in their marriage and, to make matters worse, believes that Emma is happy too. "Charles' conversation was commonplace as a street pavement," Flaubert writes, "and everyone's ideas trooped through it in their everyday garb without exciting emotion, laughter, or thought" (29).

The one area of their lives in which Emma might expect to find some of the "bliss, passion, ecstasy" that she has longed for is in their lovemaking, which she finds dull and routine. "Charles's passion was no longer very ardent," Flaubert writes. "His outbursts became regular; he embraced her at certain fixed times. It was one habit among other habits, like a familiar dessert after the monotony of dinner" (31). Emma begins to suffer from nervous depression, a kind of self-induced hypochondria. Later in the book her maid tells her about a woman who suffered from similar symptoms that stopped only after she got married. "But with me," Emma remarks, "it was after marriage that it began" (78).

Emma's final disenchantment comes when she and Charles are invited to a formal ball at La Vaubyessard, the estate of a local aristocrat who is seeking political office in the National Assembly. Here, for the first time, Emma gets a glimpse into the world of the old aristocracy that she has only read about in books. The Marquis and his wife even condescend to greet the young couple in person, indicating something about the new age of social equality. Previously, they would never even have been invited. At the dinner table sits a member of the prerevolutionary aristocracy at whom Emma can only gawk:

> At the upper end of the table, alone amongst all these women, bent over his full plate, and his napkin tied round his neck like a child, an old man sat eating, letting drops of gravy drip from his mouth. His eyes were bloodshot and he wore his hair in a little queue tied with a black ribbon. He was the Marquis's father-in-law, the old Duke de Laverdière, once on a time favorite of the Count le Vaudreuil, and had been, it was said, the lover of Queen Marie Antoinette. . . . He had lived a life of loud dissipation, full of duels, bets, elopements; he had squandered his fortune and frightened all his family. A servant behind his chair shouted in his ear, in reply to his mutterings, the names of the dishes that he pointed to, and constantly Emma's eyes turned involuntarily to this old man with hanging lips, as to something extraordinary. He had lived at court and slept in the bed of queens! (34–35)

The contrast between imagination and reality could not be more vivid. At the table sits an old man with food dribbling down his chin, but all that Emma sees is a representative of a world that she yearns for. The contrast between the clumsy Charles and the elegant men at the ball could not be more painful to the eyes. Like Cinderella at the ball, Emma realizes that her time there is limited. She is brought down to earth the next day when their small carriage breaks down on their way back home and the dinner is not ready for them when they arrive. Soon the whole episode is nothing more than a distant memory.

THE ILLUSIONS OF THE ENLIGHTENMENT

The true object of Flaubert's contempt is not the delusions of Emma, for which he feels some genuine empathy, but the middle-class idiocy of Homais, the local apothecary and relentless civic booster of the town of Yonville, where the couple have moved in the hope of curing Emma's malaise. Homais is the villain of Flaubert's work not for anything he does—he can scarcely be said to do anything—but for what he represents. His opinions crystallize a kind of cross section of the age. He is *the* representative of the new world, a man with no imagination, capable of mouthing only the most empty platitudes. He is a typical pompous small-town bore. Flaubert took a malicious glee in skewering these small-town civic boosters and joiners, whom Tocqueville regarded as the backbone of the middle-class democracies.

Madame Bovary is nothing if not a novel of upward mobility. In their first home in Tostes the Bovarys see the old aristocracy in decay, but in their new home in Yonville they encounter the new bourgeois aristocracy in its ascendency. When the Bovarys arrive in their new home, it is Homais's pharmacy that first catches their notice. The choice of profession is not accidental. Flaubert was the son of a physician, and the novel is full of often-detailed descriptions of scientific and medical procedures. Homais is a kind of low-level scientist and a vigorous advocate for public health. He is offended by the incidence of public drunkenness and wants to see the names of all those accused of intoxication written up on a board on the door of the town hall (110). A great believer in moral progress achieved through the advancement of scientific learning, he is an ardent Voltairien, a man of the Enlightenment, who mouths all the clichés of the past century. "My God," he asserts, "is the God of Socrates, of Franklin, of Voltaire, and of Béranger! I support the *Profession de Foi du Vicaire Savoyard* and the immortal principles of '89," referring both to Rousseau's *Emile* and to the Declaration of the Rights of Man and Citizen (55). Yonville seems to be the place where the great heroes and epic struggles of the Enlightenment and the French Revolution have come to die.

When Homais is first introduced to the reader, he is holding court at the local inn. He is animatedly advising the innkeeper, Madame Lefrançois, on the necessity of buying a new billiards table. "One must keep up with the times," he admonishes her, showing himself to be both progressive and up-to-date. He immediately sizes up Charles and launches into a pompous display of his knowledge of the state of public health. In an effort to make common cause with the young doctor, he warns Charles that the people of Yonville are still steeped in prejudice and superstition and that it will be a constant struggle to talk them out of their ancient habits.

Homais is a sturdy advocate of the Enlightenment who believes that the spread of scientific knowledge will contribute to happiness and the alleviation of human suffering. He boasts that he has submitted a scholarly paper entitled "Cider, Its Manufacture and Its Effects, Together with Some New Reflections on the Subject" to a scientific periodical. He has even been admitted to membership to the distinguished Agricultural Society of Rouen (96). The great dream of Diderot's *Encyclopédie* to collect and classify all forms of knowledge for the progressive betterment of humankind has now been reduced to Homais's treatise on cider making!

As a great believer in the principles of the Revolution and the age of progress, Homais is also adamantly anticlerical. He never misses an opportunity to take a jab at the local priest, Abbé Bournisien. It is priestcraft that has maintained the people in ignorance and superstition, Homais complains. In point of fact, the parish priest is as dull and insipid as Homais. They are a perfect Alphonse and Gaston. In a central moment, when Emma is beginning to contemplate adultery, she goes to the priest for help. "I am suffering," she confides to him. "So do I," he replies, assuming that she is referring to the summer heat. Later in the conversation, the priest mistakes her symptoms of anxiety and unease for indigestion and advises her to drink a little tea. He has no greater understanding of spirituality and the soul than does Homais. It is a piece of comic misunderstanding, but one that leads Emma to return home and commit an act of unpardonable cruelty (80–82).

Flaubert's point is that the consolations of religion are as false and repellent as are the platitudes about progress. The Enlightenment and the ancien régime are the mirror images of one another. This point is brought out in one of the few heavy-handed moments of the book, when Homais and the priest begin an absurd argument over Emma's deathbed. "Read Voltaire and d'Holbach," says Homais to the priest; read "The Meaning of Christianity" replies the priest. The priest sprinkles the room with holy water; Homais douses the floor with chlorine. The two glare at each other across the room, with only Emma's dying body to separate them. By the end they come to some kind of mutual understanding. "We'll end up good friends, you and I," the priest says to Homais, slapping him on the back (244). These two ignoramuses may well have ended up as the models for Flaubert's unfinished novel of education, *Bouvard and Pécuchet.*

ADULTERY

At the moment when Emma and Charles enter Yonville, the atmosphere of the book becomes hypersexualized. While Charles and Homais blather on with their pseudo-scientific inanities, Emma strikes up a conversation with a handsome young law clerk named Léon Dupuis. Before long they are discussing travel, music, and literature. Léon confesses a tenderness for poetry because it makes one weep more easily (59). He speaks of the pleasures that literature affords among all the disappointments of life. It seems as if Emma may have at last discovered her soul mate.

Emma's love for Léon is left unfulfilled when he leaves Yonville for study in Paris, but when a man named Rodolphe presents himself at the doctor's house, she is more than ready. Emma observes someone wearing a green velvet jacket and yellow gloves walking up the path one morning. He is Rodolphe Boulanger de la Huchette, who has come to see the doctor about an ailing servant. He is thirty-four years old and the owner of a considerable estate just outside Yonville, and it is only moments until he begins plotting his seduction of Emma. His clothes and manner reveal him to be a typical boulevardier, a cynical playboy who knows the ways of the world and is used to having his way with women (although his name actually means "baker"). The first thing he notices is Emma's beautiful white arms. He immediately takes an inventory of all Emma's desirable features: nice teeth, black eyes, a cute figure. What is she doing with a bumpkin like Charles, he wonders.

The seduction of Emma takes place against the backdrop of the agricultural fair, in one of the most memorable scenes in the entire novel. The scene is intended to bring into relief with almost comic absurdity the vast disproportion between the claims of the new age and the ugliness of the reality it has created. The scene begins with a display of the tricolor flag from the houses, the symbol of the Revolution now more than fifty years in the past. The town hall is a memorial dedicated to the great progressive ideals of the new century: commerce, agriculture, industry, the arts. Against this patriotic backdrop, a child in rags is seen holding a bull by a rope (98).

The first conversation we hear is the insufferable Homais lecturing some hapless housewife about the virtues of scientific agriculture. At the same time, the mayor is delivering a pompous speech on the beneficial effects of progress. He presents a heroic picture of the struggle of farmers and agricultural workers for the attainment of civilization. "Everywhere commerce and the arts are flourishing," the mayor gushes to his audience, "everywhere new means of communication, like so many new arteries in the body politic, establish within it new relations" (102). He proclaims the virtues of agriculture to be the foundation of civilization. "You, farmers agricultural laborers!" he continues. "You pacific pioneers of a work that belongs wholly to civilization" (103).

Against this backdrop, we hear Rodolphe's seduction speech to Emma, in which Flaubert parodies all the romantic clichés of the era. "Always 'duty.' I am sick of the word," Rodolphe complains. "As if one's real duty were not to feel what is great, cherish the beautiful, and not accept all the conventions of society with the hypocrisy it forces upon us" (103–4). Emma is not entirely convinced. Must one not accept the morality of society and the opinion of others, she asks. "But there are two moralities," Rodolphe explains, "the petty one, the morality of small men that constantly keeps changing, but yells itself hoarse, crude and loud like the crowd of imbeciles that you see down there. But the other, the eternal, that is about us and above, like the landscape that surrounds us and the blue heavens that give us light" (104). It would be immediately obvious to anyone how false Rodolphe's words are, but Emma hears them filtered through the romance novels on which she was brought up. Rodolphe speaks the kind of high-romantic jargon of the era that is as platitudinous as are the official speeches coming from the platform.

Behind Rodolphe's false and manipulative speech can be heard awards being given for first in show for hogs and manures. An old woman is awarded a silver medal worth twenty-five francs for fifty years of menial labor on the same farm. When she timidly approaches the stand to collect her prize, "a half century of servitude confronted these beaming bourgeois," Flaubert writes (108). Her first instinct upon receiving her medal is to give it to the priest to say an additional mass. The description of the entire scene seems intended to evoke both laughter and despair.

The most important event of the book is Emma's adultery with Rodolphe. Her corruption that began with the reading of novels is now consummated by her marital infidelity. Emma imagines herself a heroine in one of the novels she has read ("the lyric legion of these adulterous women began to sing in her memory" [117]). She plies Rodolphe with gifts, but no sooner has he won the object of his desire than he begins to tire of the relation. "It was an idiotic sort of attachment, full of admiration on his side and voluptuousness on hers" (138). Emma projects all of her romantic aspirations onto the affair, while Rodolphe, a jaded libertine, has become bored: "He had so often heard these things," Flaubert writes, "that they did not strike him as original. Emma was like all of his mistresses and the charm of novelty gradually falling away like a garment, laid bare the eternal monotony of the passions" (138). Under his tutelage, the last vestiges of decency are abandoned. "He discarded all modesty as inconvenient," Flaubert writes. "He treated her without consideration. And he made her into something at once pliant and corrupt" (138). Rodolphe leads Emma on, but when it becomes apparent that she has plans for them to elope, he devises a plan to dump her by leaving town on his own. Emma is grief-stricken.

Months after her recuperation, Emma begins another affair, with Léon, the law clerk, who has recently returned from Paris. They meet accidentally at the opera in Rouen, where the ever-attentive Charles has taken her to see a performance of *Lucia de Lammermoor* to aid in her convalescence. Having spent some time in the capital city, Léon is now over his earlier shyness, and the two soon begin to meet in a hotel room in Rouen. While in her relationship with Rodolphe Emma was the pupil, she now takes on the dominant role with Léon. "She laughed, cried, sang, sent for sherberts, wanted to smoke cigarettes, seemed to him wild and extravagant, but adorable, superb" (200). Emma has now become the agent of corruption: "He never questioned her ideas," Flaubert writes, "he accepted all her tastes; he was becoming her mistress rather than she his" (201).

The two soon grow tired of each other. Léon has received an anonymous letter warning him that his legal career may be jeopardized if he continues seeing a married woman. By this time, his earlier infatuation with music and poetry has given way to dull careerism. (Today he would probably be a recent college graduate with an entry-level consulting position at McKinsey.) For her part, Emma has discovered that she had misjudged Léon. He conceals the soul of just another dull bourgeois, no different from Charles. "She was as sick of him as he was weary of her," Flaubert writes. "Emma found again in adultery all the platitudes of marriage" (211).

After her breakup with Léon, the end comes quickly for Emma. For some time she has been living well beyond her means, borrowing money from a merchant named L'Heureux, whose name could be translated as Mr. Happy. When her debts become due she seeks help from Rodolphe, who turns her down—as do all the others who have profited from her extravagance. When her home and furniture are about to be seized and put on public auction, Emma goes to the pharmacy and swallows arsenic. Poor Charles is utterly oblivious to what has been going on. Emma's agonizing death throes are prolonged due to medical incompetence. In her last moment of life, just as she has received extreme unction from the priest, she hears the singing of a hideously disfigured blind beggar outside the window of the house. "The blind man," she cries out as the image of his hideous face becomes her last glimpse of life.

After her death, Charles is completely overcome. In a bizarre attempt to pay homage to his wife, he begins to affect Emma's extravagant manner. He buys patent leather boots, wears a white cravat, and takes up smoking. "She corrupted him from beyond the grave," Flaubert writes (250). When Charles discovers Emma's trove of love letters, however, he completely falls apart. He dies of no apparent cause, perhaps of a broken heart, and their child is sent off to work in a cotton mill. Throughout all this, Homais has prospered. The triumph of Homais represents the final triumph of the bourgeois—everything that Flaubert regards as dull, flat, and insipid. He is the perfect embodiment of what Nietzsche would later call the "last man." The final sentence of the book reads: "He has just been given the cross of the Legion of Honor" (255).

How does Flaubert regard Emma's decision? What are his views on a marriage that he treats with contempt and on adultery, which he refuses to condemn? It is the theme of adultery that most upset contemporary readers of the book. Yet Flaubert treats his subject with a scrupulous, one is tempted to say, a clinical, objectivity, refusing to pass moral judgment, either to celebrate or to condemn. Emma seems to elicit Flaubert's sympathy—her desire to flee her awkward husband and the tedium of provincial life—but Flaubert also regards her adultery as a symptom of the same lack of imagination and hypocrisy that he condemns. Flaubert's attitude toward adultery, as Dacia Maraini has suggested, is exactly the opposite of the Catholic Church's. While the church condemns the sin but pardons the sinner, Flaubert condemns the sinner but excuses the sin.[8]

Flaubert's picture of the misery of the family—his statement that Emma found in adultery all the platitudes of marriage—is an indirect reply to Rousseau's attempt in *Emile* to re-create the family on the basis of romantic love. Rousseau saw in love a basis for connectedness between a man, a woman, and their offspring that could serve as a bridge between persons and render us whole once more. It was this very picture of the family that Tocqueville built upon in *Democracy in America,* in which he depicts the bourgeois family and the differentiation of the sexes as the foundation of an orderly liberty opposed to the chaos and disorder of the European family.[9] It was this conception of the family based upon the absolute differentiation between the sexes, the willing subordination of the woman, and the self-sacrifice of both of the parents for their offspring that Flaubert finds intolerably oppressive and sterile. Trapped in a marriage from which there seems to be no escape, Emma feels that the only alternative left to her is a desperate but self-defeating struggle to find someone worthy of her love. The result is not elevating but catastrophic. *Madame Bovary* is a tale of corruption, but while Rousseau wrote a speculative history of the development and corruption of humanity, Flaubert writes in miniature, presenting the process through a single life. In this respect *Madame Bovary* is a very moral story. But while Rousseau offers some promise of redemption at the end of his story, does Flaubert promise any way out? Does he hold out any escape from the numbing dullness and stupidity of his age? The answer is: yes and no.

BEYOND GOOD AND EVIL

Madame Bovary may conclude with the triumph of Homais, but this is not necessarily Flaubert's last word. Although Emma may be the tragic victim of her own illusions, she does not represent the novel's only voice. As even the most casual reader of the book must notice, *Madame Bovary* is full of scientific and medical language. Doctors play a prominent role in the text. It is sometimes believed that this shows the influence of Flaubert's father, himself a famous surgeon. It is also argued that Flaubert's clinical language is a feature of his unflinching realism, and, to be sure, there is some truth to this. But Flaubert uses science and medicine for other ends, namely, to exhibit a hierarchy of human types that point to other possibilities.

At the bottom of the hierarchy is, of course, Charles. He first meets Emma when he is called to the Rouault home to mend her father's broken leg. Later they are invited to the ball at La Vaubeyssard because Charles has miraculously cured an abscess in the mouth of the Marquis through a timely lancing. But this is his last medical success. His monumental incompetence is revealed in the disastrous attempt to operate on the clubfoot of Hyppolite, the stable boy at the inn. Flaubert devotes an entire chapter to this incident, so it is obviously something that carries weight.

The occasion for the operation arises after Homais has read a scientific paper on a new method for curing a clubfoot. He convinces Charles that it is his patriotic duty to perform the operation. He already imagines a newspaper article he will write about this to celebrate the miracles of progress in the new scientific age. Emma also urges Charles on, hoping that for once he will live up to her ambitions. The operation ends disastrously, and another doctor needs to be called in to amputate the leg that has become hideously gangrened. Charles is crushed, but all Emma can wonder is how she could have put her faith in such an obvious bungler. She consoles herself by once more throwing herself into the arms of Rodolphe.

Just above Charles in the hierarchy is Homais. Homais is a pharmacist, still a lowly link in the medical chain. But he is more than just a pharmacist; he is a kind of propagandist for science and its link to public health. If the book had been written today, no doubt Flaubert might have made him a psychological counselor or group therapist. At the agricultural fair we hear Homais lecturing about the necessity of introducing new scientific methods into agriculture. When the innkeeper asks him skeptically whether agriculture is any of his business, he replies with the certainty of the autodidact that to cultivate the soil one must know chemistry, geology, atmospherics, soil density, and botany. "One must keep pace with science by reading publications and papers, be always on the alert to detect improvements," he asserts (96). It is Homais who convinces Charles to undertake the operation on Hyppolite as a contribution to medical progress as well as for the fame it will bring to their town.

Homais's constant preaching about progress necessarily puts him at odds with the representatives of religion and the church. Flaubert's point is that the centuries-old struggle between science and religion has now been reduced to Homais's use of scientific knowledge for the purpose of improvements in cider making. It is not science but the trivialization of science and the vanity that it induces that is the particular object of Flaubert's scorn. Homais's final triumph comes with his campaign to have the blind beggar who appears at Emma's death permanently confined to an asylum. The very existence of the beggar, a kind of leftover from a benighted age, is an affront to his belief in progress and public decency. The beggar must be banished from sight.

Above both of these figures stands Cavinet. Cavinet is described as a "famous surgeon" from Neufchâtel, and he is called in to perform the amputation on Hyppolite's leg after the operation on the clubfoot has gone bad. Cavinet is said to laugh "disdainfully" when he sees the result of the botched operation and proceeds to lecture the panicked Homais against putting one's faith in newfangled medical fads. The doctor asks Homais if he wants to witness the operation, but Homais is too squeamish. Cavinet boasts of his indifference to suffering and discomfort. He shaves with cold water and does not wear woolen underwear in winter. "It doesn't matter to me whether I carve up a Christian or the first fowl that comes my way," he tells Homais (132).

Homais cannot refrain from flattering the doctor, comparing his coolness to that of a general, something that appeals to Cavinet's vanity.

This is the same Cavinet who is later called on to attend to the dying Emma. He prescribes an emetic to make her vomit up the poison, but we learn later that it is precisely the wrong remedy. "You would have done better to put your fingers down her throat," Cavinet is told by a superior physician. Cavinet's vanity is at least momentarily humbled. "This good Cavinet, so arrogant and so verbose at the time of the clubfoot, was today very modest. He smiled an incessantly approving smile" (235).

At the top of this bizarre medical pecking order stands the mysterious physician Larivière, who enters the room before the obsequious Homais. Flaubert's description of this man is unique in the work:

> He belonged to that great school of surgeons created by Bichat, to that generation, now extinct, of philosophical practitioners, who cherishing their art with a fanatical love, exercised it with enthusiasm and wisdom. Everyone in his hospital trembled when he was angry and his students so revered him that they tried, as soon as they were themselves in practice, to imitate him as much as possible. They could be found in all the neighboring towns wearing exactly the same merino overcoat and black frock. The doctor's buttoned cuffs slightly covered his fleshy hands—very beautiful hands, never covered by gloves, as though to be more ready to plunge into suffering. Disdainful of honors, of titles, and of academies, hospitable, generous, fatherly to the poor, and practicing virtue without believing in it, he would almost have passed for a saint if the keenness of his intellect had not caused him to be feared as a demon. His glance, more penetrating than his scalpels, looked straight into your soul and would detect any lie, regardless how well hidden. He went through life with the benign dignity that goes with the assurance of talent and wealth, with forty years of a hard-working blameless life. (233–34)

Larivière instantly recognizes that nothing can be done to save Emma. Before he leaves, Homais, "who could not keep away from celebrities," insists on preparing a luncheon for him. After the lunch Homais's wife asks for a consultation. She fears her husband's blood is thickening from falling asleep after meals. "It's not his blood, I would call too thick" are the doctor's last words before leaving (236). At the end of the day it is the austere Dr. Larivière who may be Flaubert's answer to the problem of collective mediocrity. If Homais is a prefiguration of Nietzsche's last man, Larivière is a likely anticipation of his Overman.

What are we to make of this description? What is Flaubert referring to when he describes the great doctor as a philosophical surgeon, practicing virtue without believing in it? What kind of virtue does the doctor practice? Flaubert is clearly describing a certain kind of greatness of soul, even though the doctor's virtue is not the philosophic virtue of Socrates or Plato, nor is it the political virtù of Machiavelli. It is a virtue connected to the Enlightenment's project of the alleviation of human suffering through the perfection of the techniques of modern science. Larivière seems a direct connection to the great founders of the Enlightenment project like Bacon and Descartes, who had imagined the control and conquest of nature for the relief of human suffering. Yet his is a virtue that seems to have become skeptical of the Enlightenment project of humanitarianism. Thus he practiced virtue without believing in it. Perhaps this is the best description of Flaubert himself.

CONCLUSION

What does a book like *Madame Bovary* still have to teach us? Flaubert's Olympian contempt for all that he saw around him led to a retreat from politics into the private world of art and culture from which he could hurl his broadsides. His work constitutes a kind of tableau vivant of human vanities: fearful and tepid careerists, arrogant ignoramuses, smooth-talking liars and cads, pompous pseudo-intellectuals inordinately impressed with their own accomplishments. Only Emma has the courage to try to resist the collective stupidity of the age—our age—although she lacks the means to do so effectively. Her failure is a noble one, and we can sense Flaubert's sympathy for her. His famous "Madame Bovay, c'est moi" seems to confirm this.

Flaubert gives vivid expression to Tocqueville's deepest fears about the tyranny of the newly empowered middle class in his final book, *Bouvard and Pécuchet.* Here two low-level copy clerks meet accidentally on a park bench in Paris and strike up a friendship. One of them comes into a large inheritance, and they decide to quit their posts and take up their lifelong desire to achieve enlightenment through education and then spread this enlightenment to others. It is a parody of Diderot and d'Alembert's quest for universal knowledge in their great *Encyclopédie,* but in the case of Bouvard and Pécuchet everything leads to ruin. Kant helped to initiate the Enlightenment with the slogan "dare to know." Bouvard and Pécuchet turn this on its head. They are the innocent victims of what Flaubert believed to be the greatest illusion of his time, namely, that all the ills of the world can be solved through the spread of popular education.

The novel is a collection of *idées reçues*—bits of conventional wisdom—that Flaubert had been compiling for many years, a novel built on clichés, hackneyed phrases that are a substitute for real thinking. The two autodidacts decamp for Normandy to begin their studies with agriculture and the sciences before moving on to literature, the arts, political theory, religion, and eventually universal education. Of course, they misunderstand and misuse everything they touch. At one particularly crucial point in the story, their study of scientific and literary subjects is interrupted by the events of 1848. The prospect of revolution inspires an immersion in political theory from Robert Filmer, Locke, and Rousseau to Henri de Saint-Simon and Charles Fourier. At first, Pécuchet is intrigued by the prospects of socialism and its utopian plan for society divided into industrial phalanxes where each woman will be assigned three men. "That just suits me," replies Bouvard. When word eventually gets back to their Norman village of Louis Bonaparte's coup of 1851 and the return of authoritarian government, the two fall into bleak despair. "Ah, progress, what a farce," muses Bouvard. "And politics, what a filthy mess!" Never completely defeated, Pécuchet agrees that politics will never be a real science. "The art of war is better," he exclaims, "you can anticipate what is happening; should we try it?"[10] By the end of the book, the two men—by then in their seventies—have been disabused of their efforts to reform humanity through education, and they return to their jobs as desk clerks.

Tocqueville too feared the great middle classes with their materialism, their love of comfort, and sanctimonious belief in unlimited human progress. But unlike Flaubert, he did not entirely despair of his time. As an aristocrat with a sense of social responsibility, he refused to retreat to the provinces, to hunt, gamble, and become obscure. He traveled widely, first to America, later to England, Ireland, Germany, Sicily, and Algeria. He entered public life as a member of the National Assembly and sought to steer his country in a middle course between revolution and reaction. His was not a life given over to romanticizing a world we have lost or disparaging the world that is but a life of social responsibility to the world he was given.

Flaubert would have none of this. He scorns politics and society in a way that Tocqueville never would have done. There is more than a hint of Socratic irony in the way he treats the unexamined lives of his creations. But the merciless contempt with which he treated the bourgeoisie did not lead him to sympathy with the working classes. To the contrary: the workers and the capitalists were both equal partners in the collective mediocrity of the age. From this there was no escape. "I include in the word 'bourgeois,' the bourgeois in overalls as well as the bourgeois in frock coats," Flaubert wrote to the novelist Georges Sand. "It is we and we alone, that is, the educated, who are the people, or, to put it better: the tradition of Humanity."[11] Only the artist, Flaubert believes, is capable of redeeming the world. Not philosophy but art is the royal road to truth, and from truth to beauty.

There is something ultimately unsatisfying and even self-serving in Flaubert's idea of redemption through art. It sounds almost like one of those bourgeois platitudes that he would have mocked in one of his better moments. For all of his bitterness and vitriol, Flaubert is at bottom a wounded idealist who still wants to believe in some notion of salvation, even if the traditional routes are no longer available to him. Extraordinary individuals, like Larivière and even Flaubert himself, may be able to substitute science or art for religion or even philosophy. Flaubert is one in a long line who believes that the genius, someone who is above the moral categories of good and evil, the individual of superior sensitivity, occupies a privileged place as the true conscience of society.[12]

Flaubert participates in a certain mood of thought that George Armstrong Kelly once described as "Parnassian liberalism" for its retreat from the world of political competition into the world of art and culture: "It is a fairly unbudging doctrine insofar as it consents or contrives to make this sacrifice honorably, rather than striking bargains with the political forces that would control and denature it. On the other hand, it is this obstinacy that makes it suspect and even reprehensible to the democratic mentality. It is suspect not only because it questions the wisdom of popular government, but because it is 'critical,' ironical, and elitist—holding at the extreme that, in a world of perverse or prolific 'truths,' a world of opinion, faith must be constructed from intelligence, if there is to be faith at all, and that faith must be nimble enough to shift with intelligence."[13] The Parnassian spirit was in one respect aristocratic because it favored a regime based upon culture and education, but it was also liberal as it valued individual freedom, legal equality, and a limited constitutional state. The Parnassian spirit sought moderation without mediocrity, a democracy of education and taste, if that is not a contradiction in terms.

Flaubert is too misanthropic to serve as a model for political judgment. His "Axiom: Hatred of the Bourgeois is the beginning of all virtue" says more about his own need to shock and scandalize than about any identifiable features of his time.[14] Tocqueville probably shared many of Flaubert's intuitions about his age—and as a member of the ancient aristocracy he knew whereof he spoke—but he refused to retreat from history into art and "irony." Tocqueville engaged the political world not from atop Mount Parnassas but from the standpoint of a civic-minded educator and teacher. Each reader will have to determine whether the state of democracy today leads to a Tocquevillian sense of public-spiritedness and engagement or to a Flaubertian sense of nausea and disgust. How one responds to these two books will determine what kind of human being and citizen one is.

Chapter 12 The Apocalyptic Imagination:
Nietzsche, Sorel, Schmitt

"A specter is haunting Europe—the specter of communism," Marx famously wrote in the *Communist Manifesto*.[1] When he wrote this in 1848, he was half right. Along with communism, there was another and equally important specter haunting Europe—the specter of the Counter-Revolution. The theme of the Counter-Revolution continues to haunt modernity as its twin.[2] Like the related term "Counter-Reformation," the term "Counter-Revolution" was coined after the initial revolutions that constituted the founding of modernity. The counter-revolutionaries were not conservatives looking to restore the past; they were reactionaries or messianists of the Right. Their aim was not restoration but apocalypse—if possible, Apocalypse Now. Their goal was the destruction of the legacy of 1789 through an even more violent and thorough revolution that would redeem humanity, the class, or the nation through a complete negation of the present.

The idea of the Counter-Revolution took two, often contradictory, forms. The most famous is associated with Edmund Burke, who advocated a simple return to the order, stability, and legitimacy of the balanced constitution. The question asked in his seminal *Reflections on the Revolution in France* was whether it is through the idea of revolution or of tradition that politics is best understood. Burke's historicist and restorationist critique of the Revolution was based on a belief in the sanctity and inviolability of political tradition. The attempt to remake the world on the basis of Enlightenment doctrines of the "rights of man" was false to human experience. What is more, it was the result of intrusive literary men—*philosophes,* "intellectuals" of all sorts—with no feeling for the practical wisdom and ties of affection that constitute a political community. "This sort of people," Burke complained, "are so taken up with their theories about the rights of man, that they have totally forgotten his nature. . . . They have perverted in themselves, and in those that attend them, all the well-placed sympathies of the human heart."[3]

Burke was the first to introduce the trope of the two revolutions, the English and the French, as counterfoils to one another. The French Revolution was an attempt to remake society all the way down. Streets and months were renamed, historical provinces abolished, the French language regularized, and new religious cults of the Supreme Being announced. The English had not, by contrast, attempted a total revolution. Theirs, Burke believed, was an eminently conservative revolution attempting to rebalance the traditional harmony of the monarchy, the aristocracy, and the commons. "You might, if you pleased," Burke lectured his French readers, "have profited of our example and have given to your recovered freedom a correspondent dignity."[4] By drawing on an idea of the "ancient constitution," Burke offered a contrast between a "good" English (and also American) revolution and a "bad" French revolution.

But Burke's conservative reading of the Revolution was not the same as— was indeed strikingly different from—the Counter-Revolutionary doctrines that began to emerge in France. These were not restorationist attempts to reset the wheel of history but a mirror image of the very Revolution they sought to overthrow. For Joseph de Maistre, the Revolution was less a political event in time than a drama played out against the background of providential history. It was God's judgment on a society that he deemed horribly corrupt and required nothing less than radical purgation. He adopted the same apocalyptic language as had the revolutionaries, but put it in the service of the Counter-Revolutionary movement of reaction. Jacobinism was merely the agent appointed to purge a nation already mired in sin. Like Burke, Maistre opposed the revolutionary doctrines of the rights of man. "In my lifetime," he famously declared, "I have seen Frenchmen, Italians, Russians, etc.; thanks to Montesquieu, I even know that *one can be Persian.* But as for *man,* I declare that I have never in my life met him; if he exists, he is unknown to me."[5] Maistre's opposition, however, was not just to a particular doctrine but to an entire world that it was the vocation of history to redeem.

Nor was Maistre's opposition to the Revolution merely evidence of the new "sociological" approach to society focusing on the themes of national character or organic cultures rather than on the traditional emphasis on constitutions and political forms.[6] Once again, Maistre saw the Revolution as a theologico-political event in sacred time. His view is that authority is conferred not by tradition but by the mysteries of religious faith. To the question "Why should we obey the law?" his answer is that we obey because of sheer power. Central to politics is the sense of mystery. A rational, transparent society of the kind dreamed of by the Enlightenment would be a contradiction in terms. It is only mystery sustained by power that is capable of ensuring obedience. Far from being a Restoration-era legitimist, Maistre regarded ultimate authority as conferred by the power of decision. In a way that would later be appreciated by Carl Schmitt, he understood that the essence of politics is sovereignty and the sovereign is the one authorized to decide. There is a nihilistic side to this view of sovereignty as something that ultimately belies the powers of human reason.

Maistre's extreme views were scarcely an aberration. The apocalyptic imagination, as Norman Cohn has demonstrated, has deep roots in the Western tradition.[7] But Maistre does represent a first in modern politics: the revolutionary of the Right. His views on the theological basis of authority, the irrationalist character of political decision, and his idea of history as a Manichean struggle of light against darkness would provide the intellectual weapons for the rise of fascism a century later.[8] More to the point, Maistre's conception of an eternal struggle between God and his enemies presented a fundamental challenge to the Enlightenment narrative of history as a progressive movement from barbarism to civilization aided by the rise of modern science. It would only be a matter of time until the narrative of progress was turned against itself. Progress came to be seen less as the master narrative of history than a historical artifact whose time was coming to an end. To understand progress means to understand it historically, and this means to see it just as we would all other historical concepts, as a product of its time and place. This was the insight first announced by Nietzsche's epoch-making critique of historicism in *On the Uses and Disadvantages of History for Life,* included in his *Untimely Meditations.*[9]

NIETZSCHE'S CHALLENGE

Nietzsche's short treatise begins with a passage from Goethe that states as clearly as anything its author's intention: "I hate everything that merely instructs me without augmenting or directly invigorating my activity" (59). Nietzsche's point is that knowledge—chiefly, including historical knowledge—must be evaluated not only in terms of truth and falsity but also in terms of its influence on life, on how we live. History is of value only if it serves or enhances the life of action. The problem is that rather than enhancing life, modern historical scholarship has served only to stunt and disfigure it. For this reason, Nietzsche refers to his book as being "untimely," contrary to the age in which he lives. As a classical scholar, Nietzsche admits that he has no idea "what meaning classical studies could have for our time if they were not untimely" (60). His goal might seem to be like that of Herodotus, who wrote so that "time may not draw the color from what man has brought into being," or Thucydides, who claimed to provide "an exact knowledge of the past as an aid to the interpretation of the future."[10] But Nietzsche claims that his purpose is principally the critical one of exposing the "malignant historical fever" that the modern age has produced.

The question Nietzsche's work asks us to consider is the relation of history to human happiness or well-being. While animals live unhistorically, without an awareness of past or future, mankind, he asserts, is doomed to be the historical animal. We live with a sense of time, and it is our awareness of the coming into being and passing away of all things that is the source of human discontent. Memory is as much a blessing as a curse. A person incapable of forgetting would be the most miserable of beings, like the disciple of Heraclitus, who was too fearful to lift his finger for fear of what effect it would bring about. It follows that the possibility of action, especially great deeds, depends on our capacity to forget or at least to adopt a kind of willed blindness toward the past. "This is a universal law," Nietzsche announces, "a living thing can only be healthy, strong, and fruitful when bounded by a horizon," a horizon, he might have added, that provides a protective penumbra to all our actions (63). Culture depends on finding the right balance between memory and forgetfulness, between the historical and the unhistorical sense.

At the center of Nietzsche's work is his famous analysis of the three kinds of history—the monumental, the antiquarian, and the critical—that both serve and disserve life to varying degrees. Monumental history would seem closest to Nietzsche's description of himself as a child of the Greeks. The monumental historian looks to the past for heroes or exemplary models for conduct. What was once great, it is believed, can be so again with the proper encouragement. The purpose of monumental history is to encourage and inspire people of the present by turning to the glories of the past, something like Machiavelli's turn to ancient Rome to provide models for contemporary Italy. It might seem that this is just the kind of history for which Nietzsche is searching, but in fact he is quick to point out its shortcomings. The problem with monumental history is that it necessarily sanitizes and therefore distorts the past. In looking for usable models to imitate, it romanticizes the past and brushes aside everything that does not conform to its fiction. In the wrong hands, this kind of history can be a loaded weapon. Monumental history deceives by its "seductive simplicities" between the past and the present, thus enticing "the courageous to foolhardiness and the inspired to fanaticism" (71).

Antiquarian history is the virtual opposite of the monumental. It belongs to "him who preserves and reveres," who looks back "to where he has come into being with love and loyalty" (72). As it is for Tevye in *Fiddler on the Roof,* the watchword of antiquarian history is "tradition." Antiquarianism teaches respect for a people's national past as the life-giving source of tradition. This kind of history, Nietzsche avers, serves the needs of "the less favored generations and peoples" by anchoring them firmly in their past and thus protecting them from the fruitless search for novelty and ever new sources of stimulation (73). The problem with antiquarianism is, of course, that it overlooks or willfully conceals the source of tradition. Traditions were not founded by following tradition but often by breaking with some previous tradition. The danger of antiquarian history is that it distorts the very past it claims to hold in reverence. One is reminded here of Nietzsche's later barb about traditionalism: "In the ear of the Conservatives—What was formerly not known, what is known today or could be known—a *reversion,* a turning back in any sense and to any degree, is quite impossible. We physiologists know that. . . . Even today there are parties whose goal is a dream of the crabwise *regression* of all things. But no one is free to be a crab. There is nothing for it: one *has* to go forward, which is to say *step by step further into decadence.*"[11] Tradition, it appears, is self-undermining.

Critical history—Nietzsche's third type of historical understanding—comes closest to the modern conception of scientific history. History becomes the domain in which one exercises one's own critical judgment. The critical historian "must have the strength to break up and dissolve a part of the past" by "scrupulously examining it and finally condemning it" (75–76). Critical history has no problem with uprooting the sources of tradition or calling the authority of heroes into question. It happily exposes the injustices, crimes, and inhumanities papered over by the monumental and antiquarian historians but fails to question the very grounds of its own criticism. Rendering judgment is, for Nietzsche, an awesome responsibility. The critical perspective, the product of the modern Enlightenment, never probes its authority to criticize. "Ages and generations never have the right to judge previous ages and generations," Nietzsche writes, "such an uncomfortable mission falls only to individuals, and these of the rarest kind" (93). The problem with critical history is that it can destroy but cannot create. It can cut through and expose the falsehoods, myths, and illusions on which previous cultures have been based but cannot produce the ideals by which cultures can live and thrive. Critical history, like modern science and scholarship more generally, has a negative effect on culture. It fosters a skepticism that is inimical to the very possibility of culture. Rather than serving as an inspiration, it becomes an obstacle to action.

Nietzsche's point throughout *The Uses and Disadvantages* is that modern men and women have become so thoroughly imbued with history—so thoroughly historicized—that they have lost the capacity for creative action on which culture is based. Nietzsche was himself a historian, a classical philologist, and knew of what he spoke. We moderns, he complains, have become "inquisitive tourists or pedantic micrologists clambering about on the pyramids of the great eras of the past" (68). We have become encyclopedias of learning who can digest but cannot create. The most dangerous effect of the modern historical consciousness is that we have come to think of ourselves as latecomers, "born with gray hair," with no worlds left to conquer. It is this excess of history that proves the deepest challenge to the "plastic power" of life. Nietzsche accuses Hegel ("there has been no dangerous vacillation or crisis of German culture this century that has not been rendered more dangerous by the enormous and still continuing influence of this philosophy, the Hegelian" [104]) of fostering a kind of moral complacency with his belief that the modern historical consciousness represents the high point of human achievement. This insight, Nietzsche believes, has proved deadly. A people who believe that they can no longer create can only retreat into self-absorbed irony.

The question Nietzsche forces us to ask is, What can be done about this? Given that we cannot escape history, how can history be made to serve the future? It must be admitted that he provides no very precise answer to this question. He calls for a new kind of historian, one who is both a knower and a creator. "Do not believe historiography that does not spring from the head of the rarest minds," he warns (94). "He who has not experienced greater and more exalted things than others will not know how to interpret the great and exalted things of the past" (94). But where can such a rare spirit be found, especially in an age that seems to value only specialists and other professional caretakers of culture? Nietzsche advises his reader, "Satiate your soul with Plutarch," and "when you believe in his heroes dare at the same time to believe in yourself" (95). Yet, this seems less an answer than the search for an answer, especially since Plutarch's brand of moralizing history necessarily fails what is for Nietzsche the greatest test of the modern age, namely, the demand for intellectual honesty (*Redlichkeit*).

The Uses and Disadvantages concludes with a paradox. Nietzsche agrees that the search for historical truth ("objectivity") grows out of the passionate desire to render justice. Yet this call to truth is threatening to the myths, ideals, and illusions that make up culture. "All living things require an atmosphere around them, a mysterious misty vapor," Nietzsche affirms, and then adds: "If they are deprived of this envelope . . . they quickly wither and grow hard and unfruitful" (97). Cultures presuppose a distinctive horizon within which they grow and decay, take shape and develop. These horizons created by the great lawgivers of history provide the charmed circle within which later and lesser mortals are enabled to live and act. Each culture is necessarily based on a kind of blindness to every other culture. Cultures inhabit a liminal world that is neither completely historical nor completely unhistorical. There is, then, a conflict—a necessary and vital conflict—between the science of culture, which seeks to be universal and impartial, and the needs of culture, which are subjective and value laden. How is one to choose? "Is life to dominate knowledge and science, or is knowledge to dominate life?" Nietzsche asks at the end of his essay (121). His answer is clear. Science presupposes life, but life does not necessarily presuppose science. We must embrace life.

REVOLUTIONARY NIHILISM

Nietzsche's passionate appeal to embrace life, even life over science or truth, formed the basis of what came to be called "nihilism."[12] The term was coined by the German philosopher F. H. Jacobi, who maintained that all systems of philosophical rationalism necessarily led to skepticism and loss of faith.[13] Nihilism emerged as a movement of radical opposition or what Hegel called "abstract negation." The initial blast of nihilism came originally from Russia, where the term first gained currency. Intimations of nihilism can be found in the works of Mikhail Bakunin, Sergey Nechayev, and the characters in Dostoyevsky's *The Possessed,* in which the term meant literally the will to nothing, to the destruction of everything, but nihilism was initially more of an attitude than a program. Nihilism reached its heyday during the fin de siècle and cannot be entirely divorced from the emergence of the great middle-class democracies in England and France. Nihilism meant a repudiation of the world of the bourgeois. It signified a mood of disgust, of nausea, of disenchantment with the prevailing order of things, and was therefore more likely to be expressed in poems like Eliot's *Waste Land* or novels like Sartre's *Nausea* and Celine's *Journey to the End of the Night.*

The response to bourgeois society took many forms. For the Left, it meant opposition to capitalism and the hegemony of bourgeois ideology as expressed in such formulas as the rights of man, the greatest happiness for the greatest number, and the pursuit of happiness, while for the Right it meant opposition to democracy and parliamentary government, which were construed as the last gasp of a decaying Christianity. According to Leo Strauss, who diagnosed this attitude in Germany in the years following World War I, nihilism represented a moral protest against the idea of the open or cosmopolitan society.[14] The idea of an "open morality" divorced from the particularities of nation, race, or class was deemed to exist on a lower level of humanity than a "closed morality" based on such old-fashioned virtues as loyalty, duty, honor, and self-sacrifice. Strauss found this protest movement not in every respect contemptible. It was made up of "quite a few very intelligent, and very decent, if very young, Germans," among whom Strauss seems to have included himself. "What they hated," he wrote, "was the very prospect of a world in which everyone would be happy and satisfied, in which everyone would have his little pleasure by day and his little pleasure by night, a world in which no great heart could beat and no great soul could breath, a world without real, unmetaphoric, sacrifice, i.e., a world without blood, sweat and tears."[15] Behind this pacified world of trade, science, and the rights of man stood the problem of the Enlightenment.

For the young nihilists who rallied behind the flag of Nietzsche, modern civilization—the civilization of the bourgeois—was increasingly becoming a planetary society without rulers and ruled, devoted mainly to production and consumption, a pacified world in which wars, revolutions, and "great politics" had been consigned to the past and in which the higher virtues of courage, nobility, and sacrifice no longer held a place. This was the world of Nietzsche's "last man," who no longer understands love, creativity, or longing. The last man's true desires are for peace, comfort, and above all, happiness. "We have invented happiness, say the last men, and they blink," Nietzsche wrote in *Thus Spoke Zarathustra.*[16] It is the desire to be happy, not in the Aristotelian sense of possessing a well-ordered soul, but to be secure, respected, and well-liked, that Nietzsche finds to be the most contemptible feature of the modern cosmopolitan world. While it contradicts the essence of nihilism to have a plan or program for the future, for the post–World War I generation the mere abstract negation, while it may be doomed to failure, seemed a preferable alternative to the prolongation of the idea of a pacified humanity under the rule of perpetual peace, safety, and benevolence. Better to go down, like the defenders of the Alamo, with guns blazing and flags flying than to acquiesce to the world of the last man.

At the core of the critiques of both Left and Right, however, was an opposition to not just modern civilization but especially its backbone, namely, modern science, technology, and what Max Weber called the "rationalization" of the world. Here is the point where Left and Right converge. This is especially evident if we consider Georg Lukács's famous theory of "reification" in *History and Class Consciousness.*[17] Reification (*Verdinglichung*) was Lukács's term for the theory of alienation or fetishism developed in Marx's *Capital.* Reification, as the German term literally suggests, means turning a human activity into a thing, that is, taking objects or activities that are the result of human interactions and treating them as if they obeyed laws of their own, independent of their creators. It is the process in which a human social relationship takes on thing-like properties. The description of certain market relations as obeying the "law of supply and demand" or following the "iron law of wages" or the famous "iron law of oligarchy" is reifying in the sense that it ascribes certain natural, law-like characteristics to what are transitory historical phenomena. Even the categories of historical materialism are subject to change as history evolves in new and unanticipated directions. Lukács held that the attempt to turn Marxism into a form of "scientific socialism" was just another example of reification. By exposing the reified character of these processes, it would be possible to restore the primacy of praxis or human agency—the Marxian equivalent of the Nietzschean category of life—that Lukács believed was the central insight of the dialectic.

While Marx's critique applied mainly to the sphere of commodity production, Lukács applied it in a far more capacious manner to the rational and mechanical organization of society as a whole. Reification applies especially to technology and the specialization and particularization of functions in which the individual is increasingly lost. It is to expose the rational, mechanical, and predictable character of society that is the object of the theory of reification. Behind this theory stands Weber's critique of the rationalized life world. It is the very rationalism of life under capitalism that Weber and Lukács deplore. They object not so much to waste and inefficiency—what Marx had called "the anarchy of production"—as to order and "routinization." Modern industry and the workforce, for example, require a rationalized bureaucracy and legal system to ensure their efficiency. Under these conditions, "the judge is more or less an automatic statute-dispensing machine," and "the judge's behavior is on the whole *predictable*."[18] A key feature of the reification process concerns how the continuous flow of time—the Bergsonian idea of uninterrupted flux—is broken up into discrete units. "Thus time sheds its qualitative, variable, flowing nature," Lukács laments, noting that "it freezes into an exactly delimited, quantifiable continuum filled with quantifiable 'things.' "[19]

It is easy to see that the theory of reification has less to do with Marxism than with the Counter-Enlightenment's critique of rationalism. The chief culprit of this critique is modern science and its application to society. Lukács's theory of reification has been ascribed here to the tradition of romanticism and *Lebensphilosophie*, with its opposition to science and quantification in general. Lukács finds a highly suspicious affinity between the methods of modern science and the needs of capitalist society. "There is something highly problematic," he writes in the opening pages of his book, "in the fact that capitalist society is predisposed to harmonize with scientific method, to constitute indeed the social premises of its exactness."[20] This predisposition finds expression in Galileo's call for "scientific exactitude," which presupposes that "the elements remain constant."[21] The fact that modern science has developed in tandem with the structures of modern society is sufficient to cast doubt on its legitimacy. Lukács describes "the idea, formulated most lucidly by Kant but essentially unchanged since Kepler and Galileo, of nature as the 'aggregate of systems of the laws' governing what happens" as a "development out of the economic structures of capitalism."[22] Once again Lukács follows Nietzsche's lead in ascribing to science—not historical science but natural science and its methods—the chief role in the production of "the reified mind."

Lukács's theory of reification in *History and Class Consciousness* had a perfect counterpart in Heidegger's analysis of inauthenticity in *Being and Time*.[23] Although Heidegger does not link his analysis of the inauthentic self specifically to modern science and the rationalized economy, he clearly associates it with the "anonymous" conditions of everyday life prevalent in modern democracy. Like many of his contemporaries from the cultural Right, Heidegger depicted the conditions of urban life with its cosmopolitanism, restlessness, and consuming curiosity about new places and experiences as typical of the modern everyday world. While Marxists may have complained about the workers' alienation from the means of production, for Heidegger the problem was that modern life had become rootless and forgetful of terms like *Heimat* (home) and *Vaterland* (fatherland). Heidegger later turned to Hölderlin as the poet anointed with the task of showing the way to a new homeland for the German spirit. Germany, he complained, was caught in "pincers" between Anglo-American democracy to the west and Soviet communism to the east. "Situated in the center," Heidegger complained, "our nation incurs the severest pressure."[24] Although he eschewed drawing any political prescriptions from his book, it can and should be read as a response to the conditions of Weimar democracy in the years immediately after World War I.

The key feature of everyday life is represented by the emergence of the impersonal "they" or "anyone" (*das Man*) that stands as the antithesis to Heidegger's call for a more authentic mode of being. This anonymous "they" form "the great mass" who inhabit the cities and suburbs of modern life: "The Self of everyday Dasein is the *they-self*, which we distinguish from the *authentic Self*—that is, from the Self which has been taken hold of in its own way. This dispersal characterizes the 'subject' of that kind of Being which we know as concernful absorption in the world we encounter as closest to us. If Dasein is familiar with itself as they-self, this means at the same time that the 'they' itself prescribes that way of interpreting the world and Being-in-the-world which lies closest. Dasein is for the sake of the 'they' in an everyday manner."[25]

Heidegger's concept of inauthenticity bears many of the same features that other Counter-Enlightenment figures attributed to the bourgeois: shallowness, egoism, the drawing of a sense of self from the opinions of others. This everyday mode of life is increasingly dominated by "idle talk" (*Gerede*), or chatter. Although Heidegger claims—somewhat disingenuously—that he does not use the term "idle talk" in any "disparaging" way, it is clear that it carries deeply moralistic overtones. The world of chatter, he complains, "spreads in wider circles and takes on an authoritative character."[26] Eventually it becomes impossible to distinguish what is true ("what has been drawn from primordial sources") from what amounts to "the average understanding." Further, the world of chatter—consider in today's world the role of the Internet and Facebook—blocks out the possibility of originality or thinking for oneself. "The 'they,'" Heidegger writes, "prescribes one's state-of-mind, and determines what and how one 'sees.'"[27]

There is much in Heidegger's analysis of everyday life that is genuinely illuminating, but as with Lukács's theory of reification, it is not clear what he recommends doing about it. Unlike Lukács, whose reification theory remained an analysis of modern social life, Heidegger thought of inauthenticity as an ontological condition into which we have simply "fallen."[28] Our fallenness, a term with clear Christian overtones, suggests that the world we inhabit is not our creation but something given to us, from which there is, to use Sartre's phrase, "no exit." To this grim picture of an entirely rationalized, disenchanted world, Lukács offered his own theory of "totality"—a term borrowed from German romanticism—that suggests a more integrated and harmonious way of life than the one offered under the conditions of modern capitalistic organization. Heidegger similarly offered a radical critique without offering a clear alternative. His answer seems to be the conception of the authentic personality who answers to the call of conscience and who is prepared to engage in a face-to-face confrontation with death.[29]

From Lukács's critique of reification and Heidegger's analysis of inauthenticity it is but a small step to Max Horkheimer and Theodor Adorno's *Dialectic of Enlightenment*.[30] Publishing their book in the years shortly after World War II, the authors go even farther than Lukács in ascribing the horrors of the twentieth century to the Enlightenment, which they at various times conflate with positivism, capitalism, and fascism. It is the Enlightenment that they regard as being at the root of modern tyrannies, precisely for the absolutism and inflexibility of its methods. The original goal of emancipation achieved through the free use of reason has flip-flopped into a plan to render the world calculable and predictable through science and to punish every form of resistance. It is the Enlightenment that reduces thought to calculation and "instrumental rationality." Bacon, Descartes, and Leibniz are all accused of creating the methods for turning thought into computation. The story they tell is one of unending control, manipulation, and regulation that can only result in oppression. There is a steady progression from the original aims of the Enlightenment—Kant's "sapere aude"—to the death camps at Auschwitz. "For the Enlightenment, whatever does not conform to the rule of computation and utility is suspect," Horkheimer and Adorno write. "Enlightenment is totalitarian."[31]

The central themes of these works we have been considering is the depiction of modernity as a veritable wasteland created by a combination of scientific technology, instrumental rationality, and the "reification" of the world, or what Heidegger would later call "enframing" (*Gestell*).[32] What animates this repudiation has less to do with any particular evil or injustice than with the animating spirit behind society, namely, the Enlightenment, with its goal of a safe, peaceful, and tolerant world secure from conflict, war, and tragedy. No one did more to anticipate this mélange of ideas and attitudes than did a Frenchman, Georges Sorel.

THE PHILOSOPHY OF PESSIMISM

Sorel, like Nietzsche, was a bourgeois. He was born in 1847 (three years after Nietzsche) and studied engineering at the École Polytechnique. He was a capacious reader and student of history, but largely self-taught. His interests ranged from classics to the history of Christianity to political theory. He wrote a book, *The Trial of Socrates* (1889), in which he took the side of the Athenian polis against Socrates, whom he interpreted as an agent of moral decay. His book *The Illusions of Progress* (1908) was an intellectual history of the idea of progress, which he treats as an ideology of the middle class. His most famous book, *Reflections on Violence,* presented his controversial ideas on myth, violence, and apocalyptic revolution.[33] Sorel was an eclectic. At various times he was an ideological soul mate of both communism and fascism.

In the Introduction to *Reflections on Violence,* Sorel remarks that what irritated many readers of the book is the pessimistic conception of human nature on which the entire study rests (8). What did he mean by pessimism? Pessimism is best defined by what it opposes. The poles of pessimism and optimism are similar to other polarities, like realism and idealism, or William James's tough-minded and tender-minded, or Nietzsche's Dionysian and Apollonian. The optimist is associated with the Enlightenment belief that rational scientific schema or categories can serve as patterns or models of reality. For Sorel, this belief represents a profound distortion of reality that is always far more fluid, more spontaneous, and more combustible than our intellectual categories could ever allow. The world is in constant flux and motion, and any attempt to describe, control, and predict it represents a distortion of experience.

Sorel adopted the view of Henri Bergson's philosophy of vitalism, according to which all thinking, especially our theoretical concepts and categories, represents an arrest of reality, an attempt to render fixed and permanent what is in constant motion. Abstractions kill; they interrupt the flow of life. When applied to politics, this optimism is expressed in the form of utopianism. Utopias, Sorel believes, are dangerous and sterile doctrines because they postulate an ideal end state or fixed goal for human aspirations that is simply false to the unpredictability and diversity of human ends. From Plato to Marx— or at least the Marxism of his contemporaries—he regarded this aspiration to utopia as harboring deep-seated tyrannical tendencies.

In contrast to these images of optimism, Sorel means by pessimism something closer to the view that the world is governed by perpetual struggle and conflict. The pessimist is especially skeptical of the view that the human condition is amenable to piecemeal or gradual reform. Some of the most vivid moments in the *Reflections* are when Sorel is heaping scorn on the advocates of meliorism, or gradual parliamentary change toward some limited goal. The great pessimists in history were the early Christians who believed that no human effort could redeem the world and instead withdrew to await the Second Coming. The Calvinists of the sixteenth century with their harsh views on the sinfulness of man were another example of this metaphysical pessimism, as, of course, were the anarchists and revolutionaries of Sorel's own time (13).

Oddly, Sorel regards Marxism as another example of pessimism in action. He rejects the idea of Marxism as a theory of progress following a logical development of stages of modes of production culminating in communism. Rather, true Marxism, like Christianity, is a doctrine of the apocalypse. "The pessimist," Sorel writes, "regards social conditions as forming a system bound together by an iron law which cannot be evaded, as something in the form of one block, and which can only disappear through a catastrophe that involves the whole" (11). While the optimist regards life as a series of trade-offs between better and worse, the pessimist sees it as an existential struggle between all or nothing. The optimist looks into the abyss and pulls back; the pessimist looks in and says, "Bring it on."

Pessimism is ultimately more a teaching about human psychology than a theory of history or society. Optimists—today we would call them social scientists, such as economists and political scientists—believe that human beings respond to rational incentives, that at our core we are utility maximizers who rationally calculate what is in our interests for us to be or to do. Sorel is far more struck by the nonrational (although not necessarily irrational) wellsprings of human behavior. Why, he wondered, do people engage in often-violent popular upheavals and display considerable courage and self-sacrifice? Why do people risk their lives for a cause when they have little to gain in any pragmatic sense? Sorel is struck, for example, by the way medieval stonemasons sculpted statues of great beauty and yet were content to remain completely anonymous, how soldiers in Napoleon's armies were prepared to face death for glory alone, and how Christians throughout the ages have often chosen death and martyrdom. In all of these behaviors he finds a striving for perfection, for the absolute, that could never be explained by appeals to utility, self-interest, or some mercenary incentive. Something other than reason and interest is at work, but what is it?

MYTH AND VIOLENCE

Sorel's term for this nonrational source of human action is *myth*.[34] Myths are not simply false beliefs, as the Enlightenment maintained. Although Sorel rejected Plato's utopianism, he may have discovered in the Platonic analysis of *mythos*—the power of poetry, music, and song—the ability to galvanize human behavior. Myths are not simply forms of false consciousness. Throughout history, myths have given expression to people's collective aspirations. They start not from the individual but from the group and typically exalt the family, armies, communities, and other traditional modes of association. Sorel had a strangely conservative view of the myth of the proletariat. Only the producers—not the cowardly bourgeoisie—he believed, were the bearers of the true values of work, respect for family, sacrifice, order, and chastity.

One point on which Sorel insists is that myths are not the same as ideologies or utopias. "A utopia," he remarks, "is an intellectual product; it is the work of theorists who, after observing and discussing the facts, seek to establish a model to which they can compare existing societies" (28). Utopias are typically programs for reform; they offer blueprints or road maps for a future society. Because utopias are intellectual constructions, they can be discussed, and in being discussed, they can be refuted. Myth is something entirely different. Myths "are not descriptions of things but expressions of a will to act" (28). They present the future not as a possible social order but as a catastrophic event. Unlike utopias, myths cannot be refuted, because they are "at bottom identical with the convictions of a group, being the expressions of those convictions in the language of movement" (29). The two most potent myths of his day were the Marxist myth of revolution and the syndicalist myth of the "general strike."

Myths are the expression of the catastrophic or apocalyptic mentality. They are matters of faith rather than predictions of the future based on the prevailing trends of society. The idea that the source of our beliefs is ultimately a matter of faith not reason, as we shall see later, connects Sorel to the tradition of political theology. What myths depict is not a possible future social order but a theory of catastrophe. Accordingly, they are forms of collective mobilization and action: "Experience shows that the *framing of a future in some indeterminate time,* may, when it is done in a certain way, be very effective and have very few inconveniences; this happens when the anticipations of the future take the form of those myths which enclose with them all the strongest inclinations of a people, of a party, or of a class, inclinations which recur to the mind with the insistence of instincts in all the circumstances of life" (115).

Importantly, myths are not predictions about how things will work out, and so they cannot be falsified. Sorel notes how the Christian myth of the apocalypse has been indefinitely postponed but remains no less powerful for this fact. The important thing is that the myth presents itself as a comprehensive antithesis to the here and now, to the way things are. Catholics, Sorel tells us, "have always pictured the history of the Church as a series of battles between Satan and the hierarchy supported by Christ; every new difficulty that arises is an episode in this war which must finally end in the victory of Catholicism" (20).

In this respect, Marxism is another such myth that carries with it a vision of apocalyptic change, for which Sorel uses the term the "general strike":

> The general strike is indeed . . . the *myth* in which socialism is wholly comprised, i.e. a body of images capable of evoking instinctively all the sentiments which correspond to the different manifestations of the war undertaken by socialism against modern society. Strikes have engendered in the proletariat the noblest, the deepest, and the most moving sentiments that they possess; the general strike groups them all in a coordinated picture and, by bringing them together, gives to each one of them its maximum of intensity; appealing to their painful memories of particular conflicts, it colors with an intense life all the details of the composition presented to consciousness. We thus obtain that intuition of socialism which language cannot give us with perfect clearness—and we obtain it as a whole, perceived instantaneously. (118)

It is important to understand that by the general strike Sorel does not mean a labor dispute or a work stoppage. He is completely uninterested in economic subjects like wages, working conditions, and pensions. The purpose of the general strike is not to improve the material conditions of the working class. He is in fact quite contemptuous of those politicians, like his social democratic contemporary Jean Jaurès, who regarded socialism as just a means of raising the standard of living. For Sorel, every strike is simply a further step along the road to the apocalypse when the bourgeois class will meet its doom. The purpose of the general strike is not improvement but the destruction, the absolute negation, of an existing state of affairs.

Myths are by their very nature Manichean. They divide the world into two unalterably opposed camps: the children of light and the children of darkness. Every myth must construct the image of an enemy that it opposes root and branch. For classical Marxism, the enemy was the capitalist class, which was presented as robbing the proletariat of its very humanity. For Sorel, the enemy of the working class is not the capitalists—to some degree Sorel even admires them—but the intellectuals for whom ideas have become a new kind of power. Sorel's fascination with the danger of intellectuals goes back to his study of Socrates, whom, like Nietzsche, he sees as the great destroyer of Greek heroic ethics. The modern heirs of Socrates were those eighteenth-century humanists, the Encyclopedists, whose theories of progress and the rights of man were simply a means of achieving power. "During the Terror," Sorel writes in the Introduction to the *Reflections,* "the men who spilt the most blood were precisely those who had the greatest desire to let their equals enjoy the golden age they had dreamt . . . optimistic, idealistic, and sensitive, they showed themselves to be the more unyielding the greater their desire for universal happiness" (10). Sorel is part of the reactionary tradition that views groups like the Freemasons and other intellectuals as forming a conspiracy to enhance their own power. In his day, he believes, it is the social democrats with their theories of scientific socialism and historical necessity who are attempting to gain power over the working classes. It is not capital per se but the intellectuals— the scientists, the theoreticians, *philosophes* of all stripes—who must be resisted.

Central to Sorel's myth of the general strike is his call to violence. *Reflections on Violence,* like Machiavelli's *Prince,* is nothing if not a hymn to the redemptive powers of violence. For Sorel, everything of value owes its meaning to violence. "It is to violence," he writes in the last sentence of the book, "that socialism owes those high ethical values by means of which it brings salvation to the modern world" (251). Sorel displays a kind of anthropological fascination with all kinds of violence from very different parts of the world, from rural Norwegian communities, to vigilante mobs described in Denver and New Orleans, to Corsican vendettas. Violence is approved not just for its powers of destruction but because it affords an opportunity for heroism. Sorel is at his core a moralist deeply concerned with the fate of ethics in the bourgeois world. It is not peace but war and violence that he believes brings out the best in us: "The nature of lofty moral convictions . . . never depend on reasoning or on any education of the individual will; they depend upon a state of war in which men voluntarily participate and which finds expression in well-defined myths. In Catholic countries the monks carry on the struggle against the prince of evil who triumphs in this world and would subdue them to his will; in Protestant countries small fanatical sects take the place of the monasteries. These are the battlefields that enable Christian morality to hold its own, with that character of sublimity which today still fascinates many minds and which gives it sufficient luster to occasion in society a few pale imitations" (207–8). What was true of Christianity is true today for the workers—Sorel prefers to call them the producers—who will establish a new, even higher, morality based on revolutionary violence. What will this new morality look like?

THE NEW MORALITY

Sorel treats socialism simply as a comprehensive antithesis to the existing state of society. He denies that socialism is a plan or a program. Nevertheless, he does allow himself to speculate on some of the positive ideals that the myth of the general strike will bring about.

In the first place, the new society will be a society of producers. By a producer Sorel means something like a creator and, above all, an artist. Every worker will be transformed into an inventor. Most inventions and discoveries, he contends, have been advanced by largely anonymous workmen making their own innovations on the spot. "The free producer in a highly progressive workshop," he writes, "must never measure his efforts by an external standard; he finds all the models presented to him to be mediocre and wants to surpass everything that has been done before him" (244).

What most engages Sorel's imagination, however, is an idea of the practical life—the life of action and struggle—rather than theory. The goal of socialism, Sorel is convinced, is not comfort or happiness, but struggle. There is something pre-Socratic, almost Homeric, in his attempt to revive the spirit of heroic antiquity. "I am not among those," Sorel says, "who consider Homer's Achaean type, the indomitable hero, confident in his strength and putting himself above rules, as necessarily disappearing in the future" (233). Liberty, he fears, would be fatally compromised if we came to think of Homeric ethics as something consigned to the past. But where is one to look for it?

Sorel is unique among the members of the Counter-Enlightenment who see in America the land where this new ethic of producers has taken shape. For most of the Counter-Enlightenment thinkers, America was the land where a soulless rationalism and a dreary Puritan work ethic had taken root. We saw in chapter 6 how Max Weber cited Benjamin Franklin's *Autobiography* as evidence of this view. For Heidegger and his heirs in the Frankfurt School, America was the place where culture went to die, dominated by mass communication, consumerism, and Hollywood.[35] America, for these thinkers, merely represented the coming of age of certain European ideas that had been nurtured mainly in England, especially by Locke. The struggle against America was also a struggle against England and its empire. Lockean empiricism and common sense represented the debasement of everything great and noble in philosophy that was ostensibly preserved by the spirit of German philosophy.

Sorel was certainly no fan of the moderate Enlightenment represented by Locke and the "common sense" school of philosophy. Yet, what he saw—or believed he saw—in America was not a smug and prosperous middle-class society—the world represented by Flaubert's apothecary, Homais—that he would have despised but the triumph of a certain kind of anarchy and the state of nature in the Wild West. Sorel seems to have found in Theodore Roosevelt's America an example of the active life, the life of energy and struggle.[36] He chastises Nietzsche ("the professor of philology") for deploring the disappearance of the Homeric type of hero but failing to see what was under his very nose. The master type, he asserts, still exists, and it is this type that at the present time has created the extraordinary greatness of the United States. "He [Nietzsche] would have been struck," Sorel continues, "by the singular analogies that exist between the Yankee, ready for any kind of enterprise, and the ancient Greek sailor, sometimes a pirate, sometimes a colonist or a merchant; above all, he would have established a parallel between the ancient heroes and the man who sets out to conquer the Far West" (232).

Sorel's reading of America as a land of heroic producers is based largely on the work of a French economist, Paul de Rousiers—much less well known than Tocqueville—who had written a book called *American Life* (*La vie américaine*), which Sorel says describes "admirably" the mythic qualities of energy and virtue: "To become and to remain an American, one must look upon life as *a struggle and not as a pleasure* and seek in it victorious effort, energetic and efficient action, rather than pleasure, than leisure embellished by the cultivation of the arts and the refinements proper to other societies. Everywhere we have seen what makes the American succeed, what constitutes his type—it is moral character, personal energy, energy in action, creative energy" (232). In the same context, Sorel draws attention to the "strange likeness" between Andrew Carnegie, Theodore Roosevelt, and Nietzsche. All celebrate the active life of self-exertion, heroism, and conquest. I can only imagine that if Sorel had lived long enough, he would have been an admirer of the westerns of John Ford.

Sorel's reading of the American character can be described as a kind of heroic nihilism. He was an admirer of William James's *Pragmatism,* which famously distinguished between the tough-minded and the tender-minded. The tender-minded are typically rationalistic, idealistic, optimistic; the tough-minded are empiricist, pragmatist, and pessimistic. The tender-minded are those with a need for an eternal moral order, while the tough-minded are those who are prepared to constantly adjust and adapt to life's circumstances.[37]

Sorel would agree with this in part, but he would not have seen morality as the outcome of Jamesian adaptation to circumstances. The only morality worthy of the name is the one that emerges from resistance and opposition to what is, not adaptation to it. James praises the tough-minded, but perhaps he is really not so tough. Sorel regards morality as something forged in battle; it can only come into being through the act of creative destruction, especially the destruction of the old order of things. Sorel can brook no compromise with the present. Like Nietzsche, he represents the apocalyptic imagination at its most extreme.

SORELIAN LEGACIES

Sorel's writings exercised no demonstrable influence on the Marxist movement, yet it is widely believed that his ideas share a strong affinity with the political radicalism of the New Left of the 1960s. Isaiah Berlin, for example, discerns a connection between Sorel and thinkers and revolutionaries like Franz Fanon and Che Guevara, for whom "the oppressed can find themselves and acquire self-identity and human dignity in acts of revolutionary violence."[38] What connects Sorel with third-world revolutionary movements is said to be his "unyielding emphasis" on the will as the principle of action.

"He believed," Berlin continues, "in absolute moral ends that are independent of any dialectical or other historical pattern . . . this rather than a sense of the unalterable timetable of historical determinism is the mood of the majority of the rebels, political and cultural, of the last two decades."[39] The radicals of the sixties, unlike those of the Depression-era thirties, were more likely to be moved not by social and economic conditions but by the charges of hypocrisy and bad faith against the regimes and institutions under which they lived. Their protest was moral rather than economic. "This is far closer to Sorel's position," Berlin maintains, "and connects him with modern revolutionary protest."[40]

These arguments seem oddly dated today. They are based on some easy and facile affinities between the era of fin de siècle France and the culture of the 1960s. More to the point is a thinker on whom Sorel exercised real and demonstrable influence. In his 1923 work *The Crisis of Parliamentary Democracy,* Carl Schmitt was one of the first to appreciate and draw attention to Sorel's combustible appeal to violence, myth, and the general strike.[41] Schmitt admired Sorel's argument that it was myth, not reason, which alone could generate the courage and enthusiasm necessary for mass political action. "The warlike and heroic conceptions that are bound up with battle and struggle," he wrote, "were taken seriously by Sorel as the true impulse for an intensive life."[42] He further acknowledged that the Bolshevik Revolution testified to the power of the Marxist myth of the proletariat. Sorel had even dedicated the 1919 edition of *Reflections on Violence* to Lenin, calling him the greatest Russian statesman since Peter the Great. But Sorel's praise of Lenin was a mixed blessing. The Bolshevik Revolution had succeeded because Lenin had turned Marxism into a Russian national myth castigating the Westernized upper classes as the enemy of the indigenous Russian peasantry. This transformation of the proletarian myth into a Russian national myth was symbolized by the transfer of the capital from Saint Petersburg to Moscow. Russia had become Muscovite again.[43]

Schmitt drew from Sorel's depiction of the Russian Revolution an important lesson: the national myth is stronger than the class myth. Sorel's myth of the general strike remained disfigured by Marxian class analysis, an essentially economic category, and in this respect Sorel, like Marx, displayed his intellectual dependence on both his liberal and his socialist opponents. Sorel's attempt to create a morality of economic producers would eventually morph into "a rationalism and mechanistic outlook that is empty of myth."[44] For Schmitt, it was not the class enemy but the national enemy that was at the core of his famous definition of "the political" (*das Politische*). By the political, Schmitt means to distinguish not between the good and the bad (morality), the beautiful and the ugly (aesthetics), or the profitable and unprofitable (economics) but between the friend and the enemy. "The specific political distinction to which political actions and motives can be reduced," he avers, "is that between friend and enemy."[45]

On what criterion is the Schmittian myth of the friend-enemy based? About this, Schmitt is notoriously vague. Almost anyone or anything can become the object of political enmity. On one point, however, he is clear. The enemy is not necessarily someone for whom one feels personal animosity. He distinguishes between the private enemy and the public enemy (*hostis*). It is only the latter that is an object of political enmity: "The political enemy need not be morally evil or aesthetically ugly; he need not appear as an economic competitor, and it may even be advantageous to engage with him in business transactions. But he is, nevertheless, the other, the stranger; and it is sufficient for his nature that he is, in a specially intense way, existentially something different and alien, so that in the extreme case conflicts with him are possible."[46]

Schmitt takes from Sorel the idea that the myth of the enemy presupposes a world of conflict, war, and ever-present preparation for war. It is this sense of pervasive conflict that lends a sense of existential urgency to Schmitt's concept of the political. War is the "ever present possibility" of politics. Schmitt regards the whole domain of parliamentary politics as a continuous effort to overcome conflict and abolish the distinction between friend and enemy. The social contract tradition from Hobbes to Kant sought to find the device that could turn the state of war into one of peace. By turning politics into talk and debate, parliamentarianism seeks to put an end to the state of war. To wish for a pacified world, a world without war, would be to wish for a world without politics. It would also be a world without ideals, without the possibility of heroism, courage, and sacrifice.[47]

In contrast to the world of constitutional democracy, Schmitt proposed his doctrine of "decisionism," something that goes back to Maistre. By decisionism Schmitt meant the view that our deepest moral commitments cannot be established or even defended by reason, much less be used to predict what will happen on the basis of statistics or existing social trends. Rather our highest ideals and commitments are irrational in the sense that they are utterly arbitrary expressions of the will. These commitments stand in turn in a relation of radical conflict with one another. They are most clearly revealed in times of war rather than peace. It follows that morality and politics are not the domain of logrolling, compromise, and give-and-take but the arena where ultimate values play themselves out. In contrast to the classical or prudential advice of following the mean or moderate course, the nihilist will claim to follow the extreme wherever it might lead. By declaring himself in favor of will and decision, Schmitt was implicitly putting himself on the side of political theology as opposed to political philosophy. Politics is simply theology carried out by other means, namely, the arena where ultimate questions of good and evil, God and the Devil, battle one another for popular allegiance. It is a reenactment of certain biblical dramas of enmity that set Cain against Abel, Esau against Jacob, Satan against God. It would be but a short step from Schmitt's embrace of this moment of decision to Heidegger's statement praising "the inner truth and greatness" of National Socialism.[48]

In Schmitt, we find all the themes of the Counter-Enlightenment's war against civilization brought to their breaking point. Schmitt saw in the Weimar constitution—the liberal democratic constitution adopted in Germany after the First World War—a sign of the dominance of Anglo-French *Zivilisation* over German *Kultur*. Schmitt's decisionism has recently been seen as a form of political theology that had resurfaced in Germany of the 1920s.[49] By political theology Schmitt did not mean any particular religious doctrine or creed. Although raised a Catholic, like the other young nihilists of his generation, he thought of himself as an atheist. Following Nietzsche, these nihilists of the Right believed that the contemporary creeds of liberalism, socialism, and pacifism were all decayed remnants of Christianity with its belief in the equality of rights and dignity of all human beings. To face up to reality—to view it in the full light of day "with sober senses" (Marx)—it must be viewed without the illusions of religion and its humanitarian appeals to justice. But this kind of atheism was not inconsistent with faith of another sort. This is the belief, deeply embedded in the Counter-Enlightenment, that all our ultimate values and decisions are in the final analysis a matter of faith, not reason. Schmitt's political theology is ultimately not a religious doctrine but an epistemological theory about the nonrational foundations of our beliefs.

It was Leo Strauss who first identified the "theologico-political" nature of Schmitt's *Concept of the Political*.[50] Strauss, we saw earlier, was one of those youthful admirers of Schmitt's critique of liberalism, but his admiration was not without qualification. Schmitt had complained that a world without war would be a nonpolitical world. Such a world would lack a vital element of humanity. It would be a world with culture, civilization, law, morality, and the arts, but it would also be a world without moral seriousness, the kind of seriousness that can only be generated in periods of intense national crisis when the very future of society is at stake.[51] Schmitt owed his thinking to Hobbes, who presented the state of nature as one of maximal fearfulness and dread. But while Hobbes's desire was to overcome the state of war and replace it with a civil society based on economic development, the sciences, and the arts, Schmitt feared such a world precisely because it is based on the illusory belief that human nature is educable and that man, the dangerous animal, can be transformed into a peaceable bourgeois.[52]

Strauss questioned the foundations of Schmitt's insight. It is not the friend-enemy distinction per se that divides humanity into hostile camps but competing conceptions of justice and the human good. Strauss here raises the Socratic question—"How should we live?"—as the issue that truly divides humanity. At a crucial point in his critique, Strauss cites two Platonic texts—the *Euthyphro* and *Phaedrus*—to the effect that the ground of conflict has nothing to do with arbitrary distinctions between friend and enemy but always involves reasoned judgments over justice and injustice. "Agreement at any price is possible only as agreement at the price of the meaning of life," Strauss avers, "for such agreement is possible only when man abandons the task of raising the question regarding what is right, and when man abandons this question, he abandons humanity."[53] It is only disagreement over what is right—the moral question—that justifies the division of humanity into friends and enemies.

Strauss acknowledges the value of Schmitt's critique of liberalism's attempt to sidestep the issues of ultimate value, but he denies that Schmitt has gotten to the core of what these issues are. It is not, Strauss believed, political theology, with the dominance of faith and commitment, but political philosophy, with the dominance of reason and judgment, that is the ultimate arbiter of fate. With a simple turn of the screw, Strauss concluded that Schmitt's search for seriousness ultimately lacked seriousness. Schmitt's decisionism was a form of political aestheticism seeking thrills and entertainments, that is to say, it remained a captive of the same bourgeois liberalism that it struggled to overthrow. "We mean by this that his critique of liberalism takes place within the horizon of liberalism"—and that was the unkindest cut of all.[54] Strauss's critique of Schmitt points the way toward another modernity, less radical, more humane, and more in line with Tocqueville's spirit of moderation. This modernity is committed to finding a *juste milieu* between the Enlightenment and its critics.

Chapter 13 The Tragic Liberalism of Isaiah Berlin

It is generally believed that the Counter-Enlightenment is a phenomenon of the political Right. The previous chapter attempted to show that the Counter-Enlightenment has a far more capacious reach, encompassing political extremists—anarchists, revolutionaries, nihilists—of many political stripes, from Maistre and Schmitt to Sorel and Lukács. Yet it remains a deeply embedded belief that an attack on the Enlightenment must simultaneously be an attack on liberal democracy and perforce the first step on the slippery slope to fascism and other right-wing ideologies. It is as if the Enlightenment were to fall, so too would all the scaffolding upon which modern liberalism has been constructed. This is an opinion that has received powerful support from scholarly works like Zev Sternhell's *The Anti-Enlightenment Tradition* and learned screeds like Cory Robin's *The Reactionary Mind*.[1] Yet this is to wildly overstate the case for the Enlightenment's connection to liberalism, as the example of Isaiah Berlin amply demonstrates.

The name of Isaiah Berlin will always be remembered when informed people speak about liberalism. This may not, at first blush, be obvious. Berlin never wrote a systematic treatise on politics. There is no Berlinian equivalent of Locke's *Two Treatises of Government* or Rawls's *A Theory of Justice*. After his early biography of Marx written in the 1930s, Berlin in the strict sense of the term never wrote another book. Perhaps this is what led his colleague Maurice Bowra, the Oxford classicist, to quip, "Though like Our Lord and Socrates he does not publish much, he thinks and says a great deal and has an enormous influence on our times."[2]

This was not quite true, of course. Berlin wrote quite a bit, a great deal of which has only come to light posthumously. In place of the formal treatise, he wrote on a wide range of topics, employing a variety of literary genres from the history of ideas, to philosophical analysis, to a series of wonderful character sketches—éloges in the great French tradition of the funeral oration—of well-known friends and contemporaries (including the above-mentioned Bowra). He was capable of using a broad canvas as well as painting in miniature. Among philosophical writers of the last century, he is rivaled only by Michael Oakeshott as a master of English prose. Berlin once described himself as not a philosopher but a historian of ideas.[3] This, too, is only partially true. While he trafficked in the history of ideas, writing essays and monographs on thinkers and statesmen as diverse as Machiavelli, Vico, Herder, Tolstoy, Turgenev, Mill, Disraeli, Weizmann, and Churchill, these essays and other writings convey a deep philosophical teaching and focus on a single theme: the place of freedom in the overall economy of human life.

Berlin's liberalism is unique for its embrace of a strand of the romantic Counter-Enlightenment that puts him at odds with most mainstream varieties of liberal doctrine. To be sure, liberalism is not something that can be defined in a word or a phrase. Like other "isms," it has developed, evolved, and assumed different aspects at different times.[4] Classical liberalism of the form found in writers from Locke to Hume to the *Federalist* authors was largely a doctrine of individual liberty, of "freedom from" in Berlin's idiom. Liberalism in its classic, or genus, form is a doctrine that puts the liberty of the individual front and center, regarding the wants and desires of persons—what they believe contributes most to their well-being—as the only moral basis of government. The task of government is not to tell people what they ought to want but to interfere as little as possible with the wants and desires that people actually do have. Only then can the dignity and autonomy of the individual be respected. To act otherwise is to treat adults as if they were children and rational persons as in need of tutelage. Liberty is to liberalism what justice is to Plato or equality to Marx.

But this type of genus liberalism has often morphed into another version of the creed whose heroes are Kant, Hegel, and Mill. This kind of perfectionist liberalism is less concerned with the satisfaction of individual desires than with shaping the social environment within which those desires can be satisfied. On this account, individuals have the duty, not merely the option, to cultivate their physical, intellectual, moral, and aesthetic capacities to the best of their abilities. Only when we have achieved the full and complete realization of our natural capacities can we be in a position to exercise our freedom. Freedom is less an endowment than an achievement. Perfectionist liberalism has an undeniably collectivist component. Freedom is understood here not merely as a right to be protected from external interference but as a capacity that requires training and cultivation through the agencies of culture and moral self-development. It eventually becomes a plan for the rational control of society.[5]

Neither of these liberalisms is adequate for dealing with the problem of moral conflict. Genus liberalism—the standard version of which can be found in the tenth *Federalist* paper—regards all conflict as the conflict of interests. This is certainly characteristic of many kinds of conflict, but not all. The language of interests is economistic and mathematical. Interests are ultimately quantifiable and divisible. Genus liberalism is a politics of give-and-take, of compromise, and fair dealing. When interests diverge, it is in principle possible to find a means of accommodating them through the right mix of institutions by giving each of the parties to the conflict at least a part of what it desires. This was the strategy famously adopted by liberal political theorists from James Madison's tenth *Federalist* paper to Robert Dahl's *A Preface to Democratic Theory*.[6] Perfectionist liberalism, by contrast, treats moral disagreement as a problem of education. On this account, when interests conflict it is because at least some people do not understand what their true interests really are. The cure for moral conflict is Bildung in the Hegelian sense of the term, namely, bringing people to a proper awareness of what their true, or rational, selves are. Conflict is regarded here as a moral defect that can be overcome by discovering the proper technology of deliberation or self-improvement to establish social harmony and consensus.

Berlin found both of these species of liberalism defective. Genus liberalism correctly regarded politics as a means of dealing with conflict but regarded all conflict only superficially as a form of interest-based conflict. Perfectionist liberalism similarly failed to understand the permanence of conflict by reducing it to a failure to achieve understanding of our "true," or "objective," interests. Berlin offered a third form of liberalism, rooted in a deeper appreciation of the intractability of moral conflict. It is not just that we should be left alone to pursue our ends or that our ends require a process of rigorous moral cultivation, it is that our ends are various, often incompatible, and in open conflict with one another. Conflict, for Berlin, is not only about interests but also about identities. Identities are not just things we have, they define who we are. We can compromise and balance interests. We cannot so easily adjudicate our identities.

For Berlin, liberalism is concerned not only with the protection of the rights and liberties of individuals from intrusion by other individuals or from collective agencies like the state. Rather, it is also concerned with respecting and perpetuating the fundamental diversity of human beings, including national character, as expressed in language, culture, or what Wittgenstein called "forms of life."[7] This insight gleaned from the figures of German romanticism—Friedrich H. Jacobi, Johann Gottfried Herder, and Johann Georg Hamann—has given Berlin's liberalism a psychological and moral complexity deeper than the dominant Enlightenment strand of the doctrine and has turned Berlin into something of a multiculturalist *avant la lettre*. Berlin seems willing to respect a deeper and more fundamental diversity among ways of life than that ordinarily respected by most liberals, who believe that conflicts can either be accommodated or resolved in some higher synthesis. The question is whether his commitment to liberty is consistent with his defense of a deep moral pluralism. Is liberty the highest end or merely one "value" among many others? This dilemma cuts to the core of Berlin's tragic liberalism.

LIBERTY

Berlin was appointed to the Chicele Chair of Social and Political Theory at Oxford in 1957. His inaugural lecture, "Two Concepts of Liberty," has been as extensively discussed and analyzed as any text in the Anglo-American philosophical tradition. "Two Concepts" is certainly Berlin's most famous and most characteristic piece.[8] In it, Berlin laid out two of the great themes that would be the hallmark of his work: the centrality of ideas to the study of history and politics and the primacy of freedom, especially what he calls negative freedom, as the most important value of a civilized community. The first claim was intended to refute the beliefs of various Marxist and determinist thinkers who held that material causes and circumstances are what govern human behavior. At the outset of his lecture, Berlin argues emphatically not

just that ideas have consequences but that they can have devastating consequences. "Our philosophers," he writes, "seem oddly unaware of these devastating effects of their activities . . . politics has remained indissolubly
intertwined with every other form of philosophical inquiry" (192). Berlin's
statement here is directed not only against materialist thinkers but also against
those of his colleagues, the Oxford analytic philosophers, who believe that philosophy is a kind of "meta" discourse—language about language—concerned
only with the analysis and clarification of concepts rather than with the relation of those concepts to political practice.

In his belief about the centrality of freedom, Berlin also took up a controversial position. Here he set himself against a range of positions that hold that
social justice, equality, or democracy constituted the highest goal of society.
He did not dispute the genuine value of these goals—I shall have something
more to say about this later—although he denied emphatically that to maxi-
mize any one of them would automatically lead to an increase in human freedom. In one of the most arresting passages from this text, Berlin asserts the
following: "Everything is what it is: liberty is liberty, not equality or fairness
or justice or culture, or human happiness or a quiet conscience. If the liberty
of myself or my class or nation depends on the misery of a number of other
human beings, the system which promotes this is unjust and immoral. But if
I curtail or lose my freedom in order to lessen the shame of such inequality
and do not thereby materially increase the individual liberty of others, an absolute loss of liberty occurs . . . it is a confusion of values to say that although
my 'liberal,' individual freedom may go by the board, some other kind of
freedom—'social' or 'economic'—is increased" (197–98).

The core of Berlin's lecture turns on two different kinds of liberty, which
he refers to as negative and positive liberty, respectively. What is this controversial distinction intended to signify? Negative liberty is in the first instance
freedom from external impediments or controls. We are free when we are left
alone or unattended, that is, when we are not interfered with by other persons, institutions, or agencies. Negative liberty concerns itself with the space
within which persons are free to act without being coerced by others. It is described as negative because it represents freedom from external hindrances to
action. At the essence of this conception of freedom stands a theory of choice
or will. We are free to the extent that we can exercise our wills not just to *do*
this rather than that but to *become* this rather than that. Negative liberty presupposes that persons are malleable and underdetermined, that we not only
choose between values and ways of life but are the active makers and shapers

of these values and ways of life, or in one of Berlin's striking images, that we are the driver and not the horse.[9] There is a heroic quality to this idea of liberty, to which we shall return.

The theory of positive liberty, on the other hand, is ultimately less about will and choice than about human rationality. According to the positive theory of liberty, we are free only when we exercise control over our choices. The classic theorists of positive liberty understood correctly, Berlin believed, that our choices may be constrained or even determined by a range of variables over which we may have no control, such as upbringing, education, social conditioning, and the like. We are not free unless and until we exercise control over those determinants that condition our choices. Berlin associates this kind of liberty with a conception of self-mastery or self-determination. We are free not just by virtue of the choices we make but when we live our lives according to a plan or a set of rules that we have made for ourselves and that we find worth living for. The essence of this view of freedom is not choice so much as rational choice, choosing in accordance with a goal or principle that makes life worth living.

Positive liberty is what might be called teleological or perfectionist liberty. It is associated with a good or ideal against which all our choices can be judged. Indeed, every moral philosopher from Socrates to Mill has distinguished more worthy or less worthy forms of life and argued that freedom consists in choosing the more over the less worthy. Even Mill, the most resolute champion of the negative theory of liberty, found it necessary to distinguish between our "miserable individuality"—a telling phrase—and real freedom.[10] Freedom consists here not just in the act of choice but in choosing what most fully realizes our humanity.

Berlin is not simply a neutral in the debate over negative and positive liberty. He associates negative liberty with the tradition of political liberalism and positive liberty with the vast networks of tyranny and social control. He believes that positive liberty contains a coercive component that over time leads to tyranny. He did not mean to say that there is a necessary logical entailment between ideas of positive liberty and social coercion; nor did he claim (as he sometimes appears to do) that there is an invariable historical association between the two. Many positive libertarians—Spinoza and Kant, to name only the best known—strongly rejected paternalism in any of its forms. For Berlin, there was a kind of psychological affiliation—an "elective affinity," to use a different vocabulary—leading from positive liberty to totalitarianism.[11] Positive liberty contains a dogmatic belief that it knows what human beings ought to be or what is the best way of life; those who fall short of this ideal are deemed ignorant, corrupt, sinful, or greedy. In its effort to make us more rational, enlightened, or virtuous, proponents of positive liberty are bound to violate the autonomy of the individual. Positive libertarians are necessarily led to treat individuals as means to the promotion of their goals, however worthy those goals might be. And when such people feel called upon to use the state or other institutional means of coercion to achieve those ends, the result can only be despotism masquerading as freedom.

The great heroes of Berlinian liberalism are thinkers like Montesquieu, the authors of the *Federalist Papers,* Constant, Tocqueville, and Mill, all of whom defended the maximum space for human choice and action. By contrast, it was the tradition of positive liberty championed by Rousseau and his epigones (Fichte, Hegel, and Marx) that was responsible for the creation of some of the worst experiments in social control known to history. The paradox that Berlin never ceased to explore is how political ideas that aimed to liberate us from tyranny could be at the root of even more extensive forms of coercion, all in the name of political freedom. Not inaccurately, Berlin's "Two Concepts" has been described by one reader as an "anti-communist manifesto."[12]

"Two Concepts" has been subjected to a variety of criticisms from the time it was first published. Analytical philosophers have argued that there is only a single conception of liberty, of which the positive and negative variants are but interpretations.[13] Historically minded philosophers have recently argued for a third, "neo-Roman" conception of liberty as "non-domination."[14] Yet for all of these criticisms and refinements, Berlin's distinction has persevered, in large part because it captures an important aspect of our natural experience. Part of Berlin's brief for negative liberty derives from his very real dislike of paternalism in all its forms and a kind of Kantian appreciation of the individual as an end in itself. All systems of morality and government that use the individual as means or materials to achieve their goals are immoral. Here Berlin agrees with John Maynard Keynes's famous dictum that in the long run we are all dead. This means that the use of one person to achieve the greater good of others, or of one generation to achieve the good for later ones, can never be ethically justified.

Yet it is valid to wonder whether Berlin was pushing on an open door in launching his defense of liberty. As Macaulay said of Mill's *On Liberty,* Mill was crying fire in Noah's flood.[15] This judgment may have been premature. Macaulay did not live to see the rise of communism, fascism, and other modern tyrannies that would use the language of freedom to help achieve their goals of social domination. Berlin was a close friend of the Israeli political theorist Jacob Talmon, whose book revealingly entitled *The Origins of Totalitarian Democracy* argued that Rousseau and the French Revolutionaries were simply the harbingers of the twentieth century's far greater experiments in totalitarian social engineering.[16] But even if it is clear what Berlin is against, it is just as important to know what he is for. What makes liberty stand so high in the pantheon of human goods? Why is liberty preferable to justice, order, excellence, equality, or other equally worthy goals of moral aspiration? A good case can be made that liberty is not itself a virtue but a precondition for all the virtues, as all moral qualities presuppose choice at their core. A virtue that was a product of coercion or of unreflective habit could not be considered altogether praiseworthy. This was an idea pioneered long before in the second book of Aristotle's *Nicomachean Ethics*.

Berlin is so resistant to any form of teleology or perfectionism that he is loath to ask questions like "What is liberty for?" and "Freedom to do what?" There is a kind of formalism to his conception of freedom that makes it seem empty of all content as well as indifferent to context and circumstance. Is liberty good in all situations? Can there ever be too much of a good thing? It is more than arguable that the pathologies of modern life grow not from the absence of but from an excess of liberty. The sense of rootlessness, alienation, and moral drift that pervades much of contemporary life—think of the characters in Jonathan Franzen's novel *Freedom*—comes not from restrictions on liberty but from the absence of authority figures and the restraints of moral tradition that alone can give life a sense of meaning. For a thinker who famously valued the role of judgment and feared grand abstractions in political life, Berlin's praise of liberty has a peculiarly abstract ring to it. To the question "What am I free to do or to be?" Berlin's answer seems to be "How should I know?" This is the point that Burke made against the abstractness of the French Revolution's demands for the realization of absolute freedom: "Is it because liberty in the abstract may be classed amongst the blessings of mankind, that I am seriously to felicitate a madman, who has escaped from the protecting restraint and wholesome darkness of his cell, on his restoration to the enjoyment of light and liberty? Am I to congratulate a highwayman and murderer, who has broke prison, upon the recovery of his natural rights? This would be to act over again the scene of the criminals condemned to the galleys, and their heroic deliverer, the metaphysic Knight of the Sorrowful Countenance."[17] Berlin's defense of liberty stands in some conflict with his claim, which I now want to examine, that liberty may not be the highest virtue but is one extremely valuable end that may still find itself in conflict with others that may prove to be of equal importance.

MONISM AND PLURALISM

Berlin's defense of negative liberty and the liberal tradition is the best known but is only one aspect of his teaching, and in a curious way perhaps not even the most important one. Underlying Berlin's account of both positive and negative liberty is a set of assumptions about human nature and the limits of knowledge that make his views more complex and controversial than would at first blush appear. At the core of Berlinian liberalism is not just a teaching of negative liberty but also a defense of what Berlin calls "value pluralism." It is his view that our values—the ideals and aspirations that we care most deeply about—are in a condition of permanent and ineradicable conflict.

Berlin first put this thesis about value pluralism forward in the eighth and final section of "Two Concepts," entitled "The One and the Many." It was subsequently developed in the book that would become *Vico and Herder* and in his many different writings on the Counter-Enlightenment. The current debates over value pluralism have largely supplanted the debates over positive and negative liberty of a generation ago. While the debates over negative and positive liberty seem rooted in the Cold War environment and the struggle against totalitarianism, the focus on value pluralism has engaged recent controversies over liberalism and muticulturalism. The belief that not peaceful convergence on ultimate ends but rather spirited agonistic struggle between these ends is what gives Berlinian liberalism its tragic, even heroic, dimension.

Berlin associates the traditions of positive liberty and negative liberty with two very different forms of social ontology, although this is not a term that Berlin would have used. Positive liberty presupposes a kind of philosophical monism, that is, the belief that moral and political problems can be solved by the same methods or with the same degree of certainty as scientific and technical problems. This is the scientific rationalism of the Enlightenment, although Berlin regards it as a feature of very many diverse societies and thinkers stretching back to Plato and the Greeks. Positive liberty is identified with a deep-rooted fallacy that Berlin sees as putting the Western tradition on a disastrous course. This claim that the West has been disfigured by an "Ionian fallacy"—a view that Berlin shares with Heidegger, to put him in some rather uncomfortable company—can be reduced to three propositions that can be described as follows:

1. That all genuine questions can be answered, and if a question cannot be answered then it is not a genuine question.
2. That a method exists for the discovery of the correct answers to our questions, which can be learned and taught to others.
3. That the answers to all questions are compatible with one another and form parts or aspects of a single system of truth.[18]

Sometimes Berlin writes as if the entire history of moral and political philosophy rests on a mistake—the erroneous belief that there is a single right answer to questions about the best way of life or the ideal regime. The basic questions set out by thinkers as different as Plato, Aristotle, Spinoza, and Kant are, he believes, wrongly put. Underlying these questions is the false premise that leads down a slippery slope, namely, (a) that for every problem there must be an answer, (b) if there is a correct answer, then it must be in principle knowable, and (c) if such answers are knowable, then they can and even should be implemented. To attempt even to answer these questions contains the germs of coercion and tyranny. There is an unbreakable link between the rationalist view that there are moral truths and the desire to educate, coerce, or force other persons to accept them. The doctrine of positive liberty may begin with a desire to be my own master, but it invariably ends with the attempt to impose such a doctrine on others. Berlin regards this monistic fallacy as the root of all forms of tyranny, from "Victorian schoolmasters and colonial administrators" to "the latest nationalist or Communist dictator": "The rationalist argument, with its assumption of the single true solution, has led by steps which, if not logically valid, are historically and psychologically intelligible from an ethical doctrine of individual responsibility and individual self-perfection to an authoritarian State obedient to the directives of an elite of Platonic guardians" (223).

In contrast to what he believes are the monistic rationalizing tendencies of the Enlightenment tradition of positive liberty, Berlin associates negative liberty with the Counter-Enlightenment thesis of value pluralism. In political science, pluralism is generally associated with the Madisonian view of a political order in which diverse interests and groups peacefully compete with one another for a share of political rule. Berlin means something quite different. Pluralism is not just a descriptive statement about how interests compete with one another but a much deeper philosophical thesis about the structure of the moral universe. Pluralism is the view that our fundamental values and beliefs are in a condition of irreconcilable conflict with one another and, what's more, are not comparable with one another on some scale of rank. If monism is an attempt to see our differences as simply partial and incomplete aspects of a single whole, pluralism—a term possibly cribbed from the pragmatist philosophy of William James—is a celebration of multiplicity and difference as expressed in individual life choices, in distinct national communities, and entirely different ways of life.[19]

For Berlin, there simply *are* ineradicable conflicts between goods: freedom and security, justice and democracy, respect for excellence and attention to the needy. There is not some single formula for reconciling these competing values into a higher synthesis. The conflict between values is not the symptom of a defective constitution but is inseparable from human life. The recognition of the conflict between ultimate ends forms the basis of Berlin's understanding of the tragic nature of the human condition. "If as I believe," Berlin writes, "the ends of men are many, and not all of them are in principle compatible with each other, then the possibility of conflict—and of tragedy— can never wholly be eliminated from human life, either personal or social. The necessity of choosing between absolute claims is then an inescapable characteristic of the human condition" (239).

Berlin's value pluralism is frequently associated with a form of relativism, although Berlin has strenuously contested this identification. In the conclusion to "Two Concepts," he offers a quasi-Marxist objection to his theory of negative liberty and value pluralism, according to which "the ideal of freedom to choose ends without claiming eternal validity for them, and the pluralism of values connected with this, is only the late fruit of our declining capitalist civilization" (242). He then goes on to assert, "Principles are not less sacred because their duration cannot be guaranteed" and concludes with a phrase drawn from the Austrian economist Joseph Schumpeter: ' "To realize the relative validity of one's convictions,' said an admirable writer of our time, 'and yet stand for them unflinchingly is what distinguishes a civilized man from a barbarian.' To demand more than this is perhaps a deep and incurable metaphysical need; but to allow it to determine one's practice is a symptom of an equally deep, and more dangerous, moral and political immaturity" (242).

Leo Strauss has taken the passage just quoted as evidence of Berlin's endorsement of an unqualified relativism. "Berlin's statement seems to me," he writes, "to be a characteristic document of the crisis of liberalism—or a crisis due to the fact that liberalism has abandoned its absolutist basis and is trying to become entirely relativistic."[20] He took particular umbrage at Berlin's claim that it is belief in the "relative validity" of one's convictions that distinguishes a civilized person from a barbarian. To this claim Strauss offers the counter-thesis: "Berlin cannot escape the necessity to which every thinking being is subject: to take a final stand, an absolute stand in accordance with which he regards as the nature of man or as the nature of the human condition or as the decisive truth."[21] The endowment of our moral convictions with a sense of absoluteness is for Strauss not a sign of immaturity or of some pathology ("a deep and incurable metaphysical need") but is itself the mark of civiliza-tion. "If [relativism] were right," Strauss concludes, "every resolute liberal hack or thug would be a civilized man, while Plato and Kant would be bar-barians."[22]

Although Berlin chose not to address Strauss, he did respond to a similar accusation made by his friend the Italian classicist Arnaldo Momigliano.[23] Mo-migliano had argued that Vico and Herder—two of Berlin's heroes—were in fact moral relativists and that by implication so was Berlin. Momigliano's charge of relativism clearly stung, perhaps because it appeared in the presti-gious *New York Review of Books*, to which Berlin was a frequent contributor. In response, Berlin chose to define relativism as the belief that human thought and action are simply expressions of the taste or emotional attitude of an indi-vidual or group with no external standard by which to determine its objective truth or falsehood. By this standard, Berlin denied that either Vico or Herder was a relativist and, by implication, denied that he was a relativist for endorsing their views. They are more accurately described as pluralists. What is the differ-ence? Relativism is the view that our tastes and values are incommensurable. "I prefer coffee, you prefer champagne" is Berlin's example of relativism.[24] There is simply nothing more to say. Pluralism accepts the fact of moral and aesthetic diversity but regards these as different and objective modes of humanity.

Berlin puts special emphasis on our ability to imaginatively understand val-ues, ideals, and forms of life very different from our own. This does not imply an endorsement of these views but rather implies an acceptance of the fact that there are many different ways of being human. The dialogues of Plato, the religion of medieval Japan, and the novels of Jane Austen may express different moral viewpoints, but they are all recognizable ways of being human. "Intercommunication between cultures in time and space is only possible because what makes men human is common to them and acts as a bridge between them," Berlin writes.[25] Our values may differ, and conflict between them may be inevitable, but this does not prevent us from attempting to enter into and understand each other's point of view. If we could not or if we did not even try, we would cease to be human at all. Even though our forms of life may differ, Berlin believes, they are not "infinitely many" and still exist within the "human horizon."[26]

Pluralism, as I mentioned above, is not simply a descriptive statement about the competition between values or interests. It is a philosophical thesis about the human condition. How does Berlin know this? On what insight is it founded? It is a vast leap from the statement that our ends are in conflict to the view that our ends must necessarily be in conflict. Berlin takes his thesis of philosophical pluralism as proof of why civilizations are incompatible with one another and why conflict between them is inevitable. To some degree, his belief about the truth of pluralism derives from his belief in the incoherence of its opposite, of the monistic claim about the compatibility of all goods:

> The notion of the perfect whole, the ultimate solution, in which all good things coexist, seems to me to be not merely unattainable—that is a truism—but conceptually incoherent. I do not know what is meant by a harmony of this kind. Some among the Great Goods cannot live together. That is a conceptual truth. We are doomed to choose, and every choice may entail an irreparable loss. Happy are those who live under a discipline which they accept without question, who freely obey the orders of leaders, spiritual or temporal, whose word is fully accepted as unbreakable law. . . . I can only say that those who rest on such comfortable beds of dogma are victims of forms of self-induced myopia, blinkers that may make for contentment, but not for understanding of what it is to be human.[27]

As is clear from this passage, pluralism is presented as not only the truth about the moral universe; it is also an assertion of a certain view of human nature. There is something existentialist, almost Sartrean, in Berlin's anguished view that we are the beings "condemned to be free." Berlin presents this as a tragic condition. Every choice is not only the affirmation of something; it is the negation of something else that may be equally desirable or valuable. *Omnis determinatio est negatio*: to affirm one thing is to deny another. It is this necessity for choice in which our freedom resides. To avoid the necessity for choice—to find solace in vast philosophical systems like determinism and historicism that deny the primacy of freedom—is to deny what is fundamentally human in us. This insight comes as close as anything to the moral center of Berlin's thought.

THE COUNTER-ENLIGHTENMENT
AND ITS PROBLEMS

Berlin's conception of value pluralism was underwritten by a series of writings on what Berlin dubbed the Counter-Enlightenment. As he uses the term, the Counter-Enlightenment stands in direct opposition to the monistic and rationalist premises of Enlightenment thought. It has been argued with considerable plausibility that Berlin's conception of the Enlightenment is a clumsy construction, a straw man, created only to be knocked down. His description of the monolithic character of the French Enlightenment has been endorsed enthusiastically by some, but for others it looks "a trifle embarrassing" because of its sweeping reductionism.[28] For example, his failure to account for Montesquieu's appreciation of cultural diversity as a central Enlightenment value is generally regarded as evidence of the Procrustean character of Berlin's treatment of the Enlightenment. Any account of the Enlightenment that cannot include Montesquieu in its pantheon must be in need of rethinking. To be sure, Berlin often writes less as a careful intellectual historian than as a philosopher of history concerned to characterize entire epochs and movements of thought.

Like many critics of the Enlightenment—consider Alasdair MacIntyre and his description of the "Enlightenment Project" in *After Virtue*—Berlin often exaggerated its monistic character, while refusing to disavow what he believed were the Enlightenment's key values of rationality, toleration, equality before the law, and freedom of conscience. In a brief intellectual autobiography, he recalled that his interest in the French Enlightenment originally grew out of research for his book on Marx. It was here that he "acquired an admiration for the great task which the thinkers of the French Encyclopedia had set themselves, and for the great work which they did to liberate men from darkness—clerical, metaphysical, political and the like."[29] Although he later came to be critical of the foundation of these Enlightenment beliefs, he admits, "I never lost my admiration for and sense of solidarity with the Enlightenment of that period."[30]

Berlin's intentionally monistic reading of the Enlightenment is set up to serve as the perfect doppelgänger to his image of the Counter-Enlightenment. Unlike the French *philosophes,* who were said to conceive of human nature as fundamentally the same across time and place, the Counter-Enlightenment—best expressed by the German romantics—posited that there are different, but still rational and coherent, ways of being human, that cultures and nations differ from one another just as people do, and that the only way to understand this diversity is through a form of historical interpretation that regards all human institutions and activities as forms of self-expression. Just as Berlin had organized Enlightenment thought around three principles, so he sees the Counter-Enlightenment challenge as resting on a contrary set of assumptions that can likewise be reduced to three:

1. The Enlightenment's belief in the uniformity and permanence of a common human nature is false or superficial; only what is unique, individual, or particular is really authentic or true.[31]
2. The individual is what resists rules, uniformity, reduction to "cases" or "instances" of some general law. To be individual is to be self-creating, a shaper of ends as well as means; it is to turn life into art.[32] Human life is *expressive* and is most fully revealed through such media as poetry, myth, and literature.[33]
3. What is true of individuals is also true of nations and cultures—they follow no overall pattern of development, whether cyclical or progressive; they constitute distinct and irreducible ways of life for their members. Cultures are characterized by diversity. Each culture has its own special path to happiness that can only be studied and appreciated from "within," that is, through an act of imaginative sympathy, of what Vico called *fantasia* and Herder called *Einfuhlung*.[34]

The Counter-Enlightenment is central to Berlin's appreciation of negative liberty and value pluralism. The Enlightenment's rationalism blinded it to the expressive and self-created dimensions of freedom; its universalism blinded it to the plurality of values and cultures. Berlin praises the Counter-Enlightenment, especially figures like Vico, Montesquieu, and Herder, for recognizing that there is no one ideal culture or way of being human but rather a variety of values and cultures, all of which reveal the many-sided nature of humanity.[35] Perhaps the quintessential Counter-Enlightenment figure was the reactionary French philosopher Joseph de Maistre. Berlin especially enjoyed quoting Maistre's praise of pluralism against the Enlightenment's uniformitarian conception of human nature. "In my lifetime I have seen Frenchmen, Italians, Russians, etc.; thanks to Montesquieu, I even know that *one can be Persian,*" Maistre wrote. "But as for *man,* I declare that I have never in my life met him; if he exists, he is unknown to me."[36]

One especially controversial aspect of the Counter-Enlightenment is its teaching about nationalism, a concept that Berlin both explored and defended

within limits.[37] Once again, unlike the individualist and reductionist theories of the Enlightenment that tried to explain human behavior through the
operation of certain common and uniform causes such as self-interest or the
desire for power, the Counter-Enlightenment was especially attuned to the collective dimension of human life. Individual choice and creativity always take
place within the context of certain common cultural forms, particular ways
of life, which cannot be explained by the interaction of instances of individual behavior. For romantic nationalists like Hamann and Herder, to be a
human being is to be part of a culture, a group, or an ethnic identity. The
isolated individual is bare, abstract, lacking any recognizable human identity.
The group or nation is the collective expression of the individual, and the
individual is nothing outside the group. Nationalism is not simply a pathology, although it has its pathological dimensions, but also the expression of a
genuine human need for belonging to a group.[38]

One of the earliest and finest expressions of the kind of nationalism that
Berlin seems to endorse is found in Herder's theory of linguistic nationalism.
For Herder and the romantics, language is not simply one feature among other
aspects of human nature but constitutive of what it is to be a person. The language we speak determines the kinds of persons we are. Language is not an
instrument or strategic means for helping us achieve the objects of our desires; it is a form of collective self-expression by which diverse peoples give voice
to their particular "genius" in poetry, music, storytelling, and myth. Every
language is particularistic. There is no universal language, like Esperanto; if
there were one, it would be intolerably dull and flat. For Herder and ipso
facto for Berlin, it is the particularity of our natural languages that forms
the perimeters of distinct national cultures and communities, giving our lives
meaning.[39]

Berlin wrote sympathetically about the appeal of nationalism as the expression of a legitimate human need. This is especially evident in his writings on
Zionism, which he regarded as a humane and liberal expression of the nationalist sentiment.[40] He was not a religious thinker by any means and even reveals a certain tone deafness to the music of religious belief, but he believed
in the justice of Zionism and regarded the establishment of the state of Israel
as a legitimate response to the European persecution of the Jews. While assimilation may be possible in individual cases, it has proven to be unwork-
able as a collective response to the problem of anti-Semitism. The nineteenth
century—the great age of assimilationism—also produced the emergence of
anti-Semitism on a hitherto unprecedented scale. Though he could be critical

of particular aspects of Israeli policy, Berlin never doubted the essential justice of the case for Israel to take its place among the nations of the world. There is a wonderful story that he recounted about a conversation with the Russo-French philosopher Alexandre Kojève, who had his doubts about Zionism. "You're a Jew," Kojève said to him. "The Jewish people probably have the most interesting history of any people that ever lived. And now you want to be Albania?" "Yes, we do," was Berlin's reply. "For our purposes, for Jews, Albania is a step forward."[41]

Berlin treats the Counter-Enlightenment as the source of diversity, individuality, resistance to uniformity, and love of freedom where this means freedom not just to choose means but to create ends.[42] But this is not the whole of the matter. Just as Berlin posits a kind of "dialectic of Enlightenment" in which the ideas of reason and freedom flip-flop into their opposite, so the Counter-Enlightenment threatens to dissolve into forms of collectivism and group tyranny. The Counter-Enlightenment is not only the source of our ideas of moral pluralism, it is also at the root of modern irrationalism, a resistance to, even a hatred of, science, reason, and "enlightened" morality. It is often associated with the supremacy of faith over intellect and, even worse, the power of the group over the individual.

Berlin often associates the rise of collectivism with the rejection of science and the use of empirical methods, to which he always paid tribute. This goes back to Vico's method of fantasia, or the imaginative reconstruction of an institution or activity. To understand a way of life, it is necessary to see it from the "inside," to see what it means to the lives of those most affected, and to do this requires a special sort of historical empathy that Berlin himself sometimes called judgment. He insisted on a strong distinction between the methods of the natural sciences and the human sciences and rejected the Enlightenment belief in a unified scientific method equally applicable to nature and society, a fallacy known as positivism. The danger comes when the rejection of positivism becomes an opposition to scientific knowledge and empiricism *tout court.*

A key and surprising cause for the rise of this hostility to science came from an unlikely source in the Scottish philosopher David Hume.[43] Hume's skepticism about all things, including religion, would seem temperamentally close to Berlin, but Berlin had a way of showing how even the best ideas may have unintended consequences. In *A Treatise of Human Nature,* Hume famously demonstrated how reason alone was inadequate to account for causality or the necessary connections between things. From the observation that one thing seems to follow from another, Hume argued that we can never conclude that there is an actual causal relation between them. Rather we are at most entitled to infer that they are connected, a feeling that arises from the custom or habit of seeing two things so associated. Hume had no intention of denying the importance of science, but his corrosive skepticism had this effect, especially on those who came later. His goal was to show that instead of necessity governing the world, there was only chance reduced to order by custom.

It was the German romantics—Hamann and Jacobi—who extended Hume's critique of the category of causality to apply to the whole of knowledge. For these thinkers, our knowledge of reality, including our scientific knowledge, is based on a prior act of faith (*Glaube*). By faith they did not mean religion in any doctrinal sense but rather meant a direct, intuitive insight into the way things are that precedes our rational concepts and categories. What the philosophers vainly called "the principle of sufficient reason"—the belief that everything must have a reason or cause—is simply a castle built on sand. The belief that everything has a cause is just that: a belief or an act of faith, which precedes all reason. Reason is not so much a slave to custom and habit as Hume argued, but it is dependent on certain irrational "givens" that underlie all knowledge claims. By pointing out the irrationalist core of all knowledge—that reason itself presupposes a faith or belief in reason—it is only a step further to see all knowledge, including science, as but a form of "ideology" (Marx), "myth" (Sorel), or "weltanschauung" (Jaspers).

The idea that all knowledge, all philosophy, is nothing more than an expression of a particular nation, class, race, or historical epoch is an extreme outgrowth of the Counter-Enlightenment. The Leninist slogan that all theory is an expression of the class struggle is functionally no different from the execrable fascist injunction to think with the blood. In each case the role of critical judgment is subordinated to a movement or cause. Indeed, it is the collectivization of thought to which Berlin seems most strenuously to object. This occurred when the Counter-Enlightenment turned the liberal Herderian teaching about expressive freedom into not only a theory about individual flourishing and self-creation but also a doctrine of cultures and nations. When the nation becomes the locus of self-expression, it frequently becomes a cause of chauvinism and imperialism. It subordinates the individual to collective acts of self-expression to which the individual is said to "belong." In its extreme form the Counter-Enlightenment has been associated with the rise of irrationalist movements, even twentieth-century fascism and totalitarianism.

Are we to believe, then, that the Counter-Enlightenment is both a source of freedom and a cause of tyranny? Are Herder's and Vico's theories of culture a source of moral pluralism or the cause of a new kind of irrationalism that the collective exercises over the individual? Is the Counter-Enlightenment a more humane alternative to Enlightenment rationalism and universalism or does its sense of the importance of group identity leave the individual defenseless against potentially illiberal forms of collectivism?

BERLIN'S LIBERAL LEGACY

These questions force a consideration of where Berlin stands vis-à-vis the currents of the Enlightenment and Counter-Enlightenment that he so eloquently analyzed and described. There appears to be an unresolved tension in Berlin's thought between his appreciation of negative freedom and the importance of diversity. These might at first appear to be mutually consistent, but they can pull in quite different directions. Sometimes Berlin writes as if negative liberty were not simply one value among many but the highest human value. We are the beings with the gift of choice, and to be human is to be able to exercise that capacity. Freedom thus has a priority among all other goods that one might choose to have, for without freedom none of those other goods is valuable. Individual liberty is thus the metric against which all other values are to be measured. If this is true, then Berlin seems to attribute to freedom the same kind of absolute and monistic value that he had criticized the Enlightenment thinkers for endorsing.

Yet, if we are to believe that pluralism is the truth of the human condition, as Berlin frequently insists, then we must admit that freedom is one, but only one, value that human beings and even entire cultures might wish to embrace. There are other goods—security, justice, loyalty, excellence, solidarity—that may all trump freedom as the goal to be maximized. In fact, to take value pluralism seriously would be to recognize that there are whole cultures and ways of life for which freedom, as we understand it, may be only a subordinate good. Orthodox Judaism based on the primacy of Talmudic law is only one example of a way of life for which negative freedom—the freedom to choose to live apart from or outside the law of one's ancestors—is not the highest good but a kind of heresy. Value pluralism is, then, premised on the view not only that negative liberty is merely a subordinate good but that different cultures are based on different scales of values that may be unshakably opposed to one another.

The debate over value pluralism has in recent years led to a standoff. According to John Gray, Berlin's most controversial disciple, there is a clear disjunction between support for value pluralism and support for liberal democracy. For Gray, the more seriously we take the claims of value pluralism as a true account of the moral universe, the less plausible will seem the various theories of liberal democracy. Most contemporary theorists of liberalism take one particular standard—justice (Rawls), rights (Ronald Dworkin), liberty (Robert Nozick)—as the timeless core of society against which all others must be ranked. But if value pluralism is accepted, any attempt to give priority to one of these goods over the others is arbitrary at best and coercive at worst. Gray does not necessarily reject liberalism, but he believes that it should be understood simply as a modus vivendi, a pragmatic means for adjudicating conflicts between values and nothing more. If Gray is right, liberalism will have to be seen as one parochial way of dealing with the inevitable conflict of values.[44]

As we saw earlier, Berlin was aware of and concerned with the relativism to which Gray's interpretation of value pluralism could lead. If values and cultures are unalterably plural, how are people to resolve conflicts between them? Is there any way of ranking ways of life or are they simply incommensurable? Berlin's question is how people (and peoples) with vastly different scales of values can live together in a way that does justice to the plurality of ends and yet recognize their common humanity. If the "Platonic" idea of a harmonious reconciliation of interests and beliefs is not just impractical but incoherent because basic values will always collide, what kind of political order is best? Perhaps the question is wrongly stated. As F. Scott Fitzgerald famously said, "The test of a first-rate intelligence is the ability to hold two opposed ideas in the mind at the same time, and still retain the ability to function."[45] Fitzgerald got it backwards. It is genius that abhors contradiction, that demands logic, system, and coherence. Most of the rest of us, not blessed with "first-rate intelligence," manage to function quite well holding a range of contradictory beliefs and opinions. What are our great political parties but congeries of conflicting principles and tendencies? Moral purity is the privilege of philosophers and monks; everyday life demands compromises and an acceptance of a degree of moral incoherence. Most of us seem able to tolerate considerable paradox and confusion in ordinary life, much like the bumblebee that by the laws of aerodynamics should be unable to fly yet manages to do so anyway.[46]

Gray is right, however, that the acceptance of value pluralism would force some substantial revisions in the way that liberal political theory has been conventionally understood. But it also seems clear that he has taken Berlin's thinking far beyond where Berlin would have been comfortable. Berlin retained a deep attachment to liberal institutions and ways of life as more than a mere modus vivendi, regarding them rather as something desirable on their own terms. Berlin describes the aspiration to negative liberty as "a mark of high civilization on the part of both individuals and communities" that throughout history has been the desire of "a small minority of highly civilized and self-conscious human beings" (201, 232). This is more than a piece of rhetorical overkill. It shows that Berlin and Strauss are on the same page when it comes to the defense of civilization against relativism.

Berlin's defense of negative liberty as a mark of a certain kind of high civilization is sometimes at odds with his claim that political institutions should not be designed to produce the summum bonum or some perfectionist ideal of the greatest good but rather be designed as a means of preventing the worst, the systematic abuse, degradation, and humiliation of citizens. "Perhaps," Berlin writes, "the best that one can do is to try to promote some kind of equilibrium, necessarily unstable, between the different aspirations of differing groups of human beings—at the very least to prevent them from attempting to exterminate each other and, so far as possible, to prevent them from hurting each other—and to promote the maximum practicable degree of sympathy and understanding, never likely to be complete, between them."[47] Berlin acknowledges that this is not "a wildly exciting program," not "a passionate battle cry" likely to inspire heroic actions, but is intended to prevent people from killing one another. He even hopes that if such a policy were adopted it might yet "prevent mutual destruction and, in the end, preserve the world."[48]

The great debate over pluralism threatens to overshadow another, less visible but no less important, aspect of Berlin's thought, namely, his appreciation for the role of statesmanship in history.[49] Values and interests neither automatically collide nor automatically cohere. This is due to the powers of creative statecraft, of political agency, which Berlin defended against some of the dominant determinisms of his time. He realized that the idea of the statesman may seem nothing more than a "romantic illusion" in an increasingly data-driven age. Yet some of his finest essays are devoted precisely to determining the character of such commanding geniuses as Churchill, Chaim Weizmann, Franklin D. Roosevelt, and Einstein.[50] Just as he had distinguished two different theories of liberty—negative and positive—so he posited two very different models of statesmanship. "There are at least two types of political greatness, incompatible with, and indeed sometimes opposed to each other," he explained. "The first kind is that amalgam of simplicity of vision with intense, sometimes fanatical, idealism which is to be found in men compounded of fewer attributes than the normal human complement, but those larger than life. At its best such men rise to the noble grandeur of the great and simple heroes of classical antiquity."[51]

It is clear that Berlin includes Churchill—at least the wartime Churchill—as belonging to this type. Men of this type—Berlin includes others like Garibaldi, Herzl, de Gaulle, Trotsky, and Vladimir Jabotinsky—"tend to see the world in a series of simple contrasts between light and darkness, good and evil" and are able to attract followers due to "the intensity and purity of their mind, by their fearless and unbending character, by the simplicity and nobility of the central principle to which they dedicate all that they have." Much like the Tolstoyan hedgehog, they are able, through "the sheer force of conviction," to unify the manifold particulars of any situation under a single commanding vision.[52]

But there is another type of statesmanship that fits closer to the model of the fox: "The second type of political genius belongs to those who possess the gifts of ordinary men, but these in an almost supernatural degree. So far from ignoring the infinite complexity of the life which surrounds them, they have an unanalyzable capacity for integrating the tiny fragments of which it is composed into some coherent, intelligible pattern. So far from imposing their own form upon events without regard for the properties of the material, molding it by sheer force of will-power and the passionate ideal, these latter are acutely aware of the smallest oscillations, the infinite variety of the social and political elements in which they live."[53]

To this second group of leaders, Berlin associates Weizmann (the first president of Israel), but others like Mirabeau, Cavour, Lincoln, Jan Masaryk, and Roosevelt. This group may seem less inspiring than the first, but they are just as important. While Churchill's greatness derived from his continual reading of English history and his identification with its great heroes, including his own ancestor the Duke of Marlborough, Weizmann's was formed through the experience of being an Eastern European Jew in exile who needed to learn how to operate in the corridors of power. Weizmann's genius was diplomatic, not visionary. Berlin speaks of Churchill in almost Plutarchian language befitting a colossus who bestrides the world, but he speaks of Weizmann with greater warmth of affection, precisely because of his all-too-human qualities. Those like Weizmann "are regarded not with awe or religious faith—they are not figures surrounded by a kind of unearthly radiance—but with affection, confidence, admiration, sometimes not unmixed with a certain appreciative irony—a delight in their accessibility, their democratic quality, their human failings."[54] In short, Berlin might have said, for their humanity.

Berlin saw history as shaped by a succession of inspired statesmen, poets, and philosophers. This was itself testimony to the power of the Counter-Enlightenment that always gave greater credence to the role of the individual in history. It is the great thinkers and statesmen whose ideas and imaginative sympathies give form to peoples and nations. Berlin rejected any view of history as shaped by anonymous causal powers or structures. He is fond of quoting Aristotle's dictum that history is what Alcibiades did and suffered.[55] He remained a resolute methodological individualist for whom history is a theater in which personalities and individuals of great genius take priority, for good as well as ill. It was Churchill's genius to stiffen the moral spine of his countrymen during a time of frivolity and ennui. Churchill had a unique understanding of the power of language to transform and inspire. His speeches and writings evoked the older rhetorical tradition of Burke, Gibbon, and Macaulay, giving voice to the importance of liberty rivaled only in the examples of Pericles and Lincoln.

Berlin is often criticized for offering not a substantive political philosophy of his own but rather a series of vivid character sketches of notable philosophical, literary, and political figures. This is clever but not entirely accurate. Berlin showed us how to value freedom not by offering grand theories or abstract models but by showing how ideas interact with life, how the complex ways in which good ideas taken to the extreme can have bad consequences, and how even the love of freedom, if taken in abstraction from all the other goods human beings pursue, can end up turning into its opposite. At the core of Berlin's thought is his recognition of a conflict between the claims of moral diversity, pluralism, and openness and the need for order, permanence, and stability. How to achieve some kind of balance between competing goods? Berlin offers no formula for arriving at an answer—no Categorical Imperative, no "greatest happiness for the greatest number"—only an awareness that not all good things come together and that life is more often a conflict between competing sets of goods rather than between good and bad. It is this awareness that life is choice and that not all ends are compatible that forms the basis of Isaiah Berlin's liberal legacy.

Chapter 14 Leo Strauss on Philosophy as a Way of Life

"The end of philosophy," the Oxford philosopher Stuart Hampshire once wrote, "has been announced many times by modern philosophers."[1] The Hegelian and Marxist program for "the realization of philosophy" meant to close the gap between reality and rationality. In the rational state of the future there would no longer be a "contradiction" between the demands of justice and the reality of social existence. Philosophy as a speculative enterprise would simply wither away. Similarly, for the logical empiricists, the philosophy of the future would become increasingly scientific, limited to the areas of mathematical logic, the methodology of the natural sciences, and the study of everyday forms of grammar. Philosophy as the investigation of being or inquiry into the first principles of politics and ethics would simply cease to exist, along with the great metaphysical systems from Plato to Spinoza. Ludwig Wittgenstein captured the self-denying quality of this scientific empiricism when he declared at the end of his *Tractatus Logico-Philosophicus,* "Whereof one cannot speak, thereof one must be silent."[2]

What Hampshire and Wittgenstein had said about the end of philosophy in general was similarly proclaimed about political philosophy in particular. According to what might be described as the dominant view of the mid-twentieth century, political philosophy was on its way to being replaced by the modern behavioral sciences. These sciences—economics, psychology, political science—are concerned with discovering empirical regularities in human behavior that can then be tested and put forward as general theories or covering laws. These sciences are concerned not with normative questions about what ought to be but with strictly empirical matters of what is. As Max Weber, the greatest expositor of social scientific positivism, declared: "Science today is a 'vocation' organized in special disciplines in the service of self-clarification and knowledge of interrelated facts. It is not the gift of grace of seers and prophets dispensing sacred values, nor does it partake of the contemplation of sages and philosophers about the meaning of the universe."[3]

Weber's endorsement of the fact-value distinction did not rule out the possibility, even the necessity, for making normative judgments. His point was that there was simply no rational or scientific warrant for our moral and political choices, that these choices were acts of will, like matters of religious faith. Rationality would henceforth be limited to determining the means to achieve the goals that individuals and societies set for themselves. As for substantive reflection on the goals themselves, social science must remain mute. A social scientist, on this account, may prefer a liberal tolerant society to that of a closed authoritarian one, but this remains merely a preference or desire; social science cannot prove the superiority of one type of society over another. The great efforts of the classical philosophers to legislate what states of affairs ought to exist was declared officially over. As Peter Laslett proclaimed in the Introduction to the first series of *Philosophy, Politics and Society:* "For the moment, anyway, political philosophy is dead."[4]

Leo Strauss was one of those who lived at the moment when political philosophy was considered all but moribund. "Today," he wrote in his classic essay "What Is Political Philosophy?" "political philosophy is in a state of decay and perhaps of putrefaction, if it has not vanished altogether."[5] As we have just seen, many of Strauss's most distinguished contemporaries, even if they shared little else, believed that political philosophy was either dead or dying. The only task left—providing it was a task at all—was for the student of political philosophy to become a kind of cultural caretaker, entombing the great books and ideas of the past as historical artifacts in order to ensure

them a decent burial. More than anyone else, Strauss applied all of his intellectual efforts to revive the serious study of political philosophy from this kind
of antiquarianism.

"SKEPTIC IN THE ORIGINAL SENSE"

Strauss is best known to social science as a critic of the two dominant schools
of late modern thought—historicism and positivism—alluded to above. As
his late colleague and former literary executor Joseph Cropsey has written,
Strauss was first and foremost a critic of what he regarded as the decisive
premises of modernity, namely, "a historicism that implied progress without
a fixed frame of reference to recognize progress, and a scientism that lost contact with its phenomena, proclaimed itself normless, and fell into a dilemma
of skepticism and dogmatism."[6] The claim that modernity had lost its way was
not initially regarded as welcome news by members of the academy. "Inevitably," Cropsey remarked with characteristic understatement, "Strauss was
controversial."[7]

Some of the standard charges brought against Strauss are that he sought to
convey a secret teaching that contains dangerous antidemocratic sentiments,
that he favored the rule of a philosophical elite, and that he believed the masses
should be held in check through the judicious use of religion and other "noble lies."[8] The debate over Strauss—the Strauss War, as it might be called—
came to the fore with the rise of the neoconservative movement, especially
after 9/11. A raft of books, articles, and op-ed pieces alleged that Strauss gathered around him a cult of like-minded followers who thirty years after his
death gained power and influence over American foreign policy during the
administration of George W. Bush. On the more exotic fringe of the anti-
Strauss movement are those who claimed that Strauss was secretly importing
National Socialist ideology borrowed from Heidegger and Schmitt under the
guise of a traditional teaching of natural law.[9]

These polemics miss the point. Strauss was not a reactionary except if seen
from the standpoint of extreme progressivism. He was, as will be argued
below, a classical liberal who believed that present-day liberalism requires the
support of certain premodern sources of authority if it is to be sustainable.
He clearly believed in the practical superiority of liberalism or liberal democracy to any of the existing alternatives and sought ways to defend it from its
detractors on both the Right and the Left. He praised liberal democracy as
the regime most in keeping with the classical conceptions of mixed govern-

ment, the rule of law, and above all, a certain ideal of humanity. Unlike Nietzsche, Heidegger, and other radical critics of the Enlightenment, he associated modernity at its best with England and the Anglo-American way of life. He was one of those German Anglophiles for whom the language of Shakespeare, Austen, Macaulay, and Churchill stood for something higher—nobler—than did the late modernism of Dostoyevsky, James, Proust, and Eliot. The English ideal of the gentleman, altogether absent in Continental Europe, retained links to the classical tradition that Strauss saw as insulating liberalism from the progressive blasts of romanticism, historicism, and today, we might add, deconstruction.

Of greater import is the charge leveled a generation ago by an English critic, Myles Burnyeat, who wrote an excoriating attack upon Strauss in the pages of the *New York Review of Books.* Among other things, Burnyeat declared that while Strauss's writings contained much discussion of "the philosopher" there was "no sign of any knowledge, from the inside, of what it is to be actively involved in philosophy."[10] If true, this would be a damning indictment. The question, though, is whether it is true and whether Burnyeat's confidence in identifying what it means to be "actively involved in philosophy" is justified, a phrase that Burnyeat did not bother to define.

Strauss's understanding of philosophy is marked by a return to an older—a much older—meaning of the word. Philosophy in its oldest sense is *philosophia,* or, literally, the love of wisdom. But what does it mean to love wisdom? Long before philosophy became a name for an academic discipline nested within divisions of the humanities, it was associated with a way of life. To practice philosophy meant not necessarily to adhere to a specific set of doctrines, to a method, much less to anything like a system of ideas, but to practice a certain manner of living. Philosophy was not just a theoretical exercise but a practical one designed to answer the question, How ought I to live? or, What is the best way of life? or simply, Why philosophy?

There is some evidence that interest in this older conception of philosophy as a way of life is receiving renewed attention. In *Philosophy as a Way of Life,* the French classicist Pierre Hadot argues that the ancient philosophical sects—Platonists, Stoics, Epicureans—all understood philosophy first and foremost as a "spiritual exercise" designed to liberate the mind and free oneself from the grip of the passions.[11] Their aim was to create spiritual communities in which the individual members could seek to live freely and in friendship with others who had chosen a similar way of life. In a similar vein, Alexander Nehamas has sought to revive the idea of philosophy as "the art of living." While denying that he is urging readers to return to a philosophical way of life, he wants to remind analytical philosophers in particular that the type of philosophy one espouses affects the type of person one is. Philosophical discourse, like the great works of literature, shapes character, and the greatest proponents of philosophy as the art of living have been Socrates, Montaigne, Nietzsche, and Foucault.[12]

It is only when we think of philosophy in this older sense that we can begin to appreciate Strauss's role in recent philosophic debate. For Strauss, philosophy is not the kind of "spiritual exercise" Hadot associates with certain ancient ascetic cults; nor is the philosophic way of life a form of romantic self-creation, as Nehamas maintains. Philosophy, as Strauss understands it, is less a constructive or architectonic activity than a skeptical one. Philosophy, as he puts it, is "skeptic in the original sense of the term," that is, knowing that one does not know or knowing the limits of knowledge.[13] The task of the philosopher is not so much to propound answers as to anticipate problems. At the moment when the certainty of our solutions outweighs the awareness of the problematic character of the solution, the philosopher ceases to be a philosopher. He joins the camp of the partisans. This is in many ways a rigorous and demanding conception of philosophy. To use a modern category to express a Socratic insight, the philosopher must be a practitioner of "negative dialectics."[14] The passage in which Strauss defines philosophy as "skeptic in the original sense of the term" provides the key for his understanding of philosophy as a way of life. The question is, What kind of life is it? What promises and responsibilities does it hold out for its followers? And, most fundamentally, What can justify the choice of philosophy as a way of life?

PHILOSOPHY AS QUEST

Strauss is, of course, most famous as a student of political philosophy, but his understanding of political philosophy cannot dispense with some general account of philosophy. Philosophy, he explains, is the quest for "universal knowledge," or knowledge of "the whole."[15] By the whole he does not mean some kind of encyclopedic inventory, a catalogue raisonné of everything that exists; he means a knowledge of "the natures of things," that is, the basic categories of being that allow us to ask "What is . . . ?" type questions. We know a thing by knowing its nature or the category to which it belongs. Philosophy strives for categorical knowledge, not knowledge of things in their particularity. Strauss gives as examples of these categories the knowledge of God, man, and world.[16]

Philosophy as a distinctive enterprise emerges because knowledge of these natures is not immediately accessible. We have a variety of more or less reliable opinions about things, but these opinions often exhibit internal inconsistencies and may even stand in contradiction with one another. In Strauss's formulation, philosophy is "the conscious, coherent and relentless effort to replace opinions about the political fundamentals by knowledge regarding them."[17] But even as philosophy strives for knowledge of the whole, the whole is fundamentally elusive. We may have knowledge of the parts, but the whole remains mysterious, and knowledge of the parts without knowledge of the whole remains incomplete knowledge. Strauss admits that the discrepancy between the loftiness of the ambition for coherence and completeness and the puniness of the results "could appear as Sisyphean or ugly," but he then goes on to affirm that philosophy "is necessarily accompanied, sustained, and elevated by eros."[18] In other words, philosophy is first and foremost an erotic activity consisting more in the quest, the desire, for knowledge than in the completion or achievement of wisdom.

On occasion Strauss associates philosophy with a certain type of causal knowledge. "The philosopher's dominating passion is the desire for truth, i.e., for knowledge of the eternal order, or the eternal cause or causes of the whole."[19] Once again Strauss emphasizes the desire or passion—eros—that characterizes philosophy. This passion is for knowledge of the causes of the whole rather than for knowledge of any particular kind of thing. In fact, this desire for knowledge can lead the philosopher to look askance at the human things that cannot but appear "paltry and ephemeral" in comparison to the eternal order.[20] Being chiefly concerned with causes—with the form, or *eidos,* of things— philosophy seems to care little about things, including human beings, in their particularity.

Strauss is aware—deeply aware—of an obvious objection to this conception of philosophy. The ancient or Socratic conception of philosophy as "knowledge of the whole" or of an "eternal order" seems to presuppose an "antiquated cosmology," namely, one in which the universe appears as an ordered cosmos in which human beings and other species have their predetermined roles. Such an idea is completely at odds with the modern scientific conceptions of the evolution of the species and an infinitely expanding universe.[21] If all is change, the idea of knowledge of the whole is rendered incoherent. Is there a whole to have knowledge of? The teleological conception of nature seems as obsolete today as the claims of creationism and other pseudo-sciences. Does Strauss have an answer to this very pointed objection?

Strauss offers an intriguing response to the modern critique of ancient philosophy. He denies that the classical conception of human nature presupposes any specific cosmology or underlying metaphysics. The claim, for example, that classical ethics and political philosophy are disfigured by a teleological physics or a metaphysical biology misses the point. It reads back into the past the modern Enlightenment trope that natural scientific knowledge is the basis or premise for all forms of knowledge. The desire for knowledge of the whole, Strauss argues, remains precisely that—a desire. It does not dogmatically presuppose, much less claim to demonstrate, one or another specific cosmology. Strauss claims that ancient philosophy understood the human situation in terms of "the quest for cosmology" rather than any specific answer to the problem of cosmology. It is the very openness to or skepticism about knowledge of the whole that protects ancient philosophy from the charges of dogmatism and naïveté: "Whatever the significance of modern natural science may be, it cannot affect our understanding of what is human in man. To understand man in the light of the whole means for modern natural science to understand man in the light of the sub-human. But in that light man as man is wholly unintelligible. Classical political philosophy viewed man in a different light. It was originated by Socrates. And Socrates was so far from being committed to a specific cosmology that his knowledge was knowledge of ignorance. Knowledge of ignorance is not ignorance. It is knowledge of the elusive character of the truth, of the whole."[22]

Strauss's understanding of philosophy begins with a desire for knowledge of the whole and concludes with an awareness of "the elusive character of the truth." Knowledge of the whole is necessarily preceded by knowledge of the parts. Since we cannot achieve knowledge of the whole immediately, as if "shot out of the barrel of a gun" (in Hegel's famous metaphor), our access to the whole must take the form of an "ascent," a movement from the things most immediately known to us—the world of "pre-philosophic" experience—to those things that remain obscure and shrouded in mystery. Philosophy must proceed "dialectically" from premises that are generally agreed upon.[23] This ascent begins with the opinions we share, that are "first for us," namely, about the foundations of the political community, the rights and duties of its members, the relation of law and liberty, and the imperatives of war and peace. It is the "political" that provides our clearest point of departure for this ascent. Why is this the case?

Political philosophy is not simply a branch of general philosophy like ethics, logic, or aesthetics. For Strauss, political philosophy is a kind of first philosophy. The investigation of political things requires that we begin with the investigation of the opinions about the better and the worse, the just and the unjust, which give shape and meaning to political life. All politics is governed by opinion, and political philosophy takes as its starting point the investigation of opinion—the often authoritative opinions as handed down in laws, statutes, and other official documents—that govern a community. Our opinions contain *in nuce* core assumptions about the nature of political life. One cannot see a policeman as a policeman without making certain assumptions about law and authority.[24] Only in beginning from opinion can we begin the ascent to political philosophy.

If all politics is governed by opinion, all opinion is concerned with preservation or change. Change is the desire to make something better; preservation is the wish to prevent it from becoming worse. It follows, then, that all politics presupposes some opinion of better and worse by which to judge change. "Political things are by their nature," Strauss writes, "subject to approval and disapproval, to choice and rejection, to praise and blame. . . . One does not understand them as what they are, as political things, if one does not take seriously their implicit or explicit claim to be judged."[25] But judgments about better and worse presuppose some thought of the good, the good of the community or society. These opinions, while not philosophy itself, nevertheless share something with philosophy, namely, a concern for the political good, the good of the community. But what distinguishes the political philosopher from even the best citizen or statesman is not knowledge or concern for the well-being of this or that political community but a certain breadth of perspective: a search for the "true standards" that shape "the good political order."[26]

The political community is from one point of view a category of being, merely one aspect or part of the whole, but from another it is the very microcosm of the whole. The political is the most comprehensive human grouping within the order of nature. As such, the political order provides the basic structure or ranking of all other orders. Of all the perishable things, the heterogeneity of the political order is the closest expression to the heterogeneity of the eternal order. Knowledge of the whole must begin with political philosophy. Whether political philosophy becomes an end in itself or a means to an understanding of metaphysics is a problem not clearly resolved by Strauss.

THE LIBERALISM OF CLASSICAL
POLITICAL PHILOSOPHY

It should be clear that Strauss's return to classical political philosophy was not an attempt to discover recipes or formulas for contemporary use so much as an effort to elucidate the grounds or first principles for any adequate understanding of politics. Accordingly, Strauss always referred to his approach as "tentative" or "experimental," a kind of thought experiment rather than a dogmatic conclusion.[27] Such an approach was bound to be beset with difficulties, most obviously the fact that the ancient philosophers rejected democracy as a viable or legitimate regime. "The classics," Strauss wrote, "rejected democracy because they thought that the aim of human life, and hence of social life, is not freedom but virtue."[28] Liberty for Plato and Aristotle was subordinate to virtue; freedom meant not the liberty to do what we like but the educated use of freedom. Education, as the ancients conceived it, was only possible for a few, in part because education requires leisure and wealth that are not universally accessible. The best regime would be an aristocratic republic beginning from a broad or flat base and rising to a high peak of human excellence.[29]

Yet, Strauss also makes clear that classical political philosophy is not as elitist or antidemocratic as it first appears. Plato may have composed "the severest indictment" of democracy ever written, in the eighth book of the *Republic,* but he was by no means blind to the beauties of Athenian democracy. Plato described democracy as a "multicolored coat" in which every way of life, including philosophy, is allowed to flourish. Socrates was able to practice his craft until the age of seventy, something that would have been unimaginable in Sparta. Strauss cites Plato's *Seventh Letter* to the effect that the tyranny of the Thirty, in which his own relatives were implicated, made the discredited democracy look like the golden age.[30] Likewise, Aristotle praised the capacity of the demos to arrive at collective decisions that may be wiser than the judgment of a single individual.

Strauss claimed to find in the principles of classical political philosophy a "direct connection" to the defense of liberal democracy. "Liberal or constitutional democracy," he wrote, "comes closer to what the classics demanded than any alternative that is viable in our age."[31] Contrary to Karl Popper and the consensus that arose during the Cold War that regarded Plato as a precursor of modern totalitarianism, Strauss continually emphasized the value of the ancients as a support for modern democracy. Even if the best regime may be the unfettered rule of the philosopher-king, all actual regimes require a balance or a compromise between the need for wisdom and the consent of the ruled. Every decent polity will be a constitutional government ruled by law. "Wisdom," Strauss declared, "requires an unhesitating loyalty to a decent constitution and even to the cause of constitutionalism."[32]

Strauss saw in the American Constitution the closest approximation in the modern world to the classical Aristotelian or Polybian model of the "mixed regime," a power-sharing arrangement between the one, few, and many: "The classics had no delusions regarding the probability of a genuine aristocracy's ever becoming actual. For all practical purposes they were satisfied with a regime in which the gentlemen share power with the people in such a way that the people elect the magistrates and the council from among the gentlemen and demand an account of them at the end of their term of office. A variation of this thought is the notion of the mixed regime in which gentlemen form the senate and the senate occupies the key position between the popular assembly and an elected or hereditary monarch as head of the armed forces of society."[33] Even here Strauss notes "important differences" between the ancient and modern conceptions of mixed government. The ancients considered the three parts of society to form fixed estates of the realm, each of which required some measure of representation in decision making. The modern doctrine began from the natural equality of all men, and with it the assertion of the absolute sovereignty of the people.

Most important of all, Strauss found in modern liberal democracy the regime that is most open to education in the manner conceived by the classics. The ancients, as noted above, had doubts about democracy because they doubted whether the kind of education necessary for self-rule was possible for all. They associated democracy with the rule of the uneducated, and as Strauss noted, "no one in his senses would wish to live under such a government."[34] But modern social conditions made possible by the rise of modern science may have changed all this. Modern science, aided by advances in technology, has made possible an economy of abundance, or at least abundance enough to allow for the education of a great many people. Modern democracy at its best seems to be what the ancients thought of as an aristocracy that has broadened itself into a universal aristocracy.[35] In a striking formulation Strauss asserts: "The difference between the classics and us with regard to democracy consists exclusively in a different estimate of the virtues of technology."[36] Like most sober observers, he wondered whether this liberation of technology from moral and political control has produced greater opportunity for all or has led to the "dehumanization" of mankind. Has technology truly changed the human landscape for the better? Has it produced the conditions that have made possible a liberal education for all or the leveling of things great and noble? In a moment of seemingly environmental self-consciousness, Strauss asks: "Are we not crushed, nauseated, degraded by the mass of printed material, the grave-yards of so many beautiful and majestic forests?"[37]

Strauss held deep reservations about whether modern science had created a truly free and educated citizenry. Modern education has been deeply shaped by the demands of modern science, and modern science from its beginning has been governed by the imperatives of "the control of nature" and "the relief of man's estate." It is justified by its power, whether for good or evil. Modern science is Machiavellianism come of age. Its goal is not contemplation but "universal enlightenment." Yet this enlightenment, as Rousseau was but the first to note, has come at a cost. Science has produced increased specialization, which has brought a focus on "method" at the expense of vision and inspiration. It has achieved progress, but at the cost of a narrowing of the imagination. Modern science has also ushered in an age of mass culture that is necessarily the age of the mass man. The mass man of the modern age is one of Weber's "specialists without spirit, hedonists without heart." Strauss notes that democracy has tended to develop a very one-sided idea of character. In a passage that could almost be mistaken for Tocqueville, he writes: "There exists a very dangerous tendency to identify the good man with the good sport, the cooperative fellow, the 'regular guy,' i.e., an overemphasis on a certain part of social virtue and a corresponding neglect of those virtues which mature, if they do not flourish, in privacy, not to say in solitude; by educating people to cooperate with each other in a friendly spirit, one does not yet educate non-conformists, people who are prepared to stand alone, to fight alone, 'rugged individualists.' Democracy has not yet found a defense against the creeping conformism and the ever-increasing invasion of privacy which it fosters."[38] It would seem hard to argue with this point.

Despite this bleak assessment, Strauss believes that liberal education—not necessarily philosophy in the strict sense, but the cultivation of the arts and literature—has been kept alive in the great universities of the United States and England. "The classical ideal of humanity was nowhere better preserved than in Oxford and Cambridge," he wrote near the outset of World War II.[39] The task of education remains a "counterpoison" to the effects of mass culture. But even liberal education is no guarantee of liberal politics. "Karl Marx, the father of communism, and Friedrich Nietzsche, the stepgrandfather of fascism, were liberally educated on a level to which we cannot even hope to aspire."[40] Classical education is not a panacea for all that ails us, but it can serve as a prophylactic against some of our worst tendencies. Its goal is to develop an aristocracy—an aristocracy of talent and learning—within democracy and therefore to restore democracy to its ideal as a democracy of intellect.

CAVES AND CAVES BENEATH CAVES

Throughout his various writings, Strauss emphasized that his approach to philosophy was given its canonical expression in the writings of Plato and Aristotle. This was not simply because their writings came first chronologically but because the ancients stood in a privileged position in regard to the political opinion that shaped their communities. These opinions—Strauss refers to them as forming the "natural consciousness" or the "pre-philosophic consciousness"—shape the moral horizon out of which the fundamental concepts and categories of political philosophy arose and against which they can be checked.[41] Classical political philosophy, as Strauss presents it, was related directly to political life, whereas all subsequent philosophies represented modifications of this tradition and hence could only experience their world indirectly, viewing it, so to speak, through a glass darkly. Natural experience has become further distorted through a tradition of philosophy that has become at various times intermingled with theology, science, and more recently, history. Consequently, we experience the world today through a prism of concepts that prevents access to the "original position"   apologies to John Rawls—of philosophy vis-à-vis the city.[42]

Strauss seeks to account for the natural condition of philosophy through the famous Platonic metaphor of the cave.[43] Plato's cave, Strauss argues, is not simply a condition of darkness and superstition. It represents the natural horizon of everyday life, the world in which we all live and act. The "prisoners" in the cave—for that is what Plato thinks they are—are shackled to one another and are able to see only images projected on a wall from a fire burning behind them. These persons—passive and enthralled—Socrates claims are "like us." The metaphor is something like a modern movie theater or television screen where the spectators passively absorb the images they see in front of them but are never allowed to see the causes of these images. These images are in turn controlled by "puppet handlers" who allow the cave dwellers to see only what they want them to see. The puppeteers are, in the first instance, the legislators of the city, its founders, statesmen, and legislators, the bringers of its laws and codes of justice. Next to them are the poets, mythologists, historians, and artists; and below them the craftsmen, architects, city planners, and designers. All of these craftsmen contribute their share in the decoration of the various caves that constitute political life.

The novelty of our situation—and the originality of Strauss's use of the cave metaphor—is that we are no longer said to inhabit Plato's cave but have dug for ourselves a cave beneath the natural cave, an artificial cave, that has created even further obstacles to the pursuit of philosophy. It is as if

> people may become so frightened of the ascent to the light of the sun, and so desirous of making that ascent utterly impossible to any of their descendants, that they dig a deep pit beneath the cave in which they were born, and withdraw into that pit. If one of the descendants desired to ascend to the light of the sun, he would first have to try to reach the level of the natural cave, and he would have to invent new and most artificial tools unknown and unnecessary to those who dwelt in the natural cave. He would be a fool, he would never see the light of the sun, he would lose the last vestige of the memory of the sun, if he perversely thought that by inventing his new tools he had progressed beyond the ancestral cave-dwellers.[44]

What is the cause of this new pit, the cave beneath the cave?

Strauss traces the cause of this new and unprecedented condition to the errant path of modern philosophy itself and its "twin-sisters" called science and history. It must be said that he does not oppose science and history per se. It is rather the transformation of science and history into two pseudo-philosophies that go under the names of positivism and historicism, which are the greatest obstacles to the recovery of philosophy. Positivism is the belief, which "the kind of human knowledge possessed or aspired to by modern science is the highest form of knowledge."[45] Positivism necessarily depreciates the value of all nonscientific forms of knowledge, whether inherited traditional beliefs, folk wisdom, or simple common sense. Only what can stand the test of scientific scrutiny and control can count as knowledge. In the social sciences, positivists have typically insisted on a fundamental distinction between facts and values, arguing that true knowledge concerns only facts and their relations. Values or "value judgments" are said to be matters of individual choice and thus fall outside the scope of knowledge. The attempt to rank or evaluate different political regimes or claims to justice is, therefore, deemed to be impossible from the get-go.[46]

The problem with positivism is not only that it distrusts and therefore attempts to break from all forms of prescientific knowledge but that it ends up merely confirming through complicated scientific means things that "every

ten-year-old child of normal intelligence" already knows. Scientific reductionism ("telescopic-microscopic knowledge") may be valuable in certain areas,
but not when it is applied to the social and political world: "There are things
that can only be seen as what they are if they are seen in the perspective of the
citizen, as distinguished from the scientific observer."[47] With a nod to Swift,
he claims that to demand scientific exactitude can lead not to greater clarity
but to distortion, "the kind of research projects by which [Gulliver] was
amazed in Laputa."[48]

The second and even more prominent cause of our descent below the natural cave comes from historicism. Historicism is not to be confused with history,
a discipline that Strauss admired; instead, historicism involves a corruption of
history. Historicism is the belief that all knowledge—scientific, philosophical—
is historical knowledge, that is, an expression of the time, place, and circumstance in which it appeared. Positivism maintained that one kind of
knowledge, scientific knowledge, was the source of truth. Positivism at least
retained some connection, however tenuous, to the philosophic tradition. Historicism contends that even to raise the question of truth, of the "permanent
characteristics of humanity," is to relapse into a kind of "decayed Platonism"
with its ideas of timeless truths and the one correct order of society.[49]

On Strauss's account, historicism fails even on its own terms. Historicism
is the belief that all thought is the product of its time. But if all thought is the
product of its time, this must be true for historicism itself. Yet historicism in-
consistently exempts itself from the verdict of history. All thought would appear to be historical except the idea of historicism, that is, the idea that all
thought is historically relative. There is also the problem that historicism fails
to offer an adequate account of the thought of the past. The modern historical method demanded to understand the past as it actually—*eigentlich*—
happened or as it actually understood itself. But to read a book like Plato's
Republic or Rousseau's *Social Contract* as the product of its time is to fail to
understand Plato and Rousseau as they understood themselves. They were not
historicists, so it is a distortion of true historical understanding to force historicism upon their works. It is to impose on the history of thought a form of
historicism that is itself a modern construction.

How can we extricate ourselves from these dogmas that constitute the cave
beneath Plato's cave? Strauss admits that we no longer have direct access to
the original meaning of experience, of the city and its gods, that was the
pretheoretical condition for philosophy. It has been papered over by layers of
congealed tradition that have succeeded in obscuring it from view. But,

ironically, Strauss believed this was not entirely a bad thing. Due to histori-cism's deconstruction of all previous philosophies, we live at a time when the very shattering of tradition has made a rethinking of tradition possible. As Strauss claims in the passage cited above, such a rethinking will require the creation of "new and most artificial tools" if we are to emerge from the sub-basement and ascend to the natural cave that is the presupposition of all philosophy. These new tools, paradoxically, are drawn from the same toolbox of historicism that he appears to reject. While historicism may dogmatically confine philosophy to the conditions of its time and place, it can also be used against itself. Strauss holds out the possibility that by drawing attention to the conditions of philosophy, historicism might unwittingly be self-undermining: "The historian who started out with the conviction that true understanding of human thought is understanding of every teaching in terms of its particu-lar time or as an expression of its particular time, necessarily familiarizes himself with the view, constantly urged upon him by his subject matter, that his initial conviction is unsound. More than that: he is brought to realize that one cannot understand the thought of the past as long as one is guided by that initial conviction. The self-destruction of historicism is not altogether an unforeseen result."[50] Strauss's answer is that only through historical stud-ies can we think ourselves back into the original situation of philosophy. Ironically, to become more historical, we must first disenthrall ourselves from the bewitchments of historicism. Only by reacquiring the art of careful reading shall we be able to begin the slow and painstaking ascent from the artificial cave we now inhabit back into the "natural cave" that is the founda-tion for a philosophy of the future.[51]

THE PHILOSOPHER AND THE CITY

Classical political philosophy has a privileged place for Strauss because it re-veals the original or natural condition of philosophy. This condition consists in a tension between the philosopher and the city, between the needs of the mind and the political needs of the city. Strauss puts this tension in the form of a syllogism:

Major Premise: Philosophy is the attempt to replace opinion, including opinions about political things, by knowledge;
Minor Premise: Opinion is the medium of society;
Conclusion: Philosophy is necessarily at odds with society.

It is this tension between philosophy and society, given its most vivid expression in Plato's *Apology of Socrates,* which constitutes the natural situation of philosophy. The philosopher's way of life is forced to pay homage to politics. Strauss drew from this the following further conclusion: philosophy is necessarily a function of the "few," an elite that must conceal its activity from the hostility of the "many."[52]

Strauss's most developed thoughts on the tension between philosophy and politics occur in his exchange with the Hegelian-Marxist philosopher Alexandre Kojève over the nature of modern tyranny. Strauss's *On Tyranny* was an attempt to resuscitate the ancient concept of tyranny as presented in Xenophon's dialogue *Hiero* in order to better understand the phenomenon of twentieth-century totalitarianism. Unlike many of his contemporaries who emphasized the novelty of totalitarianism, Strauss, somewhat counterintuitively, saw a continuity between ancient and modern tyranny. He did not deny that modern tyrannies, supported by the powers of technology and ideology, have become vastly more dangerous than tyrannies in the past, but he wondered whether this changed the essential nature of the phenomenon ("Tyranny is a danger coeval with political life" [22]).[53] In the course of their exchange Strauss and Kojève turned the debate over tyranny into a discussion of the philosopher's responsibility to the city.[54]

Strauss begins by considering the philosopher's motives, the peculiar desire, or eros, that drives the philosophic quest. For Kojève, it is recognition above all that intellectuals crave, the desire to have their ideas "realized" by being put into practice, whether it be by a court, a president, or a tyrant. The test of the truth of an idea is its success in the public sphere. For Strauss, however, it is not public recognition but the satisfaction that derives from philosophy itself that is its own reward. The justification of philosophy is entirely internal to philosophy. "We do not have to pry into the heart of any one in order to know that, insofar as the philosopher, owing to the weakness of the flesh, becomes concerned with being recognized by others, he ceases to be a philosopher," Strauss retorts. "According to the strict view of the classics he turns into a sophist" (203).

Kojève's complaint is that Strauss's understanding of philosophy remains isolated from the life of the city, political praxis, and the historical process. This retreat has historically taken the form of the Epicurean garden, the Republic of Letters, or the academic ivory tower. These all represent efforts to escape the judgment of history by retreating into some kind of inner citadel. Strauss accepts that the philosopher's quest is a lonely one that requires liberation from "the most potent natural charm" of attachment to the city, but this does not render it absolutely self-regarding. Fully aware of the fallibility of the mind, the philosopher must seek out others of his kind with whom to share, challenge, and test his ideas. The cultivation of friendship becomes one of the highest duties of philosophy (194–95).

To be sure, Strauss agrees with Kojève regarding the danger of self-referentiality that comes from "the cultivation and perpetuation of common prejudices by a closely knit group of kindred spirits" (195). He appears to be fully cognizant of all the dangers later associated with "Straussianism." But if one danger to philosophy comes from "the snobbish silence and whispering of the sect," an even greater danger derives from the desire to turn philosophy into a mass doctrine ("propaganda"). The idea of a public philosophy is an oxymoron. "If we must choose between the sect and the party," Strauss writes, "we must choose the sect" (195). The conditional "if" suggests that Strauss is not happy with the choice, but that it may be a necessity. There will always be rival philosophical sects that check and balance one another in the search for truth. The true danger to philosophy comes not from the sect but from the attempt to turn philosophy into an ideology—a public doctrine—that would end up monopolizing the conversation.

It is in this context that Strauss confirms the skeptical or what he calls "zetetic" (seeking) nature of philosophy referred to earlier. Philosophy is a matter of knowledge, but knowledge of one's ignorance, of knowing the limits of knowledge: "Philosophy as such is nothing but genuine awareness of the problems, i.e., of the fundamental and comprehensive problems. It is impossible to think about these problems without becoming inclined toward a solution, toward one or the other of the very few typical solutions. Yet as long as there is no wisdom, but only quest for wisdom, the evidence of all solutions is necessarily smaller than the evidence of the problems. Therefore the philosopher ceases to be a philosopher at the moment at which the 'subjective certainty' of a solution becomes stronger than his awareness of the problematic character of that solution. At that moment the sectarian is born" (196).

This is Strauss's boldest statement on the nature of philosophy and surely refutes Burnyeat's charge that in Strauss's writings there is "no sign of any knowledge, from the inside, of what it is to be actively involved in philosophy." Yet Strauss leaves many questions unanswered. His affection for Socratic moderation and nonsectarianism notwithstanding, where does one draw the line between knowledge and ignorance? Even if we accept the claim that the evidence of the problems of philosophy is greater than the evidence for the solutions, does this render all solutions equally problematic? Are we not entitled to claim that some solutions are preferable to others, even if they lack certainty? Is the only choice that between dogmatism and zetetic skepticism? More seriously, Strauss's zetetic understanding of philosophy seems to under-cut the ground of political judgment. If, as he remarks above, one cannot think about the problems without becoming "inclined" toward a solution, on the basis of what is one so inclined? If knowledge of the right or good political order remains fundamentally problematic, what standard can be used for judg-ment in political life?

Strauss probably exaggerates philosophy's radical detachment from the con-cerns of the city. He recognizes that the philosopher "cannot help living as a human being who as such cannot be dead to human concerns" (199). Among these concerns are the philosopher's twin responsibilities to both philosophy and the city. The philosopher's first and primary concern must always be to philosophy itself, to ensure its survival even in the most dangerous times. "The philosopher must go to the market place in order to fish there for poten-tial philosophers" (205). These fishing expeditions will necessarily be seen by the city as an attempt to corrupt the young by weaning them away from politics and commerce to philosophy. In this way, philosophers are forced to defend themselves and their way of life, not only before other philosophers, but before the tribunal of public opinion as well.

In what does the philosopher's responsibility to the city consist? Recogniz-ing that philosophy can only take place within the context of the city, the philosopher must show a decent respect to the opinions on which the city is based. To be sure, the philosopher's public responsibilities are entirely exoteric. It is sufficient to satisfy the city "that the philosophers are not atheists, that they do not desecrate everything sacred to the city, that they reverence what the city reverences, that they are not subversives, in short, that they are not irre-sponsible adventurers but good citizens, and even the best of citizens" (205–6). Knowing that true happiness is found only in the activity of philosophy, phi-losophers will find it easy to accommodate themselves to the *nomoi* of the city. Plato's allegory of the cave always remained Strauss's Exhibit A for the intransigent hostility between philosophy and even the best social order. Strauss's philosophic politics raises the troubling question of the limits of the philosopher's accommodation to the city. Does this accommodation include acquiescence to tyranny as something "coeval with political life"? How far must the philosopher maintain the fiction that philosophy is not atheistic but reveres the gods of the city? Must tyrannical regimes be tolerated as one of the evils "inseparable from the human condition" (200)?

Strauss's answer to these questions is best summed up in a phrase he uses in regard to Judah Halevi: "The line of demarcation between timidity and responsibility is drawn differently in different ages."[55] He might also have added, "and according to the temperament and judgment of each individual." This is clearly true for Strauss himself, whose own philosophical politics displayed a combination of inner radicalism and outer conformity. There will always remain the lingering question of how far he recommended a strategy of esotericism to his own readers. As Rémi Brague observed, "Strauss excelled in the art of window-dressing and paying lip service to conservative and 'square' opinions."[56] To what degree does esotericism remain a historical thesis about the interpretation of the thought of the past or a responsibility of philosophy even in the present? This is a theme on which Strauss remained tantalizingly, and, I believe, deliberately, opaque. It is certainly far from evident that a strategy adopted by Halevi, Al-Farabi, and Maimonides, writing in times of considerable hostility to philosophy, remains applicable in a modern democratic age where the demands for intellectual probity and "transparency" have become not just private but also public virtues.[57]

THE THEOLOGICO-POLITICAL DILEMMA

The philosopher may believe—Strauss may even believe—that the philosophic life is best. The question is what makes it so. Strauss refers to the sense of satisfaction bordering on "self-admiration" felt by the philosopher. But this is not so much a proof as an expression of the philosophic life. It is also less than clear how knowledge of one's ignorance contributes to the sense of satisfaction or happiness experienced by the philosopher, but as Strauss would say, "be that as it may." Can philosophy justify itself and its way of life before the most serious alternatives? This is perhaps the central question of Strauss's philosophical writings.

The most serious alternative to philosophy, in fact the only real alternative that Strauss considers, is the challenge posed by divine revelation.[58] Other choices and other life plans—even the classical conflict between the philosophical life and the political life—pale in comparison. The alternatives of reason and revelation, or, in Strauss's idiom, Athens and Jerusalem, remain the sharpest and most comprehensive question that philosophy must confront in defending itself and its way of life. The difference between Athens and Jerusalem centers on their respective views of the role of morality in the overall economy of human life. For adherents of Jerusalem, it is the passionate quest for righteousness that represents the pinnacle of humanity, while for partisans of Athens, morality is at most instrumental to the attainment of a kind of contemplative autonomy. This contrast, even more than the famous "quarrel between the ancients and the moderns," remains *the* philosophic question because if philosophy cannot defend itself against the adherents of revelation, then philosophy itself threatens to become just another faith based upon an arbitrary decision or an act of will.[59]

Strauss states this contrast nowhere more starkly than in the pages of *Natural Right and History:* "Man cannot live without light, guidance, knowledge; only through knowledge of the good can he find the good that he needs. The fundamental question, therefore, is whether men can acquire that knowledge of the good without which they cannot guide their lives individually or collectively by the unaided efforts of their natural powers, or whether they are dependent for that knowledge on Divine Revelation. No alternative is more fundamental than this: human guidance or divine guidance."[60] There seems, then, to be a standoff between philosophy and revelation. Can either side refute the other?

In Socratic fashion, Strauss considers a variety of opinions on both sides of the argument. Consider the matter first from the side of theology. Within the Jewish tradition what is termed the Call of God is often said to be verified by a long line of tradition. This Call was given to Moses on Mount Sinai and then handed down to Joshua and to the elders and the prophets in an unbroken chain of tradition stretching to the rabbis. Is this tradition reliable?

Strauss questions the validity of this kind of historical proof. The Call of God cannot be distinguished from those who claim to have experienced the Call. In other words, the Call is only as reliable as the individuals who claim to have received it. But this makes the Call dependent on the interpretation of the believer, and such interpretations will inevitably vary from person to person and from sect to sect. A believing Jew will interpret the Call very differently from a believing Muslim. Furthermore, those who claimed to be witnesses to the revelation or the inheritors of this revelation are in all known cases already adherents of the faith. There are no impartial or neutral witnesses apart from the believers themselves.[61]

Strauss considers and rejects the various arguments used to defend the primacy of revelation, but how do things look from the standpoint of philosophy? No better. Philosophy demands that revelation defend itself before the bar of human reason. But revelation resolutely refuses to do this. The argument that revelation must justify itself rationally is circular. It presupposes what it needs to prove, namely, that revelation is a rational experience. At most philosophy can claim to have refuted the various theological arguments in defense of revelation; it has not disproved the possibility of revelation itself.

Strauss considers a number of more specific arguments against revelation, some drawn from the historical and archaeological criticism of the Bible and others from modern scientific theories (Darwinism), but he pays the greatest respect to the claims of philosophical theology, or what goes by the name of natural theology. According to the argument of natural theology, God's attributes are in principle knowable and accessible to human reason. The opening axioms and demonstrations of book 1 of Spinoza's *Ethics* is the clearest proof text of this approach. According to Spinoza, we can know the attributes of God because God *is* nature, and the operations of nature can be known through the application of unaided human intelligence. Just as everything exists within the ordered sphere of nature, so can everything be known according to the principle of sufficient reason. According to this principle, there is a perfect unity between reason and nature, and this unity is God.

Strauss takes Spinoza's argument with the utmost seriousness, but in the end finds it just as arbitrary as the assertion of revelation. The attributes of God proposed by Spinoza have all been preselected to prove God's perfect rationality and intelligibility, to deny all mystery to the universe. Whether Spinoza's disenchantment of the universe represents a form of concealed atheism or a form of higher piety is not a question that concerns Strauss. His point is that the Spinozist conception of God as *Deus sive natura* may well follow the criteria of clarity and distinctness, but clarity and distinctness are not a guarantee of truth. A clear and distinct proof for the existence of God is only clear and distinct from our point of view, from the standpoint of philosophy; it cannot begin to penetrate the existence of an infinite being whose ways may not be our ways. The *Ethics* remains a castle built on sand.

The conflict between Athens and Jerusalem seems to have concluded with a draw. Strauss writes: "All alleged refutations of revelation presuppose unbelief in revelation, and all alleged refutations of philosophy presuppose faith in revelation."[62] No common ground or neutral standpoint seems possible. But a standoff between philosophy and faith would seem to tilt the balance in favor of faith. If philosophy cannot rationally demonstrate its superiority to revelation, if every proof against revelation turns out to be hypothetical, or to rest upon "unevident premises," then one must accept that the philosophical life is itself based on faith, that is, an act of will, or on a decision that cannot in the last instance be rationally grounded. In such a competition the adherents of faith would win on a technicality.[63]

Strauss goes out of his way to make the strongest case for revelation or, what amounts to the same thing, to create the highest possible hurdle for philosophy. He often seems to demand a much higher burden of proof from philosophy than from theology. Theology merely needs to hold open the possibility of revelation, whereas philosophy is required to refute its very premises. But how can one refute a possibility? Anything less must be taken as an admission of failure. Strauss was himself a product of the early twentieth-century "reawakening of theology" associated with the names of Karl Barth and Franz Rosenzweig, who "appeared to make it necessary to investigate how far the critique of orthodox theology—Jewish and Christian—deserved to be victorious."[64] Strauss clearly took it for granted that the critique of theology had not yet proved deserving of victory.

But while the reawakening of theology alerted Strauss to the failure of the Enlightenment critique of religion, it would be a mistake to place him in the camp of Counter-Enlightenment political theology, to turn him into a defender of faith, as some have tried to do. Through his dissatisfaction with Spinoza, Strauss fought his way back not to a reaffirmation of orthodoxy but to a much older conception of philosophy as zetetic philosophy. This, I take it, is the meaning of his statement that a return to premodern philosophy is not an impossibility, only a very great difficulty.[65]

Strauss's "return" to classical political philosophy, as we saw earlier, is not an endorsement of natural hierarchy or any form of metaphysical biology. Strauss's understanding of ancient philosophy has more to do with the political problem of philosophy or the issue of the philosophic life than with a philosophy of politics as it is usually understood. This has certainly not inhibited all manner of interpreters from attributing all manner of doctrinal positions to Strauss, from neoconservatism to a nihilistic antimodernity. His concern was with the original situation of philosophy as a mode of questioning and not with the defense of any particular philosophical school or sect, much less a political movement or cause.

Strauss makes clear that the philosophic life is to be understood as a form of zetetic questioning. This is the meaning of "Platonic political philosophy" in its original sense.[66] Even here, zeteticism is a return not to the questions of the Stoa but to a whole range of topics unknown to the ancients, mainly the problem of Athens and Jerusalem, or what Strauss later called the "theologico-political dilemma" ("*the* theme of my investigations").[67] Zetetic or Platonic philosophy does not claim to have found an answer, much less *the* answer, to the reason/revelation problem; rather, it keeps that problem alive for future generations. Zetetic understanding is precisely what protects the philosopher from the twin dogmatisms of faith and unbelief. Neither of these can withstand the test of rational justification. Only the philosopher who lives in constant awareness of and engagement with the conflict between Athens and Jerusalem, who is able to engage each side with the claims of the other, is in a position to justify philosophy as a way of life.[68]

CONCLUSION

If Strauss is correct that we have lost sight of the question of the philosophic life, then it is hardly surprising that many today fail to see him as a philosopher, often mistaking him for an interpreter, a historian of ideas, or even some kind of political guru. His interest was not with the techniques or methods of philosophy, much less with advancing knowledge of concepts and propositions. His interest was with the prior question, "Why philosophy?" This is obviously not a question one would ask of activities like military strategy and business enterprise, in which the ends (victory, profit) are not fundamentally controversial. The ends of philosophy are and will always remain an open question. Strauss remained a philosophical skeptic whose task was to revive a sense of the problems besetting political life rather than advocating political solutions to them. More specifically, Strauss was concerned with what the philosophic life is and what value, if any, it confers on the life of the community. His single-minded examination of this question fulfills the office of philosopher to the highest degree.

Chapter 15 The Political Teaching of

Lampedusa's *The Leopard*

It is not obvious why a study of modernity should include a treatment of *Il Gattopardo—The Leopard*—a work by an Italian aristocrat, Giuseppe Tomasi di Lampedusa, that takes place entirely on the island of Sicily, which most would agree stands somewhat at the periphery of the modern world.[1] Yet despite its deliberately parochial setting, the book is a profound meditation on the problem of modernity. The action of *The Leopard* is set at the time of the Italian Risorgimento, the reunification of the Italian Peninsula for the first time since the age of the Roman Empire. The revolutionary and political upheavals of the era are a backdrop to the book's principal characters. While Giuseppe Garibaldi's invasion of Sicily may not exactly qualify as a world-historical event—it is not Napoleon's invasion of Russia in Tolstoy's *War and Peace*—it nevertheless provides more than enough material for the author to sketch the great theme of his novel, the decay of the aristocracy.

The plot of *The Leopard* is a simple one. The central character, Don Fabrizio Corbera, is a Sicilian prince, a vast landowner, and an accomplished astronomer. The focus of the novel is on the marriage of the prince's favorite nephew, Tancredi, to Angelica, the daughter of a member of the nouveau riche merchant class that has come to power along with the new regime. The principal tension exists between the nobles, represented by the house of Corbera, whose emblem is the leopard, and the up-and-coming merchants, represented by Don Calogero Sedàra, the father of the beautiful Angelica. Don Fabrizio reluctantly realizes that the only way to ensure the success of his impoverished nephew is to give his blessing to the union; the marriage will provide Tancredi with the money he will need to succeed in the new order, and it will bestow a title of nobility on Angelica, whose parents are only one generation removed from their peasant origins. It is Tancredi who speaks the most famous line in the book: "If we want things to stay as they are," he tells his uncle just before leaving to join Garibaldi's troops, "things will have to change" (40).

Yet *The Leopard* is more than a historical romance. It is also a deeply political book, although Lampedusa's politics are far from clear. Was the author a reactionary lamenting the decline of the traditional ruling elite, or was the work a merciless depiction of a class in its final state of decrepitude, or was it, as I believe, the work of a learned skeptic reflecting on the limits of political reform? I am less interested in the artistic merits of the book—although these are considerable—than in Lampedusa's image of Sicily as a land where the forces of nature, history, and psychology combine to confound our modern expectations about change. The book is ultimately about the transition from one world to another, from what Tocqueville called the age of aristocracy to the age of democracy, or, to use Marxist categories, from the world of feudalism to the world of the modern bourgeoisie. It is, finally, a book about the loss of collective memory.

"THE PROTAGONIST IS AT BOTTOM, ME"

The story of the author and the work's publication have become almost as famous as the book itself.[2] Giuseppe Tomasi di Lampedusa—the eleventh prince of Lampedusa—was born in Palermo in 1896. He served in the Italian army during World War I but was taken prisoner and spent much of the war in a POW camp in Hungary. After the war he returned to Sicily and later married a Latvian aristocrat who shared his passion for books and literary pursuits. The two lived together off and on in Palermo, where they cultivated a circle of friends who together spent their time reading and discussing the great works of European literature in their original languages. The couple had no children. Aware that the line of Lampedusa was coming to an end, Giuseppe began a novel that set out to describe the aristocratic world of his ancestors.

The Leopard was the first and only book written by Lampedusa. It was completed in 1956 and rejected by every publishing house to which it was submitted during Lampedusa's lifetime. It was considered too traditional and too nostalgic about the aristocracy to be accepted by the Marxist elite that then held sway over the Italian literary establishment. Lampedusa died at the age of sixty in 1957, and the next year the book was finally accepted for publication by Feltrinelli. It became an immediate success and has since come to be regarded as a classic of European literature. A film version of *The Leopard* directed by the Italian filmmaker Luchino Visconti (himself a landowning aristocrat) and starring Burt Lancaster was made in 1963.

The Leopard is a fictionalized biography of Lampedusa's great-grandfather, but it also contains strong elements of autobiography. In a letter from 1957 Lampedusa denied that the book was a "historical novel," stating that "Don Fabrizio expresses my ideas exactly."[3] Like Flaubert, who once said of his most famous creation "Madame Bovary, c'est moi," Lampedusa announced in another letter, "The protagonist is at bottom, me."[4] Like Don Fabrizio, Lampedusa was something of a brooding melancholic. He lived his life as a provincial aristocrat whose sole luxury was buying books. He was a reader more than an author. His mornings were spent at a café where he would sit reading for hours at a time before returning home by bus. In addition to Italian, he read and spoke English, French, German, and Russian. He especially loved English literature—Shakespeare's *Measure for Measure* was his favorite—and his wife once said that he always carried a volume of Shakespeare with him so that "he could console himself with it if he should see something disagreeable" on his wanderings.[5]

In addition to depicting the similarity of Lampedusa's own personality to that of the prince, *The Leopard* often contains oblique autobiographical asides. For example, the ancestral home where Lampedusa lived was destroyed by allied bombing during World War II. Late in the book, when describing the painted frescoes on the ceiling of one of the aristocratic homes in Palermo, he writes: "From the ceiling the gods, reclining on gilded couches, gazed down smiling and inexorable as a summer sky. They thought themselves eternal; but a bomb manufactured in Pittsburg, Pennsylvania, was to prove the contrary in 1943" (258). The prince's relation with Tancredi was based upon Lampedusa's own relation with his nephew, Lanza Tomasi, whom he adopted and who became his literary executor after his death.

Leaving aside Lampedusa's denial that *The Leopard* is a historical novel, history and context are vital to an understanding of the book. The action begins in the year 1860, which marks the invasion of Sicily by Garibaldi and the unification of the Kingdom of Naples, also known as the Kingdom of the Two Sicilies, with the Italian Peninsula. The movement for unification had come from the state of Savoy in the north of Italy. The force behind the Risorgimento, or "Resurgence," was Camillo Cavour, who served as the prime minister to King Victor Emmanuel of Savoy. The Risorgimento was a nationalist movement that sought to bring about a kind of modern constitutional monarchy to the divided Italian states.[6]

The greatest stumbling block to the dream of a unified Italy was the Kingdom of the Two Sicilies in the south, whose capital was Naples. Sicily remained an outpost of the Bourbon dynasty and was the area with the strongest localist traditions and hence most resistant to the modernizing and nationalizing efforts of Cavour. The Bourbons collapsed with the invasion of the island by Garibaldi and his "Redshirts," who stormed Palermo and drove out King Francis II. Later Garibaldi sailed to Naples, where he was welcomed enthusiastically. Although there was bad blood between Garibaldi, a genuinely democratic leader, and the more conservative Cavour, Garibaldi willingly handed power over to Victor Emmanuel. A series of plebiscites around the country were called, and Sicily agreed to join the new Kingdom of Italy led by Victor Emmanuel, who was proclaimed king of Italy in Turin. To be sure, not everyone was happy with these changes, and throughout *The Leopard* we hear the voices of smoldering discontent of those who feel dispossessed by the new regime.

"A SHAPE FOR LIFE FROM WITHIN"

At the center of the story is Don Fabrizio Corbera, Prince of Salina. The first thing to note about Don Fabrizio is that he is a prince. To be sure, he is not a "Machiavellian" prince full of virtù and energy. He is a traditional prince, a member of the nobility, who holds his power on the basis of heredity and ancient family ties. Properly speaking, Don Fabrizio belongs to the class of the "gentlemen" who in Machiavelli's terms "live in idleness on their abundant revenue derived from their estates" (*Discourses,* I.55). The prince is a man of great wealth who has three castles, one in San Lorenzo outside Palermo, his town palace inside the city walls, and his vast country estate in Donnafugata. He is a feudal lord who rules over his large family and countless retainers and tenants with a kind of benevolent indifference that can only grow out of the possession of old money. He is a poor businessman not because he does not have the head for business but from "a kind of contemptuous indifference about matters he considered low" (160).

The second thing that Lampedusa tells us, however, is of the prince's native melancholy. Underneath his "Jovelike frown," the prince lives in a state of "perpetual discontent," observing "the ruin of his own class and his own inheritance without ever making, less still wanting to make, any move toward saving it" (19). Only his dog, Bendicò, his constant companion (and a key player in the novel), seems to bring him any joy.

The feature that most distinguishes the old aristocracy—and something that money cannot buy—is a certain kind of refinement and manners. The prince's tact consists in his ability to put others at their ease. "There is a deity who is the protector of princes," we read later. "He is called Courtesy" (146). There is a delicacy of taste and judgment that distinguishes Don Fabrizio from the other characters in the novel. This is conveyed in a number of ways, both small and large. Consider the scene at Donnafugata, to which the prince and his family have invited their future in-laws, the barely presentable Sedàra family, for dinner:

> The Prince was too experienced to offer Sicilian guests in a town of the interior, a dinner beginning with soup, and he infringed the rules of *haute cuisine* all the more readily as he disliked it himself. But rumors of the barbaric foreign usage of serving insipid liquid as a first course had reached the major citizens of Donnafugata too insistently for them not to quiver with a slight residue of alarm at the start of a solemn dinner like this. So when three lackeys in green, gold, and powder entered, each holding a great silver dish containing a towering mound of macaroni, only four of the twenty at table avoided showing their pleased response: the Prince and Princess from foreknowledge, Angelica from affectation, and Concetta from lack of appetite (96).

Or consider Don Calogero's reflection on the prince after he has come to know him. Up until then, we learn, Sedàra, a self-made millionaire, had been accustomed to looking at the aristocracy (somewhat in the manner of Plato's Thrasymachus) as consisting "entirely of sheeplike creatures, existing merely in order to give their wool to the clipping sheers," but association with the prince has led him to change his mind. What he finds most beguiling about the prince, we are told, is "a tendency toward abstraction, a disposition to seek a shape for life from within himself and not in what he could wrest from others." Gradually, even Sedàra begins to realize just "how agreeable can be a well-bred man, who at heart is only someone who eliminates the unpleasant aspects of so much of the human condition and exercises a kind of profitable altruism" (161–62). We might call the prince a great-souled man.

It is the prince's tact that allows him to express a generosity toward those below him. The people of Donnafugata held a high degree of affection for their lord, who, we are told, often "forgot" to collect their meager rents (75). When Father Pirrone, the family priest, pays a visit to his hometown of San Cono, he is eagerly asked what it is like to live among the nobles. In particular what are they saying about the recent revolution? Are they for it or against it? Many of the prince's retainers are strongly opposed to the republic's new confiscatory tax policies and are looking for leadership from the nobles (unbeknownst to them, the prince has in fact voted in favor of the new republic at the plebiscite [130]). This is something the priest has clearly thought about but has a hard time explaining even to himself. The nobles are not like you and me: "They live in a world of their own, of joys and troubles, of their own; they have a very strong collective memory so they're put out by things which wouldn't matter at all to you and me," he explains to the local herbalist (226). Such men may occasionally be cruel, but they are never petty or small ("Rage is gentlemanly; complaints are not" [230]).

But despite their inward-looking character—"a sort of obscure atavistic instinct"—the nobles confer benefits on others. They provide shelter for the families of the poor, even if their motives are not so easily understood. "When they treat someone badly, as they do sometimes," the priest admits, "it is not so much their personality sinning as their class affirming itself" (28).

Don Fabrizio, though, is not a typical representative of his class. He stands apart both physically because of his height and great size, but also intellectually. He is, we learn, both the first and last member of an ancient family to have a genuine passion for mathematics (19). He is regarded as an "eccentric" by his peers largely because of his intellectual and aesthetic tastes. His passion for mathematics and astronomy would have been seen as bordering on blasphemy had he not also mastered the gentlemanly arts of riding, hunting, and womanizing (256). But the prince, like Lampedusa himself, is a reader. In the evenings at Donnafugata he reads to the family, even though the modern literature of Dickens, Eliot, Sand, Flaubert, and Dumas had been prohibited by Bourbon censorship (169).

Above all, the prince is an aesthete who admires beautiful things for the grace and adornment they lend to life. In his last moments of life, he goes over in his mind a list, not of the things he has failed to do, but of what has given him the greatest pleasures in life. It is an extraordinary and revealing list of what has made life most worth living: the few weeks before and after his wedding, the thirty minutes or so after the birth of his first son, the pleasure of his dogs and horses, the award given him at the Sorbonne for his astronomical discoveries, and "the exquisite sensation of one or two fine silk cravats" and "the smell of morocco leathers" (290).

But what most distinguishes the prince is his passion for abstract mathematical and astronomical investigation. In the opening pages of the book we learn that he had discovered two small planets; one he named "Salina" for his family estate and the other he named "Speedy" for a hunting dog of which he was especially fond (19). The prince's passion for astronomy displays a yearning for eternity, for what transcends the transitory and vulgar. It is not a form of escapism—although it has something of this about it—but an expression of an elevated spirit who seeks satisfaction in the realm of pure thought. The prince has something of a philosopher about him. He finds in the heavens not the Christian hope for personal immortality but something of the philosophical quest for autonomy and self-sufficiency. Like Spinoza, he views himself and the world *sub specie aeternitatis:* "The soul of the Prince reached out toward them [the stars], toward the intangible, the unattainable, which gave joy without laying claim to anything in return; as many other times, he tried to imagine himself in those icy tracts, a pure intellect armed with a notebook for calculations: difficult calculations, but ones which would always work out. 'They're the only really genuine, the only really decent beings,' thought he, in his worldly formulae" (101).

Contemplation of the heavens always means for the prince an escape from the paltriness of existence, from the worries of family and politics. It is his antidote to the pain and suffering of existence (44). "Let's leave the Bendicòs down here running after rustic prey and the cooks' knives chopping the flesh of innocent beasts," the prince thinks to himself. Seen from the aspect of his observatory, everything down here below seems to merge into a kind of "tranquil harmony": "The comets would be appearing as usual, punctual to the minute, in sight of whoever was observing them. They were not messengers of catastrophe . . . on the contrary, their appearance at the time foreseen was a triumph of the human mind's capacity to project itself and to participate in the sublime routine of the skies" (54).

After an all-night ball where Tancredi and his fiancée Angelica have been introduced to Palermo society, the prince has a disturbing conversation with one of the guests, who bemoans the condition of the new Italian state. Rather than take a carriage home with his family, the prince prefers to walk by himself, claiming he needs some air. "The truth is," Lampedusa writes, "he wanted to draw a little comfort from gazing at the stars. There were still one or two up there, at the zenith. As always, seeing them revived him; they were distant, they were omnipotent, and at the same time they were docile to his calculations; just the contrary to human beings, always too near, so weak and yet so quarrelsome." He wonders when Venus "wrapped in her turban of autumnal mist . . . [will] give him an appointment less ephemeral in her own region of perennial certitude" (272–73).

"HE FOLLOWS THE TIMES, THAT'S ALL"

In the person of Don Fabrizio, Lampedusa gives us a depiction of the ancien régime—the world of the aristocracy—at its best. But the abstract and somewhat distant and distracted character of the prince will not be the qualities valued by the new order represented by Don Calogero. If there is to be hope for the older classes, it will only be through an alignment with, rather than resistance to, the new political forces at work. Like Tocqueville, Lampedusa recognizes that the age of equality is here. Resistance is futile. Can the forces of equality be moderated by some of the habits and manners represented by the age of aristocracy? This possibility is suggested in the novel by the union of Tancredi and Angelica.

Tancredi is the prince's nephew, the son of his sister and her spendthrift husband, who have left the boy orphaned. The prince regards him as his "real son," even more than his actual son, Paolo, who is a nonentity. It is above all Tancredi's subtle wit and irony, as well as his shrewd and calculating intelligence, that most appeals to the prince. "Unless we take a hand now, they'll foist a republic on us," Tancredi tells his uncle. "If we want things to stay as they are, things will have to change," he says, and Don Fabrizio cannot help but slip a roll of gold coins into his nephew's pocket as he goes off to join Garibaldi's army (40–41).

Tancredi has inherited the prince's sense of tact and delicacy, but he does not have the money to inherit the prince's way of life. Tancredi is the true "Machiavellian" in the book, supporting Garibaldi's revolution more out of opportunism than idealism. Like Machiavelli's prince, Tancredi knows an opportunity when he sees one, even if this comes at the expense of disappointing Concetta, the prince's own daughter: "The Prince was very fond of this daughter of his. But he was even fonder of his nephew. Conquered forever by the youth's affectionate banter, he had begun during the last few months to admire his intelligence too: that quick adaptability, that worldly penetration, that innate artistic subtlety with which he could use the demagogic terms then in fashion while hinting to initiates that for him, the Prince of Falconeri, this was only a momentary pastime. . . . Tancredi, he considered, had a great future; he would be the standard-bearer of the counterattack which the nobility, under new trappings, could launch against the new social state" (87).

Of course, what Tancredi lacks is money, and this accounts for his ambition. Yet unlike Don Calogero, Tancredi is not just an opportunist. He is a man of subtlety and charm. "It is impossible to obtain the distinction, the delicacy, the fascination of a boy like him without his ancestors having romped through a half-dozen fortunes," the prince explains to Tancredi's future father-in-law (152). Don Calogero is forced to agree. In Tancredi "he had found himself dealing unexpectedly with a young noble as cynical as himself," one able to strike "a sharp bargain between his own smiles and titles and the attractions and fortunes of others" (161). Tancredi knows how to tack with the times: each man is able to read into the other some of his own admired characteristics.

Tancredi's only hope for fulfilling his ambitions is to establish a marriage with the beautiful and wealthy Angelica—even if this means marrying down. But to do this, he will need not only his uncle's support but also his complicity. So while Tancredi is away in Garibaldi's army, he writes to his uncle telling him of his love for Angelica and asking him to request her hand from her father. Tancredi knows that this will be repulsive to his uncle, so he offers the following by way of a sweetener: "Tancredi went on to long considerations of the expediency, nay the necessity, of the unions between families such as the Falconeris and the Sedàras (once he even dared write 'The House of Sedàra') being encouraged in order to bring new blood into old families, and also to level our classes, aims of the current political movement in Italy. This was the only part of the letter that Don Fabrizio read with any pleasure . . . because the style, with its hints of subdued irony, magically evoked his nephew's image: the jesting nasal tone, the sparkling malice in his blue eyes, the mockingly polite smile" (118). Later, when confiding the letter to his wife, Maria Stella, who is violently opposed to the marriage, the prince says in Tancredi's defense: "He's not a traitor; he follows the times, that's all," and Stella is consoled at having a husband "so vital and so proud" (121–22).

Even though Don Fabrizio approves of Tancredi's plan, the idea of welcoming the nouveau riche Sedàras into his family does not go down well. He compares it to "swallowing a toad." One of his underlings, the organist Don Ciccio, is appalled by the idea of a union of the house of Salina and the Sedàras (143). The prince does not try to convince him of the propriety of the wedding, but when Sedàra actually shows up at the house, Lampedusa describes the scene as a surrender: "As he [the prince] crossed the two rooms preceding the study he tried to imagine himself as an imposing Leopard with smooth, scented skin preparing to tear a timid jackal to pieces; but by one of those involuntary associations of ideas which are the scourge of natures like his, he found flicking into his memory one of those French historical pictures in which Austrian marshals and generals, covered with plumes and decorations, are filing in surrender past an ironical Napoleon; they are more elegant, undoubtedly, but it is the squat man in the gray topcoat who is the victor" (145).

When we are first introduced to Angelica she is only seventeen years old and already regarded as a great beauty. We learn that she has been sent by her parents to finishing school in Florence, where she has been completely transformed. "A real lady she's become," says one of Don Fabrizio's retainers (142). She has lost most of her harsh Sicilian accent (except for the vowels) and addresses Don Fabrizio as "Prince" and not the old-fashioned "Excellency." But if Angelica's beauty is what first attracts Tancredi, she has also acquired her father's shrewdness and ambition. Even the prince has to admit that his own daughter, Concetta, who had her eyes on Tancredi, is no match for Angelica (87).

Angelica is a quick study and eager to learn. In the most romantic scene from the novel, as she and Tancredi explore unchaperoned the vast palace rooms and apartments at Donnafugata, nothing is lost on her. Tancredi later explains what will be required by her new life: "You can be expansive and noisy only with me," he tells her, "but with all others you must be the future Princess of Falconeri, superior to many, equal to all" (251). Angelica's coming out at the ball at Palazzo Ponteleone—something like Eliza Doolittle's appearance at the embassy ball in *Pygmalion*—is a huge success. Her appearance is described as a "highly successful mixture of virginal modesty, aristocratic hauteur, and youthful grace" (251). From that night on her keen observations and judgments would win for her "the reputation of a polite but inflexible art expert" that would remain with her for the rest of her life (253).

In Angelica we find a character fully as Machiavellian as Tancredi in her desires and ambitions ("each of them full of self-interest, swollen with secret aims" [259]). We learn that despite all its promise, the marriage was not to be a happy one. "Flames for a year, ashes for thirty" is predicted by the prince (88). It is hinted that Tancredi will become a successful ambassador and Angelica will be a ruthless political manipulator in the new Parliament and Senate (167).

"THE NEW MAN"

The bourgeois world of the new middle class is depicted by Lampedusa in the character of Don Calogero Sedàra. Sedàra, we learn, is the head of the liberal party in town. He is a self-made man who was able to acquire a large estate by buying it out of foreclosure. We further learn that he has made other profitable purchases and was something of a war profiteer, making great profits on the sale of grain during the upheavals of the revolution (80–81). He has many tenants who rent land from him on harsh terms and is on his way to becoming the largest landowner in the province. It is even predicted that once the papal lands go on sale, Sedàra will pick them up at rock-bottom prices (138–39). He is a man of boundless energy who also entertains political ambitions. The mayor of his town, he will become the district's representative to the new Parliament in Turin (the capital of the new Italian state until the capital was moved to Rome). In short, Sedàra is the man of the future. What does he represent?

Sedàra is described as "the new man" (139) and as representing the "bourgeois revolution" (114). Lampedusa nowhere defines these terms exactly. But for him, as for so many artists and intellectuals, "bourgeois" is a term of abuse. To be sure, the word is most famously associated with Marx—"some German Jew whose name I can't remember" is how the prince describes Marx (213)—whose *Communist Manifesto* characterized modern history as a titanic struggle between the bourgeoisie and the proletariat. But for now, Sedàra represents the triumphant class as he first appears in the novel climbing Don Fabrizio's stairs in his ill-fitting tailcoats (92–93).

Yet not all of Lampedusa's descriptions of Sedàra are entirely negative. Despite his inappropriate clothes and bad shave, Sedàra evokes in the prince an "odd admiration" for some of his qualities. He is described as a man of "rare intelligence," energy, and boundless self-confidence: "Many problems that had seemed insoluble to the Prince were resolved in a trice by Don Calogero; free as he was from the shackles imposed on many other men by honesty, decency, and plain good manners, he moved through the jungle of life with the confidence of an elephant which advances in a straight line, rooting up trees and trampling down lairs, without even noticing the scratches of thorns and the moans of the crushed" (159).

Sedàra subsequently offers advice to the prince on how he might more efficiently manage his great estate, advice that ultimately turns to the prince's disadvantage. Lampedusa uses the occasion to make a point about the fundamental incompatibility of the two classes: "But the eventual result of such advice, cruelly efficient in conception and feeble in application by the easygoing Don Fabrizio, was that in years to come the Salina family were to acquire a reputation for treating dependents harshly, a reputation quite unjustified in reality but which helped to destroy its prestige at Donnafugata and Querceta, without in any way halting the collapse of the family fortunes" (160).

Sedàra is not evil, although three times he is described as a jackal (145, 214). When he and Angelica arrive at the ball at Panteleone, he is described as "a rat escorting a flaming rose" (251). Although his clothes lack elegance, this time at least Tancredi promises the prince that Sedàra will come with a decent shave and polished shoes. "Angelica's father lacks *chic*," is how Tancredi describes him (248). His only obvious faux pas is wearing a cross of the new order of Italy in his buttonhole, something bound to be offensive to his guests, which the observant Tancredi quickly pockets (251). As Sedàra and the prince stand next to one another at the ball, Sedàra's "quick eyes" are said to be "moving over the room, insensible to its charm, intent on its monetary value." He is something like the man Oscar Wilde would describe as knowing the price of everything and the value of nothing: "Quite suddenly Don Fabrizio felt a loathing for him; it was to the rise of this man and a hundred others like him, to their obscure intrigues and their tenacious greed and avarice, that was due the sense of death which was now, obviously, hanging darkly over these palaces" (258). When last heard, Sedàra is discussing the possible rise in the price of cheese with one of the other guests (260).

"WE THINK WE ARE GODS"

What are the political teachings of *The Leopard?* A thoughtful aristocrat after the manner of Montesquieu and Tocqueville, Lampedusa is concerned with the transition from the aristocratic to the bourgeois world and what this means. The book might well have been subtitled *The Ancien Régime and the Revolution* after Tocqueville's great work. The book presents (not always fairly to be sure) the great liberal hopes for the nationalizing and modernizing plans of the Risorgimento against the backdrop of Don Fabrizio's somber and meditative reflections on the limits of progress and political reform. It looks upon the creation of the modern state with a deep sense of classical sadness, not for what has been achieved, but for what will be lost.

At the core of the prince's view of politics is a profound sense of skepticism coupled with a mistrust of reform. The first sense we get of this is a conversation between the prince and his accountant, Don Ferrara, "who hid the deluded mind of a 'liberal' behind reassuring spectacles and immaculate cravats" (44). He greets the prince with baleful warnings about the immediate future ("so many of our fine lads are sure to get killed"), but still predicts "glorious new days will dawn for this Sicily of ours." Ferrara, like Sedàra, represents the new class of accountants, merchants, and businesspeople—think of Burke's "sophisters, economists, and calculators"—that will soon come to power. The prince refuses to engage the conversation, but he later thinks to himself, "These [changes] have been promised us on every single one of the thousand invasions we've had from Nicias onward, and they've never come. And why should they come, anyway?" (45).

The reason for the prince's skepticism is revealed later, during a conversation with his hunting partner, Don Ciccio. Don Ciccio and a few others loyal to the old Bourbon monarchy have voted "no" in the plebiscite to ratify the new revolutionary government of Victor Emmanuel. Out of the 515 registered voters in Donnafugata, 512 ballots were cast, and when they were counted there were 512 "yes" votes. We find out that the "no" votes had been nullified by Sedàra, leaving those like Don Ciccio to bear the brunt of popular antagonism. The new Italian state has been ratified through an act of willful manipulation, foretelling a regime of corruption and bad faith.

In the course of their hunting expedition, the two men stop for lunch consisting of wine, roast chicken, cake, and some of the local grapes. It is when they doze off afterward that the ants begin their attack, leading to one of Lampedusa's most vivid and unforgettable metaphors for the new regime: "Nothing could stop the ants. Attracted by a few chewed grape-skins spat out by Don Ciccio, along they rushed in close order, morale high at the chance of annexing that bit of garbage soaked with saliva. Up they came full of confidence, disordered but resolute; groups of three or four would stop now and again for a chat, exalting, perhaps, the ancient glories and future prosperity of ant hill Number Two under cork tree Number Four on the top of Mount Morco; then once again they would take up their march with the others toward a buoyant future; the gleaming backs of those imperialists seemed to quiver with enthusiasm, while from their ranks no doubt rose the notes of an anthem" (125).

The longest political discussion in the book takes place between the prince and Aimone Chevalley di Monterzuolo, a deputy from the North, who has come to Sicily to offer the prince a seat in the new Senate. Chevalley is described as "congenially bureaucratic" and "much out of his element," something like a northern carpetbagger who has come to Sicily with an idea of helping (or coercing) the Sicilians to modernize their ways (195). Chevalley's prejudices have only been inflamed by being told gruesome stories about banditry, kidnapping, and murder in the area. "This state of things won't last," Chevalley confidently tells himself, "our lively new administration will change it all" (214).

Chevalley's offer to the prince begins with a revealing slip of the tongue. Chevalley refers to the recent "annexation" of Sicily and then corrects himself, calling it a "glorious union" with the mainland. He then proceeds in grandiloquent language to offer the prince a seat in the Senate, no doubt to add a measure of legitimacy to the new state by gaining the participation of one of the oldest ruling families. When the prince asks him to explain the function of this Senate—is it like the Roman Senate?—Chevalley goes on to state that it represents "the flower of Italy's politicians" and will be in charge of approving and disapproving laws for the progress of the state. The prince then embarks on his longest political speech.

Don Fabrizio's speech, which takes nearly ten pages of text, outlines his arguments against the possibility of liberal reform. The first argument derives from the temperament or national character of the Sicilians. The spirit of reform, the prince tells Chevalley, goes against the indigenous character of the people. To govern a people one must know their character, and this is what the new administration fails to grasp. "In Sicily," Don Fabrizio says, "it doesn't matter whether things are done well or done badly; the sin which we Sicilians never forgive is simply that of 'doing' at all" (205). The Sicilians have been exposed to twenty-five hundred years of conquest and colonization, and consequently they have little taste or capacity for now joining the modern world. Rather than a new society, Sicily is an exhausted one. In a provocative image, Don Fabrizio compares Sicily to "a centenarian being dragged in a Bath chair around the Great Exhibition in London."

The prince then goes on to connect this decrepitude to political somnolence. That is Sicily's tragedy. The prince associates this resistance to modernization with a kind of primordial death wish, a longing for immobility and eternity: "All Sicilian expression, even the most violent, is really wish-fulfillment; our sensuality is a hankering for oblivion, our shooting and knifing a hankering for death; our laziness, our spiced and drugged sherbets, a hankering for voluptuous immobility, that is, for death again; our meditative air is that of a void wanting to scrutinize the enigmas of nirvana" (206).[7]

It is not only the power of history and collective psychology that resists the spirit of reform; so too does the power of nature. The very geography of the island prevents change. The heat, the barren landscape, and the "cruelty of climate" are described as "irredeemable" and have created an inertia coupled with "a terrifying insularity of mind."

Finally, the prince argues that his own family traditions and loyalties prevent him from participation in the new order. We learn that he is not indifferent to the failings of his class and the old monarchy. Early in the novel he recalls a meeting with the present king, for whom he has little respect (26–27). "Swung between the old world and the new," he says, "I find myself ill at ease in both" (209). Despite their failings, it is only with members of his own class, those with whom he shares certain collective memories, that he can feel truly at ease. The prince is a realist who cannot (or will not) engage in the type of willful self-deception necessary for political rule.

In a final effort to convince him, Chevalley asks the prince to put his objections aside. He shares the characteristically liberal belief that obstacles like geography and history can be overcome. If "honest men" withhold their support for the new order, there will be no one to protect it from the Sedàras of the world. The prince takes this argument seriously, but in the end it cannot overcome his reservations. He saves his most revealing answer for last. In an almost Nietzschean moment of self-assertion, he says that he cannot accept a seat in the Senate because as a Sicilian *"we think we are gods"* (212; emphasis in original).

Don Fabrizio identifies himself with the old ruling class, however imperfect it may be. In any case, is there any evidence that a new ruling class will be an improvement? What will be the difference, the prince asks himself at one point: "Wouldn't things be just the same? Just Torinese instead of Neapolitan dialect; that's all" (27). His resistance to change is not the result of world-weariness; it comes out of a profound meditation upon history. One ruling class will replace another in a Polybian cycle of descending order of rank. "We were the Leopards, the Lions," he thinks to himself, "those who'll take our place will be little jackals, hyenas; and the whole lot of us, Leopards, jackals, and sheep, we'll all go on thinking ourselves the salt of the earth" (214).

"MUMMIFIED MEMORIES"

The Leopard concludes in the year 1910, half a century after the main action takes place. The prince has died many years before, and the Salina sisters, now in their seventies, live as spinsters in the faded glory of the family estate. Palermo is preparing to celebrate the fiftieth anniversary of Garibaldi's invasion, and Angelica—Tancredi, too, has passed away—is one the managers of the event. She is in charge of finding housing for the veterans of the revolution and has tickets for her and Concetta to sit together in the royal box at the parade. "Don't you think it's a good idea," she asks. "A Salina rendering homage to Garibaldi! A fusion of old and new Sicily!" (308). Concetta seems less than thrilled at the prospect. Angelica is in the company of Senator Tassoni, a former comrade of Tancredi's, who has since made a fortune in the new regime as a thread manufacturer. What is Lampedusa's judgment on the new Italy, on the bourgeois democratic age?

Like Tocqueville and Nietzsche, Lampedusa regards the new society as flat, ugly, lacking in nobility or tradition. The world has become small. A manufacturer of thread that sews buttons throughout Italy has become a hero of the new order. The new ruling class represented by Angelica and Tassoni—who had a brief affair years earlier—has shed its humble origins. After forty years of marriage to Tancredi, Angelica has lost the remains of her local accent and manners, keeps up with the latest novels, and has become regarded as an authority on French architecture. She has managed to shed entirely her peasant origins, just as the democratic republic she represents has done. In one of his most memorable images, Lampedusa remarks that it is the same process of conversion that "in the course of three generations transforms innocent peasants into defenseless gentry" (162).

Most of all, what Lampedusa deplores is the loss of tradition. When Father Pirrone earlier tried to explain the way of the nobles, he referred to the fact that they have "a very strong collective memory" (226). It is memory that holds a family and a tradition together and assures its continuity over time. A loss of memory can only lead to a break with tradition. This thought appears again to Don Fabrizio as he lies dying in a Palermo hotel room considering the fate of his grandchildren: "For the significance of a noble family lies entirely in its traditions, that is in its vital memories; and he was the last to have any unusual memories, anything different from those of other families. Fabrizietto would only have banal ones like his schoolfellows, of snacks, of spiteful little jokes against teachers, horses bought with an eye more to price than to quality; and the meaning of his name would change more and more to empty pomp. . . . He would go hunting for a rich marriage when that would have become a commonplace routine and no longer a bold predatory adventure like Tancredi's" (286).

The final chapter of the book, entitled "Relics," well describes the surviving Salina sisters. Only Concetta, alone and embittered, whose father only belatedly came to recognize her as the true heir of the Salina line, has a link to a past that has now been broken forever. As Tocqueville recognized, only an aristocratic society preserves these memories; democracies tend to dissolve them. To the extent that tradition even exists, it remains "an inferno of mummified memories" locked away in the four massive wooden crates that contain Concetta's trousseau collected from half a century before or in the remains of Bendicò, now "a heap of mangy fur" embalmed forty-five years before (305). It is these memories that will finally be forgotten when she orders Bendicò's remains to be discarded where "all found peace in a heap of livid dust."

Chapter 16 Mr. Sammler's Redemption

Mr. Sammler's Planet may not be Saul Bellow's greatest book.[1] That title would almost certainly go to *Herzog,* his picaresque novel of a modern Don Quixote. Rather than being armed with the Don's manuals of chivalry, Moses Herzog is equipped with Hegel, Tocqueville, and the entire "great books" curriculum of the Hutchins College at the University of Chicago, of which he is a product. He has written a doctoral dissertation on the state of nature in English and French political philosophy, a book entitled *Romanticism and Christianity,* and a long unfinished manuscript on the social ideas of the romantics. Rather than tilting at windmills, Herzog finds himself frenetically writing letters to his mistresses, to his ex-wives, and to famous figures of the likes of Adlai Stevenson, Martin Heidegger, and J. Edgar Hoover.

Even if *Mr. Sammler's Planet* is not Bellow's greatest novel, it is the one that most deeply engages the problems of the day. Like Herzog, Sammler is an "intellectual." A Polish Jew and cultured Anglophile, Artur Sammler—he is named after Schopenhauer—spent the interwar years as a journalist in London, where he lived in

Russell Square and became associated with John Maynard Keynes, Lytton Strachey, H. G. Wells, and other figures of the Bloomsbury Circle. Having returned to Poland and survived the Holocaust, Sammler and his daughter, Shula, were rescued from a displaced persons camp by his nephew, Elya Gruner, and Sammler is now living with his niece, Margotte, in a room in her Upper West Side apartment, from where he travels every day by bus to the New York Public Library and spends what little time is left to him reading with his one good eye Meister Eckhart and other works of the German mystical tradition. In his wanderings along upper Broadway, he contemplates the combination of luxury and barbarism. Sammler has already lived through the collapse of one civilization. Could it happen again here? This is the question the book asks us to consider.

When we are first introduced to Mr. Sammler, he is just over seventy years old and is recalling an incident that he has watched daily unfolding as he takes the bus back to his room from the Forty-second Street library. An elegantly dressed black pickpocket has been plying his trade on the bus between Columbus Circle and Seventy-second Street and has caught Sammler's attention. Sammler is struck not only by the brazenness of the act but also by the pickpocket's camel hair coat, designer sunglasses, silk tie, and single gold earring, none of which can entirely hide "the effrontery of a big animal" (2). What is more, the pickpocket knows that Sammler knows what he has been doing. He has seen an older white man carrying a furled umbrella, British-style, watching him at work. Sammler is not a coward (we learn later that he even took lives during his time in the Polish resistance movement), but "he had had as much trouble in life as he wanted." When he attempts to call the police to report the man, he is told that nothing can be done about it and is made to feel under suspicion himself for reporting the crime.

The denouement of the scene occurs when the pickpocket follows Sammler home from the bus and assaults him in the lobby of his own building. Without uttering a word, the pickpocket forces Sammler against the wall, unzips his own pants, and exposes himself. It is the ultimate expression of black power. "The interval was long," Bellow writes. "The man's expression was not directly menacing but oddly, serenely masterful. The thing was shown with mystifying certitude. Lordliness. Then it was returned to the trousers. *Quod erat demonstrandum*" (40). This incident sets the logic of the novel in motion.

It is now more than forty years since the publication of *Sammler*. It has always been Bellow's most controversial work. The horrifying confrontation between Sammler and the black pickpocket led some readers to think of it as racist. Bellow's graphic depiction of the promiscuity of Elya's daughter, Angela, was taken as an attack on feminism and the sexual revolution of the 1960s, and the unforgettable scene where Sammler is shouted down by a student radical when attempting to give a lecture at Columbia was seen as a denunciation of the leftist politics of the period. For still others, the book was too didactic, using the central character simply as a mouthpiece for Bellow's ideas. In retrospect, the book seems like the first salvo of the counterrevolution that would be given full-throated expression several years later in Allan Bloom's *Closing of the American Mind*.[2]

There is, to be sure, some truth to all of these depictions of *Sammler*. But when we read the book today, I want to suggest, it seems less about race, or sexuality, or politics than about Sammler's personal redemption, his return to life from the very margins of civilization. Sammler has been twice exiled: once as a Jew living in Nazi-occupied Poland and again as a refugee haunting Manhattan's Upper West Side. But as its title suggests, *Mr. Sammler's Planet* is a call to embrace the world—the common planet that we all inhabit—and the possibilities of human goodness that it contains. The transformation that Sammler undergoes at the novel's end now suggests a deeper and richer message than it did when the novel first appeared.

"HORS D'USAGE"

More than anything else, *Sammler* is Bellow's most extended meditation on the fragility of civilization. The title character is himself a displaced person in more than one sense of the term. Not only has he survived the horrors of the Holocaust, but as a "Polish-Oxonian," he has never completely assimilated to the ways of his adopted country. Sammler had "the face of a British Museum reader" and maintained attitudes "not especially useful to a refugee in Manhattan" (3).

Sammler is not only displaced himself, he lives in a world of displaced persons. His landlady, Margotte Arkin, is the niece of his late wife, and she lives on reparation money paid by the German government. Margotte's late husband, Ussher, had been a professor of political theory at Hunter College before being killed in a plane crash on his way to deliver a lecture at the Hebrew seminary in Cincinnati. Margotte is good-hearted but hopelessly muddled—"As though to be Jewish weren't trouble enough, the poor woman was German too"—with a penchant for abstract ideas. When first introduced, Margotte is forcing Sammler into a discussion of Hannah Arendt's thesis about "the banality of evil" from her book *Eichmann in Jerusalem*, which had recently been published. Sammler recalls what Margotte's husband would have said ("Enough, enough of this Weimar *schmaltz*"), but Sammler is a gentleman as well as a boarder and cannot allow himself the luxury of such brutal honesty (11–12).

Bellow is here able to introduce one of the great themes of the novel, namely, our capacity for intellectual self-delusion. One of the great delusions that the book sets out to expose is the Enlightenment's belief that we inhabit a rational universe that can be explained by human reason alone. In the opening scene of the book, as he is waking up in his apartment, Sammler reflects on the ubiquity of explanations: "Fathers to children, wives to husbands, lecturers to listeners, experts to laymen, colleagues to colleagues, doctors to patients, man to his own soul, explained." We live in a world of explanations, of intellectual constructions: "For the most part, in one ear and out the other," Sammler muses. "The soul wanted what it wanted" (1). Man has become the explaining animal. Although "alert to the peril and disgrace of explanations," Sammler "was himself no mean explainer" (14).

Sammler is in many respects Bellow's answer to Horkheimer and Adorno's *Dialectic of Enlightenment*. It is a book about the self-destruction of reason. The young Sammler had himself been a great believer in the Enlightenment's hope to abolish war and create an international society, but "most of that nonsense had been knocked out of him" by the Holocaust and the war. In viewing his adopted city today, he is reminded of a passage from Saint Augustine that he had translated as a schoolboy ("The Devil hath established his cities in the North"). The assault on civilization today comes in the name of the Enlightenment's claim to establish a universal league of free and equal nations, each nation consisting of free and equal men and women:

> The labor of Puritanism now was ending. The dark satanic mills changing into light satanic mills. The reprobates converted into children of joy, the sexual ways of the seraglio and of the Congo bush adopted by the emancipated masses of New York, Amsterdam, London. Old Sammler with his screwy visions! He saw the increasing triumph of the Enlightenment—Liberty, Fraternity, Equality, Adultery! Enlightenment, universal education, universal suffrage, the rights of the majority acknowledged by all governments, the rights of women, the rights of children, the rights of criminals, the unity of the different races affirmed, Social Security, public health, the dignity of the person, the right to justice. (25)

The fulfillment of the Enlightenment's promise of a free, open, and prosperous society has produced a new kind of barbarism combining the "luxurious inventiveness of Versailles with the hibiscus-covered erotic ease of Samoa." Throughout the book, Sammler finds evidence of a new kind of primitivism taking hold in the center of civilization: "The dreams of nineteenth-century poets polluted the psychic atmosphere of the great boroughs and suburbs of New York. Add to this the dangerous lunging staggering crazy violence of fanatics, and the trouble was very deep. Like many people who had seen the world collapse once, Mr. Sammler entertained the possibility it might collapse twice. He did not agree with refugee friends that this doom was inevitable, but liberal beliefs did not seem capable of self-defense, and you could smell decay. You could see the suicidal impulses of civilization pushing strongly" (26).

Far from intellectuals helping to impede these impulses, Sammler wonders whether in fact "the worst enemies of civilization might not prove to be its petted intellectuals who attacked it at its weakest moments—attacked it in the name of the proletarian revolution, in the name of reason, and in the name of irrationality, in the name of visceral depth, in the name of sex, in the name of perfect instantaneous freedom" (26).

Sammler's worries about the onset of a new barbarism are richly confirmed when he accepts an invitation by a protégé, Lionel Feffer, to give a guest lecture at Columbia. Feffer is one of the more colorful, and oddly sympathetic, characters in the book. Sammler's daughter, Shula, had hired a number of university students to read to her father to spare his good eye. Most were unacceptable, but Feffer was one of those readers to whom Sammler had taken a liking. He is described as variously "sly, shrewd, meddling, as well as fresh, charming, and vigorous" (97). A kind of cross section of his age, he is more an "ingenious operator" than a student.

We learn later that Feffer had been admitted to Columbia without finishing high school, on the basis of his extraordinary entrance exams. He speculates in the stock market and is an executive for a Guatemalan insurance company covering railway workers. His academic field is diplomatic history, and he belongs to a corresponding society called the Foreign Ministers Club. On top of this, he is an adept seducer of women, while still finding time to work on behalf of handicapped children. He has a friend at NBC and is trying to get Sammler a spot on a talk show ("You should denounce New York. You should speak like a prophet, like from another world" [99–100]). Feffer "led a high-energy American life to the point of anarchy and breakdown," which of course includes psychiatric treatment. "Nothing," Bellow sardonically observes, "was omitted" (31).

Sammler agrees to Feffer's request for a lecture to a seminar group on Britain in the 1930s. Only later does he discover that he was a last-minute fill-in for another lecturer, who had promised to speak on Sorel and violence. Sammler's lecture on Orwell begins promisingly enough with background on the Russian Revolution and the utopian hopes for a world state (the *Cosmopolis* project) propagated by British intellectuals like Wells and Olaf Stapeldon, but a half-hour into the lecture Sammler slowly becomes aware that he is being interrupted by a student radical. Sammler has said something about Orwell and the British Navy that has apparently met with disapproval. The bearded revolutionary turns to the audience, "raising his palms like a Greek dancer," and shouts: "Why do you listen to this effete old shit? What has he got to tell you? His balls are dry. He's dead. He can't come" (34). In the meantime Feffer is nowhere to be found—we find out later that he is on the telephone trying to close a deal on a locomotive!—and for his own safety Sammler is escorted out of the building and back to Broadway.

The student revolutionary and the black pickpocket are the perfect bookends of the novel, the combination of black power and youth culture. Power, youth, and sexuality, the symbols of the new age, combine to render Sammler irrelevant, "*hors d'usage*" as he says later (111, 255). He is a survivor, a *revenant*, from the Old World who has somehow managed to survive in the New.

"THE AGE"

One of the lesser-noted themes of *Sammler* is the collapse of the family as the basic unit of civilization. Sammler's own family has been torn apart by the European conflagration. In addition to his niece Margotte, he and his daughter, Shula, are supported by the generosity of his wealthy nephew, Elya. Shula is one of the walking wounded. Having survived the war in a Polish convent, she is torn between her Jewish and Catholic identities and goes by two names, Shula-Slawa. She wears wigs to suggest Jewish orthodoxy but then attends Easter services. Shula had been married briefly to Eisen, a survivor of Stalingrad who now fancies himself an artist, and the two had set up house in Israel, but Eisen was paranoid and abusive, and Sammler had to bring her back to New York for her own safety. There she is able to survive on makeshift work provided by Elya, but she is a lost soul wandering the city, scavenging from trash bins, attending free lectures and sermons ("she seemed to know lots of rabbis in famous temples and synagogues"), where she was always the first to ask questions. To make matters worse, she has just stolen the manuscript of a visiting lecturer at Columbia on the possibility of creating a colony on the moon, which she believes will be of interest to her father for the biography of Wells that she remains convinced he still intends to write.

At the center of Sammler's family drama is Elya. He is in many respects Sammler's alter ego. He is the opposite of a man of ideas, a retired gynecologist who has been very successful in real estate. He is an *Ostjude* who has married up (his wife, who has since passed away, was continually bent on his social improvement), lives in a large Westchester mansion, and has a chauffeur-driven Rolls-Royce. Sammler cannot help but recall the difference between Elya's hardscrabble origins and his own privileged childhood in Cracow during the time of Franz Josef, where a family servant would serve the young Sammler chocolate and croissants while he would sit in his room reading Trollope and Bagehot, trying to become an English gentleman (49). Elya is a sentimentalist for whom Sammler fulfills a longing to have an Old World relative and all that represents ("Mr. Sammler had a symbolic character. He, personally, was a symbol. . . . And of what was he a symbol? He didn't even know." [74]). Elya embodies everything that the American dream holds out—wealth, upward mobility, material success—but he is now in the hospital with an aneurysm and has two ungrateful children who very much embody the restless energy of what Sammler refers to as "the Age."

Angela, Elya's daughter, is a sexual adventurer, "one of those handsome, passionate, rich girls who were always an important social and human category" (7). Educated (or miseducated) at Sarah Lawrence, with a degree in French literature, Angela uses Sammler as a sounding board for her various escapades. Her father says that she has "fucked-out eyes." Angela's current infatuation is Wharton Horricker, a Madison Avenue marketing executive with a "dressy third-generation-Jew name." Wharton is a Californian, a physical culturalist, and something of a dandy. He purchases custom-made clothes from London and Milan, and "you could play sacred music while he had his hair cut (no, 'styled')" (55). Wharton seems to represent everything young, carefree, and exuberant about modern America, but looks may be deceiving. Angela admits to her uncle that the two had taken a trip to Mexico, where they engaged in a hookup with another couple they had met on the beach, and Wharton is now having second thoughts about their relationship. Angela is clearly seeking Sammler's approval, but he does not wish to become entangled in her problems. "Is it an effort to 'liberalize' human existence and show that nothing that happens between people is really loathsome? Affirming the Brotherhood of Man?" he asks himself (130). For Sammler, Angela's affairs are just one more step in the direction of the democratization of society. Such behavior, he reflects, simply represents the "generational ideology" of the age and is to that extent "impersonal."

But the truly lunatic center of the modern American family is Angela's brother, Wallace. "Wallace," Bellow writes, "was a born plunger" who has run through his first fifty thousand dollars investing with a Mafia group in Las Vegas (62). When first introduced, he is discussing sports handicapping with his father's physician, a famous ex–football player from Georgia. With a look of "mental power, virility, nobility, all slightly spoiled," his life has been a series of almosts. Wallace was an almost-physicist, an almost-mathematician, and briefly a lawyer, opening an office simply to work on crossword puzzles but giving that up to become an almost-neuroscientist. At one time he had visited Morocco and Tunisia on horseback ("backward people should be seen from a horse") but had been robbed at gunpoint in his hotel room. He managed to enter Russia but was detained by the Armenian police and was only released through the intervention of Senator Javits. Now back in New York, he carelessly lost his father's Rolls-Royce and has had to take a job driving a crosstown bus to pay off gambling debts to bookies. His current project is a business venture with Lionel Feffer to take aerial pictures of country houses and sell the photographs to the owners with the names of their trees and plantings identified in both English and Latin.

Wallace wants Sammler to intercede with his father on his behalf. He needs money for the photography enterprise—renting the plane, hiring graduate students in botany and other sciences to make the proper identifications—and Elya is reluctant to bankroll another project. Furthermore, Wallace is convinced that his father has a large stash of money buried somewhere in their New Rochelle home that he has obtained through performing illegal abortions on socialite heiresses and Mafia princesses. With the money he plans to make from this new enterprise, Wallace tells Sammler, he can spend his time reading philosophy and finishing his Ph.D. in mathematics. Later Feffer, a born conman, is even more expansive on their plans for the business. Should it prove successful, they can open up regional offices around the country and hire local plant specialists to make the proper identifications. Feffer reminds Sammler of the first line from Aristotle's *Metaphysics*—"All men desire to know"—and draws from this the lesson that "if they desire to know, it makes them depressed if they can't name the bushes on their own property. They feel like phonies" (90).

"DISTINGUISH AND DISTINGUISH AND DISTINGUISH"

The longest exchange in the book takes place between Sammler and Dr. V. Govinda Lal. Dr. Lal is the author of *The Future of the Moon,* which captures all of the utopian and transformational aspirations of the 1960s. He had been lecturing at Columbia, where the only copy of his manuscript has been stolen by Shula, which in turn has led to a frantic search effort that has finally ended at Elya's Westchester home, where Margotte, Shula, and Sammler have all gathered. Dr. Lal, we learn, is a biophysicist who has been employed at NASA and at a company called Worldwide Technics, where he is an advocate of the "bang bang hypothesis." Although there is no specific mention in the book of the moon landing, he regards the colonization of space as the means of fostering a "new Adam," an attempt to escape the confines of the earth in order to create a new beginning for humanity made possible through the progress of science.

Dr. Lal's manuscript reminds Sammler of the kind of utopianism that he had once eagerly discussed with Wells and his associates. But now when he first hears of Dr. Lal's plans for the colonization of space, he is extremely skeptical. "But the moon, Uncle," Wallace enthusiastically exclaims, to which Sammler replies, "To the moon? But I don't even want to go to Europe" (151). Sammler's experiences have developed in him a sense of the limits of human aspiration and the dangers created by the illusion of the illimitable. He prefers the ocean, which at least has a floor and a ceiling, to the vast emptiness of space. "I think I am an Oriental," he tells Wallace. "I am content to sit here on the West Side, and watch, and admire these gorgeous Faustian departures for the other worlds" (151). He recalls that even Jules Verne's Captain Nemo played Bach and Handel—representatives of the Old World—while sitting in a submarine on the bottom of the ocean. Apparently, the desire for the new can never completely forsake the old.

But Dr. Lal is no vulgar missionary for science. He is a man of culture and learning and wins Sammler's respect. As a man of the East, he, too, has seen his share of human misery, and as he says to Sammler, "Perhaps it is natural that an Indian should be supersensitive to a surplus of humanity" (180). His very identity, a synthesis of East and West, bespeaks a new kind of "shared consciousness." It seems obvious to Dr. Lal that mankind cannot be restricted to life on a single planet. He regards the exploration of space as the logical extension of mankind's desire for discovery and invention. Of course, he remarks, we must acknowledge "the extremism and fanaticism of human nature," but this is no reason to refuse "the challenge of a new type of experience." He is aware of the danger of strange new diseases contracted through space travel—an obvious reference to Wells's *War of the Worlds*—but to give up would turn the earth into a prison where "the species is eating itself up."

Dr. Lal's reflections on space travel provide the occasion for Sammler's longest reflection on history and the future of mankind. While Lal is an optimist who marvels at the extraordinary state of scientific progress, Sammler is a disciple of Schopenhauer, whose namesake he is; he had been given a copy of *The World as Will and Idea* for his sixteenth birthday (172). He begins his speech with the warning that he has become "extremely skeptical of explanations" and "the modern religion of empty categories" (186). What he is referring to are the modern theories of historical explanation—by Marx, Weber, Toynbee, Spengler—that arose with the Enlightenment and created a new class of social reformers: "Through universal education and cheap printing," he tells Dr. Lal, "poor boys have become rich and powerful. Dickens, rich. Shaw, also. He boasted that reading Karl Marx made a man of him. I don't know about that, but Marxism for the great public made him a millionaire. If you wrote for an elite, like Proust, you did not become rich, but if your theme was social justice and your ideas were radical you were rewarded by wealth, fame, and influence" (174).

Sammler provides here a highly Nietzschean picture of modernity as the work of a new class of "ascetic priests" who use their knowledge—their explanatory power—to create new hierarchies and forms of social control. Sammler knows whereof he speaks. He may well have been thinking of an earlier conversation with his cousin Walter Bruch, where he contrasts distinguishing ("a higher activity") from explanation. "One had to learn to distinguish. To distinguish and distinguish and distinguish . . . Explanation was for the mental masses" (51). Apparently, distinguishing is aristocratic; explanations are plebian. In the great bourgeois period, it is the writers and explainers who have become the new ruling class. Knowledge has become power. Writers and demagogues like Rousseau, Marat, Saint-Just, and Marx made it possible for people with nothing more than "mental capital" and the power of language to achieve influence over millions: "A crazy provincial lawyer demanding the head of the King, and getting it, too. In the name of the people. Or Marx, a student, a fellow from the University, writing books which overwhelm the world. He was really an excellent journalist and publicist. . . . Like many journalists, he made things up out of other newspaper articles, the European press, but he made them up extremely well, writing about India or the American Civil War, matters of which he actually knew nothing. But he was marvelously shrewd, a guesser of genius, a powerful polemicist and rhetorician. His ideological hashish was very potent" (175).

It is this new class of public intellectuals that has created the modern passion for individuality, for liberation, for unlimited freedom that has become the cause of the chaos and disorder that Sammler observes everywhere around him. He sees clearly that this kind of freedom has been a triumph for justice, but it has also introduced its own forms of misery and suffering as people struggle with how to employ their newfound freedom. The emancipation of the individual has led to newer and ever more extravagant calls for liberation. For some, this has meant an escape into exotic religious cults (Orphism, Mathraism, and so on), while for others it has meant a bacchanalian celebration of drugs, sexuality, and other "round trips through evil, monstrosity, and orgy, with even God approached through obscenity," as modern men and women seek new forms of experience. The passion for originality, to live an interesting life, has in turn led to Sadean experiments in cruelty and blasphemy. "An *interesting* life," Sammler observes, "is the supreme concept of dullards" (189).

The most grotesque expression of this passion for originality was Chaim Rumkowski, the insane "King" of the Jewish ghetto in Lodz, whom Sammler associates with this need for theatricality and "play acting." A failure in life, Rumkowski was appointed *Judenaltester* by the Nazis and charged with carrying out their plans. He created an entire court, a parody of European royalty, while people awaited deportation to the death camps.

It is this same passion for transcending the ordinary that Sammler regards as the folly of Dr. Lal's hopes for the colonization of the moon. It is another attempt to escape the limits of the human condition. In an earlier scene, when Wallace and Sammler are being driven in Elya's Rolls, Sammler contemplates the vast disparity between the new scientific elite, represented by Dr. Lal, and the legions of those seeking escape through drugs, sex, and other experiments in living: "An oligarchy of technicians, engineers, the men who ran the grand machines, infinitely more sophisticated than this automobile, would come to govern vast slums filled with bohemian adolescents, narcotized, beflowered, and 'whole.' He himself was a fragment, Mr. Sammler understood. And lucky to be that" (149). In the name of progress and civilization, the world is being ruthlessly divided into two distinct species, much like the Morlocks and the Eloi in Wells's *Time Machine.*

Sammler's ruminations are interrupted by the most comic and absurd scene in the novel. As Sammler is speaking in Elya's home, everyone suddenly becomes aware that water is pouring into the living room from upstairs. They all assume it is a burst pipe, but in fact Wallace has been dismantling the pipes in search of what he believes is his father's hidden treasure. No one has any idea what to do until Dr. Lal finds the shut-off valve.

A MENSCH FOR ALL SEASONS

The following morning is a comedy of errors. Dr. Lal and Margotte have left together for the city in Dr. Lal's rented sports car, Wallace has left for the airport to hire a plane to begin test flights for his new business venture, and Sammler is stranded at the house with Shula, who discovers Elya's stash in a hassock on which Sammler had been sitting. Later Sammler is finally driven back to New York by Elya's chauffeur, Emil (a former driver for Lucky Luciano), to visit his nephew in the hospital. As they speed down the Henry Hudson Parkway and then along Broadway, Sammler reflects on what he sees through the window of the Rolls.

In no other Bellow novel does the city itself play such a central role. Most readers think of Bellow as a quintessentially Chicago novelist. *Augie March, Humboldt's Gift, The Dean's December,* and large parts of *Herzog* are all Chicago-based books. But the central character of *Sammler* is New York. Near the opening of the novel when Sammler is attempting to find a phone booth to report the pickpocket to the police, he cannot help but reflect on the state of putrefaction of the public facilities. A sense of decay and a kind of "orientalization" of civilization is a central motif of the book: "New York was getting worse than Naples or Salonika. It was like an Asian, an African town, from this standpoint. The opulent sections of the city were not immune. You opened a jeweled door into degradation, from hypercivilized Byzantine luxury straight into the state of nature, the barbarous world of color erupting from beneath. It might well be barbarous on either side of the jeweled door" (4). Later Sammler notes: "New York makes one think about the collapse of civilization, about Sodom and Gomorrah, the end of the world. . . . I am not sure that this is the worst of all times. But it is in the air now that things are falling apart" (252).

Sammler returns to these thoughts when he is thinking about his escape from Poland after the war. What he witnesses around him is a desire, in fact a mania, for individuality and self-expression. Here again he indulges in a kind of Nietzschean meditation on the transition from the age of aristocracy to democracy. What was once an ancient privilege—the right to live freely and creatively—has become a modern right. This is what the revolutions of the modern era have done, redistributed downward the privileges of one aristocracy onto another, but this transformation has come at a cost. "The middle class," Sammler reflects, "had formed no independent standards of honor" (119). The result of this transformation has been that the right to take life, once the prerogative of the few, has become the right of the many, whether this takes the form of Dostoyevsky's Raskolnikov or Kierkegaard's Knight of Faith. All that remains now is the desire to live creatively or authentically.

It is this passion for originality that Sammler observes while waiting for the crosstown bus: "All human types reproduced, the barbarian, redskin, or Fiji, the dandy, the buffalo hunter, the desperado, the queer, the sexual fantasist, the squaw; bluestocking, princess, poet, painter, prospector, troubadour, guerrilla, Che Guevara, the new Thomas à Becket. Not imitated are the businessman, the soldier, the priest, and the square. The standard is aesthetic" (120).

Sammler's dyspeptic, even misanthropic, reflections on the city are fortunately not his last thoughts on the subject. As he is being driven to the hospital, the Rolls is stopped in traffic, and to his horror Sammler sees that a fight has broken out between Feffer and the pickpocket. Feffer had been intrigued by the story about the pickpocket, especially his exposing himself to Sammler, and has followed him on the bus to snap pictures. Sammler wants someone to break up the fight, but a crowd is standing around smiling and laughing while waiting for the police to arrive. Finally, Sammler calls upon Eisen (Shula's former husband) to help, but rather than separate the two, Eisen smashes the pickpocket's face with a bag of heavy metal medallions—actually fashioned into Stars of David and other religious symbols—that he has been carrying with him. "You can't hit a man like this just once," Eisen says to Sammler. "You were a partisan. You had a gun. So don't you know?" (241–42).

Much might be made of the symbolism of this last act—*Sammler* was written under the shadow of the growing rift between blacks and Jews and the creation of the Jewish Defense League—but it is the very violence of the incident that stirs a sudden transformative affect in Sammler. "It was a feeling of horror," Bellow writes, "that grew in strength, grew and grew. What was it? How was it to be put? He was a man who had come back. *He had rejoined life*" (240; emphasis added). Sammler the misanthrope has been reborn, and the agent of his redemption is the very pickpocket who had victimized him earlier. Sammler, himself a victim who was left for dead in a pit in Poland, cannot help but feel a wellspring of sympathy for another human being who is now being victimized. The pickpocket no longer appears to him as an animal or predator; he is a fellow sufferer who deserves our care.

The claim that Bellow's novel bespeaks some kind of racism is completely undercut by this scene. More troubling is his depiction of Eisen, the novel's sole representative of Israel.[3] Possibly insane and certainly demented, Eisen, who has survived Stalin, Hitler, and the Israeli wars with the Arabs, has drawn the brutal lesson that it's us or them, kill or be killed. "If in—in. No? If out—out," he taunts Sammler (242). But it is this very stark either/or logic that he now finds hateful. "Sammler was sick with rage at Eisen. The black man? The black man was a megalomaniac. But there was a certain—a certain princeliness. . . . And how much Sammler sympathized with him—how much he would have done to prevent such atrocious blows!" (243). Sammler has at last returned to life. For all of its foibles and idiocies, he has learned to embrace the "planet" that we all call home.

Sammler's reconciliation with the world is made complete in the final scene of the book. Arriving at the hospital, he encounters Angela in the waiting room wearing her "sexual kindergarten dress." She is in an agitated state not because her father is dying but because Wharton has revealed to him the secret about their foursome in Mexico (perhaps she fears being disinherited). Throwing caution to the wind because he realizes that after Elya's death he might become financially dependent on Angela, Sammler says that the fault is not with Elya but with her. She should make restitution with her father. "Till forty or so," Sammler tells Angela, "I was simply an Anglophile intellectual Polish Jew and person of culture—relatively useless. But Elya, by sentimental repetition and by formulas if you like, partly by propaganda, has accomplished something good" (251). Elya may not have been perfect, but he lived life as a mensch, and no one can expect more.

Elya's simple goodness as doctor, father, friend, and benefactor restores some measure of balance and order to the "fragment" that has been Sammler's life. "Sentimental" is the word Sammler associates with Elya. He is not a man of books or learning but a man of untaught feeling, someone who has fulfilled "the terms of his contract." After Elya's death is announced, Sammler insists on visiting the body and says Kaddish for Elya. Sammler has so far shown little interest in religion, but now he returns to something like the God of his fathers. In a "mental whisper" he asks God to remember the soul of Elya Gruner. In the midst of "all the confusion and degraded clowning of this life," he showed the possibility of simple human kindness. Sammler's final words, "We all know, God, that we know, that we know, we know, we know," suggest that underlying all the explanations, intellectual constructions, and self-delusions, we can still know a good man when we see one.

Part Four **Conclusion**

Chapter 17 Modernity and Its Doubles

It is often alleged that we are currently experiencing a "crisis" of modernity, that there has been a loss of confidence in the founding principles animating the West. This loss of confidence is often traced back to the rise of historicism or relativism in the late eighteenth and early nineteenth centuries, to the belief that the West represents just one "culture" or way of life, and as such stands as only one among myriad other actual or possible cultures. Every culture, it is claimed, is particularistic, based on a principle of inclusion and exclusion. The West is no different. Its claims to freedom, openness, and toleration simply represent a new form of empire, a "false universalism," that needs to be unmasked and exposed. The result has been a slow but steady "decentering" of the West and a feeling that it has somehow lost its sense of purpose. What is needed to address this crisis, so it is affirmed, is a robust recommitment to the basic principles not merely of the American founding documents—the Declaration of Independence and the Constitution—but of certain international charters like the U.N. Declaration of Human Rights to restore our faith in the progressive mission of Western humanity.

But the problem, as I conceive it, is deeper—far deeper—than this. It is not just a matter of pessimism or a lack of confidence that we feel, as if our earlier faith in the distinctive, not to say exceptional, character of the West could be brought back to life through an act of will. Rather the problem has to do with the very character of modernity as the site of our manifold discontents. These discontents have taken two broad forms. The political Left, especially in its Marxist and progressivist variants, has accepted the basic program of the Enlightenment—its critique of hierarchy and inequality and its pursuit of a fully rational and completely emancipated society—but has argued that the institutions of the market and the state have failed to achieve these ends. In fact, they have merely exacerbated our discontents by creating new forms of inequality and alienation. The point is to change institutions, either peacefully if possible or violently if necessary, so that there is no longer a conflict between the demands of reason and the necessities of social life. The ideal society of the progressive Left might take the form of a Kantian League of Nations intended to secure "perpetual peace," the Hegelian *Rechtsstaat* with its distinct spheres of civil society and state, or even the Marxian classless society. In each case, it is believed that freedom will cease to remain an ideal that recedes the closer we get to it, and will instead become a reality embodied in the institutions and ways of life of a fully rational society. Reason and reality will at last fully coincide.

But the Enlightenment spawned a Counter-Enlightenment that offered a deeper and more profound critique of bourgeois society. The Counter-Enlightenment grew out of a deep suspicion of the program for the progressive reform of society. At the extreme end, some have argued for a radical deconstruction of the Enlightenment and the tradition of bourgeois individualism that it represents. Counter-revolutionaries like Maistre, Nietzsche, Sorel, and Heidegger—today we could add the names of Foucault and Derrida—look forward to a radical overcoming of modernity by a new "posthuman" or "transhuman" future, often going under the name of postmodernism. The very term "postmodern" suggests a new epoch in human history, one that has replaced modernity's search for rational or scientific foundations for knowledge and society ("the mirror of nature") with a pragmatic belief in the infinite malleability of our basic conceptual schemes to adapt to new realities. The quest for certainty and the related claim that the individual subject—Descartes's *ego cogitans*—is the ultimate touchstone of moral responsibility is said to have deformed modernity from the beginning. Yet the one aspect of modernity that not even postmodernists have been able to relinquish is the idea of emancipation, or liberation. The attack on the bourgeois, whether in its Rousseauean, Marxist, or Nietzschean form, is itself a piece of bourgeois ideology, unable fully to extricate itself from the very ideas of progress and freedom. Postmodernism is, in certain respects, simply the Enlightenment on steroids.

Yet, for others of the moderate Counter-Enlightenment such as Tocqueville, Berlin, and Strauss, and to whom we might add figures like Michael Oakeshott and Raymond Aron, modernity is not a problem to be overcome but a challenge to be met. As residents of late modernity, they did not share the apocalyptic belief that it was desirable either to return to a benighted past or to dream of an apocalyptic future. Their task was to discover the deeper resources built up within the Western tradition—the aristocratic Middle Ages for Tocqueville, German romanticism for Berlin, Greek philosophy for Strauss—by which to augment the Enlightenment and provide materials that could better sustain the theory and practice of liberal democracy. These writers sought to recover the preliberal and sometimes premodern roots of modernity that have continued to survive even into the present. Their aim was to rethink the foundations of liberal democracy by aligning it with sources from the premodern Western tradition, in particular a deeper appreciation of the sources of moral diversity founded in religion and national identity. These writers understood that the middle-class democracies, especially of the Anglo-American world, could make common cause with the deeper and older traditions from which they had originally drawn sustenance. These members of the moderate Counter-Enlightenment did not intend to deconstruct modernity so much as to find the tools and methods necessary to sustain it, to save it from its worst vices and excesses.

I am in agreement with the claims of the Counter-Enlightenment that the Enlightenment is based on a kind of ersatz religious faith, the faith in infinite progress. The idea of the Enlightenment was initially generated by the belief that science and the application of scientific method could provide answers to the most pressing problems—war, poverty, ignorance, and disease—facing humankind and that the progress of scientific knowledge was in principle indefinite. No one can doubt the immense benefits brought about by this humanitarian project, but the Enlightenment belief in the progressive function of science was, in some of its bolder and more confident moments, combined with another, almost eschatological faith that humanity is evolving, sometimes violently, at other times gradually, but always inevitably and inexorably, toward a more rational, secure, and prosperous future, better than anything that has existed in the past. Progress in this sense became a surrogate for religious faith, faith in the power of knowledge to liberate us from the burdens of the past.

From the beginning, the Enlightenment was connected with a program for the "progressive" transformation of society. Once one accepts the narrative of progress, the only question is how to adjust to the rhythm or tempo of change. In fact, rather than one merely accommodating to change, it becomes a duty, even an obligation, to work for the acceleration of progress. There is even an implied immorality in not working to bring about the most complete development of which humanity is capable at any moment. The progressive leader must become a mouthpiece of society ready to interpret public opinion or the public mood wherever it might go. The successful leader is one who is not only able to adapt to change but also anticipates it as society moves in ever new and unforeseen directions. Since history is always working toward the progressive improvement of human well-being, those who fail to embrace, or, even worse, resist embracing, the future are at risk of being labeled "conservatives," then "reactionaries," and ultimately "enemies of the people."

Progressivism is not the same as progress. It is the belief that all the important problems facing civilization are technical in nature and therefore can be solved through the application of the correct scientific method. To be sure, this belief is rooted not so much in science itself as in an ideology called "scientism" or "positivism," according to which whatever stands outside or apart from science simply does not count as knowledge. This ideology had its roots in the philosophies of Descartes, Bacon, and Hobbes but only came of age in the twentieth century with the rise of the social and behavioral sciences and their view of knowledge as a collaborative effort of teams of researchers building incrementally on the work of previous researchers. These sciences have increasingly emphasized the role of "big data," "large-N studies," and the quantification of every aspect of learning. Not even the traditional fields of the humanities have been immune from the intrusion of economics and computerization; witness the rise of what is called today the "digital humanities."

The progressivism of the Enlightenment has entailed far-reaching changes in our conception of politics. In America, progressivism has been associated with the philosophy of John Dewey and the relatively benign politics of the welfare state, but elsewhere it has been accompanied by far more radical social experimentation. On this account, politics ceases to be an art—the domain of prudence and practical judgment—but becomes a technical activity requiring the rule of experts. This technique allows leaders to dispense with experience as a flawed basis for knowledge and instead to rely on mathematical calculation, game theory, and other techniques to predict future probabilities. The role accorded to science, statistics, and rational-choice modeling in determining public policy accords perfectly with government by a new elite. The task for this new class of experts, as Tocqueville feared, is less to rule and guide than to reform and instruct. What we are witnessing is an end of politics and the rise of the administrative state. Once regarded as the art of keeping the ship of state afloat, politics has become swallowed up by administration. Under these conditions, the classical idea of the statesman (or what remained of it) gave rise to the new idea of the expert or policy specialist as the hero of the new age. This new priesthood—for that is what it is—is composed of sociologists, economists, and other experts who are in a position to understand the true workings of societies and markets and on the basis of this information to tell people how they should behave.

Of course, it is often contended that belief in progress was always more empirical and provisional than suggested above, that it did not endorse some lockstep theory of historical development and was not linked to the idea of the rule of experts but was based on the idea of an open-ended and indefinite future. On this account, progress is in principle indeterminable; there is no knowing whether what future generations regard as progressive would seem so to us. Virtually the one thing that is certain is that the progressives of today will end up becoming the conservatives of tomorrow as changes in taste, fashion, perhaps even rationality itself, continue to evolve and develop in new and unforeseeable directions. The question that must always be put to this claim, then, is: By what metric is change or progress to be measured? When do we know whether progress has met its limits? How are we to know exactly how much progress is enough? How do we even know that progress is actually "progressive," unless we have some standard by which to judge? To this question, the ideology of progressivism has yet to form a satisfactory answer.

I suggest that today's skepticism about progress has had less to do with the Enlightenment's failures than with its successes. The failures of defunct ideologies like communism and fascism require little comment. They are evident for all with eyes to see. Yet, it is the very success of Enlightenment ideas that has made modernity a continual site of our discontent. The belief in the liberating power of science and technology has created fears that it has brought with it new forms of domination and control. The ability of commerce and the market to promote unprecedented levels of prosperity and well-being has produced an antibourgeois backlash focused on the vulgarity and cheapening of culture as well as a heightened sensitivity to the creation of new forms of inequality. Even the narrative of progress itself has given rise to a counter-narrative of irretrievable decline and fall. Our discontents stem not so much from the failure of modern regimes to make good on their promises as from their very success in doing so. It is the success of the regimes shaped by science, the market, and democracy that have made them an object of envy, fear, loathing, and resentment. This should scarcely come as a surprise. Modernity has become inseparable from the doubts we feel about it.

If the narrative of progress is no longer sustainable, does this mean that the Enlightenment is dead? Of course not. It remains too much a part of our moral and political vocabulary for it to disappear altogether. I dare say that no American president of either party could afford to renounce the idea of progress or admit that our seemingly most intractable problems stand beyond our rational capabilities. This facile optimism worthy of a M. Homais is linked to the belief in the civilizing power of science to conquer nature and to bring peace among the nations. This utopianism, for that is what it is, has become the common faith of the West in all of its varieties.

Yet, not even the United States—the country in which modernity has reached its fullest and most comprehensive expression—has been entirely immune to feelings of skepticism, self-doubt, and even despair that the regime has generated about itself. Except in moments of willed ignorance, we no longer feel the same confidence in the unifying and humane mission of the West that was commonplace a century ago. The regime officially dedicated to the pursuit of happiness has found the attainment of happiness an increasingly elusive object of desire. We live in a composite civilization made up of competing strands of both the Enlightenment and Counter-Enlightenment that has made the emancipatory powers of reason and science seem increasingly illusory. The progressive narrative could never entirely slough off its doubles. We remain perpetually gnawed at by our manifold discontents—and that is a good thing.

Notes

1. MODERNITY IN QUESTION

Epigraph. Alfred de Vigny, *Cinq-Mars: Or, A Conspiracy under Louis XIII*, trans. William Hazlitt (London: David Bogue, 1847), 341.

1. Richard Rorty, *Philosophy and the Mirror of Nature* (Princeton: Princeton University Press, 1979).

2. John Rawls, *Political Liberalism* (New York: Columbia University Press, 1996), xvii.

3. See Robert Palmer, *The Age of the Democratic Revolution: A Political History of Europe and America, 1760–1800* (Princeton: Princeton University Press, 1959, 1964); see also Steven Pincus, *1688: The First Modern Revolution* (New Haven: Yale University Press, 2009).

4. Robert Pippin, *Modernity as a Philosophical Problem: On the Dissatisfactions of European High Culture* (Oxford: Blackwell, 1991), 29.

5. Francis Bacon, *The New Organon,* in *Selected Philosophical Works,* ed. Rose-Mary Sargent (Indianapolis: Hackett, 1999), sec. 72: "For they [the ancients] had no history worthy to be called history, that went back a thousand years. . . . In our times, on the other hand, both many parts of the New World and the limits of every side of the Old World are known, and our stock of experience has increased to an infinite amount."

6. Niccolò Machiavelli, *The Prince,* trans. Harvey C. Mansfield (Chicago: University of Chicago Press, 1998), chap. 15, p. 61.

7. Alexander Hamilton, James Madison, and John Jay, *The Federalist Papers,* ed. Jacob E. Cooke (Middletown, CT: Wesleyan University Press, 1961), No. 1, p. 3.

8. For modernity as a "secularization" of religious concepts, see Karl Löwith, *Meaning in History* (Chicago: University of Chicago Press, 1949); for an attempt to reassert the novelty of the modern experience, see Hans Blumenberg, *The Legitimacy of the Modern Age,* trans. Robert M. Wallace (Cambridge, MA: MIT Press, 1983).

9. See Isaiah Berlin, "The Counter-Enlightenment," in *Against the Current: Essays in the History of Ideas,* ed. Henry Hardy (New York: Penguin Press, 1982), 1–24; for a genealogy of the term, see Robert Wokler, "Isaiah Berlin's Enlightenment and Counter-Enlightenment," in *Isaiah Berlin's Counter-Enlightenment,* ed. Joseph Mali and Robert Wokler (Philadelphia: American Philosophical Society, 2003), 13–31.

10. Max Horkheimer and Theodor Adorno, *Dialectic of Enlightenment,* trans. John Cummings (New York: Seabury Press, 1972).

11. Jacob Talmon, *The Origins of Totalitarian Democracy* (New York: Norton, 1970).

12. Jean-Jacques Rousseau, *Discourse on the Sciences and the Arts or First Discourse,* in *The Discourses and Other Early Political Writings,* trans. Victor Gourevitch (Cambridge: Cambridge University Press, 1997), 9.

13. This story has been brilliantly told by Albert O. Hirschman, *The Passions and the Interests: Political Arguments for Capitalism before Its Triumph* (Princeton: Princeton University Press, 1977); Ralph Lerner, "Commerce and Character," *The Thinking Revolutionary: Principle and Practice in the New Republic* (Ithaca: Cornell University Press, 1987), 195–221.

14. Immanuel Kant, "Idea for a Universal History with a Cosmopolitan Intent," *Political Writings,* ed. Hans Reiss, trans. H. B. Nisbet (Cambridge: Cambridge University Press, 1970), 49.

15. Jean-Jacques Rousseau, *Emile or On Education,* trans. Allan Bloom (New York: Basic Books, 1979), 40.

16. Karl Marx, *The Communist Manifesto,* in *The Marx-Engels Reader,* ed. Robert Tucker (New York: Norton, 1976), 476; see also Marshall Berman, *All That Is Solid Melts into Air: The Experience of Modernity* (New York: Penguin, 1988).

17. Heinrich Heine, *Concerning the History of Religion and Philosophy in Germany,* in *The Romantic School and Other Essays,* ed. Jost Hermand and Robert C. Holub (New York: Continuum, 1985), 168.

18. Karl Marx, *Capital,* trans. Samuel Moore and Edward Aveling (London: Lawrence and Wishart, 1970), 176.

19. Friedrich Nietzsche, *Beyond Good and Evil,* trans. Walter Kaufmann (New York: Random House, 1966), sec. 252.

20. Friedrich Nietzsche, *Thus Spoke Zarathustra,* trans. Walter Kaufmann (Harmondsworth: Penguin, 1968), 17–18.

21. Martin Heidegger, *Being and Time,* trans. John Macquarrie and Edward Robinson (San Francisco: Harper Collins, 1962), 211–14.

22. Carl Schmitt, *Political Theology: Four Chapters on the Concept of Sovereignty,* trans. George Schwab (Cambridge, MA: MIT Press, 1988), 59.

23. See Jennifer Ratner-Rosenhagen, *American Nietzsche: A History of an Icon and His Ideas* (Chicago: University of Chicago Press, 2012).

24. Jeffrey Herf, *Reactionary Modernism: Technology, Culture, and Politics in Weimar and the Third Reich* (New York: Cambridge University Press, 1986); see also Zeev Sternhell, *The Anti-Enlightenment Tradition,* trans. David Naisel (New Haven: Yale University Press, 2010).

25. Alexis de Tocqueville, *Democracy in America,* trans. Harvey C. Mansfield and Delba Winthrop (Chicago: University of Chicago Press, 2000), II, ii, 8 (pp. 500–503).

26. Leo Strauss, "What Is Liberal Education?" in *Liberalism Ancient and Modern* (New York: Basic Books, 1968), 4.

27. Strauss, "What Is Liberal Education?" 5.

2. MACHIAVELLI'S *MANDRAGOLA* AND THE PROTEAN SELF

Epigraph. Machiavelli to Giovan Battista Soderini, September 1506, in *Machiavelli and His Friends: Their Personal Correspondence,* trans. and ed. James B. Atkinson and David Sices (Dekalb: Northern Illinois University Press, 2004), 135.

1. Niccolò Machiavelli, *The Prince,* trans. Harvey C. Mansfield (Chicago: University of Chicago Press, 1985), 22–24.

2. Roger Masters, *Fortune Is a River: Leonardo da Vinci and Niccolò Machiavelli's Magnificent Dream to Change the Course of Florentine History* (New York: Free Press, 1998).

3. Jacob Burckhardt, *The Civilization of the Renaissance in Italy,* trans. S. G. C. Middlemore (New York: Penguin, 1990), 98–103, 120–23.

4. Thomas Hobbes, "The Verse Life," in *Human Nature and De Corpore Politico,* ed. J. C. A. Gaskin (New York: Oxford University Press, 1994), 258.

5. See Kenneth Minogue, "Theatricality and Politics: Machiavelli's Concept of Fantasia," in *The Morality of Politics,* ed. Bhikhu Parekh and R. N. Berki (London: George Allen and Unwin, 1972), 148–62; see also, Maurizio Viroli's description of Machiavelli as "a realist with imagination" in *Redeeming the Prince: The Meaning of Machiavelli's Masterpiece* (Princeton: Princeton University Press, 2014), 66–91.

6. Niccolò Machiavelli, *Mandragola,* trans. Mera J. Flaumenhaft (Long Grove, IL: Waveland Press, 1981); references will be to act and scene number given in the text.

7. Cited in J. R. Hale, *Machiavelli and Renaissance Italy* (New York: Collier, 1966), 159.

8. Machiavelli to Francesco Guicciardini, October 21, 1525, in *Machiavelli and His Friends,* 371; see also Roberto Ridolfi, *The Life of Niccolò Machiavelli,* trans. Cecil Grayson (Chicago: University of Chicago Press, 1954), 220–31.

9. The tragic motif in Machiavelli has been explored by Ronald L. Martinez, "Tragic Machiavelli," in *The Comedy and Tragedy of Machiavelli: Essays on the Literary Works,* ed. Vickie B. Sullivan (New Haven: Yale University Press, 2000), 102–19.

10. Niccolò Machiavelli, *Discourses on Livy,* trans. Harvey C. Mansfield and Nathan Tarcov (Chicago: University of Chicago Press, 1996), I.61; see also Leo Strauss, "Niccolò Machiavelli," in *Studies in Platonic Political Philosophy,* ed. Thomas L. Pangle (Chicago: University of Chicago Press, 1983), 221.

11. Ridolfi, *The Life of Niccolò Machiavelli,* 170.

12. Livy, *The Rise of Rome: Books One to Five,* trans. T. J. Luce (Oxford: Oxford University Press, 1998), I.57–60; references will be to book and section number in the text.

13. All references are to Saint Augustine, *City of God,* trans. Henry Bettenson (Harmondsworth: Penguin, 1972), I.19.

14. Machiavelli, *Discourses on Livy,* III.2.

15. Machiavelli, *Discourses on Livy,* III.5.

16. Machiavelli, *Discourses on Livy,* III.26.

17. Machiavelli, *Prince,* 67, 72.

18. Machiavelli, *Discourses on Livy,* III.6.

19. Machiavelli is probably referring to Tacitus's statement: "I acquiesce in the present and, while I pray for good Emperors, I can endure whomsoever we may have." Tacitus, *The History,* in *The Complete Works,* trans. Alfred John Church and William Jackson Brodribb, ed. Moses Hadas (New York: Modern Library, 1942), IV.8.

20. For reading *Mandragola* as a political allegory, see Carnes Lord, "Allegory in Machiavelli's *Mandragola,*" in *Political Philosophy and the Human Soul,* ed. Michael Palmer and Thomas L. Pangle (Lanham, MD: Rowman and Littlefield, 1995), 149–73; I disagree, as will be clear below, with Lord's identification of Lucrezia with the Florentine *popolo,* simply waiting for a master. For some useful comments on using *Mandragola* as a template for reading *The Prince,* see Mikael Hörnqvist, *Machiavelli and Empire* (Cambridge: Cambridge University Press, 2004), 1–4, 34–37.

21. Machiavelli, *Prince,* 101.

22. For this suggestion, see Harvey C. Mansfield, "The Cuckold in *Mandragola,*" in *The Comedy and Tragedy of Machiavelli,* 27–28.

23. Thomas Babington, Lord Macaulay, "Machiavelli," in *Literary Essays* (Oxford: Oxford University Press, 1923), 73.

24. Thucydides, *The Landmark Thucydides: A Comprehensive Guide to the Peloponnesian War,* ed. Robert B. Strassler (New York: Free Press, 1996), VII.86.

25. Machiavelli, *Discourses on Livy,* Preface to book 1.

26. Immanuel Kant, "Perpetual Peace," *Political Writings,* ed. Hans Reiss (Cambridge: Cambridge University Press, 1970), 123.

27. Mera J. Flaumenhaft, "The Comic Remedy in Private Spectacle: Machiavelli's *Mandragola,*" *The Civic Spectacle: Essays on Drama and Community* (Lanham, MD: Rowman and Littlefield, 1994), 91; Mark Hulliung, *Citizen Machiavelli* (Princeton: Princeton University Press, 1983), 118: "Ligurio is the perfect Machiavellian."

28. Leo Strauss, *Thoughts on Machiavelli* (Seattle: University of Washington Press, 1958), 9.

29. Hörnqvist, *Machiavelli and Empire,* 2.

30. See Hanna F. Pitkin, *Fortune Is a Woman* (Berkeley: University of California Press, 1984), 110–14; see Susan Behuniak-Long, "The Significance of Lucrezia in Machiavelli's *La Mandragola,*" *Review of Politics* 51 (1989): 270–72.

31. The feminist reading of Lucrezia has been provocatively argued by Heather Hadar Wright, "Lucrezia in *Mandragola:* Machiavelli's New Prince," *Interpretation* 36 (2009): 155: "Lucrezia is Machiavelli's new prince, perfectly exemplifying his *virtù.*" See also

Michelle Tolman Clarke, "On the Woman Question in Machiavelli," *Review of Politics* 67 (2005): 229–55.

32. Machiavelli, *Prince,* 70.

3. THE EXEMPLARY LIFE OF RENÉ DESCARTES

Epigraph. Cited in René Descartes, *Discours de la méthode,* ed. Gilbert Gadoffre (Manchester: University of Manchester Press, 1964), xxi.

1. David Lachterman, *The Ethics of Geometry: A Genealogy of Modernity* (New York: Routledge, 1989); Stephen Toulmin, *Cosmopolis: The Hidden Agenda of Modernity* (New York: Free Press, 1990); John Cottingham, "A New Start? Cartesian Metaphysics and the Emergence of Modern Philosophy," in *The Rise of Modern Philosophy: The Tensions between the New and Traditional Philosophies from Machiavelli to Leibniz,* ed. Tom Sorrell (Oxford: Clarendon, 1993), 145–66.

2. Richard Rorty, *Philosophy and the Mirror of Nature* (Princeton: Princeton University Press, 1979), 136–37: "Descartes's invention of the mind . . . gave philosophers new ground to stand on . . . it provided a field within which *certainty,* as opposed to mere *opinion,* was possible"; for the Cartesian aspiration toward a unified science, see Thomas Spragens, *The Irony of Liberal Reason* (Chicago: University of Chicago Press, 1981), 35–40; see also Edwin Curley, *Behind the Geometrical Method: A Reading of Spinoza's Ethics* (Princeton: Princeton University Press, 1984), 4–6.

3. Alexis de Tocqueville, *Democracy in America,* trans. Harvey Mansfield and Delba Winthrop (Chicago: University of Chicago Press, 2000), II.i.1 (p. 405); likewise Friedrich Nietzsche, *Beyond Good and Evil,* trans. Walter Kaufmann (New York: Random House, 1966), no. 191, p. 104, calls Descartes "the father of rationalism," adding parenthetically, "and hence the grandfather of the Revolution."

4. Martin Heidegger, *Nietzsche,* vol. 4: *Nihilism,* trans. Joan Stambaugh, David Krell, and Frank Capuzzi (San Francisco: Harper's, 1991), 28: "Modern metaphysics first comes to the full and final determination of its essence in the doctrine of the Overman, the doctrine of man's absolute preeminence among beings. In that doctrine, Descartes celebrates his supreme triumph." See Emmanuel Faye, *Heidegger: The Introduction of Nazism into Philosophy,* trans. Michael B. Smith (New Haven: Yale University Press, 2009), 92–96, 266–72.

5. References to Descartes will be given by volume and page number to the *Philosophical Writings of Descartes,* trans. John Cottingham, Robert Stroothoff, and Dugald Murdoch (Cambridge: Cambridge University Press, 1985); henceforth cited as *PW.*

6. For Descartes's answer to the *crise pyrrhonienne,* see Richard Popkin, *The History of Scepticism: From Savonarola to Bayle* (Oxford: Oxford University Press, 2003), 143–57; Richard Tuck, *Philosophy and Government, 1572–1651* (Cambridge: Cambridge University Press, 1993), 284–94; see also Bernard Williams, "Descartes's Use of Scepticism," in *The Skeptical Tradition,* ed. Myles Burnyeat (Berkeley: University of California Press, 1983), 337–52.

7. For the genre of exemplary history, see Timothy Hampton, *Writing from History: The Rhetoric of Exemplarity in Renaissance Literature* (Ithaca: Cornell University Press,

1990); Descartes's use of the method of *exempla* is treated in Lachterman, *The Ethics of Geometry,* 131–34.

8. The phrase originally comes from Cicero, *De oratore,* 2.ix.36.

9. See Gilbert Ryle, *The Concept of Mind* (New York: Hutchinson, 1949), 15–18.

10. The sources of Descartes's conception of the self have been a cause of controversy; for the Christian and Augustinian sources, see Charles Taylor, *Sources of the Self: The Making of the Modern Identity* (Cambridge, MA: Harvard University Press, 1989), 143–58; for the importance of Montaigne's ethical skepticism for Descartes, see Karl Joachim Weintraub, *The Value of the Individual: Self and Circumstance in Autobiography* (Chicago: University of Chicago Press, 1978), 173, 177–78.

11. The full title in French reads: *Discours de la méthode pour bien conduire sa raison, et chercher la vérité dans les sciences: Plus la dioptrique, les météores et la géométrie qui sont des essais de cette méthode.*

12. For the background of intimidation, see Leo Strauss, *Persecution and the Art of Writing* (Chicago: University of Chicago Press, 1980), 17, 22, 33.

13. See Galileo Galilei, "The Assayer," in *Discoveries and Opinions,* trans. Stillman Drake (New York: Doubleday, 1957), 237–38: "Philosophy is written in that great book, the universe, which stands continually open to our gaze. But the book cannot be understood unless one first learns to comprehend the language and read the letters in which it is composed. It is written in the language of mathematics, and its characters are triangles, circles, and other geometric figures, without which it is humanly impossible to understand a single word of it; without these, one wanders about in a dark labyrinth."

14. For Baconian humanitarianism, see Francis Bacon, *New Organon,* 1, art. 129, in *Selected Philosophical Works,* ed. Rose-Mary Sargent (Indianapolis: Hackett, 1999), 145–47; see also Robert Faulkner, *Francis Bacon and the Project of Progress* (Lanham, MD: Rowman and Littlefield, 1993), 62–65.

15. The story of Descartes's remarkable illumination is told by Adrien Baillet, *La vie de M. Des-Cartes* (1691; reprinted New York: Garland, 1987), 1: 77–86; John R. Cole, *The Olympian Dreams and Youthful Rebellion of René Descartes* (Urbana: University of Illinois Press, 1992), 61–77; Geneviève Rodis-Lewis, *Descartes: His Life and Thought,* trans. Jane Marie Todd (Ithaca: Cornell University Press, 1998), 33–44.

16. Compare Michel de Montaigne, "Of Cannibals," in *The Complete Essays,* trans. Donald Frame (Stanford: Stanford University Press, 1971), 152: "I think there is nothing barbarous and savage in that nation, from what I have been told, except that each man calls barbarism whatever is not his own practice."

17. Descartes's *morale par provision* has often been translated as "provisional morality" (*morale provisoire*), but it has recently been claimed that *par provision* is only misleadingly rendered as "provisional"; see John Marshall, *Descartes's Moral Theory* (Ithaca: Cornell University Press, 1998), 16–17. I agree with the question of translation but still believe that the morale par provision is adopted by Descartes as a temporary stopgap during periods of sustained moral doubt and uncertainty, rather than a developed moral theory. See also Pierre Mesnard, *Essai sur la morale de Descartes* (Paris: Boivin,

1936), 46–66; Geneviève Rodis-Lewis, *La morale de Descartes* (Paris: Presses Universitaires de France, 1957), 9–23.

18. For a more general treatment of this problem, see Myles Burnyeat, "Can the Skeptic Live His Skepticism?" in *The Skeptical Tradition,* 117–48.

19. Descartes provides internal evidence for doubting the sincerity of his ethics. In conversation he is reported to have said: "The author does not like writing on ethics, but he is *compelled* to include these rules [of the morale par provision] because of people like the Schoolmen; otherwise, they would have said that he was a man without any religion and faith and that he intended to use his method to subvert them"; John Cottingham, ed., *Descartes' Conversation with Burman* (Oxford: Clarendon, 1976), 49. The issue of Descartes's sincerity has been investigated by Hiram Caton, "The Problem of Descartes's Sincerity," *Philosophical Forum* 2 (1971): 355–70; see also William Bluhm, *Force or Freedom? The Paradox in Modern Political Thought* (New Haven: Yale University Press, 1984), 311–13.

20. See Sheldon Wolin, "Political Theory as a Vocation," in *Machiavelli and the Nature of Political Thought*, ed. Martin Fleischer (New York: Atheneum, 1972), 38–39; Raymond Polin, "Descartes et la philosophie politique," in *Mélanges Alexandre Koyré* (Paris: Hermann, 1964), 388, speaks of the "reticence" of Descartes and the "conservatism" of the *Discourse;* likewise Spragens, *The Irony of Liberal Reason,* 70–72, regards Descartes's moral science as "a logically unstable mixture of old and new ideas" and regards him as "very orthodox and subservient to authority" in religious matters.

21. See Montaigne, "Of the Art of Discussion," in *Complete Essays,* 714: "My reason is not trained to bend and bow, it is my knees." See also Tvetan Todorov, *Imperfect Garden: The Legacy of Humanism,* trans. Carol Cosman (Princeton: Princeton University Press, 2002), 56–57.

22. Thomas Babington, Lord Macaulay, "Lord Bacon," in *Literary Essays Contributed to the Edinburgh Review* (London: Oxford University Press, 1923), 399.

23. Marshall, *Descartes's Moral Theory,* 18–19.

24. For the limits of Descartes' stoicism, see Rodis-Lewis, *La morale de Descartes,* 21–22.

25. Baruch Spinoza, *Theological-Political Treatise,* trans. Samuel Shirley (Indianapolis: Hackett, 1998), 228.

26. Descartes's attachment to any particular place may be doubted. See Descartes's letter to the Princess Elizabeth, June/July 1648: "Staying as I am, one foot in one country and the other in another, I find my condition very happy, in that it is free." Quoted in Todorov, *Imperfect Garden,* 55.

27. Descartes expressed such alarm at the case of Galileo that he told Mersenne that he had burned some of his papers and had hidden others, for, he said, "I did not want to publish a discourse in which a single word could be found that the Church would have disapproved of; so I preferred to suppress it rather than to publish it in a mutilated form"; Letter to Mersenne, late November, 1633 (*PW,* 3:41).

28. Leon Kass, "Mortality and Morality: The Virtues of Finitude," *Toward a More Natural Science* (New York: Free Press, 1988), 299–317.

29. Joseph Cropsey, "On Descartes' 'Discourse on Method,'" in *Political Philosophy and the Issues of Politics* (Chicago: University of Chicago Press, 1977), 289.

30. The best treatment of this theme remains Richard Kennington, "Descartes and the Mastery of Nature," *Organism, Medicine, and Metaphysics,* ed. Stuart F. Spicker (Dordrecht: Reidel, 1978), 201–23.

31. The "Machiavellianism" of Descartes is a subject little discussed in the English-language literature. The principal evidence is the letter to Elizabeth of September 1646, where Descartes offers a commentary on *The Prince,* a work he deems "excellent," and a second letter of October/November 1646, where he refers to Machiavelli as the "Physician of Princes" and says, "I have recently read his discourse on Livy and found nothing bad (*mauvais*) in it" (*PW,* 3:292, 297). The fullest treatment of the subject is Mesnard's *Essai sur la morale de Descartes,* 190–212, which speaks of "le prétendu machiavélisme de Descartes"; Polin, "Descartes et la philosophie politique," 394–95, stresses Descartes's anti-Machiavellianism and his indebtedness to the classical political theories of Plato and Aristotle; see also Richard Kennington, "René Descartes," in *History of Political Philosophy,* ed. Joseph Cropsey and Leo Strauss (Chicago: Rand McNally, 1972), 395–96; Bluhm, *Force or Freedom,* 33; Rodis-Lewis, *La morale de Descartes,* 102–5. At several points Descartes excuses himself from offering political advice, on the grounds that his private manner of life makes him an inappropriate guide to public responsibilities; see the letter to Elizabeth of May 1646: "I lead such a retired life, and have always been so far from the conduct of affairs, that I would be no less impudent than the philosopher who wished to lecture on the duties of a general in the presence of Hannibal if I took it on me to enumerate here the maxims one should observe in a life of public service" (*PW,* 3:287–88).

32. For the role of generosity in Descartes's ethical thought, see Kennington, "Descartes," 406–8; Marshall, *Descartes's Moral Theory,* 148–66; Geneviève Rodis-Lewis, "Le dernier fruit de la métaphysique Cartésienne: La générosité," *Les études philosophiques* 1 (1987): 43–54.

33. See Ernst Cassirer, *Descartes, Corneille, Christine de Suède,* trans. Madeleine Francès and Paul Schrecker (Paris: J. Vrin, 1942), 101–21.

34. See Cassirer, *Descartes, Corneille, Christine de Suède,* 72–75; Taylor, *Sources of the Self,* 153.

35. Rodis-Lewis, "Le dernier fruit de la métaphysique Cartésienne," 43–54.

36. On the differences between Christian charity and Cartesian generosity, see Rodis-Lewis, *La morale de Descartes,* 95–97.

37. Kennington, "Descartes," 395.

38. Tuck, *Philosophy and Government,* 285.

39. This aristocratic code can be seen also in Spinoza, *Ethics,* III, Prop. 59S: "All actions that follow from affects related to the Mind insofar as it understands I relate to strength of character (*fortitudo*), which I divide into tenacity (*animositas*) and nobility (*generositas*)." *The Collected Works of Spinzoa,* trans. and ed. Edwin Curley (Princeton: Princeton University Press, 1985), 529; see also Steven B. Smith, *Spinoza's Book of Life: Freedom and Redemption in the "Ethics"* (New Haven: Yale University Press, 2003) 114–16.

40. Tocqueville, *Democracy in America*, II.i.1 (p. 403).

41. Tocqueville, *Democracy in America*, II.i.1 (p. 403).

4. WAS HOBBES A CHRISTIAN?

Epigraph. Jean-Jacques Rousseau, *Of the Social Contract*, in *The Social Contract and Other Later Political Writings*, ed. Victor Gourevitch (Cambridge: Cambridge University Press, 1997), IV.8 (p. 146).

1. Thomas Hobbes, Epistle Dedicatory to *De Corpore*, in *The English Works of Thomas Hobbes*, ed. William Molesworth (London: Bohn, 1839), I.ix.

2. This idea is perhaps most widely associated with Max Weber, "Politics as a Vocation," in *From Max Weber: Essays in Sociology*, ed. H. H. Gerth and C. W. Mills (New York: Oxford University Press, 1958), 78.

3. I use Edwin Curley's edition of *Leviathan* (Indianapolis: Hackett, 1994); references will be provided in parentheses to book, chapter, and section number.

4. For an early appreciation, see J. G. A. Pocock, "Time, History, and Eschatology in the Thought of Thomas Hobbes," in *Politics, Language, and Time: Essays on Political Thought and History* (New York: Atheneum, 1973), 148–201; Eldon J. Eisenach, *Two Worlds of Liberalism: Religion and Politics in Hobbes, Locke, and Mill* (Chicago: University of Chicago Press, 1981), 13–71; Eric Nelson, *The Hebrew Republic: Jewish Sources and the Transformation of European Political Thought* (Cambridge, MA: Harvard University Press, 2010), 53–56, 122–28.

5. Leslie Stephen, *Hobbes* (Ann Arbor: University of Michigan Press, 1962), 152.

6. Stephen, *Hobbes*, 155.

7. See Howard Warrender, *The Political Philosophy of Hobbes: His Theory of Obligation* (Oxford: Oxford University Press, 1957); for a useful critique, see Brian Barry, "Warrender and His Critics," in *Hobbes and Rousseau: A Collection of Critical Essays*, ed. Maurice Cranston and Richard S. Peters (Garden City: Doubleday, 1972), 37–65; John Plamenatz, "Mr. Warrender's Hobbes" and Warrender's "A Reply to Mr. Plamenatz," in *Hobbes Studies*, ed. Keith Brown (Oxford: Blackwell, 1965), 73–87, 89–100.

8. See F. C. Hood, *The Divine Politics of Thomas Hobbes* (Oxford: Oxford University Press, 1960); A. L. Martinich, *The Two Gods of Leviathan* (Cambridge: Cambridge University Press, 1992); for a valuable critique, see Edwin Curley, "Calvin or Hobbes, or, Hobbes as an Orthodox Christian," *Journal of the History of Philosophy* 34 (1996): 257–71.

9. See Quentin Skinner, "The Context of Hobbes' Theory of Political Obligation," *Hobbes and Rousseau*, 109–42.

10. Leo Strauss, *The Political Philosophy of Hobbes: Its Basis and Genesis*, trans. Elsa M. Sinclair (Chicago: University of Chicago Press, 1966), 71; see also Leo Strauss, *Hobbes's Critique of Religion and Related Writings*, trans. Gabriel Bartlett and Svetozar Minkov (Chicago: University of Chicago Press, 2011), 23.

11. Carl Schmitt, *The Leviathan in the State Theory of Thomas Hobbes: Meaning and Failure of a Political Symbol*, trans. George Schwab and Erna Hilfstein (Westport, CT: Greenwood Press, 1996), 53

12. Schmitt, *The Leviathan in the State Theory of Thomas Hobbes,* 57–58.

13. See Leo Strauss, "Comments on Carl Schmitt's *Der Begriff des Politischen,*" in Carl Schmitt, *The Concept of the Political,* trans. George Schwab (New Brunswick, NJ: Rutgers University Press, 1976), 81–105.

14. See Strauss, *The Political Philosophy of Hobbes,* 108–28; for another view on Hobbes as a philosopher of the bourgeoisie, see C. B. Macpherson, *The Political Theory of Possessive Individualism: Hobbes to Locke* (Oxford: Oxford University Press, 1962).

15. Michael Oakeshott, ed., *Leviathan* (Oxford: Blackwell, 1946); Oakeshott offered his own critical assessment of Strauss's work in "Dr. Leo Strauss on Hobbes," in *Hobbes on Civil Association* (Indianapolis: Liberty Fund, 1975), 141–58.

16. Michael Oakeshott, "Introduction to *Leviathan,*" in *Hobbes on Civil Association,* 67.

17. Oakeshott, "Introduction to *Leviathan,*" 67.

18. Mark Lilla, *The Stillborn God: Religion, Politics, and the Modern West* (New York: Knopf, 2007), 88.

19. For the importance of Epicureanism in shaping modernity, see Stephen Greenblatt, *The Swerve: How the World Became Modern* (New York: Norton, 2012). Unfortunately this book hardly touches upon either Hobbes or Spinoza. For a better understanding of the importance of Lucretius for the Enlightenment's critique of religion, see Leo Strauss, *Spinoza's Critique of Religion,* trans. Elsa M. Sinclair (New York: Schocken, 1965), 37–52; see also James H. Nichols, *Epicurean Political Philosophy: The "De rerum natura" of Lucretius* (Ithaca: Cornell University Press, 1976), 188–90.

20. See Leo Strauss, *Natural Right and History* (Chicago: University of Chicago Press, 1971), 168–69.

21. For some useful reflections, see Pierre Manent, *The City of Man,* trans. Marc A. LePain (Princeton: Princeton University Press, 1998), 130–33.

22. Niccolò Machiavelli, *The Prince,* trans. Harvey C. Mansfield (Chicago: University of Chicago Press, 1985), 88.

23. See Strauss, *The Political Philosophy of Hobbes,* 79–107.

24. For Hobbes's ignorance of Hebrew, see Noel Malcolm, "Hobbes, Ezra, and the Bible," in *Aspects of Hobbes* (Oxford: Clarendon Press, 2002), 413.

25. Ronald Beiner, *Civil Religion: A Dialogue in the History of Political Philosophy* (Cambridge: Cambridge University Press, 2011), 53–55.

26. Gershom Scholem, "Toward an Understanding of the Messianic Idea in Judaism," in *The Messianic Idea in Judaism and Other Essays in Jewish Spirituality* (New York: Schocken, 1971), 1–36.

27. See Beiner, *Civil Religion,* 55; Warren Zev Harvey, "The Israelite Kingdom of God in Hobbes' Political Thought," *Hebraic Political Studies* 1 (2006): 310–27.

28. For Hobbes's creative interpretation of the heresy laws, see Thomas Hobbes, *A Dialogue Between a Philosopher and a Student of the Common Laws of England,* ed. Joseph Cropsey (Chicago: University of Chicago Press, 1971), 122–32; see also Thomas Hobbes, *Behemoth or The Long Parliament,* ed. Ferdinand Tönnies (Chicago: University of Chicago Press, 1990), 8–18.

29. Cited in Samuel I. Mintz, *The Hunting of Leviathan: Seventeenth-Century Reactions to the Materialism and Moral Philosophy of Thomas Hobbes* (Cambridge: Cambridge University Press, 1962), 57.

30. Henning Graf Reventlow, *The Authority of the Bible and the Rise of the Modern World* (Philadelphia: Fortress Press, 1985), 221–22.

31. Pocock, "Time, History, and Eschatology in the Thought of Thomas Hobbes," 162.

32. Thomas Hobbes, "The Verse Life," in *Human Nature and De Corpore Politico,* ed. J. C. A. Gaskin (New York: Oxford University Press, 1994), 254.

33. John Aubrey, *Brief Lives,* ed. Andrew Clark (Oxford: Clarendon Press, 1898), I:397; see the very useful discussion by Edwin Curley, ' "I durst not write so boldly' or How to Read Hobbes' Theologico-Political Treatise," in *Hobbes e Spinoza,* ed. Daniela Bostrenghi (Naples: Bibliopolis, 1992); see also Stephen, *Hobbes,* 156, 228; Strauss, *Hobbes' Critique of Religion,* 23, 32.

34. Strauss, *The Political Philosophy of Hobbes,* 74.

35. See Strauss, *Natural Right and History,* 199.

36. For attacks on Hobbes, see Mintz, *The Hunting of Leviathan.*

37. Shirley Letwin, "Skepticism and Toleration in Hobbes' Political Thought," *Early Modern Skepticism and the Origins of Toleration,* ed. Alan Levine (Lanham, MD: Lexington Books, 1999), 176; see also Oakeshott, "Introduction to *Leviathan,*" 11–13.

38. See Alan Ryan, "A More Tolerant Hobbes, *Justifying Toleration,* ed. Susan Mendus (Cambridge: Cambridge University Press, 1998), 37–59; Richard Tuck, "Hobbes and Locke on Toleration," in *Thomas Hobbes and Political Theory,* ed. Mary G. Dietz (Lawrence: University of Kansas Press, 1990), 153–71; Edwin Curley, "Hobbes and the Cause of Religious Toleration," *The Cambridge Companion to Hobbes' Leviathan,* ed. Patricia Springborg (Cambridge: Cambridge University Press, 2006), 309–34; see also Stephen, *Hobbes,* 233, who anticipates this view by more than a century: "Hobbes would thus seem to be in favour of complete religious toleration and absolute indifference of the State in religious matters."

39. Hobbes, *Behemoth,* 62: "Suppression of doctrine does but unite and exasperate, that is, increase both the malice and power of them that have already believed them."

5. WHAT KIND OF JEW WAS SPINOZA?

Epigraph. John Aubrey, *Brief Lives,* ed. Andrew Clark (Oxford: Clarendon Press, 1898), I:397.

1. See Steven B. Smith, *Spinoza, Liberalism, and the Question of Jewish Identity* (New Haven: Yale University Press, 1997); see also Adam Sutcliff, *Judaism and Enlightenment* (Cambridge: Cambridge University Press, 2003); Daniel B. Schwartz, *The First Modern Jew: Spinoza and the History of an Image* (Princeton: Princeton University Press, 2012).

2. See Harry A. Wolfson, *The Philosophy of Spinoza,* 2 vols. (Cambridge, MA: Harvard University Press, 1934); Shlomo Pines, "Spinoza's 'Tractatus Theologico-Politicus,' Maimonides, and Kant," *Scripta Hierosolymitana* 20 (1968): 3–54.

3. Cited in Yirmiyahu Yovel, *Spinoza and Other Heretics: The Marrano of Reason* (Princeton: Princeton University Press, 1989), 3.

4. Baruch Spinoza, *The Theologico-Political Treatise,* trans. Samuel Shirley (Indianapolis: Hackett, 1998); references to the text will be to chapter and page number.

5. Hermann Cohen, "Spinoza über Staat und Religion, Judentum und Christentum," in *Jüdische Schriften,* ed. Bruno Strauss (Berlin: Schwetscheke, 1924), 3:360, 361, 371.

6. Emmanuel Levinas, "The Spinoza Case," *Difficult Freedom: Essays on Judaism,* trans. Séan Hand (London: Athlone Press, 1990), 108.

7. Moses Hess, *The Holy History of Mankind and Other Writings,* ed. Shlomo Avineri (Cambridge: Cambridge University Press, 2004).

8. George Eliot, *Daniel Deronda,* ed. Graham Handley (Oxford: Clarendon Press, 1984), 498.

9. Joseph Klausner, "The Jewish Character of Spinoza's Teaching," in *The Jewish Political Tradition: Membership,* ed. Michael Walzer, Menachem Lorberbaum, and Noam J. Zohar (New Haven: Yale University Press, 2003), 419.

10. See Mark Lilla, *The Stillborn God* (New York: Alfred A. Knopf, 2007), 86–145.

11. For a reading of the *TTP* as an engagement with the Dutch politics of Spinoza's era, see Michael Rosenthal, "Why Spinoza Chose the Hebrews: The Exemplary Function of Prophecy in the *Theologico-Political Treatise,*" in *Jewish Themes in Spinoza's Philosophy,* ed. Heidi M. Ravven and Lenn E. Goodman (Albany: SUNY Press, 2002), 225–60; see also Susan James, *Spinoza on Philosophy, Religion, and Politics: The Theologico-Political Treatise* (Oxford: Oxford University Press, 2012), 282–89.

12. For Spinoza's relation to the history of biblical criticism, see J. Samuel Preuss, *Spinoza and the Irrelevance of Biblical Authority* (Cambridge: Cambridge University Press, 2001).

13. See Josephus, *Anti-Apion,* trans. H. St. J. Thackeray (London: William Heinemann, 1926), vol. 1, book 2, chap. 164; see also Gershon Weiler, *Jewish Theocracy* (Leiden: Brill, 1988).

14. Thomas Hobbes, *Leviathan,* ed. Edwin Curley (Indianapolis: Hackett, 1994), II.XXIX.1.

15. For Spinoza's "Erastianism," see Eric Nelson, *The Hebrew Republic: Jewish Sources and the Transformation of European Political Thought* (Cambridge, MA: Harvard University Press, 2010), 130–34.

16. Emil L. Fackenheim, *To Mend the World: Foundations of Future Jewish Thought* (New York: Schocken, 1982), 44.

17. Leo Strauss, "Preface to *Spinoza's Critique of Religion,*" *Liberalism Ancient and Modern* (New York: Basic Books, 1968), 246.

18. Strauss, "Preface to *Spinoza's Critique of Religion,*" 246.

19. For an imaginative reconstruction of a Jewish community situated in Alaska, see Michael Chabon, *The Yiddish Policemen's Union* (New York: Harper Collins, 2007).

20. See Smith, *Spinoza, Liberalism, and the Question of Jewish Identity,* 101–3; Yovel, *Spinoza and Other Heretics,* 190–93.

21. Isaac Deutscher, "The Non-Jewish Jew," *The Non-Jewish Jew and Other Essays* (Oxford: Oxford University Press, 1968), 25–41.

6. BENJAMIN FRANKLIN'S AMERICAN ENLIGHTENMENT

1. Benjamin Franklin, *The Autobiography,* in *Writings* (New York: Library of America, 1987); all references will be provided parenthetically to this text.

2. C. A. Sainte-Beuve, "Franklin," in *Causeries du lundi* (Paris: Garnier, 1947), 7:136, 138.

3. Sainte-Beuve, "Franklin," 181.

4. Karl Marx, *Capital,* trans. Samuel Moore and Edward Aveling (London: Lawrence and Wishart, 1970), 326.

5. Max Weber, *The Protestant Ethic and the Spirit of Capitalism,* trans. Talcott Parsons (New York: Scribner's, 1958), 53.

6. Weber, *Protestant Ethic,* 53–54.

7. Weber, *Protestant Ethic,* 52.

8. D. H. Lawrence, *Studies in Classic American Literature,* ed. Ezra Greenspan, Lindeth Vasey, and John Worthen (Cambridge: Cambridge University Press, 2003), 180.

9. Lawrence, *Studies in Classic American Literature,* 185.

10. See Stefana Sabin, "Autobiography as Self-Apology: From Deism through Transcendentalism to Atheism: Benjamin Franklin, Ralph Waldo Emerson, Henry Adams," *Religious Apologetics—Philosophical Argumentation,* ed. Yosef Shvarts and Volkhard Krech (Tübingen: Mohr Siebeck, 2004), 111.

11. John Stuart Mill, *On Liberty,* ed. David Spitz (New York: Norton, 1975), 12; Alexis de Tocqueville, *Democracy in America,* trans. Harvey C. Mansfield and Delba Winthrop (Chicago: University of Chicago Press, 2000), II.ii.8.

12. Immanuel Kant, "Idea for a Universal History with a Cosmopolitan Purpose," *Political Writings,* ed. Hans Reiss (Cambridge: Cambridge University Press, 1970), 46; Isaiah Berlin, *The Crooked Timber of Humanity,* ed. Henry Hardy (Princeton: Princeton University Press, 1990), xi, 19, 48.

13. See Henry May, *The Enlightenment in America* (New York: Oxford University Press, 1976), 126–32.

14. See Gerald Stourzh, "Reason and Power in Benjamin Franklin's Political Thought," in *From Vienna to Chicago: Essays in Intellectual History and Political Thought in Europe and America* (Chicago: University of Chicago Press, 2007), 40.

15. See Alasdair MacIntyre, *After Virtue* (Notre Dame: Notre Dame University Press, 1981), 171.

16. See Steven Forde, "Benjamin Franklin, Hero" in *The Noblest Minds: Fame, Honor, and the American Founding,* ed. Peter McNamara (Lanham, MD: Rowman and Littlefield, 1999), 39–58.

17. See Sabin, "Autobiography as Self-Apology," 112.

18. See Peter Gay, *The Party of Humanity: Essays in the French Enlightenment* (New York: Knopf, 1964).

19. See Jürgen Habermas, *The Structural Transformation of the Public Sphere: An Inquiry into a Category of Bourgeois Society,* trans. Thomas Burger (Cambridge, MA: MIT Press, 1991), 91–93.

20. For the early arguments in favor of political party, see Harvey C. Mansfield, *Statesmanship and Party Government: A Study of Burke and Bolingbroke* (Chicago: University of Chicago Press, 1965).

21. Reinhart Koselleck, *Critique and Crisis: Enlightenment and the Pathogenesis of Modern Society* (Cambridge, MA: MIT Press, 1988), 76–77.

22. De Maistre, cited in Koselleck, *Critique and Crisis,* 81.

23. Bernard Faÿ, *The Revolutionary Spirit in France and America,* trans. Ramon Guthrie (London: Allen and Unwin, 1928), 154.

24. Faÿ, *The Revolutionary Spirit,* 157–58.

25. See Ralph Lerner, "Franklin, Spectator," *The Thinking Revolutionary: Principle and Practice in the New Republic* (Ithaca: Cornell University Press, 1987), 41–59.

26. Douglass Adair, "Fame and the Founding Fathers," in *Fame and the Founding Fathers,* ed. Trevor Colbourn (Indianapolis: Liberty Fund, 1998), 9.

7. KANT'S LIBERAL INTERNATIONALISM

Epigraph. Heinrich Heine, *Concerning the History of Religion and Philosophy in Germany,* in *The Romantic School and Other Essays,* ed. Jost Hermand and Robert C. Holub (New York: Continuum, 1985), 213.

1. Immanuel Kant, *The Contest of Faculties,* in *Political Writings,* ed. Hans Reiss (Cambridge: Cambridge University Press, 1970), 182.

2. Immanuel Kant, *Critique of Pure Reason,* trans. Norman Kemp Smith (New York: Saint Martin's 1965), 9.

3. Kant, *What Is Enlightenment?* in *Political Writings,* 54.

4. For one of the many places to find this story, see Ernst Cassirer, *Kant's Life and Thought,* trans. James Haden (New Haven: Yale University Press, 1981), 86; for Kant's influence on Rousseau more generally, see Richard Velkley, *Freedom and the End of Reason: On the Moral Foundation of Kant's Critical Philosophy* (Chicago: University of Chicago Press, 1989), 36–38, 52–60; Susan Meld Shell, *Kant and the Limits of Autonomy* (Cambridge, MA: Harvard University Press, 2009), 34–36.

5. Immanuel Kant, *Observations on the Feeling of the Beautiful and Sublime and Other Writings,* ed. Patrick Frierson and Paul Guyer (Cambridge: Cambridge University Press, 2011), 104–5.

6. Kant, *Observations,* 95.

7. Kant, *Observations,* 96.

8. Immanuel Kant, *Groundwork of the Metaphysics of Morals,* trans. H. J. Patton (New York: Harper, 1964), 6.

9. Immanuel Kant, *Critique of Practical Reason,* trans. Lewis White Beck (New York: Library of Liberal Arts, 1956), 166.

10. Jean-Jacques Rousseau, *Of the Social Contract,* in *The Social Contract and Other Later Political Writings,* trans. Victor Gourevitch (Cambridge: Cambridge University Press, 1997), I.6 (pp. 49–51).

11. Kant, *Perpetual Peace,* in *Political Writings,* 112.

12. Kant, *Perpetual Peace,* 99–100.

13. Kant, *Perpetual Peace,* 93–96.

14. Kant, *Perpetual Peace,* 104.

15. Kant, *Perpetual Peace,* 106.

16. Hannah Arendt, *The Origins of Totalitarianism* (Cleveland: World Publishing, 1958), 277.

17. Kant, *Perpetual Peace,* 107.

18. Kant, *Perpetual Peace,* 107–8.

19. Kant, *Perpetual Peace,* 105.

20. Kant, *Perpetual Peace,* 113–14.

21. The paradox involved in fighting to achieve peace has recently been explored by Alexander S. Kirshner, *A Theory of Militant Democracy: The Ethics of Combatting Political Extremism* (New Haven: Yale University Press, 2014).

22. Kant, *Perpetual Peace,* 100.

23. Kant, *Perpetual Peace,* 108.

24. Kant, *Idea for a Universal History with a Cosmopolitan Purpose,* in *Political Writings,* 41–53 (all subsequent citations will be in parentheses in the text).

25. Kant, *Pure Reason,* 313.

26. See Kant, *Pure Reason,* 549–69.

27. Kant, *Pure Reason,* 635.

28. See Arthur Schopenhauer, *Parerga and Paralipomena: Short Philosophical Essays,* trans. E. F. J. Payne (Oxford: Clarendon Press, 1974), II, chap. 31, sec. 396; see also Michael Oakeshott, "Talking Politics," *Rationalism in Politics and Other Essays* (Indianapolis: Liberty Press, 1991), 460–61.

29. Kant, *Perpetual Peace,* 111.

30. Kant, *Perpetual Peace,* 114.

31. Susan Shell, "Kant's Idea of History," *History and the Idea of Progress,* ed. Arthur M. Melzer, Jerry Weinberger, and M. Richard Zinman (Ithaca: Cornell University Press, 1995), 85.

32. Kant, *Perpetual Peace,* 125.

33. Kant, *Perpetual Peace,* 123.

34. This idea was pioneered by Michael Doyle, "Kant, Liberal Legacies, and Foreign Affairs, Parts 1 and 2," *Philosophy and Public Affairs* 12 (1983): 205–35, 323–53; see also Bruce Russett, *Grasping the Democratic Peace: Principles for a Post–Cold War World* (Princeton: Princeton University Press, 1993).

35. See William A. Galston, *Kant and the Problem of History* (Chicago: University of Chicago Press, 1975), 23–38.

36. G. W. F. Hegel, *Elements of the Philosophy of Right,* trans. H. B. Nisbet (Cambridge: Cambridge University Press, 1991), Addition to para. 324 (p. 362).

37. Carl Schmitt, *The Concept of the Political,* trans. George Schwab (New Brunswick: Rutgers University Press, 1976), 30.

38. Schmitt, *The Concept of the Political,* 31–32.

39. Schmitt, *The Concept of the Political,* 54.

40. Schmitt, *The Concept of the Political,* 53.

8. HEGEL AND THE "BOURGEOIS-CHRISTIAN WORLD"

1. For some recent considerations, see Z. A. Pelczynski, ed., *The State and Civil Society: Studies in Hegel's Political Philosophy* (Cambridge: Cambridge University Press, 1984);

Manfred Riedel, *Between Tradition and Revolution: The Hegelian Transformation of Political Philosophy,* trans. Walter Wright (Cambridge: Cambridge University Press, 1984); Steven B. Smith, *Hegel's Critique of Liberalism: Rights in Context* (Chicago: University of Chicago Press, 1989).

2. Michael Walzer, "The Civil Society Argument," in *Dimensions of Radical Democracy: Pluralism, Citizenship, and Community,* ed. Chantel Mouffe (London: Verso, 1992), 106.

3. G. W. F. Hegel, *Elements of the Philosophy of Right,* trans. H. B. Nisbet, ed. Allen Wood (Cambridge: Cambridge University Press, 1991), 21; references will be cited by paragraph number; Hegel's Remarks are indicated by "R" and his Additions by "A."

4. See Riedel, *Between Tradition and Revolution,* 132, 136.

5. Adam Ferguson, *An Essay on the History of Civil Society,* ed. Fania Oz-Salzberger (Cambridge: Cambridge University Press, 1996), 172–80.

6. David Hume, "Of Refinement in the Arts," in *Essays Moral, Political, and Literary,* ed. Eugene Miller (Indianapolis: Liberty Fund, 1985), 274.

7. Hume, "Of Civil Liberty," in *Essays Moral, Political, and Literary,* 88.

8. Hume, "Of Civil Liberty," 92.

9. Hume, "Of Civil Liberty," 94.

10. See Montesquieu, *The Spirit of the Laws,* trans. Anne M. Cohler, Basia Carolyn Miller, and Harold Stone (Cambridge: Cambridge University Press, 1989), V, xix (p. 70).

11. Quoted in George Lukács, *The Young Hegel,* trans. Rodney Livingstone (Cambridge, MA: MIT Press, 1975), 170; for Hegel's indebtedness to Steuart, see Raymond Plant, *Hegel* (London: Allen and Unwin, 1973), 64–68; Laurence Dickey, *Hegel: Religion, Economics, and the Politics of Spirit, 1770–1807* (Cambridge: Cambridge University Press, 1987), 192–99.

12. George Lichtheim, *George Lukács* (New York: Viking Press, 1970), 88–89.

13. Franz Gabriel Nauen, *Revolution, Idealism, and Human Freedom: Schelling, Hölderlin, and Hegel and the Crisis of Early German Idealism* (The Hague: Martinus Nijhoff, 1971), 2–3.

14. Immanuel Kant, "On the Common Saying: 'This May Be True in Theory, but It Does Not Apply in Practice,'" in *Political Writings,* trans. H. B. Nisbet (Cambridge: Cambridge University Press, 1970), 77–78.

15. Kant, "Theory and Practice," 78.

16. G. W. F. Hegel, *Lectures on the History of Philosophy,* trans. E. S. Haldane and Frances H. Simson (London: Routledge and Kegan Paul, 1955), 2:209.

17. Jürgen Habermas, "Labor and Interaction: Remarks on Hegel's Jena *Philosophy of Mind,*" in *Theory and Practice,* trans. John Viertel (Boston: Beacon Press, 1974), 166–67.

18. Karl Marx, *Critique of Hegel's "Philosophy of Right,"* trans. Joseph O'Malley (Cambridge: Cambridge University Press, 1970), 77.

19. Marx, *Critique of Hegel's "Philosophy of Right,"* 78.

20. Karl Marx, "On the Jewish Question," in *The Marx-Engels Reader,* ed. Robert Tucker (New York: Norton, 1978), 42

21. Marx, "On the Jewish Question," 34.

22. Marx, "On the Jewish Question," 45–46.

23. Karl Löwith, *From Hegel to Nietzsche: The Revolution in Nineteenth-Century Thought,* trans. David Green (New York: Doubleday, 1967), 17–18, 23–24, 238–42.

24. See G. W. F. Hegel, *The Philosophy of History,* trans. J. Sibree (New York: Dover, 1956), 18–19.

25. G. W. F. Hegel, *Philosophy of Mind,* trans. William Wallace and A. V. Miller (Oxford: Clarendon Press, 1971), sec. 482 (pp. 239–40).

26. John Locke, *The Second Treatise of Government,* ed. Peter Laslett (Cambridge: Cambridge University Press, 1991), sec. 27.

27. See Locke, *Second Treatise,* sec. 34.

28. George Armstrong Kelly, *Idealism, Politics, and History: Sources of Hegelian Thought* (Cambridge: Cambridge University Press, 1969), 347.

29. Cited in Alexander Altmann, "Moses Mendelssohn on Education and the Image of Man," in *Studies in Jewish Thought: An Anthology of German Jewish Scholarship,* ed. Alfred Jospe (Detroit: Wayne State University Press, 1981), 389.

30. Adam Smith, *An Inquiry into the Nature and Causes of the Wealth of Nations,* ed. R. H. Campbell and A. S. Skinner (Indianapolis: Liberty Fund, 1981), V, i (p. 783).

31. Smith, *Wealth of Nations,* V.i (p. 782).

32. Ferguson, *History of Civil Society,* 172–75.

33. Ferguson, *History of Civil Society,* 174.

34. Löwith, *From Hegel to Nietzsche,* 267.

35. See Daniel Patrick Moynihan, ed., *Understanding Poverty: Perspectives from the Social Sciences* (New York: Basic Books, 1969).

9. ROUSSEAU'S COUNTER-ENLIGHTENMENT

1. Iris Murdoch, *The Fire and the Sun: Why Plato Banished the Poets* (Oxford: Oxford University Press, 1977), 7.

2. For a useful account, see Carnes Lord, *Education and Culture in the Political Thought of Aristotle* (Ithaca: Cornell University Press, 1982).

3. Georg Lukács, *Ästhetik* (Berlin: Luchterhand, 1963); Allan Bloom, *The Closing of the American Mind: How Higher Education Has Failed Democracy and Impoverished the Souls of Today's Students* (New York: Simon and Schuster, 1987).

4. For the reception of his opera, see Jean-Jacques Rousseau, *The Confessions and Correspondence, Including the Letters to Malesherbes,* trans. Christopher Kelly (Hanover, NH: University Press of New England, 1995), 314–25.

5. Jean-Jacques Rousseau, *Discourse on the Sciences and the Arts or First Discourse,* in *The Discourses and Other Early Political Writings,* ed. Victor Gourevitch (Cambridge: Cambridge University Press, 1997), 6.

6. Immanuel Kant, "What Is Enlightenment?" in *Political Writings,* ed. Hans Reiss, trans. H. B. Nisbet (Cambridge: Cambridge University Press, 1970), 54.

7. Rousseau, *First Discourse,* 6.

8. Rousseau, *First Discourse,* 24.

9. Rousseau, *First Discourse,* 26.

10. Rousseau, *First Discourse,* 26.

11. Cited in Lorraine Daston, "The Ideal and the Reality of the Republic of Letters in the Enlightenment," *Science in Context* 4 (1991): 374.

12. See Carol Pal, *The Republic of Women: Rethinking the Republic of Letters in the Seventeenth Century* (Cambridge: Cambridge University Press, 2012).

13. Cited in Daston, "The Republic of Letters," 382.

14. See François Furet, *Interpreting the French Revolution* (Cambridge: Cambridge University Press, 1988), 187.

15. See Bryan Garsten, *Saving Persuasion: A Defense of Rhetoric and Judgment* (Cambridge, MA: Harvard University Press, 2006), 44–45.

16. Reinhart Koselleck, *Critique and Crisis: Enlightenment and the Pathogenesis of Modern Society* (Cambridge, MA: MIT Press, 1988), 113–14.

17. Koselleck, *Critique and Crisis,* 118.

18. For a useful discussion, see Arthur M. Melzer, *Philosophy Between the Lines: The Lost History of Esoteric Writing* (Chicago: University of Chicago Press, 2014), 249–59.

19. Jean Le Rond d'Alembert, *Preliminary Discourse to the Encyclopedia of Diderot,* trans. Richard N. Schwab (Chicago: University of Chicago Press, 1995), 74, 75.

20. D'Alembert, *Preliminary Discourse,* 80.

21. D'Alembert, *Preliminary Discourse,* 80.

22. D'Alembert, *Preliminary Discourse,* 103–4.

23. Jean-Jacques Rousseau, *Letter to d'Alembert and Writings for the Theatre,* trans. Allan Bloom, Charles Butterworth, and Christopher Kelly (Hanover, NH: University Press of New England, 2004); all references will be provided in parentheses in the text.

24. For an excellent discussion, see Eileen Hunt Botting, *Family Feuds: Wollstonecraft, Burke, Rousseau and the Transformation of the Family* (Albany: SUNY Press, 2006).

25. Thucydides, *The Peloponnesian War,* the Crawley translation (New York: Modern Library, 1982), II.45.

26. Judith Shklar, "Rousseau's Images of Authority," in *Hobbes and Rousseau: A Collection of Critical Essays,* ed. Maurice Cranston and Richard S. Peters (Garden City, NY: Doubleday, 1972), 333–65.

27. Jean-Jacques Rousseau, *Of the Social Contract,* in *The Social Contract and Other Later Political Writings,* ed. Victor Gourevitch (Cambridge: Cambridge University Press, 1997), II.7.

28. Rousseau, *The Social Contract,* II.10.

29. Jean-Jacques Rousseau, *Julie or the New Heloise,* trans. Philip Stewart and Jean Vaché (Hanover, NH: University Press of New England, 1997), 492–99.

30. Rousseau, *Considerations on the Government of Poland,* in *The Social Contract and Other Later Political Writings,* 180.

31. Rousseau, *Government of Poland,* 183.

32. Rousseau, *Government of Poland,* 184–86.

33. Benjamin Constant, "The Spirit of Conquest and Usurpation and Their Relation to European Civilization," in *Political Writings,* ed. Biancamaria Fontana (Cambridge: Cambridge University Press, 1988), 106: "I believe that the subtle metaphysics of the *Social Contract* can only serve today to supply weapons and pretexts to all kinds of

tyranny, that of one man, that of several and that of all, to oppression either orga-
nized under legal forms or exercised through popular violence." See also Isaiah Berlin,
"Two Concepts of Liberty," in *Liberty,* ed. Henry Hardy (Oxford: Oxford University
Press, 2002), 208–10.

34. For Rousseau as a precursor of nationalism, see Alfred Cobban, *Rousseau and the
Modern State* (London: Archon Books, 1964), 99–125; Anne M. Cohler, *Rousseau and
Nationalism* (New York: Basic Books, 1970).

35. Emmanuel Joseph Sieyès, "What Is the Third Estate?" in *Political Writings,* trans.
Michael Sonenscher (Indianapolis: Hackett, 2003), 97.

36. Robert Wokler, "The Enlightenment and the French Revolutionary Birth Pangs of Modernity," in *Rousseau, The Age of Enlightenment, and Their Legacies,* ed. Bryan Garsten
(Princeton: Princeton University Press, 2012), 197.

37. Rousseau, *Emile or On Education,* trans. Allan Bloom (New York: Basic Books, 1979), 40.

38. See Isaiah Berlin, "Montesquieu," in *Against the Current: Essays in the History of Ideas,*
ed. Henry Hardy (New York: Viking Press, 1980), 130–61.

39. Karl Löwith, *From Hegel to Nietzsche: The Revolution in Nineteenth-Century Thought,*
trans. David E. Green (New York: Doubleday, 1967), 232–37.

40. Rousseau, *Government of Poland,* 184.

41. Cited in Cobban, *Rousseau and the Modern State,* 116.

10. TOCQUEVILLE'S AMERICA

Epigraph. Abraham Lincoln, "House Divided Speech," in *The Writings of Abraham Lincoln,* ed. Steven B. Smith (New Haven: Yale University Press, 2012), 126.

1. For Tocqueville's debt to Rousseau, see "Editor's Introduction," in *Democracy in
America,* trans. Harvey C. Mansfield and Delba Winthrop (Chicago: University of
Chicago Press, 2000), xxxvi–xxxix; henceforth references will be given to the vol-
ume, part, chapter, and page number in parentheses.

2. This argument has been made most famously by Robert Putnam, *Bowling Alone: The
Collaspse and Revival of American Community* (New York: Simon and Schuster, 2000).

3. Françoise Mélonio, *Tocqueville and the French,* trans. Beth G. Raps (Charlottesville:
University of Virginia Press, 1998), 5.

4. Jean-Jacques Rousseau, *Of the Social Contract,* in *The Social Contract and Other Later
Political Writings,* ed. Victor Gourevitch (Cambridge: Cambridge University Press,
1997), II, 6.

5. The debate over one Tocqueville or two goes back to Seymour Drescher, "Tocqueville's
Two *Démocraties,*" *Journal of the History of Ideas* 25 (1964): 201–16; the issues are re-
viewed in James T. Schleifer, *The Making of Tocqueville's "Democracy in America"* (Cha-
pel Hill: University of North Carolina Press, 1980); Jean-Claude Lamberti, *Tocqueville
and the Two Democracies,* trans. Arthur Goldhammer (Cambridge, MA: Harvard
University Press, 1989).

6. Letter to Louis de Kergolay, January 1835, in *Alexis de Tocqueville: Selected Letters on
Politics and Society,* trans. and ed. Roger Boesche and James Toupin (Berkeley: University of California Press, 1985), 95.

7. Letter to John Stuart Mill, November 10, 1836, in *Memoirs, Letters, and Remains of Alexis de Tocqueville* (Boston: Ticknor and Fields, 1862), 2:38.

8. Cited in Lamberti, *Tocqueville and the Two Democracies*, 120.

9. Alexander Hamilton, James Madison, and John Jay, *The Federalist Papers,* ed. Jacob E. Cooke (Middletown, CT: Wesleyan University Press, 1961), No. 9, p. 50.

10. On the role of *inquiétude,* which can be translated variously as restiveness, restlessness, or even anxiety, see Pierre Manent, *Tocqueville and the Nature of Democracy,* trans. John Waggoner (Lanham: Rowman and Littlefield, 1996), 59–60.

11. Aristotle, *Politics,* trans. Carnes Lord (Chicago: University of Chicago Press, 1984), 3 (1281a–b); see also Hélène Landemore, *Democratic Reason: Politics, Collective Intelligence and the Rise of the Many* (Princeton: Princeton University Press, 2013), 59–64.

12. Isaiah Berlin, "Two Concepts of Liberty," in *Liberty,* ed. Henry Hardy (Oxford: Oxford University Press, 2002), 175.

13. Lamberti, *Tocqueville and the Two Democracies,* 219.

14. Madison, *The Federalist* No. 55, p. 374.

15. For some of the better studies of the postrevolutionary era, see Pierre Rosanvallon, *Le Moment Guizot* (Paris: Gallimard, 1985); George A. Kelly, *The Humane Comedy: Constant, Tocqueville, and French Liberalism* (New York: Cambridge University Press, 1992); Arulien Craiutu, *Liberalism under Siege: The Political Thought of the French Doctrinaires* (Lanham, MD: Lexington Books, 2003).

16. Sheldon Wolin, *Tocqueville between Two Worlds: The Making of a Political and Theoretical Life* (Princeton: Princeton University Press, 2001), 261.

17. For the origins of the administrative state in America, see Stephen Skowronek, *Building a New American State: The Expansion of National Administrative Capacities, 1877–1920* (New York: Cambridge University Press, 1982); for the failure of progressivism, see Eldon Eisenach, *The Lost Promise of Progressivism* (Lawrence: University of Kansas Press, 1994); and for the development of progressivism in comparative context, see James Kloppenberg, *Uncertain Victories: Social Democracy and Progressivism in European and American Thought, 1870–1920* (New York: Oxford University Press, 1986).

18. François Furet, "De Tocqueville and the Problem of the French Revolution," in *Interpreting the French Revolution,* trans. Elborg Forster (Cambridge: Cambridge University Press, 1985), 159.

19. Alexis de Tocqueville, *The Old Regime and the Revolution,* trans. Alan Kahan, ed. François Furet and Françoise Mélonio (Chicago: University of Chicago Press, 1998), I:142–43.

20. Tocqueville, *The Old Regime,* I:143.

21. Karl Marx, *Capital,* trans. Samuel Moore and Edward Aveling (London: Lawrence and Wishart, 1970), 82.

22. Albert O. Hirschman, *The Passions and the Interests: Arguments for Capitalism before Its Triumph* (Princeton: Princeton University Press, 1977).

23. Hirschman, *The Passions and the Interests,* 32.

24. Montesquieu, *The Spirit of the Laws,* trans. Anne M. Cohler, Basia Carolyn Miller, and Harold Stone (Cambridge: Cambridge University Press, 1989), IV.xx; for the role

of *doux commerce* in the debates of the era, see Hirschman, *The Passions and the Interests,* 70–81; Catherine Larrère, "Montesquieu on Economics and Commerce," *Montesquieu's Science of Politics: Essays on The Spirit of the Laws,* ed. David Carrithers, Michael Mosher, and Paul Rahe (Lanham: Rowman and Littlefield, 2001), 335–70.

25. Montesquieu, *Spirit of the Laws,* IV.xx.1.

26. Montesquieu, *Spirit of the Laws,* V.xx.2.

27. Montesquieu, *Spirit of the Laws,* IV.xx.2.

28. Montesquieu, *Spirit of the Laws,* I.v.6.

29. Montesquieu, *Spirit of the Laws,* IV.xx.7.

30. Montesquieu, *Spirit of the Laws,* IV.xx.6.

31. For some useful comparisons to Marx, see Raymond Aron, *Main Currents in Sociological Thought: Volume One,* intro. by Daniel J. Mahoney and Brian C. Anderson (New Brunswick, NJ: Transaction, 1998), 237–38, 247–48, 330–32.

32. This belief has recently been contested by Thomas Picketty, *Capital in the Twenty-First Century,* trans. Arthur Goldhammer (Cambridge, MA: Harvard University Press, 2014).

33. See Hirschman, *The Passions and the Interests,* 122–25.

34. Alexis de Tocqueville, *The Old Regime and the Revolution,* trans. Alan Kahan, ed. François Furet and Françoise Mélonio (Chicago: University of Chicago Press, 2001), 2: 296.

35. Edmund Burke, *Reflections on the Revolution in France,* ed. Connor Cruise O'Brien (Harmondsworth: Penguin, 1986), 193–94.

36. Cited in Steven Lukes, *Individualism* (Oxford: Blackwell, 1979), 4.

37. Karl Marx, *Grundrisse: Foundations of the Critique of Political Economy,* trans. Martin Nicolaus (Harmondsworth: Penguin, 1973), 83.

38. See Joseph Hamburger, *John Stuart Mill on Liberty and Control* (Princeton: Princeton University Press, 1999), 168–75.

39. Tocqueville, *The Old Regime and the Revolution,* I:162–63.

40. Louis Hartz, *The Liberal Tradition in America* (New York: Harcourt, Brace and World, 1955).

41. Hartz, *Liberal Tradition in America,* 6.

42. Hartz, *Liberal Tradition in America,* 11.

43. Hannah Arendt, *The Origins of Totalitarianism* (Cleveland: Meridian, 1958).

44. Arendt, *The Origins of Totalitarianism,* 338.

45. Arendt, *The Origins of Totalitarianism,* 317.

46. Arendt, *The Origins of Totalitarianism,* 478.

47. Michael Oakeshott, "The Masses in Representative Democracy," in *Rationalism in Politics and Other Essays* (Indianapolis: Liberty Press, 1991), 363–83.

48. Oakeshott, "The Masses in Representative Democracy," 364–70.

49. Oakeshott, "The Masses in Representative Democracy," 373.

50. See Oakeshott, "The Masses in Representative Democracy," 376–79.

51. Michael Oakeshott, *On Human Conduct* (Oxford: Clarendon Press, 1975), 310.

52. Leo Strauss, "Liberal Education and Responsibility," in *Liberalism Ancient and Modern* (New York: Basic Books, 1968), 24.

11. FLAUBERT AND THE AESTHETICS OF THE ANTIBOURGEOIS

Epigraph. Friedrich Nietzsche, *Beyond Good and Evil*, trans. Walter Kaufmann (New York: Random House, 1966), no. 218.

1. Gustave Flaubert, *Madame Bovary*, ed. and trans. Paul de Man (New York: W. W. Norton, 1965); all references to this volume will be provided in parentheses in the text.

2. For the attempt to situate Flaubert in the currents of his time, see Pierre Bourdieu, "Flaubert's Point of View," trans. Priscilla Parkhurst Ferguson, *Critical Inquiry* 14 (1988): 539–62.

3. Flaubert to his niece Caroline, October 25, 1872, in *The Letters of Gustave Flaubert, 1857–1880*, trans. Frances Steegmuller (Cambridge, MA: Belknap Press of Harvard University Press, 1982), 196.

4. Flaubert to Louis Bouilhet, September 30, 1855, in *The Letters of Gustave Flaubert, 1830–1857*, trans. Frances Steegmuller (Cambridge, MA: Belknap Press of Harvard University Press, 1980), 217.

5. Flaubert to Louise Colet, September 19, 1852, in *The Letters, 1830–1857*, 170.

6. Tom Perrotta, *Little Children* (New York: St. Martin's Press, 2004).

7. Perrotta, *Little Children*, 194–95.

8. See Dacia Maraini, *Searching for Emma: Gustave Flaubert and Madame Bovary*, trans. Vincent J. Bertolini (Chicago: University of Chicago Press, 1998), 25.

9. See Alexis de Tocqueville, *Democracy in America*, trans. Harvey C. Mansfield and Delba Winthrop (Chicago: University of Chicago Press, 2000), II.iii.8, 12 (558–63, 573–76).

10. Gustave Flaubert, *Bouvard and Pécuchet*, trans. A. J. Krailsheimer (Harmondsworth: Penguin, 1976), 168, 172.

11. Flaubert to Georges Sand, May 17, 1867, in *Letters, 1857–1880*, 105.

12. For some thoughts on genius, see Darrin M. McMahon, *Divine Fury: A History of Genius* (New York: Basic Books, 2013).

13. George Armstrong Kelly, *The Humane Comedy: Constant, Tocqueville, and French Liberalism* (Cambridge: Cambridge University Press, 1992), 222–23.

14. Flaubert to Georges Sand, May 17, 1867, in *Letters, 1857–1880*, 105.

12. THE APOCALYPTIC IMAGINATION

1. Karl Marx, "Manifesto of the Communist Party," in *The Marx-Engels Reader*, ed. Robert Tucker (New York: W. W. Norton, 1978), 473.

2. For the best study of counter-revolutionary thought, see Darrin M. McMahon, *Enemies of the Enlightenment: The French Counter-Enlightenment and the Making of Modernity* (New York: Oxford University Press, 2001).

3. Edmund Burke, *Reflections on the Revolution in France*, ed. Connor Cruise O'Brien (Harmondsworth: Penguin, 1986), 156.

4. Burke, *Reflections on the Revolution*, 121.

5. Joseph de Maistre, *Considerations on France*, trans. Richard Lebrun (Cambridge: Cambridge University Press, 1994), 53.

6. See Brian Barry, *Sociologists, Economists, and Democracy* (Chicago: University of Chicago Press, 1970), 7–8; for the intellectual sources of the sociological school, see Émile Durkheim, *Montesquieu and Rousseau: Forerunners of Sociology* (Ann Arbor: University of Michigan Press, 1970).

7. See Norman Cohn, *The Pursuit of the Millennium: Revolutionary Millenarians and Mystical Anarchists of the Middle Ages* (New York: Oxford University Press, 1970).

8. See Isaiah Berlin, "Joseph de Maistre and the Origins of Fascism," in *The Crooked Timber of Humanity: Chapters in the History of Ideas,* ed. Henry Hardy (Princeton: Princeton University Press, 1990), 91–174.

9. Friedrich Nietzsche, *Untimely Meditations,* trans. R. J. Hollingdale (Cambridge: Cambridge University Press, 1983); all references to this text will be provided in parentheses; for an excellent consideration of this frequently neglected text, see Peter Berkowitz, *Nietzsche: The Ethics of an Immoralist* (Cambridge, MA: Harvard University Press, 1995), 25–43.

10. Herodotus, *The History,* trans. David Grene (Chicago: University of Chicago Press, 1985), I.1; Thucydides, *The Peloponnesian War,* trans. Crawley (New York: Random House, 1982), I.22.

11. Friedrich Nietzsche, *Twilight of the Idols,* trans. R. J. Hollingdale (Harmondsworth: Penguin, 1979), 96.

12. For a valuable overview of the history of this concept, see Michael Gillespie, *Nihilism before Nietzsche* (Chicago: University of Chicago Press, 1995).

13. See Friedrich Heinrich Jacobi, *The Main Philosophical Writings and the Novel "Atwill,"* trans. George de Giovanni (Montreal: McGill-Queen's University Press, 1994), 519; see Frederick Beiser, *The Fate of Reason: German Philosophy from Kant to Fichte* (Cambridge, MA: Harvard University Press, 1987), 123–24; Steven B. Smith, *Spinoza's Book of Life: Freedom and Redemption in the "Ethics"* (New Haven: Yale University Press, 2003), 185–90.

14. Leo Strauss, "On German Nihilism," *Interpretation* 3 (1999): 357–78; this essay was originally given as a seminar paper at the New School for Social Research on February 26, 1941. For a valuable study, see Susan Shell, ' "To Spare the Vanquished and Crush the Arrogant': Leo Strauss's Lecture on 'German Nihilism,' " in *The Cambridge Companion to Leo Strauss,* ed. Steven B. Smith (New York: Cambridge University Press, 2009), 171–92.

15. Strauss, "On German Nihilism," 360.

16. Friedrich Nietzsche, *Thus Spoke Zarathustra,* trans. Walter Kaufmann (Harmondsworth: Penguin, 1978), 17.

17. Georg Lukács, *History and Class Consciousness: Studies in Marxist Dialectics,* trans. Rodney Livingstone (Cambridge, MA: MIT Press, 1971).

18. Lukács, *History and Class Consciousness,* 96.

19. Lukács, *History and Class Consciousness,* 90.

20. Lukács, *History and Class Consciousness,* 7.

21. Lukács, *History and Class Consciousness,* 25.

22. Lukács, *History and Class Consciousness,* 136.

23. For a suggestive comparison between the two, see the work by Lukács's student Lucien Goldmann, *Lukács and Heidegger: Toward a New Philosophy,* trans. William Q.

Boelhower (London: Routledge and Kegan Paul, 1977); see also Lucio Colletti, *Marxism and Hegel,* trans. Lawrence Garner (London: New Left Books, 1973), 168–73.

24. Martin Heidegger, *An Introduction to Metaphysics,* trans. Ralph Manheim (New Haven: Yale University Press, 1987), 38.

25. Martin Heidegger, *Being and Time,* trans. John Macquarrie and Edward Robinson (San Francisco: Harper and Row, 1962), 167.

26. Heidegger, *Being and Time,* 212.

27. Heidegger, *Being and Time,* 213.

28. See the barb by Saul Bellow, who asks, if we have "fallen" into being, where were we before, in *Herzog* (Harmondsworth: Penguin, 1991), 55.

29. Heidegger, *Being and Time,* 304–11.

30. Max Horkheimer and Theodor Adorno, *Dialectic of Enlightenment,* trans. John Cumming (New York: Seabury Press, 1972); see some of Colletti's caustic comments, *Marxism and Hegel,* 173–75.

31. Horkheimer and Adorno, *Dialectic of Enlightenment,* 6.

32. Martin Heidegger, "The Question Concerning Technology," in *Basic Writings,* ed. David Farrell Krell (New York: Harper and Row, 1977), 301–5.

33. Georges Sorel, *Reflections on Violence,* ed. Jeremy Jennings (Cambridge: Cambridge University Press, 1999); all references to this text will be provided in parentheses.

34. For a useful treatment of the concept, see Henry Tudor, *Political Myth* (London: Pall Mall, 1972).

35. See Horkheimer and Adorno's analysis of the "culture industry" in *Dialectic of Enlightenment,* 120–67.

36. See Theodore Roosevelt, "The Strenuous Life," in *The Strenuous Life: Essays and Addresses* (New York: Dover, 2009), 1–10.

37. See William James, *Pragmatism and The Meaning of Truth* (Cambridge, MA: Harvard University Press, 1978), 13–14, 127–28.

38. Isaiah Berlin, "Georges Sorel," in *Against the Current: Essays in the History of Ideas* (Harmondsworth: Penguin, 1979), 328; for a similar view, see Irving Louis Horowitz, *Radicalism and the Revolt against Reason: The Social Theories of Georges Sorel* (Carbondale: Southern Illinois University Press, 1968), v–xviii.

39. Berlin, "Georges Sorel," 329–30.

40. Berlin, "Georges Sorel," 330.

41. See Carl Schmitt, *The Crisis of Parliamentary Democracy,* trans. Ellen Kennedy (Cambridge, MA: MIT Press, 1985).

42. Schmitt, *Crisis of Parliamentary Democracy,* 70.

43. Schmitt, *Crisis of Parliamentary Democracy,* 74–75.

44. Schmitt, *Crisis of Parliamentary Democracy,* 73.

45. Carl Schmitt, *The Concept of the Political,* trans. George Schwab (New Brunswick, NJ: Rutgers University Press, 1976), 26.

46. Schmitt, *Concept of the Political,* 27.

47. Schmitt, *Concept of the Political,* 35.

48. Heidegger, *An Introduction to Metaphysics,* 199.

49. The theological dimension of Schmitt's thought has been most fully developed by Heinrich Meier, *The Lesson of Carl Schmitt: Four Chapters on the Distinction between Political Theology and Political Philosophy*, trans. Marcus Brainard (Chicago: University of Chicago Press, 1998); see also Mark Lilla, *The Reckless Mind: Intellectuals in Politics* (New York: NYRB, 2001), 49–76.

50. Leo Strauss, "Comments on Carl Schmitt's 'Der Begriff des Politischen,'" in *The Concept of the Political*, 81–105.

51. Schmitt, *Concept of the Political*, 53; see Strauss, "Comments," 98.

52. Strauss, "Comments," 89–90.

53. Strauss, "Comments," 101.

54. Strauss, "Comments," 104–5.

13. THE TRAGIC LIBERALISM OF ISAIAH BERLIN

1. Zev Sternhell, *The Anti-Enlightenment Tradition*, trans. David Maisel (New Haven: Yale University Press, 2010); Cory Robin, *The Reactionary Mind: Conservatism from Edmund Burke to Sarah Palin* (New York: Oxford University Press, 2013).

2. In Noel Annan, "A Man I Loved," in *Maurice Bowra: A Celebration*, ed. Hugh Lloyd-Jones (London: Duckworth, 1974), 53.

3. See Isaiah Berlin, *Concepts and Categories: Philosophical Essays* (Harmondsworth: Penguin, 1978), vii–viii.

4. The following remarks draw on J. David Greenstone, "Against Simplicity: The Cultural Dimensions of the Constitution," *University of Chicago Law Review* 55 (1988): 428–49.

5. For the rise of this perfectionist liberalism, see Shirley Robin Letwin, *The Pursuit of Certainty: David Hume, Jeremy Bentham, John Stuart Mill, Beatrice Webb* (Cambridge: Cambridge University Press, 1965).

6. See Robert A. Dahl, *A Preface to Democratic Theory* (Chicago: University of Chicago Press, 1956); for a sharp critique of Dahl, see Harvey C. Mansfield, "Social Science and the Constitution," in *America's Constitutional Soul* (Baltimore: Johns Hopkins University Press, 1993), 137–62.

7. Ludwig Wittgenstein, *Philosophical Investigations*, trans. G. E. M. Anscombe (New York: Macmillan, 1968), sec. 19: "And to imagine a language means to imagine a form of life."

8. Isaiah Berlin, "Two Concepts of Liberty," in *The Proper Study of Mankind*, ed. Henry Hardy and Roger Hausheer (New York: Farrar, Straus and Giroux, 2000); henceforth cited as *PSM*. All references to this essay will be provided parenthetically in the text.

9. Isaiah Berlin, "John Stuart Mill and the Ends of Life," in *Liberty*, ed. Henry Hardy (Oxford: Oxford University Press, 2002), 222.

10. See Joseph Hamburger, *John Stuart Mill on Liberty and Control* (Princeton: Princeton University Press, 1999), 168–75, 226–28.

11. The psychological depths of Berlin's views on liberty have been recently explored in Gina Gustavsson, "The Psychological Dangers of Positive Liberty: Reconstructing a

Neglected Undercurrent in Isaiah Berlin's 'Two Concepts of Liberty,'" *Review of Politics* 76 (2014): 267–91.

12. Leo Strauss, "Relativism," in *The Rebirth of Classical Political Rationalism,* ed. Thomas Pangle (Chicago: University of Chicago Press, 1989), 16.

13. See Gerald MacCallum, "Negative and Positive Freedom," *Philosophical Review* 76 (1967): 312–34.

14. Quentin Skinner, "A Third Concept of Liberty," *Proceedings of the British Academy* 117 (2001): 237–68; for a fuller account, see Philip Petit, *Republicanism: A Theory of Freedom and Government* (Oxford: Oxford University Press, 1997).

15. Cited in Gertrude Himmelfarb, *On Liberty and Liberalism: The Case of John Stuart Mill* (New York: Knopf, 1974), 163.

16. Jacob Talmon, *The Origins of Totalitarian Democracy* (New York: Norton, 1970); for Berlin's association with Talmon, see Joshua L. Cherniss, *A Mind and Its Time: The Development of Isaiah Berlin's Political Thought* (Oxford: Oxford University Press, 2013), 171–74.

17. Edmund Burke, *Reflections on the Revolution in France,* ed. Connor Cruise O'Brien (Harmondsworth: Penguin, 1986), 90.

18. See Isaiah Berlin, "The Decline of Utopian Ideas in the West," *The Crooked Timber of Humanity: Chapters in the History of Ideas,* ed. Henry Hardy (Princeton: Princeton University Press, 1990), 24–25.

19. See William James, *Essays in Radical Empiricism: A Pluralistic Universe* (New York: Longmans, 1958); for some other sources of Berlinian pluralism, see Cherniss, *A Mind and Its Time,* 44–52.

20. Strauss, "Relativism," 17; Strauss's claim has been repeated by Michael Sandel, "Introduction," in *Liberalism and Its Critics* (New York: New York University Press, 1984), 1–11.

21. Strauss, "Relativism," 17.

22. Strauss, "Relativism," 17.

23. See Arnaldo Momigliano, "On the Pioneer Trail," *New York Review of Books,* November 11, 1976, 33–38.

24. Berlin, "The Pursuit of the Ideal," in *The Crooked Timber of Humanity,* 11; see also "My Intellectual Path," in *The Power of Ideas,* ed. Henry Hardy (Princeton: Princeton University Press, 2002), 11–14.

25. Berlin, "The Pursuit of the Ideal," 11; see also "Alleged Relativism in Eighteenth-Century Thought," in *The Crooked Timber of Humanity,* 76–78.

26. Berlin, "The Pursuit of the Ideal," 11.

27. Berlin, "The Pursuit of the Ideal," 13–14.

28. Robert Wokler, "Isaiah Berlin's Enlightenment and Counter-Enlightenment," *Isaiah Berlin's Counter-Enlightenment,* ed. Joseph Mali and Robert Wokler (Philadelphia: American Philosophical Society, 2003), 18.

29. Berlin, "My Intellectual Path," 4.

30. Berlin, "My Intellectual Path," 4.

31. Berlin, "The Counter-Enlightenment" and "Herder and the Enlightenment," in *PSM,* 250, 392.

32. Berlin, "The Counter-Enlightenment," in *PSM,* 252, 261–62.

33. Berlin, "Herder and the Enlightenment," in *PSM,* 386–87.

34. Berlin, "The Divorce Between the Sciences and the Humanities," 354–56; "Herder and the Enlightenment," in *PSM,* 403–4.

35. Berlin, "The Counter-Enlightenment," 254–55; "Herder and the Enlightenment," in *PSM,* 426–27.

36. Cited in Berlin, "Joseph de Maistre and the Origins of Fascism," in *The Crooked Timber of Humanity,* 100.

37. See his essays "Nationalism: Past Neglect and Present Power," in *PSM,* 581–604; and "The Bent Twig: On the Rise of Nationalism," in *The Crooked Timber of Humanity,* 238–61.

38. Berlin, "Herder and the Enlightenment," in *PSM,* 412–13.

39. Berlin, "The Counter-Enlightenment," in *PSM,* 254.

40. For Berlin's views on Zionism and Israel, see especially "The Origins of Israel" and "Jewish Slavery and Emancipation," in *The Power of Ideas,* 143–61, 162–85; for a recent study dealing with Berlin's lifelong struggle, see Arie Dubnov, *Between Zionism and Liberalism: Isaiah Berlin and the Dilemma of the Jewish Liberal* (New York: Palgrave Macmillan, 2012).

41. In Ramin Jahanbegloo, *Conversations with Isaiah Berlin* (London: Pater Halban, 1992), 86.

42. Berlin, "Herder and the Enlightenment," in *PSM,* 425–26.

43. See Isaiah Berlin, "Hume and the Sources of German Anti-Rationalism," in *Against the Current: Essays in the History of Ideas* (New York: Viking Press, 1980), 162–87.

44. See John Gray, *Isaiah Berlin* (Princeton: Princeton University Press, 1996), 141–68; for a response to Gray's thesis, see William A. Galston, "Value Pluralism and Liberal Political Theory," *American Political Science Review* 93 (1999): 769–78.

45. F. Scott Fitzgerald, *The Crack Up,* ed. Edmund Wilson (New York: New Directions, 1945), 69.

46. I owe this example to the late Joseph Cropsey.

47. Berlin, "The Decline of Utopian Ideas," 47.

48. Berlin, "The Decline of Utopian Ideas," 47–48.

49. For one of the few efforts to put the role of statesmanship back in Berlin's writings, see Ryan Patrick Hanley, "Political Science and Political Understanding: Isaiah Berlin on the Nature of Political Inquiry," *American Political Science Review* 98 (2004): 327–39.

50. See Berlin's *Personal Impressions,* ed. Henry Hardy (Princeton: Princeton University Press, 2001).

51. Berlin, "Chaim Weizmann's Leadership," in *The Power of Ideas,* 186.

52. Berlin, "Chaim Weizmann's Leadership," 186.

53. Berlin, "Chaim Weizmann's Leadership," 187–88.

54. Berlin, "Chaim Weizmann's Leadership," 188.

55. Berlin, "Winston Churchill in 1940," in *PSM,* 614.

14. LEO STRAUSS ON PHILOSOPHY AS A WAY OF LIFE

1. Stuart Hampshire, *Thought and Action* (London: Chatto and Windus, 1970), 270.

2. Ludwig Wittgenstein, *Tractatus Logico-Philosophicus,* trans. D. F. Pears and B. F. Mc-Guiness (London: Routledge, 1971), 7.

3. Max Weber, "Science as a Vocation," in *From Max Weber: Essays in Sociology,* ed. H. H. Gerth and C. Wright Mills (New York: Oxford University Press, 1958), 152.

4. Peter Laslett, ed., *Philosophy, Politics and Society* (New York: Macmillan, 1956).

5. Leo Strauss, "What Is Political Philosophy?" in *What Is Political Philosophy and Other Studies* (New York: Free Press, 1959), 17.

6. Joseph Cropsey, "Leo Strauss," in *International Encyclopedia of the Social Sciences (Biographical Supplement),* ed. David Sills (New York: Free Press, 1979), XVIII:747.

7. Cropsey, "Leo Strauss," 747.

8. Strauss's most devoted critic over the years has been Shadia Drury, *The Political Ideas of Leo Strauss* (New York: St. Martin's Press, 1988); see more recently Nicholas Xenos, *Cloaked in Virtue: Unveiling Leo Strauss and the Rhetoric of American Foreign Policy* (New York: Routledge, 2008); for a response to many of the political attacks, see Catherine and Michael Zuckert, *The Truth about Leo Strauss: Political Philosophy and American Democracy* (Chicago: University of Chicago Press, 2006); see also Peter Minowitz, *Straussophobia: Defending Leo Strauss and Straussians from Shadia Drury and Other Accusers* (Lanham, MD: Lexington, 2009).

9. See Stephen Holmes, *The Anatomy of Anti-Liberalism* (Chicago: University of Chicago Press, 1993), 61–87; see more recently William H. F. Altman, *The German Stranger: Leo Strauss and National Socialism* (Lanham, MD: Lexington Books, 2010); for an admirable response to both works, see Robert Howse, *Leo Strauss: Man of Peace* (Cambridge: Cambridge University Press, 2014).

10. Myles Burnyeat, "Sphinx Without a Secret," *New York Review of Books,* May 30, 1985, 32.

11. See Pierre Hadot, *Philosophy as a Way of Life,* trans. Michael Chase, ed. Arnold I. Davidson (Oxford: Blackwell, 1995).

12. See Alexander Nehamas, *The Art of Living: Socratic Reflections from Plato to Foucault* (Berkeley: University of California Press, 1998).

13. Leo Strauss, "Restatement on Xenophon's *Hiero,*" in *On Tyranny: Including the Strauss-Kojève Correspondence,* ed. Victor Gourevitch and Michael S. Roth (Chicago: University of Chicago Press, 2001), 196; see also Strauss, "Progress or Return?" in *The Rebirth of Classical Political Rationalism,* ed. Thomas Pangle (Chicago: University of Chicago Press, 1989), 259–60.

14. For the emphasis on Strauss as a zetetic, or skeptical, thinker, see Daniel Tanguay, *Leo Strauss: An Intellectual Biography,* trans. Christopher Nadon (New Haven: Yale University Press, 2007); the language of "negative dialectics" belongs, of course, to Theodor Adorno.

15. Leo Strauss, "What Is Political Philosophy?" 11; see also Strauss, *Natural Right and History* (Chicago: University of Chicago Press, 1953), 30–31.

16. Strauss, "What Is Political Philosophy?" 11.

17. Strauss, "What Is Political Philosophy?" 12.

18. Strauss, "What Is Political Philosophy?" 40.

19. Strauss, "Restatement," 197–98.

20. Strauss, "Restatement," 198.

21. Strauss, *Natural Right and History,* 7–8; "What Is Political Philosophy?" 38–39.

22. Strauss, "What Is Political Philosophy?" 38.

23. Strauss, "What Is Political Philosophy?" 93.

24. Strauss, "What Is Political Philosophy?" 16.

25. Strauss, "What Is Political Philosophy?" 12.

26. Strauss, "What Is Political Philosophy?" 12.

27. Leo Strauss, *The City and Man* (Chicago: University of Chicago Press, 1964), 11.

28. Strauss, "What Is Political Philosophy?" 36.

29. Leo Strauss, "Liberal Education and Responsibility," in *Liberalism Ancient and Modern* (New York: Basic Books, 1968), 12.

30. Strauss, "What Is Political Philosophy?" 55.

31. Strauss, *On Tyranny,* 194.

32. Strauss, "Liberal Education and Responsibility," 24.

33. Strauss, "Liberal Education and Responsibility," 15.

34. Strauss, "What Is Political Philosophy?" 37.

35. Strauss, *Liberalism Ancient and Modern,* 4.

36. Strauss, "What Is Political Philosophy?" 37.

37. Strauss, *Liberalism Ancient and Modern,* 5.

38. Strauss, "What Is Political Philosophy?" 38.

39. Leo Strauss, "On German Nihilism," *Interpretation* 3 (1999): 372.

40. Strauss, "Liberal Education and Responsibility," 24.

41. Strauss, "What Is Political Philosophy?" 75–76.

42. The idea that there remains some primordial prephilosophic ground of experience is indebted to Husserl's ideas about the "lifeworld," but it is left undertheorized in Strauss; see *Natural Right and History,* 31–32; for some interesting comments on the problem, see Robert Pippin, "The Unavailability of the Ordinary: Strauss on the Philosophic Fate of Modernity," *Political Theory* 3 (2003): 335–58, esp. 341–44.

43. Plato, *Republic,* trans. Allan Bloom (New York: Basic Books, 1968), VII.514a–17a; this paragraph draws from my *Political Philosophy* (New Haven: Yale University Press, 2012), 60–63.

44. Strauss, "How to Study Spinoza's 'Theologico-Political Treatise,'" in *Persecution and the Art of Writing,* 155–56.

45. Strauss, "What Is Political Philosophy?" 23.

46. Strauss, "What Is Political Philosophy?" 18–26; *Natural Right and History,* 34–80.

47. Strauss, "What Is Political Philosophy?" 25.

48. Strauss, "What Is Political Philosophy?" 25.

49. Strauss, "What Is Political Philosophy?" 25–26.

50. Strauss, "How to Study Spinoza's 'Theologico-Political Treatise,'" 158.

51. Strauss, "How to Study Spinoza's 'Theologico-Political Treatise,'" 157.

52. This is the central thesis of "Persecution and the Art of Writing," in *Persecution and the Art of Writing,* 22–37; see also Strauss, "On a Forgotten Kind of Writing," in *What Is Political Philosophy?* 221–22.

53. References to *On Tyranny* will be given in parentheses in the text.

54. The best commentary on this debate still remains Victor Gourevitch, "Philosophy and Politics, I and II," *Review of Metaphysics* 22 (1968): 58–84, 281–328; see also Robert Pippin, "Being, Time, and Politics: The Strauss-Kojève Debate," *History and Theory* 22 (1993): 138–61; Steven B. Smith, "Tyranny Ancient and Modern," in *Reading Leo Strauss: Politics, Philosophy, Judaism* (Chicago: University of Chicago Press, 2006), 131–55.

55. Strauss, "The Law of Reason in the *Kuzari,*" in *Persecution and the Art of Writing,* 110.

56. Rémi Brague, "Athens, Jerusalem, Mecca: Leo Strauss's 'Muslim' Understanding of Greek Philosophy," *Poetics Today* 19 (1998): 238.

57. For the importance of "probity," see Strauss, "Preface to *Spinoza's Critique of Religion,*" in *Liberalism Ancient and Modern,* 255–56; for Strauss's references to the Nietzschean origins of this concept, see his notes 24–28 on p. 258.

58. For Strauss's treatment of this theme, see "Progress or Return?" 227–70; "Preface to *Spinoza's Critique of Religion,*" 224–59; "Jerusalem and Athens: Some Preliminary Reflections," in *Studies in Platonic Political Philosophy,* ed. T. Pangle (Chicago: University of Chicago Press, 1983), 147–73; "Reason and Revelation," in Heinrich Meier, *Leo Strauss and the Theologico-Political Problem* (Cambridge: Cambridge University Press, 2006), 141–80.

59. The claim that the entire Straussian project rests upon a Nietzschean "will to power" has been argued provocatively by Stanley Rosen, *Hermeneutics as Politics* (Oxford: Oxford University Press, 1987), 107–23; see also Laurence Lampert, *Leo Strauss and Nietzsche* (Chicago: University of Chicago Press, 1996); Lampert treats Strauss as a weak Nietzschean.

60. Strauss, *Natural Right and History,* 74.

61. Strauss, "Progress or Return," 261–62.

62. Strauss, "Progress or Return," 269.

63. For the theistic interpretation of Strauss's thought, see Kenneth Hart Green, *Jew and Philosopher: The Return to Maimonides in the Jewish Thought of Leo Strauss* (Albany: SUNY Press, 1993); Susan Orr, *Jerusalem and Athens* (Lanham, MD: Rowman and Littlefield, 1995).

64. Leo Strauss, "Preface to *Hobbes Politische Wissenschaft,*" in *Jewish Philosophy and the Crisis of Modernity,* ed. Kenneth Hart Green (Albany: SUNY Press, 1997), 453.

65. Strauss, "Preface to *Spinoza's Critique of Religion,*" 257.

66. This may help to explain why Strauss planned a book entitled *Studies in Platonic Political Philosophy* that contained only two essays specifically dealing with Plato. The term "Platonic" meant for him a certain style of philosophizing rather than a doctrine or system attributable to Plato.

67. Strauss, "Preface to *Hobbes Politische Wissenschaft,* 453.

68. Strauss, "Progress or Return," 270: see also the following remark from Goethe cited by Strauss in "The Law of Reason in the *Kuzari,*" 107, n. 35: "The actual, only and most

profound theme of world and human history, the theme under which all others are subsumed, remains the conflict between unbelief and belief."

15. THE POLITICAL TEACHING OF LAMPEDUSA'S *THE LEOPARD*

1. Giuseppe Tomasi di Lampedusa, *The Leopard,* trans. Archibald Colquhoun (New York: Random House, 1960); all references are provided parenthetically in the text.
2. For biographical information, see David Gilmour, *The Last Leopard: A Life of Giuseppe di Lampedusa* (London: Quartet Books, 1988).
3. Cited in Eduardo Saccone, "Nobility and Literature: Questions on Tomasi di Lampedusa," *MLN* 106 (1991): 160.
4. In Saccone, "Nobility and Literature," 160.
5. In Javier Marías, *Written Lives,* trans. Margaret Jull Costa (New York: New Directions, 2006), 30.
6. The prehistory to these events is told by Benedetto Croce, *History of the Kingdom of Naples,* trans. Frances Frenaye (Chicago: University of Chicago Press, 1970).
7. Lampedusa's use of the Freudian term "wish-fulfillment" is one of the few anachronisms in the book, perhaps influenced by his wife, Licy, who was a psychoanalyst. It is hard to imagine the prince using psychoanalytic language.

16. MR. SAMMLER'S REDEMPTION

1. Saul Bellow, *Mr. Sammler's Planet* (New York: Penguin, 2004); all references are provided in parentheses in the text.
2. For the claim that "Bloom" was simply a fiction created by Bellow as a mouthpiece for his own ideas, see Robert Paul Wolff's review in Robert L. Stone, ed., *Essays on "The Closing of the American Mind"* (Chicago: Chicago Review Press, 1989), 18–21; for another review that associates Bloom with Bellow, see Louis Menand, "Mr. Bloom's Planet," *New Republic,* May 25, 1987, 38–41.
3. For a fuller reflection, see Bellow's nonfiction work *To Jerusalem and Back: A Personal Account* (New York: Viking Press, 1976).

Index

Rousseau as voice of, 15, 175–76, 193–94; Straussian views and, 293; value pluralism thesis and, 276, 281; wide-ranging reach of, 267

Counter-Revolution, 14, 243–44, 348

Creation, 58–59

creative destruction, 262

critical history, 247, 248–49

Cropsey, Joseph, 61, 292

culture, 12–13, 253, 278–85, 300; historicist and relativist view of, 303, 347; Nietzsche critique of, 18–19; original agricultural meaning of, 16; science of vs. needs of, 249

Cyrus the Great, 28, 62

Dahl, Robert, *Preface to Democratic Theory,* 269

Dasein, 253

das Man ("they"), 19, 253

death, 73–74, 75, 254

Declaration of Independence, 10–11, 347

Declaration of the Rights of Man and the Citizen, 4, 230

deconstruction, 293

Defoe, Daniel, *Robinson Crusoe,* 10, 29, 49

de Gaulle, Charles, 288

deism, 116, 117

democracy, 5, 140, 195, 222, 250, 253, 271; ancients and, 201, 298, 299; Cartesian method and, 46–47, 64; clubs and societies and, 180; as conformity, 300; direct, 203, 206; middle-class, 21, 197, 230; positive effects of, 214; theocracy and, 101; Tocqueville and, 197–203, 214, 217, 242; transition to age of, 314, 342; tyranny of the majority and, 200, 201–9, 218. *See also* liberal democracy

democratic despotism. *See* soft despotism

Derrida, Jacques, 348

Descartes, René, 4, 9–10, 27, 28, 46–66, 75, 179, 181, 182, 221, 254, 350; *cogito ergo sum,* 10, 29, 48, 58, 164, 348; contributions of, 46–47; critics of, 47; four rules of method, 10, 53–55, 94, 119; generosity ethic, 50, 59, 60, 61–64, 65; hyperbolic doubt and, 10, 48; reluctance to publish, 49, 58–59; works: *Discourse on Method,* 47–62, 63, 64, 65, 66; *Passions of the Soul,* 62; *Principles of Philosophy,* 48; *The World (Le monde),* 58

despotism, 70, 91–92, 150, 212, 215–16. *See also* soft despotism; tyranny

determinism, 263, 279, 287

Dewey, John, 350

dialectic, 11, 13–15, 167, 257

Diderot, Denis, 10, 231, 239

dignity. *See* human dignity

Disraeli, Benjamin, 268

divine election. *See* chosen people

division of labor, 156, 169–70

Dostoyevsky, Fyodor, 293; *The Possessed,* 250

Dunkers, 119

Dutch Republic, 93–94; commercial society and, 157; as liberal haven, 57–58, 65, 93, 102, 105. *See also* Amsterdam

duty, 112, 134–35

Dworkin, Ronald, 286

education, 10, 115, 160, 171, 240, 298, 299; Bildung and, 144, 167, 168–69; Descartes critique of, 51–52; Franklin and, 113–16, 129; liberal, 22, 300–301; moral, 167, 176; universal, 339

Einstein, Albert, 287

Elijah, 95

Eliot, George, *Daniel Deronda,* 90

Eliot, T. S., 293; *The Waste Land,* 250

Emerson, Ralph Waldo, 121; *American Scholar,* 130

empiricism, 7, 261, 283, 290